A Friedman Lecture Fund Monograph

THE CHINA MIRACLE

Development Strategy and Economic Reform

The Hong Kong Centre for Economic Research

The Centre was set up as a research and educational trust under a trust deed signed in 1987. It supports research and publishes studies on public policy issues to promote understanding of economic affairs and provide alternative policy choices.

The Centre's work is assisted by an international board of advisers:

The Centre is an approved tax-exempted charitable trust controlled by Trustees and financed by sales of publications and voluntary contributions from individuals, organizations and companies.

Prof. Y. C. Richard Wong, Director

The Hong Kong Centre for Economic Research
School of Economics and Finance
The University of Hong Kong
Pokfulam Road, Hong Kong
Tel: (852) 2547 8313   Fax: (852) 2548 6319

The International Center for Economic Growth

Since 1985 the International Center for Economic Growth, a nonprofit international policy institute, has contributed to economic growth and human development in developing and post-socialist countries by strengthening the capacity of indigenous research institutes to provide leadership in policy debates. To accomplish this the Center sponsors a wide range of programmes — including research, publications, conferences, seminars, and special projects advising governments — through a network of over 300 correspondent institutes worldwide.

The Center is affiliated with the Institute for Contemporary Studies and is headquartered in Panama with the administrative office in San Francisco, California.

For further information, please contact the International Center for Economic Growth, 1 Sansome Street, Suite 2000, San Francisco, CA 94104, U.S.A. Phone: (415) 984-3193; Fax: (415) 984-3196

ICEG Board of Overseers

A Friedman Lecture Fund Monograph

The China Miracle

Development Strategy and Economic Reform

Revised Edition

Justin Yifu LIN
Fang CAI
Zhou LI

Published for

The Hong Kong Centre for Economic Research

and

The International Center for Economic Growth

by

The Chinese University Press

The China Miracle
By Justin Yifu Lin, Fang Cai and Zhou Li

ISBN 962–201–985–4

First edition 1996
Revised edition 2003

THE CHINESE UNIVERSITY PRESS
The Chinese University of Hong Kong
SHA TIN, N. T., HONG KONG
Fax: (852) 2603 6692
(852) 2603 7355
E-mail: cup@cuhk.edu.hk
Web-site: www.chineseupress.com

Printed in Hong Kong

The Friedman Lecture Fund

The Friedman Lecture Fund was established from proceeds obtained from a public lecture given by Dr. Milton Friedman on 24 September 1988 in Hong Kong. The purpose of the Fund is to support research that leads to an improved understanding of the role of markets in economic life. To this end the Fund supports the work of individual scholars and institutions. The Fund is operated jointly by the Hong Kong Centre for Economic Research and the School of Economics and Finance of The University of Hong Kong.

To

Professor D. Gale Johnson

for his continuous encouragement and support

Contents

Foreword to the First Edition by Y. C. Richard Wong xix

Foreword to the First Edition by D. Gale Johnson xxi

Preface to the Revised Edition xxv

Preface to the First Edition xxxi

The Authors xliii

Chapter 1. Introduction 1

1.1 Economic Development Since Reform, and Prospects for the 21st Century 3

1.2 Policy Barriers to Persistent Growth 19

1.3 Key Questions 25

Chapter 2. The Leap-forward Strategy and the Formation of the Traditional Economic System 29

2.1 Logical Starting Point: Heavy-industry as the Priority of Development 30

2.2 Basic Characteristics of Heavy Industries vs. China's Economic Reality 37

2.3 The Macro-policy Environment for the Heavy-industry-oriented Development Strategy 39

2.4 The Planned Resource-allocation System 46

2.5 Micro-management Institutions Characterized by Nationalization and the People's Commune System 52

2.6 The Trinity of the Traditional Economic System: An International Comparison 59

Chapter 3. Economic Performance and China's Development Strategy 69
3.1 Economic Growth Before Reform 70
3.2 Distorted Structures Under the Traditional Economic Strategy 74
3.3 Lack of Incentives and Low Efficiency 84
3.4 Leap-forward Strategies: An International Comparison 91

Chapter 4. The Comparative-advantage-following Strategy 103
4.1 Different Interpretations of the East Asian Miracle .. 104
4.2 An Alternative Development Strategy 108
4.3 Comparative Advantage and Upgrading the Factor-endowment Structure 115
4.4 The Government's Role in Economic Development 120
4.5 The Comparative-advantage-following Strategy and the Asian Financial Crisis 127

Chapter 5. Economic Reform in China 137
5.1 Differences between Pre-1978 and Post-1978 Reforms 138
5.2 Reform of the Micro-management Institution 140
5.3 Reform of the Planned Resource-allocation System 156
5.4 The Reform of the Macro-policy Environment 171
5.5 The Economic Logic of "Crossing the River by Groping the Stones" — China's Approach to Reform 177

Chapter 6. Success of the Economic Reform 183
6.1 Improvement of Incentives and Efficiency 184
6.2 Correction of the Industrial Structure 190
6.3 Exploitating Comparative Advantage 197

Chapter 7. Problems with China's Reform 203
7.1 The Cyclic Nature of Reform and Development 204
7.2 Rent-seeking and Corruption 210
7.3 Difficulties in the Reform of State-owned Enterprises 215
7.4 Non-performing Loans and Malpractice in the Financial System 221
7.5 The Aggravation of Uneven Regional Development 223
7.6 The Potential of Grain Supply 231

Chapter 8. The Internal and External Environment for Economic Reform and Sustainable Development 237
8.1 Coordination of the State-owned Enterprise Reform and the Reform in Economic System 237
8.2 Further Reform and Prevention of Financial Crises 252
8.3 Exploiting Comparative Advantages to Realize Sustainable Economic Development 254

Chapter 9. Deflation in China since 1998 257
9.1 The Demand Side of Deflation 258
9.2 Serious Over-supply Is the Main Cause of Deflation 265
9.3 The Effects of Excess Capacity and Deflation 271
9.4 The New Village Movement and Solution to Deflation 275

Chapter 10. WTO Accession and China's Reform 283
10.1 WTO Accession and China's Agriculture 285
10.2 Accession's Potential Impacts on Financial Sector .. 289
10.3 WTO Accession and SOE Reform 293

Chapter 11. The Characteristics and General Implications of China's Reform 307

11.1 The Starter and Propellers of Reform 308

11.2 The Approach and Characteristics of Economic Reform 314

11.3 General Implications of China's Reform Approach 325

Chapter 12. Concluding Remarks 339

Bibliography 347

Index 375

LIST OF ILLUSTRATIONS

Tables

1.1 Average Annual Growth Rates (1980–90 and 1990–99) in China and Other Types of Economies 4

1.2 Real GDP Growth in Eastern Europe, the Baltic States, and the Commonwealth of Independent States 5

1.3 Inflation in Eastern Europe, the Baltic States, and the Commonwealth of Independent States 7

1.4 Estimate of China's Per Capita GDP 12

1.5 The Economic Scales of 10 Largest Economies in the World 14

2.1 Exchange Rate Adjustments 42

2.2 Comparisons of Consumer Price Indexes before the Reform 45

2.3 Index of Major Agricultural Products' Output and Sales before the Implementation of the State Monopoly on Procurement and Marketing 51

2.4 Comparison of the Rate of Loanable Funds in Countries Adopting Different Development Strategies 66

2.5 Income Distribution in Countries Adopting Different Development Strategies 66

3.1 Basic Indices for Economic Growth from 1952 to 1978 71

3.2 Changes in Investment Structure, 1952–1978 75

3.3 Sectoral Composition of National Income, 1952–78 76

3.4 Changes in Employment Structure, 1952–78 76

3.5 Predicted Level of Urbanization at Different Income (GNP) Levels 81

3.6	Changes in the Level of Consumption for Urban and Rural Residents	82
3.7	Changes in International Trade, 1952–78	83
3.8	Material Consumption Rate for Per Unit of GDP: An International Comparison	89
3.9	Share of Working Capital in Total Assets: An International Comparison	89
3.10	Growth of Total Factor Productivity: An International Comparison	90
3.11	Structure of Output Value in China and India	96
3.12	Growth Index of Agricultural Output Value in China and India	97
3.13	Employment Structure of China and India in 1980	98
4.1	Key Industries in Different Development Stages of Japan and the Four Little Dragons	110
5.1	Pre-reform Decentralization and Re-centralization Cycle	139
5.2.	The Scale of Government Bonds and Its Proportion in Government Expenditures	167
5.3	Development of the Stock Market in Mainland China since the 1990s	169
5.4	Changes in Price Controls	172
6.1	Output Growth Rate and Total Factor Productivity	186
6.2	Changes in the Structure of Industrial Output Value	187
6.3	Changes in the Structure of the Total Retail Sales of Commodity	188
6.4	Changes in the Chinese Economy's Trade Dependence Ratio	195
6.5	Total Investment in Fixed Assets by Source of Funds and Its Changes	196

6.6 Total Investment in Fixed Assets by Ownership and Its Changes 196
6.7 The Composition of China's Economic Growth Rate 198
7.1 Changes in the Gini Coefficient of Per Capita Income and Consumption in Urban and Rural Areas (1978–97) 226
7.2 The Contribution of Intra- and Inter-RID to the Overall RID in the Per Capita Income 227
7.3 Contribution of Rural-, Urban- and UR-RID to the Overall RID 228
7.4 Gini Coefficient Calculated on the Basis of County-level Data, 1992 230
7.5 Per Capita Daily Nutrition and Its Source (1995) . . . 232
7.6 Proportions in the Total Purchase of Agricultural Products under Different Price-setting Mechanisms 234
9.1 Interest Rate Reductions by the People's Bank of China since 1996 260
9.2 Money Supply Growth Rate, After Seasonal Adjustment 261
9.3 Money Velocity 262
9.4 The Structure of Households' Financial Assets 263
9.5 The Structure of Finance in Chinese Enterprises 264
9.6 Utilization Rates of Existing Production Capacity of Major Industrial Products in 1995 267
9.7 Number of Durable Consumer Goods Owned Per 100 Households and the Net Income Per Capita 277

Figures

2.1 Wage levels in Mainland China before the 1978 reform 44
2.2 China's traditional economic system 60

3.1 GDP structure in 1981 78
3.2 Development strategy and production efficiency 79
3.3 Production under two calculating prices 85
6.1 Annual growth rate of state industries and commerce and their shares in total output value and total volume of retail sales 188
6.2 Changes in the sown areas of major agricultural crops 191
7.1 Cyclical fluctuations in economic growth and inflation 204
7.2 Price control and rent-seeking 211
8.1 Mechanism of the endogenous inflation 242
8.2 Price effect and elasticities of supply and demand .. 245
9.1 Annual consumption growth rate 265
9.2 The leading coefficient of fixed asset investment growth over consumption growth 268
9.3 The leading coefficient of the growth of net value of fixed assets over final consumption 269
11.1 The effect of shock therapy 319
11.2 The effect of incremental reform 320
11.3 Voting model for reform opinions 335

Foreword to the First Edition

The HKCER Paperbacks are planned to be studies of medium length in which economists would analyze a policy issue from an economic perspective. Authors are invited, in particular, to consider the circumstances which encouraged or inhibited the translation of ideas into policy.

The opening of China in the 1980s has brought momentous change to the life of people of China. The sustained rapid rate of economic growth compares favourably with the experience of other transitional economies. In this important study, the authors, Justin Yifu Lin, Fang Cai, and Zhou Li of the China Center for Economic Research at Peking University, provide critical insights into the reform process. This is a highly readable account of the Chinese reforms and penetrating economic analysis of China's development strategy.

We are particularly pleased that this study is issued jointly by both the International Center for Economic Growth and our Centre.

The Trustees, Advisers and Director of the Hong Kong Centre for Economic Research must formally dissociate themselves from the conclusions of the Paperback, while welcoming its timely contribution to an issue of great importance in the world.

Y. C. Richard Wong
June 1996

Foreword to the First Edition

There have been many articles and books written about Chinese economic reforms. Not one does so with the insights and sweep of *The China Miracle*. This book is unique in several respects. The significant implications of the policy decision to adopt a heavy industry strategy, from the beginning of the People's Republic of China, are spelled out in considerable detail and with great clarity. This policy resulted in a resource allocation that was strikingly inconsistent with the resource availability of a poor country with very little capital, either physical or human, and a great deal of labour. It was this strategy, adopted from the Soviet Union and most strikingly epitomized by the Great Leap, that led to policy errors culmination in the greatest famine the world has ever known.

The specific implications of the strategy are described, in particular its emphasis on a very high rate of investment, allocation of nearly all investment funds to heavy industry to the neglect of agriculture, light industry and the services, an emphasis on low interest rates and low wages to minimize the costs of developing heavy industry, an overvalued exchange rate to minimize the cost of imported equipment and machinery, and low prices for agricultural products to make it possible for the urban workers to survive on their low wages. In other words, enormous distortions were introduced that were designed to minimize the apparent costs of the priority on heavy industry.

With the large departures from efficient utilization of resources resulting from the heavy industry or leap forward strategy, there was no alternative but to replace market institutions by a planning process. Not only did that planning process replace nearly all of the market functions in the exchange of goods among enterprises but it also left little or no room for discretion by the managers of enterprises with respect to employment, wages, investment or technology. Consequently, the strategy adopted dictated the major elements of national economic policy rather than these elements having been imposed by socialism.

Another aspect of the book is that it shows that China's emphasis on heavy industry and a leap forward policy was not unique. Not only was such a policy adopted in Central and Eastern Europe, but also in capitalist economies such as India, Argentina, Brazil, Uruguay, Chile and the Philippines. In these countries there was emphasis on significant state intervention and import substitution policies. These policies ignored the comparative advantages each country possessed. Countries that emphasized their comparative advantages, such as Australia, Hong Kong, Taiwan and South Korea, were much more successful in increasing the real per capita incomes of their populations.

The book is also unique in that it provides a balanced picture of the reforms that were begun in the late 1970s. The picture was balanced in several respects — it includes a discussion of both rural and urban reforms, it discusses why the reforms were, overall, highly successful through improving incentives for farmers, workers and managers, and by permitting China's comparative advantages to emerge in response to market signals. But the warts are not ignored and several shortcomings of the reform process are noted and evaluated, especially with respect to the state-owned enterprises, the reasons why it has not been possible to follow a consistent macroeconomic policy, and the widening income disparities between the countryside and the city and among the regions.

The authors make a strong case for an incremental approach to economic reform rather than the shock therapy that has been followed in most countries in Central and Eastern Europe. They make the valid point that incremental reform, at least as carried out in China, did not result in a decline in national output or serious unemployment as was the case in Central and Eastern Europe. In the latter countries, the sharp falls in output and increases in unemployment reduced support for economic reform and often resulted in the need to retrench and slow the reform process. It may be argued that China started its reform process with an important advantage compared to the successor states of the USSR and the countries of Eastern Europe and thus had the luxury of gradualism. In nearly all of the European states there was a large macroeconomic imbalance at the time the reform process started while China had a relatively modest imbalance. Because of the much greater importance of agriculture in China, it may well have been that the structural imbalance overall was less than in the other economies.

But this is a very minor quibble. China has made a gradual reform process work, something that Hungary was unable to do. This book contributes enormously to understanding how and why China has succeeded in so many ways while noting with care a number of shortcomings. A very important contribution was to develop with care and detail how the adoption of the heavy industry strategy set the policy agenda for China from the early 1950s until the late 1970s. Had the policy been based on a different strategy, the development of China would almost certainly have been very different than it was over the three decades from 1950 to 1980.

D. Gale Johnson
University of Chicago
June 1996

Preface to the Revised Edition

The first edition of this book was jointly published in simplified Chinese in 1994 by the Shanghai Sanlian Bookstore and the Shanghai People's Publishing House under the title *The China Miracle: Development Strategy and Economic Reform.* The Chinese Univer-sity of Hong Kong Press published an edition in traditional Chinese in 1995 and an English edition in 1996. Editions in Japanese, Korean, French, and Vietnamese soon followed. At the request of the Chinese University Press, the Linking Publishing Company (Taiwan), the Shanghai Sanlian Bookstore, and the Shanghai People's Publishing House, we revised and updated the original text. The revised Chinese edition was published in Taiwan and Shanghai. It was then translated into Russian and Korean and published in the spring of 2001.

Since the publication of the first edition, economic development and reform in China have made further progress, and several major events have occurred in the regional as well as in the world economy. Because the first edition has enjoyed a large readership in several different countries, and especially because it is widely used as a textbook about China's economic development and reform in universities in Mainland China, Hong Kong, the United States, Japan, and Korea, we have received a great deal of valuable feedbacks about our work. In response to the latest development in economic theory, policy, and practice, as well as to the comments from our friends and colleagues, we have re-examined and expanded the ideas presented in the first edition. Our refined analyses have partially appeared in papers (published in journals and newspapers) and in *Reform of China's State-owned Enterprises* (published in Mainland China under the title *Sufficient Information and Reform of State-owned Enterprises*). Readers may be better equipped to understand our theory and its policy implications if we take a moment to discuss the principles governing the revisions that led to the current edition.

Many reviews of the first edition have been printed in China and other places. Most of the reviewers appreciate the rigour of our logic. In the book, we begin with the contradiction between the traditional development strategy and the economy's factor endowment in China. Then we analyze the logic of the endogenous formation of China's pre-reform economic system and apply the same analysis to other countries and regions. The analyses lead to the conclusion that whether the development strategy is in line with the comparative advantage, the economy's factor endowment is the ultimate determinant of the nature of the economic system and of economic performance. In fact, the logic of the formation of economic institutions in China, as developed in the book, can powerfully explain the formation of economic institutions and the economic performance in other countries. We are also delighted to find that the theory developed in the book about Chinese economic development and reform can make a contribution to development economics. In this revised edition we further expound upon the logic behind this theory.

It is heartening for us to note that more and more economists in China are attaching importance to the issues we stress in the book. In particular, people have begun to view the transition of Chinese economy from the perspective of the economic development strategy. Economists used to concentrate on analyzing one aspect of the economic system in isolation and making policy recommendations accordingly. Now they have reached a higher level of understanding, by being more attentive to the intrinsic logic of the economic system.

Of course, no consensus has been reached on issues such as the general character of Chinese economy, the formation of the old economic system, and the steps still to be taken in pursuit of further economic reforms. Differences of opinion on these matters will persist for a long time. We expect that this diversity of opinion will serve to further refine our theory. In fact, the very existence of debates gives us opportunities to communicate our views on a wide range of issues and policies. For example, after the first edition was published in Mainland China, *Strategy and Management*, a Beijing-based magazine, published a series of discussions on the book's major analyses over a period of two years. Debates with economists and other scholars prompted us to review the historical evolution of development economics, and especially the way development economists in the past interpreted the development or stagnation of a nation. Drawing on the results of the debates, we rewrote Chapter 4, "The Comparative Advantage Strategy", in this revised edition.

This book explores the question of why a backward country adopted a leap-forward strategy in an attempt to overtake developed countries, why such a strategy failed to achieve its goal, and what alternative strategy could help a developing country successfully develop its economy. We base our analyses mainly on the experience of Mainland China. In the years after the publication of the first edition, economic reform and development in China have progressed considerably. The congruence of the issues discussed in the book and the measures of reforms taken in China in recent years have strengthened our confidence in the theory developed in this book.

We argue that China's pre-reform economic system was formed to facilitate the development of capital-intensive heavy industries in a capital-scarce economy. The system was characterized by the trinity of (1) a macro-policy environment that distorted prices for outputs and factors of production, (2) highly centralized planned resource allocation, and (3) a micro-management mechanism that was characterized by a lack of management autonomy, under which state-owned enterprises (SOEs) were deprived of autonomy and agricultural production was organized in collective farms. China's reform, being a gradual process with Pareto-improvement characteristics, started with the improvement in the micro-management mechanism by the way of granting partial autonomy to farmers and SOEs and allowing them to retain a portion of profits. This reform was originally intended to improve the incentive mechanism and micro efficiency. However, its implementation disrupted the internal consistency of the original centralized system. To make the delegation of autonomy successful, the government then progressively pushed the reform of the resource-allocation system and the macro-policy environment, and eventually abandoned the pre-reform development strategies. Over the past several years, the steps of reform have increasingly followed this approch.

However, we should point out that under this approach, the reform in the macro-policy environment often lagged behind that in the micro-management mechanism and the resource-allocation system, resulting in the incompatibility of institutional arrangements in the economic system and giving rise to a series of problems in the development and reform process. As is particularly noteworthy, because of the policy burdens that the heavy-industry-oriented development strategy imposed on SOEs, it was impossible to further the reform of SOEs and many other problems emerged consequently, including cyclical economic fluctuation, rent seeking, rampant corruption, stumbling financial reform, widening regional income disparities, and unstable grain production. The major prerequisite to solving these problems is to eliminate SOEs' policy burdens and restore the internal consistency of the institutional arrangements within the economic system, and make such arrangement compatible with the development strategy. Given the divergent understanding of these topics within academic circles, we devote much of Chapter 7 and Chapter 8 to elaborating on the arguments outlined above.

As economists, we do not live in an ivory tower. What has happened in the world during the past several years has been so dramatic that we have had to struggle to keep pace. In the first edition of the book, we compared the development experience in China and the four Little Dragons — Taiwan, Hong Kong, South Korea, and Singapore. We also compared the path of reform in China with those in the former Soviet Union and Eastern European countries. We attempted to identify the general implications of Chinese experience in development and reform. The World Bank cited our book in its *World Development Report 1996* (whose theme was "From planning to market"), referring it as "an outstanding work on socialist economy". For a long time, economists argued that China's approach to economic reform, though successful, was not applicable to other countries because of China's unique economic and political conditions. Nevertheless, countries that adopted radical reform measures (also called "shock therapy" or "big bang approach") have fallen by now into an economic morass. Many countries, including Russia, not only have not been able to reap the fruits of their economic reform but are still suffering from the devastating effects of financial crisis. This has led more and more economists and policy-makers to rethink the reform approaches taken in the past. At the same time, economists are becoming increasingly interested in China's success.

A financial crisis hit East Asian economies unexpectedly in 1997. As the saying goes, "something must be rotten before worms multiply." The crisis offered us an opportunity to reassess our theory, leading us ultimately to reaffirm its soundness. We believe that the eruption of the crisis was due to the economic development strategies adopted by these economies and to serious flaws in their economic systems, especially their financial systems. Although we have developed the theory of comparative-advantage-following development strategy in the book mainly in the light of the development experiences of Japan and the four Little Dragons, we have noticed that East Asian economies also have an internal drive for adopting strategies that defy their comparative advantages and attempt to leap forward and overtake advanced economies. Especially for South Korea, as it was moving into the rank of newly industrialized countries, it began to neglect its comparative advantages in factor endowment, striving instead to catch up with and surpass industrialized Western countries. Deviating from its successful development strategy, it spent lavishly to expand capital-intensive and technology-intensive conglomerates that failed to exploit the country's comparative advantages. Conse-quently, it suffered huge losses in the financial turmoil. We have supplemented relevant chapters of the book, including Chapter 4 and Chapter 8, with discussions on the East Asian financial crisis, hoping to show the explanatory power of our theory on the new phenomena in the world and regional economies. The revised edition adds two new chapters, one on the current deflation and the other on the implication of China's accession to WTO. The deflation is a new phenomenon in China. It started to appear in 1998. Chapter 9 analyzes the causes of the current deflation and why, in spite of many efforts by the Chinese government to stimulate investment and consumption demands, deflation persists. The chapter also discusses the possible ways for China to get out of the current deflation in the near future. Chapter 10 discusses the implication of WTO accession on China's reform. After 15 years of endless efforts, China finally became a formal member of WTO in November 2001. The Chinese government claims the accession to WTO to be the second most important policy change after the reform started in 1978. However, there are many concerns about the ability of Chinese economy to meet the challenges brought about by the accession. The chapter analyzes its possible impacts on agriculture and finance and discusses its implications for SOEs reforms in light of the theory developed in the book.

This edition of the book applies economic analysis to discuss questions related to the structure of factor endowment, development strategy, the economic system, and economic reform in China. We have omitted several related issues, including the environment and sustainable development, the rule of law, and the reform of the political system, and hope to highlight the logic and themes most important to our theory.

Preface to the First Edition

I

We began our research for this book in late 1988. At that time, China was experiencing its worst inflation of recent decades. There were numerous discussions in economic policy-making and academic circles about the origins and mechanisms of and the policy options for controlling inflation. Our research was prompted by participation in some of these discussions. At that time, the Chinese central government had adopted the retrenchment and consolidation policy package to deal with the difficult economic situation. Meanwhile, it organized economists to participate in a study of how the Chinese economy could extract itself from the situation. In the research process, we came to the conclusion that China's main economic problem is the chronic cycle in which liberalization leads to vigour, which in turn leads to chaos, which then leads to retrenchment, which goes on to cause sterility, which once again leads to liberalization, or in short the vigour/chaos cycle. Since during the reform process the reform of the macro-policy environment lagged behind that of the micro-management institution and resource-allocation mechanism, the frequency and amplitude of the vigour/chaos cycle increased. Therefore, without studying the inherent logic of the traditional economic system and the factors that caused the cycles described above, it would be impossible to come up with an effective policy to solve the problem.

The issue of economic transition has become a focal point of academic research. This is also an era for the advancement of and interaction between new institutional economics and development economics. China's reform and development experience provides an unprecedented opportunity and challenge for economists. In the last few decades, China's traditional economic system has undergone formation, operation and transformation. The economy has been characterized by sharp differences in economic performances at different stages. Its experience thus provides us with abundant material for studies of economic reform and development.

At the same time, there has been a wave of economic reforms around the world, thus calling for a generalization of the Chinese experience. Economists are expected to come up with a new theoretical and analytical framework for summarizing the experience of China's reform and for making contributions to the advancement of development economics and new institutional economics. We are honoured to be among the group who shoulder this responsibility.

During the research process, we were impressed by the richness of the Chinese experience, and were inspired by colleagues within and outside China. We have gained a deeper understanding of the issues relating to economic reform, and have gradually formed and refined a theoretical framework capable of analyzing China's economic reform and development. Based on this theoretical framework, we can explain the logic of the traditional Chinese system, the success of its economic reform, the existence of the vigour/chaos cycle, and the general implications of China's experience for other reforming economies. Because the framework is logically complete and the implications of the framework are consistent with the empirical observations in China and many other countries, we felt compelled to write a book summarizing our recent research as a way to solicit advice from fellow economists and all readers who are concerned about China's economic reforms and future.

II

The starting point for the formation of the traditional economic system in China was the adoption of a leap forward type of heavy industry-oriented development strategy. After the founding of the People's Republic of China in 1949, the government adopted this strategy as a way to achieve the goal of rapid industrialization so that China could catch up with or even forge ahead of advanced countries. But the capital-intensive nature of heavy industry contradicted the capital-scarce nature of China's endowment structure at that time. It was impossible to accelerate the development of heavy industry through the normal market mechanism. Therefore, it became necessary for the government to step in, artificially suppressing the interest rate, exchange rate, prices of raw material, wages and prices of daily necessities, so as to reduce the costs of developing heavy industry. In such a distorted macro-policy environment, resources had to be allocated through a highly centralized planning mechanism. The highly centralized planned resource-allocation mechanism was the result. To control the surplus produced by enterprises and implement the monopolized procurement and marketing of major agricultural products in rural areas, the government introduced the nationalization of industries and the collectivization of agriculture. In addition, state enterprises were deprived of autonomy for fear of managerial discretion under the distorted macro-policy environment. This micro-management institution was consistent with the distorted macro-policy environment and the planned resource-allocation mechanism. We can see that the result of the choice of a heavy industry-oriented development strategy in a capital-scarce economy led to the trinity of the traditional economic system — namely, the distorted macro-policy environment, the highly centralized planned allocation mechanism and the puppet-like micro-management institution. The trinity of the traditional economic system was endogenous, mutually dependent and mutually conditional.

The analytical framework of the traditional economic system described above is useful for our analysis of the problems with the traditional economic system. The trinity of the economic system has led to distortion in production structure and a suppression of incentive, thus hampering economic growth and causing people's standard of living to remain low. China is not the only country whose economic development before the implementation of reforms proves the ineffectiveness of a heavy industry-oriented development strategy in achieving the goal of catching up and forging ahead. Other countries adopting a similar development strategy found themselves in a similar situation.

In addition, the trinity of the traditional economic system helps us explain why the vigour/chaos cycle occurs repeatedly throughout the reform process. China's reform began by decentralizing administrative control of the micro-management institution and allowing micro- units to share part of the newly created profits so as to improve the micro-incentive mechanism. The planned resource-allocation mechanism was subsequently relaxed. As a result, the dual-track price system and resource-allocation mechanism appeared. Although economic vitality increased, reform of the macro-policy environment lagged behind reform of the micro-management institution and resource-allocation mechanism, thus producing an incompatibility in the institutional structure. The result was the observed vigour/chaos cycle, characterized by the repeated appearance of bottle-necks for growth, aggravated inflation, the emergence of corruption and the return to traditional institutional arrangements. Moreover, the frequent occurrence of the cycle slowed down the reforms necessary for increasing the competitiveness of large- and medium-sized state enterprises and for narrowing regional income gaps.

Finally, from the internal logic of the economic system, we can clearly see the characteristics of China's economic reform and the general implication of China's experience. China's reform started by improving micro-incentive through decentralizing and allowing micro-units to share newly created profits. The improvement in the micro-incentive mechanism produced a new stream of resources. Micro-management units obtained the right to allocate part of the newly created resources, and pressed for subsequent reform of the resource-allocation mechanism. Moreover, under the profit motive, the micro-management units allocated more resources under their control to the suppressed labour-intensive industries, leading to a further increase in the wealth of society. The reform at this stage was a Pareto improvement. Because of the increase in wealth, when the process proceeded logically to the reform of the macro-policy environment, it was possible for the state to subsidize vested interest groups which would be hurt during price reforms. Therefore, a non-Pareto improvement price reform became a Kaldor improvement. It was thus possible to continue carrying out the reform at a comparatively low cost.

III

There are ten chapters in this book. The first briefly describes China's economic reforms over the past 16 years. It also makes a simple prediction: if China's economic reform can continue to move in the right direction, and if the Chinese economy can remain healthy and expand quickly, China's economy is expected to catch up with and overtake that of the United States and Japan in the first half of the 21st century, becoming the largest in the world. The book attempts to analyze the reasons behind the miracle of China's expanding economy and to explore the necessary policies that will enable China — the sleeping lion — to rise again. Four related questions are raised in this chapter: (1) why the Chinese economy grew slowly before the implementation of reform and quickly afterwards; (2) why the vigour/chaos cycle became part of China's reform process; (3) whether the trend of China's reform and development can continue; (4) why China's reform has been tremendously successful while the reforms of the former Soviet Union and Eastern European countries have encountered dreadful difficulties.

Chapters Two to Four discuss the relationship between development strategies and economic systems, and between economic systems and economic achievements, through a comparative study of development strategies. Chapter Two — "Leap Forward Development Strategy and Formation of the Traditional Economic System" — describes from historical as well as economic points of view the choice of a leap forward type of heavy industry-oriented development strategy and the formation of the trinity of the macro-policy environment, resource-allocation mechanism and micro-management institution in the economic system. At the same time, we examine the cases of the former Soviet Union and other countries such as India and South and Central American countries. We find that these countries have adopted a development strategy similar to China's, and that their resulting economic systems were also similar to China's. Chapter Three — "Pre-Reform Economic Development in China" — reviews China's development experience before the reform in the areas of speed of economic growth, economic efficiency and incentive mechanisms. This chapter also examines the experience of other countries implementing a similar development strategy. It concludes that the anti-comparative advantage leap forward strategy[1] cannot accelerate economic development. Chapter Four — "Comparative Advantage Strategy" — provides another alternative economic development strategy generalized from the successful experiences of the four Little Dragons in Asia. In addition, the chapter theoretically and empirically discusses the macro-policy environment required for the comparative advantage development strategy and why this strategy encourages economic development. Keeping in mind the urgency of China's reform and development, this chapter points out that at the core of economic reform is the change in development strategy.

The fifth chapter — "Economic Reform in China" — and the sixth chapter — "Results of China's Economic Reforms" — summarize, from the logical sequences manifested by the reform itself, the stages, process, and main content of each stage of China's reform, and the differing economic performances witnessed after reforms were implemented. China's economic reform started with the micro-management institution. Through decentralizing and allowing enterprises to share profits, the micro-incentive mechanism improved, and the economy became more efficient. The creation of a new stream of resources and the appearance of non-state enterprises called for corresponding reform in the resource-allocation mechanism, thus forming the dual-track resource-allocation and price system. Through the newly formed market mechanism, the newly created stream of resources was allocated to the labour-intensive sectors which had been suppressed under the traditional strategy, so the distortion in the production structure was ameliorated. The improvement in economic efficiency and the adjustment in production structure have promoted economic growth and resulted in an average annual growth rate of nearly 10 percent for

1. In this revised edition, "anti-comparative-advantage leap forward strategy" is either rephrased as "comparative-advantage-defying strategy" or "leap-forward strategy".

the past 16 years in China. In particular, the phenomenal growth in China's coastal regions proves that the key to economic growth is to make good use of an economy's comparative advantage.

Chapters Seven and Eight focus on the analysis of problems and difficulties that have emerged during China's reform process, and suggest the appropriate direction for future reforms to take. Chapter Seven — "Problems with Economic Reforms" — makes use of the theoretical framework that points out the integrity and mutual dependence of the traditional institutional arrangements to clearly explain the reasons for the appearance of speed-constraining bottlenecks, inflation, and corruption. The chapter also points out that the recurrence of the vigour/chaos cycle, the difficulty of increasing the vitality of state enterprises, and the problems with narrowing regional disparity all share the same root. That is, reform of the macro-policy environment lags behind reform of the micro-management institution and resource-allocation mechanism, and the shift in the development strategy is thus incomplete. It has become increasingly clear that reform of the macro-policy environment, and particularly of the factor-price formation mechanism, is imperative so as to complete the transformation of China's development strategy. The acceptance of a market economy as the goal of economic reform, and a better theoretical understating of economic reform, provide the necessary conditions for eradicating the vigour/chaos cycle and overcoming obstacles which stand in the way of reform.

Chapter Nine — "Lessons of China's Reform" — discusses, through comparisons, the general implications and advantages of China's incremental approach to reform. On the one hand, through relaxing control of the incremental resources created by the reform of the micro-management institution, China's reforms were pushed forward to the resource-allocation mechanism and the macro-policy environment. Therefore, the reforms followed an internally logical sequence. On the other hand, the allocation of newly created resources to the suppressed sectors increased the profits of the micro-management units and the tax revenue of the government. Better still, virtually no vested interest groups were hurt in this process. Therefore the reform received nationwide support and became irreversible. When the reform was expanded to include the macro-policy environment, society was able to provide subsidies to groups whose interests suffered as a consequence of reform. Thus a non-Pareto improvement price reform was carefully transformed into a Kaldor improvement. Moreover, the reform of the macro-policy environment was implemented after reform of the micro-management institution and resource-allocation mechanism made the macro-policy environment reform indispensable. The price reform was carried out through a dual-track approach; that is, adjustments to planned prices were made incrementally, and market prices were simultaneously allowed to emerge alongside planned prices. When planned prices were continuously adjusted to a level close to market equilibrium price, and resources allocated at the market price increased to an important proportion, the liberalization of all prices at once became less risky. Therefore, through narrowing the chasm step by step, crossing it became possible. This type of incremental reform provided society with a continuous opportunity to make choices, hence maintaining a balance between speed and stability in the reform progress. Political radicalism and social unrest were thus avoided. As this book illustrates, all other countries which are currently undergoing economic reform or major adjustments have adopted a development strategy similar to China's. Their economic structures are similar, and they have experienced similar problems. Therefore, the successful experience of China's reform should be relevant to these reforming economies.

Chapter Ten concludes the book with a summary, and provides brief answers to questions raised in the Introduction. First, the fundamental cause of China's slow economic development before reform was the adoption of a heavy industry-oriented development strategy, and the key to the rapid development after the reform was the better use of China's comparative advantages which was brought about by reforming the trinity of the traditional economic system. Second, the origin of the vigour/chaos cycle was the internal inconsistency in the economic system due to some institutional arrangements' reforms lagging behind reforms of other institutional arrangements. The key to eliminating the vigour/chaos cycle is to make the reform of the macro-policy environment further reaching as soon as possible, and to uproot the heavy industry-oriented development strategy. Third, if the reform can continue moving in the right direction, China will be able to overcome the difficulties and barriers of the reform process. The continued success brought about by the reform will support persistent, rapid and healthy economic growth. Therefore, it is very likely that by the first half of the 21st century, China's economy will surpass the economies of the United States and Japan, becoming the largest in the world. And fourth, the success of China's reform was guaranteed by the adoption of an incremental approach, which is characterized by low opportunity cost, small risks and immediate benefits. On the other hand, countries of Eastern Europe and the former Soviet Union chose a different approach for their reforms, which produced enormous friction and social unrest. So far their reforms have not resulted in much economic growth. Since the economic systems as well as the difficulties encountered in the countries currently undergoing reform or adjustment are all similar, the road to reform should have something in common. Therefore, China's reform experience has general implications.

IV

We have tried to achieve two goals in writing this book. We have targeted readers from different walks of life, both in China and elsewhere. We hope to satisfy their curiosity as to how China's miracle occurred, whether it can sustain itself and whether China can become a powerful nation in the next century. We have also targeted fellow economists. We use familiar economic terminology to describe the process of China's economic reform and to explain our analytical framework. We hope to prompt further economic research into the Chinese experience.

In attempting to achieve these two aims simultaneously, dilemmas have been unavoidable. To satisfy the needs of the general reader, we have had to use a simple approach to express our views and to describe the process of China's economic reform. On the other hand, for an audience of economists, we have had to start with basic economic assumptions, and to rigorously propose and prove our theory using economic logic. Nevertheless, these two aims are in many ways complementary. The miracle of the economic development achieved by China's reform in the past 16 years has excited the curiosity of economists as well as others. In the course of human history, the Chinese economy has fallen from its one-time height into serious decline. As a result of the recent reform, in just 16 short years China has regained the hope of once again becoming a powerful economy. Understanding this miracle, and identifying the implications for other countries undergoing reform and for China's future reform itself are all of great importance. Therefore, it is our ultimate goal to explore the reasons for the success of China's reform as well as to help readers theoretically understand and empirically grasp its process.

The spirit of modern economics is its analytical approach. Economic analysis is based on the behavioural assumption of rationality. In other words, a decision maker, faced with several alternatives, will choose the one that benefits him/her most. According to economists, this provides the best explanation for the observed economic phenomena. As economists, we are obliged to start our analysis with the correct theoretical assumption, and to give readers an appropriate analytical framework with which to observe and reflect upon China's reform, so as to obtain an objective and truthful understanding of its development. In this book, we assume that consumers, producers and the government are all rational economic agents. We conclude that the set of institutional arrangements in the traditional system and the consequences of adopting them are the result of rational choices made by economic agents. They are endogenous. Understanding this is helpful for explaining the complicated phenomena that have arisen throughout the reform process. The rationality assumption can also guarantee that the analysis in this book is built on the foundation of a scientific approach. Finally, the goal of economics is to help manage society in order to benefit people. So when we theoretically explore China's economic development and reform, we hope not only to contribute to the development of economics, but also to enhance readers' understanding of the cause, course, and consequences of China's reform, to inspire their interest in its continuation, and to recommend China's approach of incremental reform to other economies undergoing reform.

V

It took us over a year to write this book. We started to research China's development strategy and economic reform more than seven years ago. During this period, we received support from many senior colleagues, and we wish to take this opportunity to express our sincerest thanks to them. First of all, we would like to thank Mr. Du Run-Sheng. He has shown great concern for our project and has carefully read drafts at every stage of our research. He also gave relevant criticism, recommendations and suggestions. His support was very encouraging. Mr. Zhang Jinfu and Mr. Ma Bin, two senior economists in China, were also very helpful. They held some of our research results in high regard, and increased our confidence in our work. Mr. Zhang also hosted our seminar which addressed on "How to Extract the Economy from Its Difficult Position." Justin Yifu Lin is Adjunct Professor at the Australian National University. Part of his research was carried out during his visit to ANU, and he received support and help from Professors Ross Garnaut and Peter Drysdale of the Research School of Pacific and Asian Studies at ANU. Fang Cai and Zhou Li also received much support and guidance from Professor Liu Guoguang, the former Deputy President of the Chinese Academy of Social Sciences, and from Professor Chen Jiyuan, Director of the Rural Development Research Institute of the Chinese Academy of Social Sciences. Many senior colleagues and friends supported and inspired our work. We would like to mention, especially, Professor Wu Jinglian, from whose work we have learned a great deal. Professor Yue-chim Richard Wong of the University of Hong Kong and Mr. Chen Xin, Director of Shanghai People's Press, provided encouragement. Shen Minggao and Zen Qiongrui helped us with much tedious work. Professor Richard Wong has been instrumental in arranging for the publication of both the Chinese and the English edition of this book. Finally, thanks go to our families, particularly Mrs. Lin Chen Yunying, Mrs. Cai Xu Tao and Mrs. Li Tian Airu, for their support and understanding over the years. Their hard work undoubtedly contributed to the completion of this book. However, the authors alone are responsible for any mistakes it may contain.

The Authors

Justin Yifu Lin is Professor and Founding Director of the China Center for Economic Research (CCER) at Peking University, and Professor at the Hong Kong University of Science and Technology. His articles have appeared in various academic journals such as *American Economic Review* and *Journal of Political Economy*.

Fang Cai is Research Fellow and Director of the Institute of Demography, the Chinese Academy of Social Sciences, Beijing.

Zhou Li is Deputy Director of the Institute of Rural Development, the Chinese Academy of Social Sciences, Beijing.

CHAPTER 1

Introduction

In pre-modern times, technological inventions and scientific discoveries depended on the experiences of craftsmen and farmers as well as on the observations of geniuses. As a populous country, China did not lack skillful craftsmen, experienced farmers, and geniuses. Hence, it had comparative advantages in developing science and technology. China was the most prosperous nation in the world; it led other nations in scientific discovery, technological innovation, productivity, industrialization, and wealth creation until about two or three hundred years ago. In the past, compared with China, "the West ... was essentially agrarian and ... was poorer and underdeveloped."[1]

As world history moved into the modern era, scientific discoveries and technological inventions began relying on scientific experiments. China's large population no longer constituted a comparative advantage in making scientific and technological progress. Meanwhile, the rigid imperial examination system — the civil service examination aiming to train obedient officials — became an obstacle to the development of human capital needed to ignite a scientific revolution. As a consequence, China, an ancient and once-glorious civilization, fell into obscurity during the scientific revolution that swept the Western world.[2] The result was that the

1. Carlo M. Cipolla, *Before the Industrial Revolution: European Society and Economy, 1000–1700*, 2nd ed. New York: Norton, 1980, p. 171.
2. Justin Yifu Lin, " The Needham Puzzle: Why the Industrial Revolution Did Not Originate in China", *Economic Development and Cultural Change*, Vol. 43, No. 2 (January 1995), pp. 269–92.

Western nations reaped the fruit of the scientific and industrial revolution that enabled them to pull ahead economically and eventually to achieve economic modernization, while China saw its national power lag far behind that of the West.

In the modern times, it was not necessary for developing countries to invent independently the science and technology essential for their economic development. Rather, developing countries could develop their economies by learning from other developed countries and by borrowing technology. Beginning in the 1950s, China accelerated its industrialization and tried to achieve economic modernization by launching a series of political movements. However, the results were far from satisfactory. Before the recent reform (which went into effect in the late 1970s) began, the gap between China and more advanced countries widened rather than narrowed. For example, in 1950, China's gross domestic product (GDP) was more than twice that of Japan, but it was only 90% of Japan's in 1980.[3]

In the late 1970s, China initiated a full-scale economic reform in rural and urban parts of the country. The outcomes were impressive. Since 1978, China has been one of the world's fastest-growing economies, with an annual GDP growth rate averaging 9.6%, a record level for the country since the founding of the People's Republic of China in 1949. Meanwhile, China's per-capita GDP growth rate averaged 8.4% annually, a rate comparable to the growth rates of the four Little Dragons during the period of their most rapid development. In particular, during this period China's five coastal provinces, which altogether have four times the area and five times the population of the four Little Dragons combined, have maintained a GDP growth rate of 12%, surpassing the growth rates of the four Little Dragons at their height. Such growth is unprecedented. If the conditions favorable to China's economic growth can be maintained or improved upon, we predict that in the near future China's

3. Angus Maddison, *Monitoring the World Economy, 1820–1992*. Paris: OECD, 1995, pp. 183, 191.

economic scale will become larger than that of the United States and Japan and that the country will thus be the biggest economy in the world.

China, whose population makes up two-thirds of the population of all developing nations, is undergoing a series of economic reforms. It has been scoring remarkable success in its transition from a centrally planned economy to a market economy. It is likely to rise as a major world power after more than two centuries of decline. The possibility that China may become the only country in world history to have fallen from the zenith of human civilization into the trough and to have again climbed to the apex will undoubtedly draw the attention of academics, among others. The aims of this book are to analyze the causes of the "China miracle", to use this analysis to determine the most productive direction for further reform in China, and to discuss the general implications of China's experience for other developing nations undergoing similar economic transition.

1.1 Economic Development Since Reform, and Prospects for the 21st Century

In the late 1970s, China began to reform its highly centralized and inefficient economic system. The first step in this process was to introduce the household responsibility system (HRS) in rural areas. In urban areas, reform focused on decentralizing powers to state-owned enterprises (SOEs) and on allowing them to share profits. Moreover, non-collectively-owned enterprises were permitted. Along with the reform of the highly centralized planned allocation mechanism, prices for products and production factors were gradually readjusted or partially liberalized. The government also adopted an open-door policy to attract foreign capital, allow foreign direct investment (FDI), establish joint ventures or exclusively foreign-owned enterprises and expand foreign trade. The reforms that have been carried out over the past two decades have increased China's economic efficiency and adjusted its economic structure. The Chinese economy has been transformed from a typical centralized planned economy into one where the market plays a major role in

Table 1.1 Average Annual Growth Rates (1980–90 and 1990–99) in China and Other Types of Economies (%)

Economy	GDP		Agriculture value added		Industry value added		Services value added	
	1980–90	1990–99	1980–90	1990–99	1980–90	1990–99	1980–90	1990–99
China	10.1	10.7	5.9	4.3	11.1	14.4	13.2	9.2
Low-income	4.4	2.5	3.0	2.5	5.4	1.1	5.7	4.7
High-income	3.1	2.4	—	0.8	—	2.6	—	2.2
World average	3.2	2.5	2.7	1.6	—	3.0	—	2.5

Source: The World Bank, *World Development Report, 2000/2001*. Oxford: Oxford University Press, 2001, pp. 294–95.

resource allocation. The reform has made China one of the fastest-growing and most robust economies in the world.

According to the *World Development Report 2000/2001* released by the World Bank in 2000, China's annual GDP growth rates in 1980–90 and 1990–99 averaged 10.1% and 10.7%, respectively. These rates were the highest in the world during these two periods. They were 6.9 and 8.2 percent points higher than the world averages, 7.0 and 8.3 percent points higher than the rates of developed countries, 5.7 and 8.3 percent points higher than the rates of low income countries. Table 1.1 shows that several significant economic indicators in China were twice or even three times as high as those of other countries and the world average.[4]

The contrast is even sharper between the economic growth of China and that of the former Soviet Union and Eastern European countries, whose economies were on the verge of collapse after economic reform. Table 1.2 and Table 1.3 show that from 1988 to 1998 the former Soviet Union and most Eastern European countries reported negative economic growth and high inflation rates. In fact,

4. The World Bank, *World Development Report, 2000/2001*. Oxford: Oxford University Press, 2001, pp. 294–95.

Table 1.2 Real GDP Growth in Eastern Europe, the Baltic States, and the Commonwealth of Independent States (%)

Country	1988	1989	1990	1991	1992	1993	1994	1995	1996	1997	1998	Estimated 1997 GDP*	Forecast 1998 GDP**
Total				–11.0	–9.5	–4.7	–5.4	–0.1	–0.2	2.0	–1.0	73	72
Eastern European Countries and the Baltic States				–11.0	–3.8	0.4	3.9	5.5	4.0	3.6	3.1	96	99
Albania				–30.0	–7.2	9.6	9.4	8.9	9.1	–7.0	10.0	80	88
Bulgaria	2.5	–1.9	–9.1	–12.0	–7.3	–1.5	1.8	2.1	–10.9	–6.9	4.0	63	66
Croatia				–29.0	–11.7	–8.0	5.9	6.8	6.0	6.5	4.8	76	80
Czechoslovakia	2.5	1.4	–0.4	–14.0	–3.3	0.6	3.2	6.4	3.9	1.0	–0.5	98	98
Estonia				–13.0	–14.2	–9.0	–2.0	4.3	4.0	11.4	5.0	73	77
Macedonia				–11.0	–21.1	–9.1	–1.8	–1.2	0.8	1.5	5.0	56	59
Hungary	–0.1	–0.2	–4.0	–12.0	–3.1	–0.6	2.9	1.5	1.3	4.4	4.6	90	95
Latvia				–8.0	–34.9	–14.9	0.6	–0.8	3.3	6.5	4.0	56	58
Lithuania				–13.0	–21.3	–16.2	–9.8	3.3	4.7	5.7	3.0	61	63
Poland	4.0	0.2	–11.6	–7.0	2.6	3.8	5.2	7.0	6.1	6.9	5.2	112	118
Romania	1.4	–6.9	–7.4	–14.0	–8.7	1.5	3.9	7.1	4.1	–6.6	–5.2	82	78
Slovakia	2.5	1.4	–0.4	–16.0	–6.5	–3.7	4.9	6.9	6.6	6.5	5.0	95	100
Slovenia				–9.0	–5.5	2.8	5.3	4.1	3.1	3.8	4.0	99	103

Table 1.2 (Cont'd)

Country	1988	1989	1990	1991	1992	1993	1994	1995	1996	1997	1998	Estimated 1997 GDP*	Forecast 1998 GDP**
Commonwealth of Independent States				–11.0	–14.2	–8.9	–13.1	–4.6	–3.4	0.9	-3.6	57	55
Armenia				–12.0	–52.6	–14.8	5.4	6.9	5.8	3.1	6.0	38	40
Azerbaijan				–2.0	–22.6	–23.1	–19.7	–11.8	1.3	5.8	6.7	40	42
Belarus				–3.0	–9.6	–7.6	–12.6	–10.4	2.8	10.4	5.0	71	75
Georgia				–25.0	–44.8	–25.4	–11.4	2.4	10.5	11.0	9.0	32	35
Kazakhstan				–8.0	–2.9	–9.2	–12.6	–8.2	0.5	2.0	1.0	63	63
Kyrgyzstan				–5.0	–19.0	–16.0	–20.0	–5.4	7.1	6.5	4.0	57	60
Moldova				–12.0	–29.1	–1.2	–31.2	–3.0	–8.0	1.3	–2.0	35	34
Russia	4.5	1.9	–3.6	–11.0	–14.5	–8.7	–12.7	–4.1	–3.5	0.8	–5.0	58	55
Tajikistan				–9.0	–29.0	–11.0	–18.9	–12.5	–4.4	1.7	3.4	40	41
Turkmenistan				–7.0	–5.3	–10.0	–18.8	–8.2	–8.0	–26.0	5.0	42	44
Ukraine	2.3	4.1	–3.4	–14.0	–13.7	–14.2	–23.0	–12.2	–10.0	–3.2	0.0	37	37
Uzbekistan				–1.0	–11.1	–2.3	–4.2	–0.9	1.6	2.4	2.0	87	88

* The estimate takes the GDP level in 1989 as 100, and the GDP level in 1997 are in real terms.

** The forecast takes the GDP level in 1989 as 100, and the GDP level in 1998 are in real terms.

Source: *Economics of Transition*, Vol. 1, No. 3 (1993), pp. 370–78; *Economics of Transition*, Vol. 6, No. 2 (1998), p. 545.

Table 1.3 Inflation in Eastern Europe, the Baltic States, and the Commonwealth of Independent States (%)

Country	1988	1989	1990	1991	1992	1993	1994	1995	1996	1997
Eastern European Countries and the Baltic States										
Albania				36.0	236.6	30.9	15.8	6.0	17.4	42.1
Bulgaria	2.2	10.0	64.0	334.0	79.4	63.8	121.9	32.1	310.8	578.5
Croatia				123.0	938.2	1149.0	–3.0	3.5	3.4	3.8
Czechoslovakia	0.2	2.3	10.8	57.0	12.7	18.2	9.7	7.9	8.6	10.0
Estonia				212.0	953.5	35.6	42.0	29.0	15.0	12.0
Macedonia				115.0	1925.2	229.6	55.4	9.0	–0.6	2.6
Hungary	16.1	17.0	28.9	91.0	21.6	21.1	21.2	28.3	19.8	18.4
Latvia				172.0	959.0	35.0	26.0	23.1	13.1	7.0
Lithuania				225.0	1161.1	188.8	45.0	35.5	13.1	8.5
Poland	60.2	251.1	585.7	70.0	44.3	37.6	29.4	21.6	18.5	13.2
Romania	2.6	0.9	7.4	161.0	199.2	295.5	61.7	27.8	56.9	151.4
Slovakia	0.2	2.3	10.8	61.0	9.1	25.1	11.7	7.2	5.4	6.4
Slovenia				115.0	92.9	22.8	19.5	9.0	9.0	8.8
Median					199.2	35.6	26.0	21.6	13.1	10.0
Average				85.0	510.2	165.6	35.1	18.5	37.7	66.4
Commonwealth of Independent States										
Armenia				100.0	na	10896.0	1885.0	31.9	5.8	21.8
Azerbaijan				138.0	1395.0	1293.8	1788.0	84.5	6.5	0.4
Belarus				80.0	1159.0	1996.0	1960.0	244.0	39.0	63.0
Georgia				81.0	1176.9	7487.9	6474.4	57.4	14.3	7.1
Kazakhstan				91.0	2984.1	2169.0	1160.0	60.4	28.6	11.3
Kyrgyzstan				85.0	1259.0	1363.0	95.7	31.9	35.0	14.7
Moldova				98.0	2198.0	837.0	116.0	213.8	15.1	11.2
Russia		2.0	5.6	93.0	2506.1	840.0	204.4	128.6	21.8	10.9
Tajikistan				103.0	1364.0	7344.0	1.1	2133.0	40.5	163.6
Turkmenistan				90.0	644.0	9750.0	1328.0	1262.0	446.0	21.5
Ukraine	0.3	2.2	4.2	91.0	2730.0	10155.0	401.0	182.0	39.7	10.1
Uzbekistan				82.0	910.0	885.0	1281.0	117.0	64.0	50.0
Median					1364.0	2082.5	1220.5	100.8	31.8	13.0
Average				101.0	1666.0	4584.7	1391.2	363.0	63.0	32.1

Note: Figures for 1997 are estimated figures.

Source: *Economics of Transition*, Vol. 1, No. 3 (1993), pp. 370–78; *Economics of Transition*, Vol. 6, No. 2 (1998), pp. 545.

in most of these countries, the real GDP in 1998 was even lower than it had been in 1989.

Following the implementation of reform, China's economic growth underwent a momentous change. During the period 1978–2000, GDP increased from RMB 362.4 billion to RMB 8,940.4 billion, and per capita GDP increased from RMB 379 to RMB 7,063. Using comparable prices, the average annual growth rates were 9.5% and 8.1%, respectively; these were, respectively, 66% and 125% higher than the average annual growth rate of national income (5.7%) and than the average annual growth rate of per capita national income (3.6%) from 1952 to 1977.[5] Meanwhile, the average annual growth rates for primary industry, secondary industry, and tertiary industry were 4.7%, 11.4%, and 10.3%, respectively, while the rates for agriculture, industry, and service sectors[6] in 1952–77 were only 1.8%, 10.8%, and 4.5%, respectively. This represents an increase of 163%, 6%, and 128%.[7] During the period 1978–2000, growth in international trade was even more rapid. The total value of imports and exports increased from US$20.64 billion to US$474.3 billion and enjoyed an average annual growth rate of 15.3%. Exports increased from US$9.75 billion to US$249.2 billion, with an average annual growth rate of 15.9%, while imports increased from US$10.89 billion to US$225.1 billion, with an average annual growth rate of 14.8%.[8] Both surpassed the average annual GNP growth rate,

5. The GNP indicators for national economic statistics were first adopted in 1978, and therefore they could not be used to compare economic growth before and after the reform. Of the three substitute indicators — aggregate social value, gross industrial and agricultural value, and national income — the first involves duplicate calculations; the second neglects construction, transportation, and commerce and also involves duplicate calculation; the third approximates GNP and is the one we have chosen to use here.
6. The three industrial statistics were first calculated in 1978. Because we cannot compare economic growth of the primary, secondary and tertiary industry before and after reform, we use agriculture, industry, and services industry instead.
7. National Bureau of Statistics of China, *China Statistical Yearbook, 2001*. Beijing: China Statistics Press, 2001, p. 52.
8. National Bureau of Statistics of China, *China Statistical Yearbook, 2001*. Beijing: China Statistics Press, 2001, pp. 26–27.

indicating the increasing integration of the Chinese economy with the world economy.

With rapid economic growth, the income of rural and urban households increased significantly. The net income of rural households increased from RMB 133.6 in 1978 to RMB 2,253 in 2000, while the average annual disposable income of urban households increased from RMB 343.5 to RMB 6,280. Eliminating the effect of inflation, the real average annual growth rates were 7.4% and 6.3%, respectively, while the average annual growth rates were only 2.9% and 1.4% in the 21 years before the reform began. The proportion of income derived from financial assets in total income also increased steadily. In 2000, savings of rural and urban households reached RMB 6,433.2 billion, 303.5 times the 1978 level of RMB 21.2 billion, with an annual growth rate of 29.7%. In addition, urban and rural households had more than US$70 billion in foreign reserves, RMB 1,600 billion in various bonds, RMB 1,609 billion in stocks, more than RMB 100 billion in stock options, and RMB 1,465 billion in cash. Total financial assets exceeded RMB 11,800 billion.[9]

These changes raised the living standards of the Chinese people and improved their quality of life considerably. The per capita consumption level rose from RMB 184 in 1978 to RMB 3,397 in 2000. Using comparable prices, the average annual growth rate of consumption index was 7.2% in 1978–2000, 3.3 times the rate in 1952–77 (2.2%).[10] Moreover, changes occurred in the consumption structure. The Engel's coefficient (the ratio of consumption expenditure on food to total expenditure for daily life) for urban and rural residents decreased respectively from 57.5% and 67.7% in 1978 to 39.2% and 49.1% in 2000, a decrease of 18.3 and 18.6 percent points respectively.

Compared with historical figures, these changes in percentages

---

9. National Bureau of Statistics of China, *China Statistical Yearbook, 2001*. Beijing: China Statistics Press, 2001, various pages.
10. National Bureau of Statistics of China, *China Statistical Yearbook, 2001*. Beijing: China Statistics Press, 2001, p. 66.

are particularly dramatic. From 1952 to 1978, China's per capita annual consumption of major foodstuffs such as grain and edible oils actually decreased. The per capita consumption of poultry held steady. The per capita consumption of meats, eggs, and aquatic products increased by less than 100%, with an absolute increase of less than or slightly more than 1 kilogram. Only consumption levels for sugar and liquors, for which initial figures were very low, increased — sugar by 276% and liquors by 125%, an absolute increase of 2.5 kilograms and 1.4 kilograms, respectively. However, between 1978 and 2000, with the exception of a slow increase in the per capita consumption of grain, which resulted from its low income elasticity, the per capita consumption of other major foodstuffs increased significantly, some doubling and some even quadrupling. According to researches conducted by the Ministry of Health, the present average nutrition level in China has reached that of middle-income countries.

As for consumer durables, not only did the amount owned by households increase dramatically during the period 1978–2000, but the consumption structure also changed considerably. Household surveys conducted by the Statistical Department show that in the 1970s consumer durables were mainly watches, bicycles, sewing machines, and radios, each of which was valued at around RMB 100. In the 1980s, the major consumer durables were television sets, refrigerators, washing machines, and cameras, each worth about RMB 1,000. In the 1990s, the major durables included air conditioners, telephones, video cassette recorders, and video cameras, each valued at about RMB 5,000, as well as personal computers worth about RMB 10,000 apiece. In recent years, people have begun to buy items costing around RMB 100,000 each, including apartments and cars.

The economic development of the past 22 years, along with domestic and international conditions favourable for sustainable and rapid growth, has imbued China with the new hope of becoming one of the most prosperous economies in the world. In fact, the phenomenal changes in the Chinese economy have led many foreign observers to conclude that China, for centuries a "sleeping lion", is awakening and is likely to become the largest economy in the world in the early decades of the 21st century.[11] Will the sleeping lion actually wake up? In response to this question, we offer a forecast and analysis.

In 2000, China's GDP reached RMB 8,818.9 billion. Calculating at the average foreign exchange rate of 2000, this is equivalent to US$1,076 billion, which ranked China the sixth largest economy in the world, after the United States (US$9,883 billion), Japan (US$4,677 billion), Germany (US$1,870 billion), United Kingdom (US$1,413 billion) and France (US$1,286 billion).[12]

Since initiating its reform, China has devalued its currency several times. The rate of the RMB to the dollar dropped from 1.7:1 in 1978 to 8.28:1 in 2000. This change has had a great impact on the growth rate of the GDP, which is calculated based on the official exchange rate. Moreover, since many products and services are classified as non-trade items, the large gap between developed and undeveloped countries' prices for these products tends to underestimate the economic scale of the developing nations based on the official foreign exchange rate. Some economists specializing in comparative international economies believe that China's actual economic scale far exceeds the estimate based on the official exchange rate, and they have attempted to come up with more accurate estimates of China's economic scale.

For example, economists at the International Monetary Fund (IMF) adopted the purchasing power parity (PPP) method to calculate China's GDP in 1992. Their estimate was US$1,700 billion, which is 4.7 times the figure based on the official exchange rate.[13] The World Bank also came up with an estimate using the PPP approach. Its estimate of China's GDP was US$2,740.44 billion in 1993, which is 4.8 times the figure based on the official foreign

---

11. "When China Wakes, A Survey of China", *The Economist,* 28 November 1992.
12. Data Source: http://www.worldbank.org/data/countrydata/countrydata.html
13. Hu Zuliu, "The Road to Prosperity — How China's Economic Position Is Evaluated in the World", *Economic Research Materials*, No. 21 (Nov. 1993).

exchange rate.[14] Ross Garnaut, an Australian economist, assumed that a similar consumption level implies a similar per capita GNP in economies with similar consumption habits. He compared China's consumption level with the levels of other Asian economies, particularly those of Taiwan, Hong Kong, and Singapore. He concluded that China's actual GDP was three times the official estimate.[15]

Because different samples, different data, and different estimation methods have been used, estimates of China's GDP may differ in spite of the fact that the same PPP method was used. However, all the estimates reach the same conclusion: that China's GDP, which is based on the official foreign exchange rate, undervalues real purchasing power. In Table 1.4, according to Heston Summers the GDP calculated using the PPP method is about eight times the value based on the official foreign exchange rate. Rand and the IMF

Table 1.4 Estimate of China's Per Capita GDP
(unit = US dollar)

	Year	Based on official rate	PPP	PPP/ Estimate based on official rate
Heston Summers	1986	300	2,444	8.15
Rand	1990	370	1,031	2.49
Lawrence Summers	1990	370	2,140	5.78
BAST University	1991	370	1,680	4.54
IMF	1992	470	1,600	3.40
The World Bank	1993	485	2,120	4.37
Foreign Ministry of Australia	1994	530	1,500–2,500	2.83–4.72
The World Bank	1995	620	2,920	4.71

Source: Zheng Jingping, "How Many US Dollars Is China's Per Capita GNP?" *Economics Information*, 13 September 1996; The World Bank, *World Development Reports, 1990–97.* Beijing: China Finance and Economic Press, 1990–97; Harry Xiaoying Wu, *Measuring China's GDP* (EAAU Briefing Paper Number 8). Sydney: Department of Foreign Affairs and Trade of Australia, 1997.

14. The World Bank, *World Development Report, 1995*, pp. 162, 220.
15. Ross Garnaut and Ma Guonan, *Grain in China*. Canberra: East Asia Analytical Unit, Department of Foreign Affairs and Trade, 1993.

estimate that it should be about two to three times the value. Estimates reached by the World Bank and Ren Ruoen of Beijing Aeronautics and Space Technology University place the GDP at four times the value based on the foreign exchange rate, which lies somewhere in the middle of the four estimates mentioned above. We shall use the World Bank estimates for further analysis. As indicated in Table 1.5, in 1991, based on the official foreign exchange rate, the size of China's economy ranked tenth in the world. However, it ranked third when GDP was estimated using PPP calculations. In 1995, it ranked seventh based on the official foreign exchange rate and second based on the PPP method. Over the past five years, China's growth rate has been much higher than that of the other most affluent countries in the world, and the trend continues. Many scholars predict that if China can overcome internal and external constraints and can maintain this trend for the next 20 to 30 years, it will become the largest economy in the world.

Generally speaking, a country's economic growth rate is determined by three factors: (1) the increase of various production factors, especially capital; (2) the upgrading of industrial structure from low-value-added industry to high-value-added industry; and (3) the technological innovation. Among these factors, technological innovation is the most important. For production factors, natural resource endowment can be seen as given, while an increase in the labour force can make only a small difference. The only production factor that can differ greatly is the rate of capital accumulation. However, the rate of capital accumulation and the upgrading of industrial structure are constrained by the speed of technological innovation. If technology does not change, the continuous accumulation of capital will eventually lead to diminishing marginal returns, which in turn lower the incentive to accumulate more capital. Similarly, if there is no technological advancement in the economy, there will be no upgrading in the industrial structure.

To begin with, the fact that the Chinese economy can maintain a high growth rate can be attributed to its high capital accumulation rate. Such a high capital accumulation rate can provide strong support for rapid economic growth. Advancement in an economy's

Table 1.5 The Economic Scales of 10 Largest Economies in the World

1991							1995						
Based on exchange rate (1)			Based on PPP (2)			Difference (2)/(1)	Based on exchange rate (1)			Based on PPP (2)			Difference (2)/(1)
Rank	Nations	GNP	Rank	Nations	GNP		Rank	Nations	GNP	Rank	Nations	GNP	
1	United States	56100	1	United States	56100	1.00	1	United States	70984	1	United States	70984	1.00
2	Japan	33600	2	Japan	23700	0.71	2	Japan	49629	2	China	35046	4.71
3	Germany	15700	3	China	16600	3.86	3	Germany	22531	3	Japan	27682	0.56
4	France	12000	4	Germany	12500	0.80	4	France	14519	4	Germany	16437	0.73
5	Italy	11500	5	France	10400	0.87	5	United Kingdom	10940	5	India	13012	
6	United Kingdom	10100	6	India	10000		6	Italy	10879	6	France	12218	0.84
7	Canada	5800	7	Italy	9800	0.85	7	China	7441	7	Italy	11366	1.04
8	Spain	5300	8	United Kingdom	9000	0.89	8	Brazil	5795	8	United Kingdom	11267	1.03
9	Brazil	4500	9	Brazil	7900	1.76	9	Canada	5736	9	Brazil	8597	1.48
10	China	4300	10	Mexico	6000		10	Spain	5323	10	Indonesia	7345	

technological structure is closely linked to the upgrading of the economy's endowment structure from a relative scarcity in capital to a relative abundance in capital. This means that relatively large capital accumulation is required for persistent technological advancement, which in turn leads to rapid economic growth. China is one of the few economies that can maintain a high rate of capital accumulation. Since the reform began, annual capital accumulation has accounted for about 40% of China's GDP. This characteristic will have a significant positive impact on maintaining rapid economic growth in China.

The second factor is the upgrading of the industrial structure, especially the shift of labour forces to higher-value-added industries, which can provide strong support for economic growth. With the rise of average income, the labour force will shift from the primary sector to the secondary and tertiary sectors. Given that China has followed a heavy-industry-oriented development strategy for a long time, the allocation of the labour force is greatly distorted, with 70% of the total labour force still concentrated in the low-value-added agricultural sector. With further economic growth in China, the development of the labour market, and improvement in related institutions, the labour force will shift from low-value-added sectors to high-value-added production sectors. Owing to the low overall development level and to the great disparity in regional development, the shift of labour from agricultural sectors with low marginal productivity to non-agricultural sectors with higher marginal productivity will take at least several decades. Thus, this process will contribute significantly to maintaining rapid economic growth in China.

The third factor is China's so-called "advantage of backwardness" in technology. There are two ways to realize technological innovation: (1) through conducting independent research and development (R&D) by self-investment, and (2) through learning from, imitating, or purchasing advanced technologies from other countries. For the developed countries, the former is the most important way for them to achieve technological innovation because they have already adopted the best technologies in their production.

The chance that investments in the R&D of the new technology will achieve success is very low. Statistically, 95% of investments in R&D can not produce the desired technology. Even among innovations that do succeed, only a small fraction have commercial value. Thus, R&D in new technologies requires a huge investment but carries a high risk of failure. Therefore, technological innovation is costly, and progress is rather slow in the developed countries. In contrast, a developing country like China that lags far behind in technology can choose to use "the advantage of backwardness" to effect technological innovation. It can do this by imitating developed countries' technology and by purchasing technology from these countries. Many studies have shown that buying patents costs no more than one-third of the cost of independent research. In addition, the purchased patented technologies have already been proven to have commercial value.

The Japanese economy maintained rapid growth for about 40 years, from the 1950s to the late 1980s. The four Little Dragons have also enjoyed rapid economic growth since the early 1960s. Their economic growth rates are incredible. All these countries and regions introduced or imported advanced technologies from developed countries to achieve rapid technological progress, a swift economic transition, and a high degree of economic growth.

At the end of 1978, China began to implement its economic reform. Since then, it has embarked on the same path of rapid growth that was taken by Japan and the four Little Dragons, which relied on importing technology. In 1978, the technological gap between China and the advanced countries was much wider than that between the advanced countries and Japan in the early 1950s, and that between the advanced countries and the four Little Dragons in the early 1960s. If relying on that technological gap to obtain low-cost technological innovation could help Japan and the four Little Dragons maintain a high economic growth rate for 40 years, it seemed logical that it would help China do the same. In addition, even by the 1990s, the percentage of China's population working in the low-value-added agricultural sector was much higher than the corresponding percentages in Japan in the 1950s and in the four Little Dragons in the

1960s. Therefore, the potential for resource reallocation from low-value-added sectors to higher-value-added ones was greater in China. Meanwhile, China's capital accumulation rate is about 40% of the GDP, which is among the highest in the world. All these factors indicate that there is great potential for rapid development in China and that the Chinese economy should be able to maintain a high growth rate for at least 30 more years.

Two more factors contribute to China's potential for achieving rapid economic growth. First, the country's potential for improving institutional efficiency is still considerable. Although China has made great strides in economic development since adopting a gradual reform policy, the task of economic transition is yet to be completed. Through further reform, resource allocation efficiency can be pushed closer to the production possibility frontier (PPF). It will then be possible to further unleash the productive forces that were previously suppressed by the traditional economic system. Although institutional improvement has mainly a one-time effect, it can exert significant impact. In the early stage of reform, China improved its resource-allocation mechanism in the agricultural sector by giving up the collective farming and adopting the household responsibility system (HRS). This institutional change released farmers' incentives that had been suppressed under the People's Commune System, shifting agricultural production efficiency closer to the PPF and greatly stimulated agricultural growth. We believe that further reform of SOEs with an emphasis on the creation of markets for fair competition will greatly improve the production efficiency in China.

Second, China's size is an important factor in maintaining rapid economic growth. Generally speaking, in countries or regions with small economic scales, internal disparity is also relatively small, and it takes less time to bridge the gap between internal technological structures. However, the case is quite different for large countries. Because of the great disparity within such countries, more time is needed to narrow the internal gap between internal technological structures. China is a large country with a huge imbalance in the technological structures of its different regions. Efforts to narrow the technological gap began in the eastern coastal regions. These regions have contributed significantly to the country's rapid economic growth of the last 20 years. However, there is still a wide gap between the coastal areas of China and developed counties. This gap offers a great deal in terms of development potential. In addition, there is an enormous disparity not only between the eastern part of China and developed countries but also between China's central and western regions and its eastern regions. Thus, the growth potential in the central and western regions is even more impressive than the growth potential of the eastern regions. Since the cost of transferring technology within a single economy is usually much lower than that of transferring it across countries, such a transfer will contribute even more to economic growth.

China's comparative advantage in scientific and technological innovation that resulted from its large population was lost as it lagged behind the Western world in scientific discoveries and technological innovation through the approach of science cum experiment. In the last 20 years, both formal and informal education has improved significantly in China, and the education gap between China and developed countries is narrowing. Therefore, considering China's large population, not only will the absolute number of skilled labourers in the country be large, but also the number of gifted scientists. The more scientists, the bigger the advantage that scientists as a group will have. The larger the economic size of the economy, the larger the impact exerted by the individual scientist, and the better the conditions for technological progress. China's size may thus become an important factor in its reassertion of economic leadership in the world after losing its position in the wake of industrial revolution.

Many scholars and research institutes have already conducted research on China's future GDP. For example, according to the Rand Institute of the United States, by 2010 China's GDP will surpass the GDPs of the United States and Japan. The Department of Foreign Affairs and Trade of Australia estimated that China's GDP will surpass that of the United States and that China will become the world's largest economy by 2015. August Madison, a renowned scholar in the field of long-term economic development, has made a similar prediction. Economists at the World Bank have predicted that if China can maintain its present economic growth rate until 2020.[16] If the GDPs of United States and Japan are 109 units and 43 units respectively in 2020, that of China will be 140 units. Even if we make a conservative estimate based on the official exchange rate (that is, if China, the United States, and Japan maintain the annual average growth rates they enjoyed between 1980 and 1995), China's economic size will surpass that of the United States and Japan in around 2035. (The average growth rates of the three countries during this period were 9.6%, 4.0%, and 2.7% respectively.[17]) In short, if China can maintain a long-term rapid economic growth rate, it will become the largest economy in the world in the first half of the 21st century.[18]

1.2 Policy Barriers to Persistent Growth

China's economy has sustained a growth rate of 10% for nearly 22 years, which makes it rather eye-catching in the world. If China can maintain a total of 50 years of rapid growth, it will be able to reach

16. Harry Xiaoying Wu, *Measuring China's GDP* (EAAU Briefing Paper No. 8). Sydney: Department of Foreign Affairs and Trade of Australia, 1997, p. 25; Xu Tianqing, *World Pattern and the Economic Development Strategy of China — The Theoretical Meditation at the Turn of the Century*. Beijing: Economic and Science Press, 1998, pp. 26–27; Augus Maddison, *Chinese Economy: Performance in the Long Run*. Paris: OECD, 1998.
17. The World Bank, *World Development Report, 1995*. Beijing: China Finance and Economics Press, 1995, pp. 164, 167.
18. This forecast coincides with the prediction of former Vice President and Chief Economist of the World Bank, Professor Lawrence Summers. He once predicted that if China and the United States maintained their growth trends of the past fourteen years, then in 2015 China would surpass the United States and become the largest economy in the world. He also thinks that China is the only country possessing the potential to surpass the United States (Hu Zuliu, "The Road to Prosperity — How China's Economic Position Is Evaluated in the World", *Economic Research Materials,* No. 21 (Nov. 1993)). Paul Krugman also holds the view that China is the only country with the potential to surpass the United States (Paul Krugman, "The Myth of Asia's Miracle", *Foreign Affairs*, Vol. 73, No. 6 (November/December 1994), pp. 62–78.).

the target of becoming a middle-income country in the first half of the 21st century. Of course, we cannot know whether China will be able to maintain altogether half a century's unparalleled growth. Delays in structural transition or mistakes in development strategy could slow the growth process or even derail it altogether. In particular, even though the Chinese economy has grown enormously in the past 22 years since the beginning of reform, accompanying such rapid growth have been a series of problems that may impede China's sustained, rapid economic growth. These obstacles are outlined below.

1. Cyclical Fluctuations in the Economy

Although the average annual growth rate has reached quite a high level since the economic reform began in 1978, the figures have varied considerably from year to year. In some years the annual growth rate reached 13–14%, while in others they were only 3–4%. There have been four cycles over the past 22 years, each lasting an average of 4 to 5 years. If the cyclical fluctuations had been stable or convergent, their negative impact might have been easier to endure. Unfortunately, the degree of these fluctuations displayed an increasing trend, which not only interfered with the goal of achieving a stable and high growth rate but also gave rise to the fear that China's economy might crash during the fluctuations. If this state of affairs cannot be ameliorated, the hope to become the world's largest economy by the first half of the 21st century will be dashed.

2. An Increase in Serious Corruption

During the past 20 years, the market has played an increasingly important role in China's resource allocation. However, China's central government still controls the allocation and pricing of many resources (e.g., capital and licenses). The difference between planned prices and market prices is known as the institutional rent. Using unscrupulous means to gain from the institutional rent is called rent-seeking. Government officials are reluctant to give up its allocation power, since that constitutes an important source of their own income. They take every opportunity to emphasize how indispensable they are and even claim that they are upholding a bastion of a socialist market economy. As the reform proceeds, the government increasingly encourages enterprises to secure resources through market, instead of from the allocation plan of the country. However, as long as there is institutional rent, enterprises will not cease rent-seeking. In recent years, the incentives for enterprises to engage in rent-seeking activities have become increasingly powerful, while the means of undertaking such activities have become increasingly unscrupulous. Thus, corruption has grown rampant. The situation has caused the corruption of government officials, who have the power to allocate cheap resources. This has not only discredited the reform but has also caused widespread discontent among the Chinese people.

3. Problems in the Banking System

It is estimated that the proportion of non-performing and bad loans in China's commercial banks is about 25% or more. This rate is even higher than the corresponding rates of Thailand, Malaysia, Indonesia, and South Korea, all of which were hit hard by the recent Asian financial crisis. The reason China was able to avoid the financial turmoil is primarily that its capital account is not open and because RMB is not convertible. However, if the proportion of non-performing and bad loans continues to rise, depositors will eventually lose confidence in the banking system. In addition, the risk of the banking system being attacked by foreign speculators will increase as the openness of the financial market increases after the WTO accession. These two factors combined may trigger a panic in the banking system and a financial crisis in China, which in turn will threaten the overall economic development.

4. Serious Losses of State-owned Enterprises

Before the reform, government revenue came mainly from the taxes and profits of SOEs. Since the reform, SOEs have performed poorly. In 1997, in some industries all SOEs suffered losses and the government had to subsidize them. SOEs' losses and their subsidies were the major reason for the government's poor financial performance. If SOEs' performance does not improve, the government will eventually be unable to bear the losses they incur. If a large number of SOEs go bankrupt simultaneously, many workers will be laid off. This will further threaten social stability, not to mention rapid economic growth.

5. Widening of the Interregional Disparities

At the initial stages of reform, the gaps among China's eastern, central, and western regions and the gap between rural and urban areas were narrowing. However, after 1985, the gaps widened again. By the early 1990s, the disparities were even greater than they had been before the reform. This made the central and western regions demand different policies from the eastern regions. While the eastern regions hope that the central government will continue to effect decentralization and marketization, the central and western regions would prefer that the government emphasize centralization so as to give fiscal transfers. It is difficult for the central government to make and implement policies that satisfy everyone. In addition, because of the gaps, many peasants in the central and western regions grew dissatisfied with the livelihood they could look forward to in agricultural production, and they moved *en masse* to the eastern region in search of jobs.

The number of rural migrants in Chinese cities is now estimated at between 80 and 100 million. In periods of economic recovery and boom, cheap rural labour forces constituted a vital contribution to economic development in the east. In addition, many rural migrants saved their money and send it home, thereby providing the major source of capital accumulation and income increase in the central and western regions. However, in the event of economic recession, large numbers of rural migrants in the cities could become the root of social unrest.

6. Problems of Grain Production

"No food leads to instability" is a political truism that has been adopted by politicians over thousands of years of Chinese history. To ensure that the people were fed is the reason the government tolerated the implementation of the household contract system in the late 1970s. Since the onset of reform, the total amount of grain produced in China has met the people's needs, despite some fluctuations. However, China lacks arable land, and the amount of arable land it does have is affected by infrastructure construction and non-agrarian industry development. China's growing population and the improvement in food consumption structure will lead to an increase in the demand for grain. Whether China can produce enough grain and whether it can regulate production fluctuations through international markets without imposing too much of an adverse effect on other regions in the world will become important questions. If the problem is not be effectively addressed, China will be unable to maintain rapid economic growth

7. Deflation after 1998

From the beginning of 1998 to the present day, the Chinese economy has encountered a deflation. The monthly wholesale price index of production materials, compared to the index in the same period of the previous year, has been falling. The monthly retail price index, compared to the same period of the previous year, has also been falling. In 1998, 1999 and 2000, the yearly retail price index dropped, respectively, by 2.6%, 3.0% and 1.5%. Accompanying the drops in price index was the slowdown in the economic growth rate. The gross domestic product (GDP) growth rate reached only 7.8% in 1998, 7.1% in 1999, 8.0% in 2000 and 7.3% in 2001, all lower than the average 9.5% of the past 23 years.

Chinese economy has never encountered the problem of deflation in the past. Once a deflation occurs in an economy, it is often very difficult for the economy to regain dynamic growth. However, in the past two decades, the main feature of the Chinese economy was rapid growth. The old system was reformed in a period of rapid growth so that it was possible for everyone to gain from the reform, and the friction of and resistance to reform was reduced. This is the key to China's successful reform of the past 20 years. Keeping the economic growth at a high level is essential to the completion of the complicated social and economic reform in China. Therefore, if the current deflation cannot be eliminated soon, China may not be able to complete the transition to a market economy smoothly.

8. Challenges of WTO Accession

After 15 years of effort, China has finally become a formal member of the World Trade Organization (WTO) on 10 December 2001. The basic spirit of the WTO is to lower tariff rates, to eliminate non-tariff barriers, and to allow market entries so that production could be allocate globally according to the principle of comparative advantage. Top Chinese leaders regard the WTO accession as the second most important change in China's economic policy regime, following Deng Xiaoping's reform and open-door policy in 1978. Some analysts are very positive about the accession. They believe that any drawback will be overwhelmed by the efficiency gains, injecting new growth impetus into China's reform and economic development. However, China's transition to a market economy has not complete. In its economy there exist many sectors which are not competitive. It is also possible that the market competition after the WTO accession may do more harm than good to the Chinese economy, even causing the bankruptcy of economy and the disintegration of society.

How the eight aforementioned issues are dealt with will have a critical effect on whether China will be able to maintain long-term rapid economic growth in the 21st century. The exacerbation of any one of the problems may lead to the collapse of the national economy. Moreover, the issues are closely linked. These problems need to be taken seriously as we investigate the prospects of economic development and the road toward further reform. We will explore the first six issues in more depth in Chapters 7 and 8. Chapters 9 and 10 will be devoted separately to the issues of deflation and WTO accession.

1.3 Key Questions

The miracle that has unfolded in China as a result of economic reform and development since the late 1970s has received worldwide attention. Why was China able to catch up so fast and to achieve such tremendous economic progress in just two decades or so? Will China be able to maintain its rapid growth? These are questions that everyone — Chinese and otherwise — would like answered. China is a developing transitional economy. The nature of its experiences in development and reform and the question of whether the experiences have general implications are of great interest to other economies undergoing similar types of development and transition. As Chinese economists, apart from our responsibility to our country and our desire to make professional contributions, we feel an obligation to seek answers to the following questions, and we attempt to address them in the book.

The first question is why China's economy was developing so slowly before the reform was implemented but has been developing so rapidly afterwards. To speed up economic development in order to catch up developed nations has been the dream of many Chinese leaders in recent history. Nevertheless, reality was often very different. After the founding of the People's Republic of China in 1949, the Chinese Communist Party explicitly set out to catch up with and overtake advanced economies in the West. For this purpose, China established a series of policies and institutions to maximize resource mobilization, so to divert resources into capital-intensive industries. However, in the 30 years prior to the late 1970s, the goal of economic advancement was not achieved. The living standards of the Chinese people remained at a subsistence level with almost no improvement. In the late 1970s, about 200 million farmers still lacked adequate nutrition and clothing. At the end of the decade, China began its economic reform and gradually abandoned the traditional economic system, which was characterized by grossly suppressed product and factor prices, a rigidly planned resource-allocation mechanism, and a puppet-like micro-management institution. Since then, market mechanisms began to play an increasingly important role in resource allocation. Moreover, the economy enjoyed a historically unprecedented growth rate. Undoubtedly, reform was the catalyst for such dramatic changes. Therefore, it is important that we summarize China's reform experience and, through historical comparisons, that we identify the reasons for the slow economic growth in the pre-reform period and for the accelerated growth afterwards.

The second question is why China's reform has been slow in some areas and why the problems mentioned in the last section have recurred throughout the reform process. Up to now, China's economic reform has not been free of ups and downs. In fact, the Chinese reform and phenomenal economic growth have been accompanied by bottlenecks that hinder further growth, including inflation pressures, corruption, and the recurring vigour/chaos cycle. If the root of the vigour/chaos cycle is not eliminated, or if the cycle becomes a divergent phenomenon, China's development and reform will eventually encounter insurmountable difficulties. Therefore, we must explore the reasons behind the cycle and try to find solutions to the problem.

The third question is whether the momentum of China's reform and development can be sustained. Undoubtedly, China's reform and development have been successful over the past 22 years. However, the reform is far from complete. This makes it even harder for China to realize its potential for economic growth and to achieve top ranking in terms of world economic development. In order to achieve these goals, China must continue the reform and must maintain the development momentum. Yet, China still faces many barriers to reform and development. If these obstacles cannot be overcome, the current momentum of reform and development will not be sustainable. Thus, one of our central goals is to determine the logical direction of China's future reform and the right approach to overcoming the above-mentioned barriers.

The fourth question is why China's reform has been so successful, compared with the reforms of the former Soviet Union and Eastern European countries. The former Soviet Union and Eastern European countries were once highly centralized planned economies. Much like China, they experienced slow economic growth before the reform as a result of low efficiency and poor incentives under the traditional economic system. This is why they decided to implement economic reform. Nevertheless, the outcomes of the reforms in these countries varied greatly. During the reform process, China has moved closer and closer to a market economy. It has controlled the pressure of inflation, relaxed growth-constraining bottlenecks, and eliminated political disturbances to realize persistent and rapid economic growth. However, those countries that proclaimed the goal of establishing a completely liberalized market economy at the very beginning of their reform have not established new institutions of higher efficiency. Instead, the economic growth rates there have declined. The countries have experienced serious inflation, unemployment, and political instability. The former Soviet Union and Eastern European countries were not fundamentally different from China at the outset of their reforms, nor do they differ in their final reform objective. The most likely explanation for the dramatic dissimilarity in the reform results lies in the differences in reform approaches. Therefore, it is important for us to sum up the experiences of China's economic reform and to explore its implications for other economies undergoing reform or adjustment.

CHAPTER 2

The Leap-forward Strategy and the Formation of the Traditional Economic System

After the Opium War in 1840, China, once an influential nation, began to decline. Chinese political leaders and intellectuals devoted their lives to the ideals of reconstructing China as a strong nation and making the people prosperous. When the People's Republic of China was founded in 1949, leaders of the new regime had to choose a development strategy and the proper administrative institutions to quickly achieve these ideals.

The first step was to choose an economic development strategy, namely, to choose a development path leading to rapid and direct realization of a strong, independent nation. The Chinese leaders chose the heavy-industry-oriented development strategy. Their choice was based not only on the international and domestic political and economic environment but also on their economic vision.

However, heavy industries are capital-intensive industries whose fundamental characteristics conflicted with China's economic reality at that time, namely, the scarcity in capital endowment. This made it hard to give priority to heavy industries through a market mechanism. To solve this problem, institutional arrangements were made, and the barriers to heavy-industry development were lowered artificially. The government had to suppress capital formation costs for heavy industries by lowering the prices of capital, foreign exchange, energy, raw materials, agricultural produce, and labour. As a result, a macro-policy environment with distorted prices was established. In accordance with this macro-policy environment, the government had to impose a series of institutional arrangements like the centralized planning system in the allocation and administration of economic resources, the establishment of state ownership on industry and commerce, the People's Commune System in rural areas, and other micro-management mechanisms that deprived the enterprises of decision-making power.

The traditional economic system was first formulated to implement the heavy-industry-oriented development strategy in an economy short of capital. The economy was characterized by a macro-policy environment with distorted factors and products prices, a highly centralized planned resource-allocation system, and a micro-management mechanism without decision-making power in enterprises. To explain the traditional economic system and the vigour/chaos cycle, or to discuss reform policies and the prospects for future reform and development, we first need to make clear the logic behind the formation of the traditional economic system and the historical sequence of the related events.

2.1 Logical Starting Point: Heavy-industry as the Priority of Development

China's economic development began when China was a poor, agrarian economy, which constitutes an important factor in the choice of economic development strategy. When the People's Republic of China was founded in 1949, the gross output value of national industrial and agricultural products was RMB 46.6 billion, and per capita national income was only RMB 66.10. The total output of agriculture accounted for 70% of the gross value of national industrial and agricultural output, with industry accounting for 30% and the heavy industry accounting for just 7.9%.[1] At the same time, China lacked a favourable external economic environment. It had to prepare itself for war that could break out at any time, because of political isolation and the United States–led economic embargo against China engineered by Western countries that were unhappy with China's change to a socialist regime. The Chinese leaders were aware that under such circumstances the determinant for the very

1. *China's Economic Yearbook 1981* (abridged edition). Beijing: Economic Management Press, 1982, pp. VI–4.

survival of the nation as well as for the regime was whether the economy could quickly recover and develop so as to become independent. According to China's development level and the knowledge available to its leaders at that time, industrialization was virtually synonymous with economic development and the goal of eliminating poverty and backwardness.

When New China — China under the socialist government — first came into being, Chinese leaders chose the heavy-industry-oriented development strategy for three reasons.

The first reason was international competition. Industrialization is related to the increasingly-large role played by the heavy industry in the industrial structure, according to Walter Hoffmann's study on industrial structures in some countries.[2] Hoffman used the ratio between consumer goods industries (light industries) and production goods industries (heavy industries) as an index (later referred to as the "Hoffmann Coefficient") to divide industrialization periods and found that the higher the level of industrialization in a country, the higher the proportion of its heavy industries. Perhaps the Chinese leaders were unaware of the "Hoffmann Law" when they chose heavy industries as a development priority. But an analysis of economic structure in developed countries would have clarified that heavy industries meant modern industries and that a higher heavy industry proportion was indicative of a country's economic development level and strength.

Most developing countries achieved political independence and began national economic construction after World War II. These countries took heavy industries or import substitution as a basic development path. They hoped this could help to reach a higher level of industrialization and leap over some economic development phases. They thought to quickly realize independence a country had to adopt a heavy-industry-oriented development strategy.

The second reason was the constraints imposed by the international political and economic environment. The Korean War broke

2. Walter Hoffmann, *Growth of Industrial Economics*. Manchester: Manchester University Press, 1958.

out in June 1950, and by October the United States had pushed the war to the Yalu River, the borderline between Korea and China. China entered the war for the sake of its own security. In the meantime, China was also in military confrontation with the Kuomintang regime in Taiwan. This political and military situation meant that the fledging People's Republic had to quickly increase its national defense strength and war mobilization capacity. In addition, the Western capitalist countries led by the United States imposed political isolation and an economic embargo to cut off China's channel of normal international economic exchange and trade. This international political, economic, and military climate forced China to try to quickly build a relatively comprehensive and self-contained industrial structure with heavy industries as the core.

The third reason was China's limited ability to effect industrial accumulation. China was an economically backward country and a dual economy, with its rural population accounting for 80% to 90% of the total population, and with the large part of the rural population living in poverty. Limited by their lack of knowledge and experience, the leaders of the Chinese Communist Party believed that if they made it a priority to develop light industries or consumption industries, they would face a limited market and inadequate demand, which would hinder China's attempt to achieve the capital accumulation it needed. Leaders and experts in Chinese economic construction had learned from the experiences of the former Soviet Union and the reality in China that heavy industries had the characteristics of self-service and self-cycle. Although peasants living in absolute poverty could not generate the demand needed for industrial development, developing heavy industry could overcome this obstacle. Therefore, the Chinese leaders thought they could carry out industrialization by skipping the development of light industries. This point is elaborated upon at more length later.

The logic by which the leaders identified their strategic development objectives closely resembled that adopted by the leaders of the former Soviet Union during the corresponding historical period. Many people hold that China's economic construction principles and institutional patterns were copied or inherited from the former Soviet Union.[3] Indeed, the two nations faced similar conditions, but while it is true that China's economic logic mirrored that of the former Soviet Union during the corresponding historical period, it is also the case that, once objectives were chosen and a starting point established, China's leaders had to formulate a special economic system based on China's particular economic and social characteristics. To understand the similarities and differences, it is helpful to review a debate that took place in the former Soviet Union in the 1920s concerning industrialization and choices of strategies.

From 1921 to 1924, the Soviet national economy recovered quickly by carrying out the New Economic Policy according to Lenin's theory. At that time the proportion of Soviet modern industries in the economy as a whole was very small. A backward agricultural economy and farmers in poverty still dominated the economic structure. Under these circumstances, heated debates broke out among Soviet political leaders and economists about how to accumulate funds for industrialization, how to solve the problem of inadequate market demand for industrial growth, what mechanism should be adopted to adjust the national economy, and so forth. On one side of the debates was the "balanced development" camp, represented by Nikolai Bukharin. E.A. Preobrazhensky represented the other side, which was known as the "hyper-industrialists".[4]

3. Xue Muqiao, a well-known Chinese economist, holds such view (Xue Muqiao, *A Study of Problems Concerning China's Socialist Economy*. Beijing: People's Publishing House, 1979, p. 181); the World Bank takes a similar point of view but mentions that "China adopted the Soviet economic system but made changes in many aspects." (The World Bank, *PR China: Development of Socialist Economy*. Washington, DC: The World Bank, 1983, p. 46).
4. The focus of the debate and the hyper-industrialization camp's main theory are reflected in E.A. Preobrazhensky's book, *New Economics* (Beijing: Sanlian Bookstore, 1984). See also two papers on the debate by Western economists (Raj K. Sah and Joseph E. Stiglitz, "Price Scissors and the Structure of the Economy", *The Quarterly Journal of Economics*, Vol. 102 (1987), pp. 109–34; Raj K. Sah and Joseph E. Stiglitz, *Peasants Versus City-dwellers*. Oxford: Clarendon Press, 1992).

Bukharin stressed the importance of the peasants and the peasant-worker coalition, pointing out that agricultural labour productivity and rates of commercialized agricultural products were the basis for industrial accumulation and development. Sacrificing peasants' rights and interests would not only slow the industrialization process but would also jeopardize the proletarian dictatorship, he believed. He held that funds needed by industrialization should be achieved through normal accumulation means such as self-accumulating, attracting deposits, imposing explicit taxes, and the like. He emphasized that the national economic plan should not deviate from the market mechanism and that the agricultural economy should be guided onto the socialist road via the establishment of market relations. Therefore, the state should expand its demand for light-industry products through agricultural development to boost light industry development and increase the supply of consumer goods. The demand for heavy industry products would follow. Meanwhile, agricultural development would create a huge market for industrialization.

What the hyper-industrialists saw, however, was the inconsistency between a quick realization of industrialization and small-scale, state-run industrial sectors. They believed that the latter could not meet the need of capital formulation through self-accumulation. Preobrazhensky believed that in the transition period, there were two alternative and mutually exclusive coordination mechanisms, namely, the law of the socialist primitive accumulation and the law of value. Each mechanism had its own adjusting range, with the former gradually replacing the latter. In addition, since planning was contradictory to the market system, the hyper-industrialists held that the state should impose forced industrialized accumulation through means such as a state monopoly, an unequal exchange between industrial products and farming products, heavy taxes on non-socialist economic ownership, inflationary policy, and so forth. To this end, the market mechanism should be prohibited.

At the same time, the hyper-industrialization camp claimed to have solved theoretically the problems of creating a market for industrial growth in a country dominated by a small-scale peasant economy. The theory exerted a tremendous influence on the formulation of the traditional socialist economic system. G.A. Feldman, who worked in the Soviet State Planning Commission, formulated the first socialist growth model on the basis of Marx's and Lenin's theories on the law of preferential growth of productive materials. According to this model, economic development was pushed forward by a closed cycle of metallurgy, machinery, and subsidiary industries (the so-called heavy industry complex), while agriculture just passively provided funds and labour for industrial growth.[5]

This debate began in 1924 and ended in 1927, after economists from the hyper-industrialization camp were purged from the party. Nevertheless, just one year later, the leap-forward strategy, which featured speeding up and prioritizing the development of heavy industries, was put forward again, and it was fully manifested in the Soviet Five-year Plan, which went into effect in 1929. This plan made developing heavy industries its top priority and sacrificed contemporary consumption. For instance, the plan stipulated that net investment should rise to account for one-fourth or even one-third of national income. And three-fourths of net investment were to be invested in heavy industries.[6] This development strategy, which was the first of its kind, formed the basis for the economic administration system of the former Soviet Union.

In Mainland China, the theory behind the heavy-industry-oriented development strategy was not even thoroughly discussed before it was stipulated in the national economic plan.[7] After the economic recovery of 1950–52, the development strategy was first

5. See E. D. Domar, "The Growth Model of the Soviet", in *Essays on the Theory of Economic Growth*. Beijing: Commercial Press, 1983, Chapter 9; Hywel G. Jones, *An Introduction to Modern Theories of Economic Growth*. New York: McGraw-Hill, 1976.
6. Tom Kemp, *Modern Industrialization Models — The Soviet Union, Japan and Developing Countries*. Beijing: China Outlook Press, 1985, p. 76.
7. The first extensive debate over the capital-goods-growth-first theory took place between the late 1950s and the mid-1960s. See *Debate on Important Questions Concerning Plutonomy Since the Foundation of the PRC (1949–1980)*. Beijing: China Finance and Economics Press, 1981.

fully manifested in the First Five-year Plan for national economic development. Li Fuchun, the then vice premier and head of the State Planning Commission, pointed out explicitly in the First Five-year Plan report that "socialist industrialization is the primary task of our country in the transitional period. The key component of socialist industrialization is giving priority to the development of heavy industries."[8] The drafting of the First Five-year Plan came into effect in 1951 and was implemented from 1953 to 1957, and the First Five-year Plan was constantly revised and reformulated in the process of implementation. In fact, it was not finalized and announced until the first half of 1955, when the Congress of the Communist Party of China (CPC) and the Second Session of the First People's Congress approved the plan.

The primary tasks of the First Five-year Plan included carrying out industrial construction to build up China's socialist industrialization base. This construction project centered around 156 key projects designed with aid from the former Soviet Union, and it included 694 other important projects. Also part of the Plan was the development of collectively-owned agricultural production cooperatives and handicraft industrial cooperatives, the purpose of which was to establish the foundation for socialist reconstruction of agriculture and handicraft and to build the foundation for socialist reformation of private industries and commerce by bringing capitalist industries and commerce into various forms of state capitalism. The public finance, bank credit, materials and people's lives were arranged according to these tasks.

According to the First Five-year Plan, the development of heavy industry was put in a strategically favourable position. The heavy industries to be developed under the plan included electrical power, coal, petroleum, metallurgy (modern steel, nonferrous metals, and basic chemicals), large metal-cutting machine tools manufacturing, electricity-generating equipment, metallurgy equipment, ore-

8. CPC Central Committee, Documentation and Research Office, *Documents of the Second Session of the First National People's Congress of the PRC*. Beijing: People's Press, 1955, pp. 160–61.

extracting equipment, automobiles, tractors, and airplanes. The 156 key projects designed with aid from the former Soviet Union were all related to heavy industries and newly emerged sectors created to fill the gap and improve the industrial system. During the period of the First Five-year Plan, investment in basic construction of heavy industry accounted for 85% of the total industrial investment in basic construction and 72.9% of the total agricultural and industrial investment in basic construction.[9]

2.2 Basic Characteristics of Heavy Industries vs. China's Economic Reality

Given that resources are allocated by the market mechanism, producers decide what to produce and what technology to adopt according to market prices of products and production factors. During the initial period of China's economic development, capital was in short supply; hence the market interest rate was naturally high, while the cost of labour was low. Developing capital-intensive heavy industries was thus extremely costly, and such industries could not hope to be viable in an open, free market economy.[10] If resources had been allocated by the market mechanism, investment would not have flowed to heavy-industry sectors. Rather, industrialization featuring light industry would have occurred, which would have been contradictory to the goal of implementing the heavy-industry-oriented development strategy.

For a developing country, heavy industry has three basic characteristics: (1) a long construction cycle, (2) the need to import most equipment, and (3) a very large scale of initial investment. Far from being able to meet these needs, China's economy at the time of

9. National Bureau of Statistics of China, *China Statistical Yearbook, 1992*. Beijing: China Statistics Press, 1992, p. 158.
10. Justin Yifu Lin and Tan Guofu, "Policy Burdens, Accountability, and Soft-budget Constraint", *American Economic Review*, Vol. 89, No. 2 (May 1999), pp. 426–31. Justin Yifu Lin, "Development Strategy, Viability and Economic Convergence" (Inaugural D. Gale Johnson Lecture, Department of Economics, the University of Chicago, 14 May 2001).

the First Five-year Plan was lacking on three basic fronts: (1) capital was scarce and interest rates were high; (2) there was a lack of foreign exchange, a low export capacity, and a high exchange rate; and (3) the economic surplus was small and it was difficult to mobilize funds. The characteristics of heavy industry thus conflicted with China's economic reality. This conflict is explored in more detail below.

First, there was the conflict between the long construction cycle of heavy industry and the scarcity in capital endowment. Heavy industry requires a much longer cycle for basic construction to achieve its production capacity than does light industry. Owing to its highly capital-intensive nature, heavy industry also needs continued investment, but it takes a long time before any returns on investment can be realized. In the initial years of the People's Republic of China, China's economic development was still at a very low level. The national income per capita was only RMB 104 in 1952. This impeded capital accumulation. Scarcity of capital would certainly have led to high interest rates if market forces had been allowed to take their natural course. In the early 1950s, the monthly market interest rate was 2–3%. Suppose that the compound annual rate was 30%. A RMB 1 investment, calculated at compound interest, would require a repayment of RMB 3.71 in 5 years and RMB 13.79 in 10 years. It is clear that in the 1950s, such a high capital cost could have made it impossible to develop heavy industry at the time.

Second, there was the conflict between the source of heavy industry equipment and the scarcity of foreign exchange. For a country at a primitive stage of development, the construction of a heavy-industry project required not only a high level of technology, but also implied importing a large amount of technology and equipment. Given that heavy industry development was the core component of industrialization, a large amount of machinery and equipment had to be imported, thus implying a strong need for foreign exchange. At that time, China was basically a closed autarkic economy. The products that could be exported were limited in variety and quantity. Therefore, the ability to trade and earn foreign exchange was very low. In addition, the relationship between China and other advanced capitalist countries was not normalized. The ability to obtain foreign exchange was thus further circumscribed. Under these conditions, foreign exchange was relatively scarce. If the exchange rate, that is, the price of foreign currency, had been determined by market, it would have been much higher, which would have made it more costly to develop the heavy industry in China.

The third conflict was between the funds required for a heavy industry project and the economy's ability to mobilize such funds. Compared with projects in other industries, a heavy industry project requires a longer construction period and a larger initial investment, because heavy industry is an industry that is typically characterized by economies of scale. When heavy industry becomes the core of industrial development, and especially when a whole series of industrial projects are undertaken simultaneously, the conflict becomes more evident. In such a case, it is vital that the nation is able to mobilize funds and other resources in need. At the initial stage of China's economic development, the capital was scarce, the economic surplus was small and was scattered in rural areas throughout China. Therefore it was extremely difficult to mobilize the funds necessary for heavy industry development. For example, in 1952 the year-end total asset value of state-owned banks was only RMB 11.88 billion, and the total deposit was RMB 9.33 billion. They accounted for only 20.2% and 15.8%, respectively, of the GNP in 1952.[11] In a free market economy, this conflict between the endowment conditions and the strong desire to develop heavy industry were irreconcilable.

2.3 The Macro-policy Environment for the Heavy-industry-oriented Development Strategy

The development strategy implemented by the Chinese government in the 1950s was the leap-forward strategy.[12] The strategy was thus

11. Sheng Bin and Feng Lun, eds., *Census Report on China*. Shenyang: Liaonin People's Press, 1991, p. 521.
12. Years later, when this type of development strategy was formulated, the national slogan "Catch up with the United State and overtake Britain" illustrates this.

named because of the enormous gap between the industrial objectives of the strategy and the industrial structures required by China's factor endowment. In an open and competitive market economy, an industry whose capital intensity is far from the capital intensity of the economy's factor endowment cannot produce socially acceptable profits; such an industry will often create huge losses, and thus is not viable.[13] This applies for relatively capital-intensive heavy industry in an economy with scarce capital as well as for relatively labour-intensive light industry in an economy rich in capital. China's development strategy was thus aimed at developing non-viable industries, and the government was faced with the question of how to mobilize resources to achieve its goal.

Because of the simultaneous development of many large scale heavy industrial projects, if the government had relied on direct fiscal subsidies to finance these projects, it would have had to collect heavy explicit taxes from the economic sectors that were generating a surplus. But such a surplus would have come only from the small and scattered agricultural sector, making tax collection difficult and costly. As a result, heavy explicit tax collection was impossible. Clearly, a macro-policy environment was needed to allocate resources in a way that would encourage the development of heavy industries. The cost of developing heavy industries had to be decreased artificially, while the ability of resource mobilization — including the supply of cheap labour, funds, raw materials, imported equipment, and technology — had to be improved. The key to creating such a macro-policy environment was to completely suppress the functions of market mechanisms and to distort artificially the relative prices of factors and products. Such a policy environment includes the following:

(1) A low-interest-rate policy. Heavy industry cannot develop under high interest rates when the project has a long construction

13. Justin Yifu Lin and Tan Guofu, "Policy Burdens, Accountability, and Soft-budget Constraint", *American Economic Review*, Vol. 89, No. 2 (May 1999), pp. 426–31. Justin Yifu Lin, "Development Strategy, Viability and Economic Convergence" (Inaugural D. Gale Johnson Lecture, Department of Economics, University of Chicago, 14 May 2001).

cycle. Therefore, the most important condition needed for fast, low-cost growth of heavy industry is low price for capital, i.e., a low and stable interest rate. In the initial months after the founding of the People's Republic of China, the new government adopted an austere monetary policy of high interest rates to eliminate the hyper-inflation caused by the previous regime. From 1949 to early 1950, the People's Bank's of China's industrial credit rate rose to 144% per year. By the first half of 1950, inflation had been brought under control, and the interest rate began to fall. Using the 3.0% monthly rate of industrial credit in May 1950 as a benchmark, we can observe that the interest rate was adjusted many times and that it fell dramatically within a short time. The monthly rate for loans to SOEs underwent similar changes. This rate was adjusted to 2.0% on 31 July 1950, to 1.5–1.6% by April 1951, to 0.6–0.9% by January 1953, and to 0.456% by 1954; the rate was maintained at this level for a long time. The loan rate was readjusted to 0.6% in June 1960 but was reduced again to 0.42% in August 1971.[14]

(2) A low-exchange-rate policy. The foundation of heavy industries is capital-intensive equipment, most of which, in the early stages of economic development, need to be imported, requiring payment in foreign exchange. The exchange rate is the price of foreign exchange measured in home currency. In the early 1950s in China, exportable goods were highly limited. Foreign exchange was as scarce as capital. Thus, the market-determined exchange rate would have been too high for the development of capital-intensive heavy industries. To ensure that key projects could import critical equipment at low prices, the Chinese government had to interfere in the formation of the foreign exchange rate by artificially over-valuing domestic currency and by instituting a low-exchange-rate policy.[15]

14. Zheng Xianbing, *An Introduction to Interest Rate*. Beijing: China Finance Press, 1991, pp. 115 –20.
15. The low exchange rate policy can also be used to lower the domestic price paid for the export of primary products, thus imposing an indirect tax on exports. This is equivalent to collecting indirect taxes on export to subsidize the import for heavy industry.

The suppression of the exchange rate began in 1950. In just over a year — from March 1950, when the National Finance Conference opened, to May 1951, the exchange rate of RMB against the U.S. dollar was adjusted downward 15 times. On 13 March 1950, the exchange rate was RMB 420 (old RMB converted into new currency) for US$100. The exchange rate was lowered to RMB 223 for US$100 on 23 May 1951 (see Table 2.1). From 1952 to 1972, the exchange rate of RMB was no longer listed; it was main-tained at a low level by internal control of the government. From 1 March 1955 to December 1971 the exchange rate was maintained at RMB 246.18 for US$100. In December 1978, when the U.S. dollar depreciated by 7.89%, the exchange rate of RMB also began to change. In 1978, the exchange rate was RMB 172 to US$100.[16]

Table 2.1 Exchange Rate Adjustments*
(US$100 and Sterling £100 = RMB ¥)

Date	U.S. Dollars		Pounds Sterling	
	Exchange rate	Extent of Adjustment (%)	Exchange rate	Extent of Adjustment (%)
March 13, 1950	420.00	—	—	—
July 1, 1950	375.00	–10.71	989.00	—
July 8, 1950	360.00	–4.00	956.00	–3.34
July 26, 1950	360.00	0.00	932.00	–2.51
August 7, 1950	350.00	–2.78	914.40	–1.89
September 5, 1950	322.00	–8.00	812.20	–11.18
May 23, 1951	223.00	–30.75	—	—
December 1971	246.18	10.39	—	—
July 1978	172.00	–39.07	—	—

* New RMB ¥1 yuan equals 10,000 Old Yuan.
Source: State Administration for Exchange Control, *Exchange Rate Manual.* Beijing: China Finance Press, 1986; Ma Hong and Sun Shangqing, eds., *Contemporary Dictionary of Chinese Economic Events.* Beijing: China Finance and Economics Press, 1993, p. 960.

16. See State Administration for Exchange Control, *Exchange Rate Manual.* Beijing: China Finance Press, 1986; Ma Hong and Sun Shangqing, eds., *Contemporary Dictionary of Chinese Economic Events.* Beijing: China Finance and Economics Press, 1993, p. 960.

(3) A policy of low nominal wages and low prices for energy and raw materials. When national economic development was at a low level, traditional economic sectors usually constituted a large proportion of the country's national economy. Since the economic surplus generated by the traditional sectors was very limited, the funds available for capital accumulation was small in size in the whole economy. Furthermore, the level of monetization in the economy was low, which made it difficult to transfer surplus from one sector to another. Therefore, it was extremely hard to raise funds at the time. Furthermore, at that time the People's Republic of China was newly founded. To consolidate the newborn regime and to strengthen the coalition with the peasants, the adoption of a low-tax policy in a certain period was highly necessary. Therefore, the high accumulation rate required for developing heavy industry could not be obtained through the direct transfer of surplus through tax, but had to depend largely on the heavy industry's own ability of accumulation. As we know, the potential for accumulation in an industry is determined by its profitability, and the level of profit is determined by the difference between the total value of outputs and the total cost of inputs. Therefore, the suppression in the cost of labour, energy and raw materials for heavy industry became one important measure for the heavy industry to achieve a high accumulation rate.

Take the wage level as an example. The uniform wage system was introduced in the early 1950s. According to the total wage fund appropriated by the government and the average-wage plan, an eight-grade wage system for production workers was adopted. From 1956 onwards, the wage standard in all government departments and enterprises was identical throughout the country. The wage standard, the determination of the wage-grade and the method of promotion were all regulated by the central government. Local governments and individual enterprises were not allowed to make any adjustment. Under this unified system, the nominal wage rate was suppressed to a very low level for many years. Until 1978, the average nominal wage for workers was below RMB 600. Even based on the distorted official exchange rate of RMB 246.18 to US$100, the average wage level for workers throughout the country was merely US$200 or so in

Figure 2.1 Wage levels in Mainland China before the 1978 reform (RMB per year per worker)

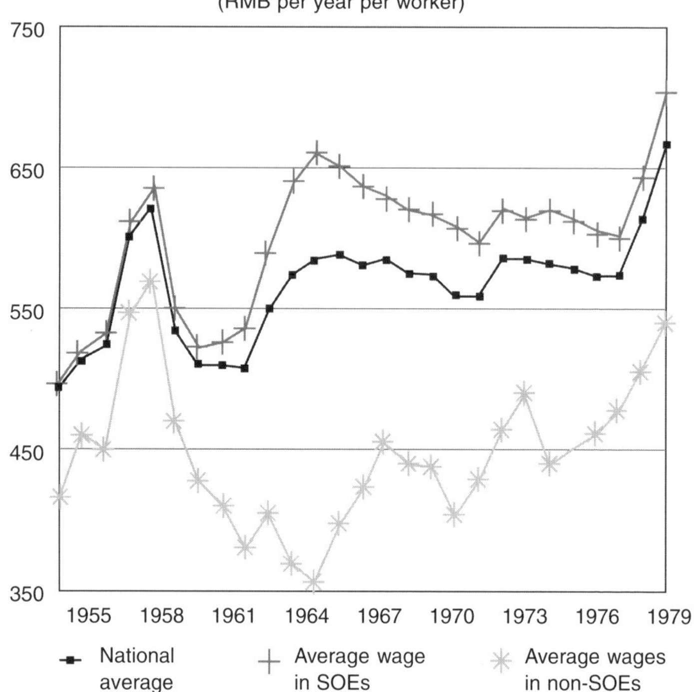

those years (see Figure 2.1) the low nominal wage reduced the labour cost for industrial development. Together with the low prices for energy and other raw materials, the low input-price policy became one important component in the macro-policy environment necessary for the heavy-industry-oriented develop-ment strategy.

(4) A policy of low prices for agricultural products and other essential goods and services. Such essentials included food, daily-use articles, housing, medical care, education, fuels for domestic use, and various living services. The low-wage policy held down the purchasing power of urban residents. If essential goods and services had been priced through the market mechanism, they would have been out of reach for most workers. This in turn would have threatened social stability and the labour supply because of the inadequate

reproduction of labour forces. The solution was to lower the prices for agricultural products and other essential goods and services. Because large-scale industries were concentrated in urban areas, the low-cost policy was targeted toward urban populations, and rural populations had no access to this privilege. In fact, a large proportion of the costs of heavy-industry development, through such a mechanism, were transferred to traditional economic sectors such as agriculture.

The low-price policy serving the heavy-industry development strategy distorted the prices of essential goods and services such as agricultural products and institutionalized the distortion. The distortion is apparent from the price index of consumer goods from 1952 to 1978 (see Table 2.2). Here we use the rural fair price index to indicate the price-changing trend required by the market. Since the macro-policy environment suppressed the national consumer-goods price index, its change deviated from the demands of market. If we take into consideration the serious and prevalent shortage of consumer goods in China, the comparison more clearly reflects the distortion caused by the macro-policy environment.

Table 2.2 Comparisons of Consumer Price Indexes before the Reform (1950 = 100)

Year	The Nation (1)	Rural Fair Market (2)	Degree of Distortion (1)/(2)
1952	113.3	111.0	1.02
1957	122.5	120.9	1.01
1962	155.6	354.8	0.44
1965	138.2	192.3	0.72
1970	137.8	197.7	0.70
1975	143.0	259.5	0.55
1976	143.4	269.8	0.53
1977	147.8	263.3	0.56
1978	150.0	246.0	0.61

Data source: National Bureau of Statistics of China, *China Statistical Yearbook, 1992*. Beijing: China Statistics Press, 1992.

2.4 The Planned Resource-allocation System

In a competitive market, the prices of products and production factors are the market clearing prices. On the one hand, the supply and demand determine the equilibrium price, on the other hand, the price can affect and adjust the market supply and demand. When the price of a product or a production factor is artificially set below its equilibrium price, the demand will be stimulated and the supply will be suppressed. The quantity demanded and the quantity supplied will deviate from the equilibrium level, and a shortage will thus be created.

If price depression is a stabilized institutional arrangement, the gap between supply and demand will persist, that is, shortage will become normal.[17] A macro-policy environment that distorts prices of products and production factors will inevitably lead to a serious disequilibrium between the supply and demand of funds, foreign exchange, raw materials, agricultural products, and various living necessities. In this kind of economy with prevalent shortages, it becomes necessary to replace the market mechanism with a planned resource-allocation system in order to ensure that the limited supplies of resources will be allocated to the government-determined priority industries.

Under the circumstances described above, low interest rates reduced people's incentive to save, thus decreasing the source of funds. At the same time, the low rates also increased enterprises' demand for funds. Moreover, the low exchange rate suppressed the incentive to export but stimulated the impulse to import. The low prices of energy and raw materials resulted in a short supply and excessive demand. A large gap was thus created between the supply and demand of funds, foreign exchange, and energy and raw materials. If the market had been allowed to direct resource

17. We attribute the shortage phenomenon to the macro-policy environment due to the introduction of the leap-forward strategy. J. Kornai, who is well known for his study on the shortage phenomenon in socialist economies, admits that shortages exist in non-socialist developing counties (J. Kornai, *Shortage Economics*, Vol. 1. Beijing: Economic Science Press, 1986, p. 12).

allocation, the policy of suppressing prices could not have ensured that these resources would flow to strategic sectors. As a result, the government needed to create an order of priority for industrial development and investment projects. Meanwhile, it had to replace the market mechanism with a series of planned administrative means in resource allocation.

In addition, owing to the development of heavy industries or import substitution policy regardless of the economic reality at the time, corresponding industries could not compete in the international market. To protect such industries and secure scarce foreign exchange for them, foreign trade had to be carried out under unified regulation. To implement the First Five-year Plan which was the embodiment of the heavy-industry-oriented development strategy, a series of administrative bureaus were established to regulate resource allocation in the mid-1950s. With the establishment of these bureaus and the strengthening of their position, a highly centralized planned resource-allocation system was gradually put into place.

The first step in creating the system was to establish an administrative institution of the financial sector. If a bank's deposit rate is lower than the opportunity cost or shadow price of funds, this will usually reduce currency holders' incentive to save. The funds absorbed by banks will be less than society's potential supply. Savings will flow into other financial channels, if any exist. But since the policy to suppress the interest rate was designed to facilitate the development of heavy industries, and since financial channels outside state control could not take on the task of supporting heavy industry, financial monopoly had to be imposed. When loan interest rates were lower than the opportunity cost or the shadow price, enterprises tended to demand as much funds as possible. In the face of such a heavy demand for funds, an effective and centralized resource-allocation system was required to ration funds to enterprises and sectors so as to serve the state's development goal.

To fulfill this requirement, between 1949 and 1952, China gradually nationalized its banks and created a financial system around the People's Bank of China (PBC). PBC then became the country's centre for cash, clearance, and credit, and it assumed overall responsibility for financial transactions. To carry out the heavy-industry-oriented development strategy and the First Five-year Plan, PBC in 1953 instituted a planned credit-and-loan administrative system at all levels of banks so as to draft and implement the overall credit-and-loan plans. PBC also correspondingly adopted an internal control system of unified management of deposits and loans. All deposits absorbed by local branches had to be delivered to the head office, and loans were granted according to quotas, which were determined by the head office. The bank stipulated uniform deposit and loan rates. Under this system, limited funds were funneled to priority projects. In this way, a link was formed between allocating funds according to strategic development objectives and the macro-policy environment of low interest rates.

The second step was to establish a management system for foreign trade and exchange. The foreign exchange rate was suppressed below the equilibrium level, which had two consequences. For producers of exportable, a low exchange rate meant that products' prices measured in foreign currency were lower than the prices measured in domestic currency, making export unprofitable. But if nobody was willing to export, sources of foreign exchange would dry up. For users of imported products, a low exchange rate meant that imported goods were cheaper than locally-made products, so industries tended to demand as many imported goods as possible. To solve this problem, the state was forced to make a unified arrangement for imports and exports by imposing a monopoly over foreign trade and a highly controlled regulatory system over foreign trade and exchange.

Control over foreign trade was implemented in February 1950, when the State Council issued the *Decision on the Unified Implementation Measures for International Trade*. This publication stipulated that the Central Department of Trade would control all business concerning foreign trade, while the District Trade Departments and the Provincial Bureau of Commerce (or the Bureau of Commerce and Industry) would be concurrently in charge of trade with foreign countries in their localities. Under the leadership of the Central Department of Trade, several nationwide specialized foreign trade companies were created. This organizational form was maintained even after the Ministry of Foreign Trade was established in 1952.

The national planning administration controlled four aspects of foreign-trade activities. (1) It imposed an import and export permit system to strictly control import and export quantities, prices, trade terms, conditions, and time, as well as business components and foreign trading partners. (2) It controlled foreign exchange, stipulating that all foreign exchange earnings of social groups, enterprises, and individuals be sold to state banks at the official exchange rate and that any use of foreign exchange be approved by governing bodies and that the exchange be bought from state banks. (3) It stipulated that private import and export enterprises (before nationalization) and foreign-funded companies be registered with the state. (4) It imposed protective tariffs and a quality inspection system on import and export commodities. From the mid-1950s onward, the state controlled all foreign trade.

In 1958, the State Council stipulated that all international trade should be monopolized by the Ministry of International Trade under the principle of unified policy, unified plan, and unified action. It also stipulated that all foreign exchange rates should be determined by PBC and foreign reserves be managed jointly by PBC, the Ministry of International Trade, and the Ministry of Finance. The international trade and foreign exchange administrative system to coordinate the low exchange rate policy was thus established.

The third step was to establish a system to manage materials. In a fully competitive market, when materials are in short supply, their prices will increase until the equilibrium level is reached and the market will be cleared as a result. When prices are artificially suppressed, demand is stimulated while the incentive to supply decreases, creating an imbalance between supply and demand. Under such circumstances, China's government had to establish a highly centralized system to manage materials to ensure that heavy industries would be adequately supplied.

To implement the First Five-year Plan and the policy stipulating low energy and raw-materials prices, the State Planning Commission was established in 1953. Its function was to allocate important materials across the country. The commission classified the materials into three categories: (1) materials under the unified allocation of the state; (2) materials under allocation by state industrial ministries and commissions under the State Council; and (3) materials under the allocation of the local administration. From 1953 to 1957, industrial products directly distributed by the State Planning Commission increased from 110 kinds to 300, whose value increased to 60% of the total value of industrial output. Meanwhile, materials under unified distribution of ministries increased from 227 kinds to 532.[18] The state-managed allocation system for materials was thus established.

Finally, the state established a monopoly over the purchase and marketing of agricultural products. The low-price policy for agricultural products suppressed peasants' incentive to produce and sell products to the state. If the state-run commercial department had been a competitor in a competitive market for agricultural and sideline products, it could not have fulfilled its procurement task had prices be as low as they were. To obtain sufficient agricultural products, such as grain, cottons and edible oils, and to guarantee enough supply to cover the daily consumption of urban residents and to supply raw materials for processing enterprises, it was imperative that the state monopolize the procurement of major agricultural products. As the low-price compulsory procurement reduced peasants' incentive to produce, it was also imperative that the state created an institutional arrangement that would ensure its control of argricultural production. Toward this end, an agricultural collectivization movement was launched, and it led to the People's Communes, which came into existence in 1958. Leaders of the communes were appointed by the government and were responsible for the communes. With suppressed prices and consequently

18. Liu Guoguan, ed., *On China's Economic Reform Models*. Beijing: China Social Sciences Press, 1988, p. 238. There is another piece of data which indicates that there were 231 kinds of materials under unified distribution by the state and 301 kinds under unified distribution by the ministries (see Li Debin, *A Concise Economic History of the PRC (1949–1985)* . Changsha: Hunan People's Press, 1987, p. 272), but everyone admits that the number of types of materials under planned allocation increased dramatically.

insufficient supply, it was necessary to establish a planned sales system to supply agricultural products in urban areas.

For a period after the People's Republic of China was founded, state-owned commercial organizations competed with private merchants to procure agricultural and sideline products. As the industrialization process sped up, state-owned commercial departments carried the increasingly heavy burden of supplying agricultural and sideline products for urban residents (see Table 2.3). Once the low-price policy for purchasing agricultural products was implemented, these organizations lost their competitive advantage over private enterprises. They were no longer able to adjust supply and demand so as to stabilize market prices and ensure that the needs of urban people and national construction were met.

After the autumn harvest of 1953, the state failed to realize its grain purchase plan on time in many regions, while the sale of grain far exceeded the plan's specifications, resulted in an imbalance between purchases and sales. In response, the CPC Central Committee and the State Council issued mandates to implement the planned procurement and supply of edible oils and grain. In September 1954, the State Council issued another mandate concerning the implementation of the planned purchase of cotton. In

Table 2.3 Index of Major Agricultural Products' Output and Sales before the Implementation of the State Monopoly on Procurement and Marketing

Year	Grain		Cotton		Edible oils	
	Quantity produced	Sales of state commerce	Quality produced	Market sales	Quantity produced	Sales of state commerce
1950	100	100	1936=100	100	100	N/A
1951	110	192	123	133	na	100
1952	133	366	152	156	141	N/A
1953	135	542	139	231	about 141	over 150

Data source: Calculated on data on pp. 47–49 in Wang Dafu, ed., *Commerce in the Transitional Period*. Shanghai: New Knowledge Press, 1955.

August 1955, it promulgated the *Temporary Methods of State Monopolized Purchase and Marketing of Grain in Rural Areas*, which clearly stipulated the methods on how to decide the amount of grain production, purchase, and sales. After the establishment of monopolized purchase and sales of grain, cotton, and edible oils, the state named more commodities that were to be purchased by state quotas, including critical sideline products and raw industrial materials such as flue-cured tobacco, cotton, live pigs, tea, silkworms, wool, and cowhide.

In 1958, the State Council announced the *Measures of Administration According to the Product Categories* for agricultural products and other commodities, and further institutionalized and legalized the state-monopolized procurement and marketing system and the state-arranged procurement system in the related areas. The "First-category commodities" included those that were of essential importance for the national economy and people's livelihood, those for which production was concentrated but consumption was scattered, and those that were important export commodities. The First-category commodities were managed directly by the central government. The "Second-category commodities" consisted of goods with concentrated production but had to be provided to widespread areas or industries, or those for which production was scattered but needed to ensure the supply to important regions, or those that were required for special use. The central government made inter-regional transfers to make up the regional balance for these commodities. The commodities such as non-staple foods and agricultural and sideline products which were not included in the above two categories made up the third category. The commodities in this category were managed by the local government and inter-regional trade would be arranged by the higher-level commercial departments when necessary.

2.5 Micro-management Institutions Characterized by Nationalization and the People's Commune System

In the discussion that follows, we trace the formation of the industrial ownership structure in the economy dominated by state-owned sectors. The low-interest-rate and low-exchange-rate policies lowered the barriers for capital formation in industries. The low-price policy for energy and raw materials and the low-nominal-wage policy reduced enterprises' production costs. These policies were designed to increase the profits and accelerate the accumulation of existing enterprises. They did create the necessary macro-policy environment for industrial construction at the early stages of economic development. However, these policies alone were not sufficient to make the heavy-industry-oriented industrial development successful. If enterprises were owned and run by private agents, they would have had the right to allocate profits and choose investments, which would have deviated from the heavy-industry-oriented development strategy.

As a matter of fact, such profit-oriented private enterprises would allocate their resources to the sectors that yielded the highest returns. For instance, there was a strong demand for products of light industry because of insufficient market supply; at the same time, the technological structure of light industries catered well to the comparative advantages of the Chinese economy. With the state focused on developing heavy industry, investment in the suppressed light industries would tend to yield high returns. Therefore, for the purpose of securing policy-distortion-induced profits for heavy industry projects, the state had to nationalize private enterprises to the greatest possible extent, and let SOEs become dominant in the industrial structure. Furthermore, it was imperative to establish, on the basis of this ownership arrangement, a compulsory production planning system and a unified revenue and expenditure system.

According to the New Democracy Policy, upon the founding of the People's Republic of China, national capitalist industries and commerce were expected to coexist with socialist industries and commerce for quite a long period.[19] However, with the

19. In the Third Plenary Session of the Seventh Central Committee of the CPC, Mao Zedong criticized people who suggested eliminating capitalism and implementing socialism at an earlier time. He said, "This idea is erroneous; it

implementation of the First Five-year Plan, the heavy-industry-oriented development strategy became increasingly incompatible with the coexistence of different ownerships in the economy, and the Party began to change its stance. In 1954, the state began to transform large-scale private factories into joint state-private ventures, with new investments from the state to expand or restructure them. For medium-sized and small private enterprises, the transformation started with joint state-private ventures of a few enterprises and spread to the whole industry, ending with the establishment of new enterprises. Whole-industry joint state-private ventures began to appear in Beijing in early 1956 and then spread to other cities in the country. After joint ventures were established in the whole industry, the practice of allocating profits to private owners within a single enterprise was changed to uniformly award private owners throughout the industry with a fixed dividend that was determined according to the entire industry's profits. Former private owners lost their right to manage their own enterprises. Private enterprises became virtually state run. In 1956, the output value of state-run enterprises made up 67.5% of the total industrial output, and the output value of joint state-private ventures made up 32.5%. Private industry had almost completely vanished.[20]

By issuing a series of compulsory indicators to SOEs, the state was directly managing the economy. In an enterprise owned by the state, the interests of the managers and workers came into conflict with national interests. The national objective was to accumulate the maximum possible amount of industrial capital and to continuously expand capital accumulation. However, managers and workers tended to maximize their own wages and benefits. Whenever possible, they would over-report production costs or under-report output value to deliver less profits to the state. As a consequence, the enterprises and individuals encroached upon national assets and

---

is not suitable to the conditions of our country." See Zhao Dexin, ed., *The Economic History of the PRC*. Zhengzhou, Henan People's Press, 1989, p. 118.

20. Xue Muqiao, *A Study of Problems Concerning China's Socialist Economy*. Beijing: People's Press, 1979, p. 38.

profits. Because of information asymmetry, monitoring costs for the state was prohibitively high. In particular, since prices were distorted by macro policy, profits and losses could no longer reflect management performance. When competition was eliminated after private enterprises were artificially destroyed, and the allocation of goods and resources was carried out merely by the state, profits and losses for enterprises in an industry ceased to be a function of their market competitiveness.

Under these conditions, if SOEs had been granted the autonomy in production and management, it would have been impossible to prevent them from encroaching on the surplus. As a result, the state chose to deprive SOEs of any autonomy. All production materials used by SOEs were supplied by the government through planning, and all their output was sold to and allocated by the state. All revenue was remitted to the state, and all expenditures were approved and allocated by the state. SOEs remitted not only profits but also depreciation to the state, both of which were included in the government revenues. Investments in basic construction, funds for renovating fixed assets and for technological upgrading, expenses for pre-production tests, and funds for miscellaneous capital acquisition were all appropriated by the state. In addition, funds for working capital were appropriated in fixed amounts by the departments of finance in government. The seasonal and temporal capital beyond the pre-approved amount were provided by the bank. Both workers' recruitment and their wages were arranged by the state according to plan.

Next came the collectivization of agriculture through the People's Communes. Establishing a state-monopolized purchase and marketing system was merely the first step toward forming a collectively organized agricultural economy. The establishment of the People's Commune System was actually the bench-mark for completing the agricultural system that was required by the distorted macro-policy environment.[21] In accordance with the *Overall*

21. Mao Zedong admitted at that time that the state monopoly of purchase and marketing was an important step toward achieving socialism, see Mao

Guidelines and Tasks in the Transitional Period at that time, farming cooperatives that were organized to take advantage of economies of scale after the land reform should base on the free will of individual farmers and provide mutual assistance and cooperation during the peak seasons. Usually it took between three and five households to cooperate voluntarily in this way during the harvest season. The main mode of cooperation was the mutual-aid team, which was based on individual household farm management. However, with the implementation of the heavy-industry-oriented development strategy, the formation of a distorted macro-policy environment, and the introduction of a state monopoly of purchase and marketing, agricultural collectivization suddenly accelerated to ensure the low-price purchase of agricultural products.[22]

When the nationwide land reform programme ended in 1952, farming households participating in mutual-aid teams made up only 39.9% of the total rural households, whereas only 0.1% of the households participated in agricultural production cooperatives. Moreover, all the agricultural cooperatives were elementary cooperatives, which consisted of 20 to 30 households. Afterwards, although there was some development in the agricultural collectivization movement, the major mode of mutual assistance and cooperation was still the mutual-aid team. This was the case until 1955, when 50.7% of peasants' households participated in mutual-aid teams, and of these only 14.7% participated in elementary cooperatives. At that time, Mao Zedong estimated that the socialist transformation in agriculture would not be completed until the 1960s. However, it was

---

Zedong, *Collection of Mao Zedong's Works*, Vol. 5. Beijing: People's Press, 1977, p. 335. Before long, he logically pointed out that the "People's Commune is better because it integrates workers, peasants, businessmen, students and soldiers. It is easier to govern in this way." See "Mao Zedong's Visit to the Villages in Shandong", *People's Daily*, 13 August 1958.

22. From our knowledge of economics, we know that the monopolized purchase of agricultural products only allows the state to procure agricultural products at a low price. If the state wants to increase the quantity of agricultural product purchase, it must exercise direct control over agricultural production. Collectivization is an institutional arrangement by which the government can exercise its direct control over agricultural production.

completed in 1956. The proportion of peasants participating in agricultural cooperatives jumped from 14.2% of the total in late 1955 to 80.3% in early 1956 and rose to 96.3% in December of the same year. Meanwhile, advanced cooperatives consisting of about 200 households developed very quickly. The proportion of households participating in this type of cooperatives increased from 30.7% in early 1956 to 87.7% at the end of that year.[23]

Launched in 1958, the Great Leap Forward Movement in economic construction proposed that China surpass the United Kingdom's level of economic development and catch up to that of the United States. Heavy industries were emphasized, especially the iron and steel industries. Several unrealistically high targets of industrial development were proposed. Owing to the sudden expansion in the construction scale of basic infrastructure, the number of workers in SOEs increased by 85% in just one year. Because of the inappropriate ratio of accumulation to consumption and because of the shortage of consumption funds, and also because agricultural production could not meet increasing needs, the government had to increase compulsory procurement quotas. In 1958, grain production increased by only 2.55%, but the quantity procured rose by as much as 22.3%.

This was actually an experiment that magnified the policy distortion of the heavy-industry-oriented development strategy, thus, a more rapid approach to the corresponding micro-management was also required. The result was the rapid expansion of the People's Communes. The transition from the establishment of the first People's Commune to national communization was almost completed between August and early November of 1958. By then, the number of agricultural households participating in communes had reached 127 million (i.e., 99.1% of all agricultural households).[24]

The consequences were disastrous. From 1952 to 1958, during the agricultural collectivization, agricultural production rose steadily.

23. Su Xing, *The Socialist Transformation of Agriculture in China*. Beijing: People's Press, 1980, p. 156.

24. Zhao Dexin, ed., *The Economic History of the PRC*. Zhengzhou: Henan People's Press, 1980, p. 449.

However, in 1959 a severe agricultural crisis broke out and lasted for three years.[25] Grain production in 1959 and 1960 underwent a continuous 15% reduction, as compared with the previous year. In 1961, its output barely matched the 1960 level. This led to an unprecedented famine that claimed 30 million lives.[26] Although the People's Commune System was not abolished after the crisis, the scale of production units was reduced. Collective ownership was divided among a People's Commune, a brigade, and a production team (the so-called "Three-level System"), with the production team being the basic accounting unit. Production management accounting and income distribution were put in the charge of the production team. Each production team conducted its business accounting independently and assumed full responsibility for its own profits and losses. Through this type of institutional arrangement, the state retained its control over agricultural production, consumption, and the allocation of agricultural resources.

In the late 1950s or early 1960s, in order to deal with the difficulties appearing in the economy, a few adjustments were made

25. Agriculture activities are hard to monitor because of their long production cycle and wide range. The success of agricultural cooperatives therefore depends on the self-discipline of the participating peasants. But self-discipline can only be maintained in cooperatives that are formed by the peasants voluntary requests. Justin Yifu Lin believed the change from a voluntary to a compulsory membership in the cooperatives was the main reason for the failure of China's collectivization in 1959. During the transitional period from mutual aid teams to the advanced cooperatives, peasants had the right to exit (i.e., they were willingly participating in the cooperatives at that time). However, beginning in late 1958, during the formation of People's Communes, peasants were deprived of their right to exit. Under these circumstances, self-discipline could not be maintained, and production incentives decreased. Therefore, a crisis broke out. See Justin Yifu Lin, "Collectivization and China's Agricultural Crisis in 1959–1961", *Journal of Political Economy*, Vol. 98, No. 6 (December 1990), pp. 1228–52. U.S. academics debated Yifu Lin's hypothesis. See *Journal of Comparative Economics*, Vol. 17 (June 1993).
26. See Basil Aoton, Kenneth Hill, Alan Piazza and Robin Zeitz, "Famine in China, 1958–1961", *Population and Development Review*, Vol. 10 (December 1984), pp. 613–45.

in the micro-management institutions. However, these adjustments made no changes to the nature of the micro institutions, which was endogenous to the strategic goal, the distorted macro-policy environment and the planned resource-allocation mechanism. On the contrary, several regulations and resolutions were adopted to further institutionalize and refine the system. Therefore, the 1960s was a period in which the trinity of the traditional economic system — the macro-policy environment, the resource-allocation mechanism and the micro-management institution — was fully established.

2.6 The Trinity of the Traditional Economic System: An International Comparison

The above analysis traces the historical development of China's traditional economic system. The choice of a heavy-industry-oriented development strategy led first to the formation of a macro environment with distorted product and factor prices, then to a highly centralized planned resource-allocation mechanism, and finally to a puppetlike micro-management institutional system. We term these components *the trinity of the traditional economic system.*

Figure 2.2 summarizes this sequence. It shows that the economic development strategy is exogenously determined by political consideration. In China's agrarian economy, where capital was scarce, the trinity of the traditional system was formed in response to the government's adoption of a heavy-industry-oriented development strategy. All three elements of the trinity are endogenously determined by the exogenously-given factor endowments of the economy and the politically-determined development strategy. Given the resource-allocation mechanism, the corresponding economic structure followed; and given the micro-management institutional system, it will generate a certain level of incentives accordingly, leading to a specific level of economic performance. This will be discussed in the next chapter.

China was not the only country that adopted this kind of leap-forward development strategy. The former Soviet Union adopted a similar development strategy. Indeed, many other countries did the

Figure 2.2 China's traditional economic system

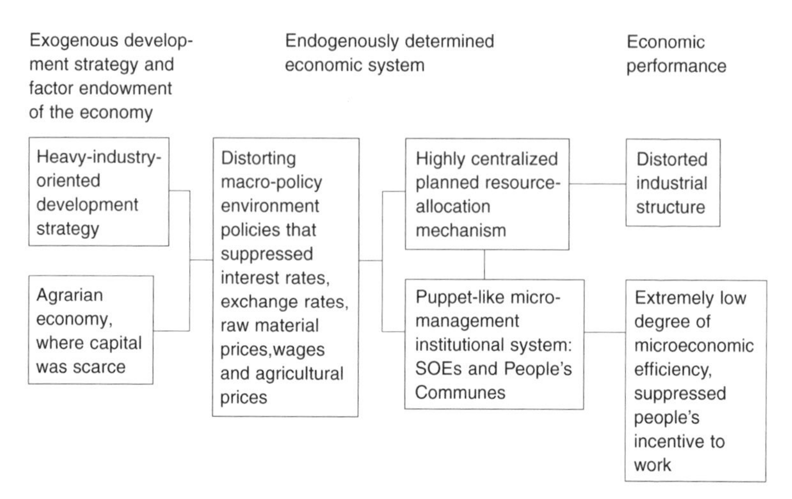

same. In fact, in addition to socialist countries, many non-socialist developing nations, notably those in South Asia and Latin America, made similar choices, and their economic systems had many features in common with the Chinese system.

For instance, under the leadership of the late premier Nehru, Mahalanobis drafted India's heavy-industry development plan. During the period of its First and Second Five-year Plans, the development of heavy industries was India's main economic objective. Subsequently, Indian government investment also focused on heavy industries. Of the Indian government investment in 1976–77, the investment in the iron and steel industry made up 28.5%, that in the chemical and pharmaceutical industry 18.7%, the coal industry 11.5%, the heavy machine-building industry 7.3%, the mining industry 6.4%, and the oil industry 6.2%. These totalled 78.6%.[27]

Apart from the reasons discussed above, which are specific to China, we can briefly summarize a number of common theoretical

27. Chen Licheng, et al., *The Economic Development Strategy in Developing Countries and the New International Economic Order*. Beijing, Economic Science Press,1987, p. 147.

and practical factors that contributed to the widespread selection of such a strategy.

First was the strong desire of the developing countries to catch up with and overtake advanced economies. After World War II, a large number of colonial or semi-colonial countries became politically independent. How to develop the economy independently so as to achieve a rapid economic take-off and eliminate poverty was a central task on every government's national agenda. However, compared with developed countries, these developing countries had an extremely low economic growth rate and per capita GNP, high birth and death rates, a low education level, an insufficient number of capable managers, and a rigid political system. In order to change these conditions quickly, many developing countries thus had strong incentives to pursue the rapid industrializtion approach.

Second, the radical view of economic development also significantly affected the strategies in developing countries. Most developing countries used to be colonies or semi-colonies. Their leaders were deeply influenced by the views held by radical economists at that time. They believed that market system would lead to serious polarization in their economies and result in economic backwardness, and that conducting foreign trade at the time was in essence a loss of valuable resources. Based on these assumptions, they expected that the terms of trade for the primary products, which were their major export items, would deteriorate continuously. Therefore, national leaders and economists in these countries tended to think that while the economic development was highly unbalanced in the world, if developing countries did not establish their own independent industrial systems and merely depended on their export of primary products, they would continue to be the peripheries of advanced economies and would remain in a state of backwardness forever.[28]

28. "The Issues of Economic Development and Under-development from a Historic Perspective", in Charles K. Wilber, ed., *The Political Economy of Development and Under-development*, Part 2. Beijing: China Social Science Press, 1984.

Third, under the influence of Keynesianism, the mainstream theories in development economics at the time held that the market encompasses insurmountable defects and that the government was a powerful supplementary means to accelerate the pace of economic development.[29] Many development economists opposed conventional economics. They emphasized market imperfections in developing countries, despite the positive role of market and price mechanisms. They advocated the implementation of centralized and detailed planned management so that the national economy could operate smoothly. Academic exchanges — including the hiring of economists from developed countries as economic advisers, and the participation of international organizations such as the World Bank — greatly affected developing countries' choice of development strategy.

Both the radical development theory prevalent in developing countries and the economic development theories influenced by Keynesian theory in advanced economies emphasized the idea that the characteristics of economic development in developing countries were different from those in the classic capitalist economies. Hollis B. Chenery summarized the basic assumptions of such theories: (1) it was not necessary for the prices of production factors to reflect their opportunity costs accurately; (2) since production factors were partially the outputs in the production process, their quality and quantity could be changed greatly with time; (3) in many production sectors, economies of scale associated with the existing size of the market were very important; and (4) the complementarity between commodities greatly affected the demands of producers and consumers. The economic-development strategy based on these assumptions emphasized the continuous acceleration of the

29. Until the mid-1970s, most development economists were anti price system, pro planning, pro intervention, and anti trade. Although they conducted positive analyses, they pointed out the ineffectiveness of the market. When they conducted normative analyses, they advocated intervention. See Deepak Lal, *The Poverty of Development Economics*. Cambridge, MA: Harvard University Press, 1985, pp. 5–16.

economic growth rate and the increasing use of production factors. It ignored the functions of the market, comparative advantages, and inter-national trade, which would provide continuous sources of impetus for economic development.[30]

Because of the influence of these ideas on the choice of development strategy, and because of the impact of the development strategy on the formation of the macro-policy environment, the resource-allocation mechanism, and institutional micro management, many developing nations — whether socialist, such as China, the former USSR and those in Eastern Europe, or non-socialist, such as those in Asia and Central and South America — had a similar trinity within their economic systems.

Some developing nations, notably those in Latin America, called their economic development strategy the "import-substitution strategy". Their aim was to satisfy domestic demand with locally produced industrial products so as to reduce imports and promote the nation's industrialization. The preferential development of heavy industries was a necessary component of this strategy, which was called "secondary import substitution". The heavy-industry-oriented development strategy and the import-substitution strategy are in essence the same. Along with the term "leap forward", China used the slogan "surpass the United Kingdom and catch up to the United States" in the late 1950s. In May 1958, the Second Plenary Session of the Eighth Central Committee of the CPC proclaimed that China's economy should surpass the level of the United Kingdom's within about 5 years and should catch up to or even surpass that of the United States within about 15 years. This was set up as the goal of economic development and led to the Great Leap Forward Movement.

During the 1950s, most developing nations shared a common trait: they had a rich labour pool or natural resource endowment. At the same time, they all had scarce capital. In attempting to surpass or

30. Hollis B. Chenery, "Comparative Advantage and Development Policy", *American Economic Review*, Vol. 51 (March 1961), p. 21.

overtake developed countries, these countries were trying to bypass a necessary stage of development. "Leaping forward" thus vividly describes the heavy-industry-oriented development and the import-substitution strategy. We use the expression to refer to the goals of all of the countries that blindly sought to overtake more advanced economies regardless of their own comparative advantages in factor endowment.

At the core of such an economic strategy lies a macro-policy environment with distorting product and factor prices. Since they are in conflict with the comparative advantages of resource endowment, sectors given priority in the leap-forward strategy lack the endogenous ability to survive in a competitive free-market environment. Without exception, all countries adopting the leap-forward strategy used a series of administritive methods to distort the price system so as to create a policy environment favourable to the development of the priority sectors. These countries usually established policies that suppressed interest rates, exchange rates, raw material prices, and agricultural prices. We call these policy measures the distortion or price-distorted macro-policy environment.

All countries implementing this type of economic strategy had to establish a highly controlled administrative management system that was used to guarantee the implementation of price-distortion policies. Artificially distorted product and factor prices implied the limitation or suppression of market functions and competition. Therefore, they necessitated the use of various regulations, as well as different types of discrimination and protection, to replace the functions of market and price mechanism. The set of administrative management systems that carried out the distortion policies included the following:

(1) The nationalization or pursuit of an exceedingly high proportion of SOEs to control the lifeline of the economy. For instance, SOEs in India played a leading role in almost all important industrial sectors. They produced 22% of the net domestic product value in the 1980s. Brazil also adopted a typical import-substitution strategy. In 1984, among the

200 largest enterprises in the country, 81 were state-owned. Their assets and revenues made up 74.2% and 56.3% respectively of the total assets and net revenue of the 200 largest enterprises.[31]

(2) Government involvement in the allocation of scarce resources, a monopoly of trade, and the support of infant industries through the establishment of an industrial protection system and erecting entry barriers. Countries that pursued the heavy-industry-oriented strategy almost invariably adopted protective trade measures such as custom duties, multiple exchange rates, quantitive limitations, and domestic discriminating policies such as production permits and a national monopoly.

(3) Financial suppression, including the erection of credit ceilings and the restriction of financial activities, to ensure that priority industries enjoyed preferential credit conditions. If we compare the countries adopting the heavy-industry-oriented strategy with advanced countries or with countries and regions adopting different development strategies, we can see this institutional feature in the former countries, and as a consequence of their financial suppression, the banking system was underdeveloped, and loanable funds were insufficient. The figures in Table 2.4 show that because of the implementation of the low-interest-rate policy and the financial-suppression policy, loanable funds in their banks (the M2 to GNP ratio) were much more meagre than those in the banks of other types of economies.

(4) Adoption of an urban-biased social welfare policy to encourage industrial development. This feature can also be observed by looking at the degree of unequal income distribution — one of the consequences of this discriminating policy for rural areas (see Table 2.5).

31. Chen Licheng, et al., *The Economic Development Strategy in Developing Countries and the New International Economic Order*. Beijing: Economic Science Press, 1987, p. 34.

Table 2.4 Comparison of the Rate of Loanable Funds in Countries Adopting Different Development Strategies (M2 to GNP ratio)

Country/region	Year	Rate of average loanable fund
Economies adopting the leap-forward strategy:		
Brazil	1960–75	0.168
Argentina	1960–75	0.222
India	1960–75	0.276
Philippines	1960–75	0.205
Advanced industrial economies		
Belgium	1960–75	0.573
France	1960–75	0.533
Sweden	1960–75	0.638
The United States	1960–75	0.665
Economies adopting other strategies		
Japan	1975	1.087
Korea	1975	0.334
Taiwan	1975	0.750
Hongkong	1975	0.702

Source: John Cody, et al., eds., *Industrial Development Policies in the Developing Countries*. Beijing: Economic Science Press, 1986, pp. 98–99.

Table 2.5 Income Distribution in Countries Adopting Different Development Strategies

Country/region	Year	Gini Coefficient on household basis
Economies adopting leap-forward strategy		
Argentina	1961	0.425
Brazil	1970	0.500
India	1964–65	0.428
Philippines	1971	0.490
Economies adopting other strategies		
Korea	1970	0.351
Taiwan	1964 –1977	0.321*
Hong Kong	1971	0.434

* Arithmatic mean

Source: Jacques Lecaillon, et al., *Income Distribution and Economic Development*. Geneva: International Labour Office, 1984, pp. 26–27; and Hu Shengyi, *Economic Development and Social Welfare*. Taipei: Zhongyang Wenwu Gongyingshe, 1980, p. 39.

To sum up, the formation of the traditional economic system as a result of the adoption of a heavy-industry-oriented development strategy was not unique to China or particular to the socialist system. Therefore, the formation, consequences, and reform process of China's traditional economic system have valuable implications for other socialist economies and developing countries that had adopted similar development strategies.

CHAPTER 3

Economic Performance and China's Development Strategy

Giving priority to the development of heavy industry and creating a corresponding economic system yielded an accumulation rate of over 15%[1] and resulted in a relatively comprehensive industrial economic system in China, in spite of its extremely economic backwardness. However, in terms of economic efficiency, the cost of implementing this strategy was extremely high.

Economic development under the traditional Chinese economic system was repressed in two ways. The first is reflected in a distorted industrial structure, and the second is in the low economic efficiency at the micro level. Giving priority to heavy-industry development ran counter to China's comparative advantage and distorted the economic structure so much that development was slower than it could have been. The capital-intensive industrial structure constrained the full play of comparative advantage in labour resources, and fortified the dual structure of the traditional and modern sectors. As a result, an originally attainable level of employment and urbanization became impossible to realize. To maintain economic growth under such a development strategy, a high accumulation rate was required and resulted in the distortion of national income distribution, which then led to slow improvement in people's living

1. Lewis points out that "the central question of an economic development theory is to understand the process of how a society with less than 4% or 5% of saving and investment turned into an economy with voluntary increase to over 12% to 15% of the national income." W. A. Lewis, *Economic Dualism*. Beijing: Beijing Economics Institute Press, 1989, p. 15; W. A. Lewis, "Economic Development with Unlimited Supplies of Labour", *Manchester School of Economics and Social Studies*, Vol. 28 (1954), pp. 139–91.

standards, and the distorted industrial structure created an inward-looking economy. Hence, the economy could not use international trade to exploit its comparative advantages or complement its own comparative disadvantages. As for the enterprise system, the SOEs obtained all inputs from the state and submitted all their products to it. The state covered all the production cost of SOEs and the SOEs remitted all their revenues to the state. Under these conditions, the SOE's development was not linked to its economic performance, and workers income had nothing to do with their contribution. All these factors suppressed people's incentive to work and resulted in an extremely low economic efficiency. Production could only be conducted inside the production possibility frontier (PPF).

As previously mentioned, trying to effect rapid development by giving priority to heavy industry was the choice not only of the Chinese leaders but also of leaders in many other developing countries. After making international comparisons, we can see that none of these countries achieved what they had hoped for, and they certainly did not catch up with or overtake developed countries. Other developing countries that had adopted the heavy-industry development strategy are now facing difficulties similar to those China is grappling with. Therefore, we can assume that the fundamental cause for the high cost and inefficiency of China's pre-reform economy was the poorly chosen development strategy.

3.1 Economic Growth Before Reform

From 1952 to 1978, China's overall economic size increased substantially. The average annual growth rates of the total social output value, total output value of industry and agriculture, and the total national income calculated on a comparable prices basis were as high as 7.9%, 8.2%, and 6.0%, respectively (see Table 3.1). This economic growth rate was higher than the world average and was only a bit lower than the growth rates of South Korea and Taiwan. During this period, China underwent dramatic changes in its economic structure and established a comprehensive industrial system.

In 1978, China's industrial sectors accounted for 46.8% of the

Table 3.1 Basic Indices for Economic Growth from 1952 to 1978 (%)

	Total social output value	Total output value of industry and agriculture	GDP	National income	Accumulation ratio
First Five-year Plan	11.3	10.9	9.1	8.9	24.2
Second Five-year Plan	–0.4	0.6	–2.2	–3.1	30.8
1963–1965	15.5	15.7	14.9	14.7	22.7
Third Five-year Plan	9.3	9.6	6.9	8.3	26.3
Fourth Five-year Plan	7.3	7.8	5.5	5.5	33.0
1976–78	8.1	8.0	5.8	5.6	33.5
1953–78	7.9	8.2	6.0	6.0	29.5

Note: The growth rate is based on comparable prices; the accumulation ratio is based on current prices.

Source: National Bureau of Statistics of China, National Economic Balance Statistics Division, *National Income Statistics Data Compilation (1949–1985)*. Beijing: China Statistics Press, 1987, pp. 2, 45–46.

total national income, an increase of 34.2 percent points from 1949's 12.6%. In the same period, the share of agriculture in the total national income decreased from 68.4% to 35.4%; that of the construction sector rose from 0.3% to 4.1%; transportation from 3.3% to 3.9%; whereas commerce decreased from 15.4% to 9.8%. From 1952 to 1980, the total industrial investment reached RMB 359.92 billion, with newly added fixed assets reaching RMB 273.45 billion. In 1980, the total industrial output value was RMB 499.2 billion, which was 13.5 times higher than the RMB 34.33 billion of 1952 after price adjustment.[2]

Why, then, did China, with its high economic growth rate, fail to achieve economic modernization? The conditions of economic development in China were similar to those in surrounding regions, including South Korea and Taiwan, in the early 1950s. From the 1950s to the 1970s, all the three economies also shared a similar rate

2. Ma Hong, ed., *Dictionary of Economic Affairs in Contemporary China*. Beijing, China Social Sciences Press, 1982, pp. 79, 153.

of economic growth.[3] However, China's per capita GNP was still very low in 1978. Per capita GNP was US$52 in 1952 and US$210 in 1978.[4] By 1978, China had not yet attained a per capita income of US$265, the minimum level for a middle-income developing nations.[5] In the following two sections, we discuss in more detail the reasons that China's per capita GNP increased so slowly. Here, we briefly explain the coexistence of the apparently high growth rate and the actual low development level.

Without sufficient evidence, it is unwise to assume that economic growth data from 1952 to 1978 is unreliable. However, as is shown below, the growth rate figures cannot fully reflect reality. In other words, these figures may help illuminate that the seemingly high growth rate does not represent real growth.

First, China's economic growth started from a very low level. The absolute total output value of industry and agriculture was only RMB 46.6 billion in 1949, based on 1952 prices, and RMB 82.7 billion in 1952. Per capita total output value of industry and agriculture were RMB 86.03 and RMB 143.87, respectively. The total figures and per capita figures of national income, GNP, and GDP were very low. Compared with other developing economies that won their independence after World War II, the relatively low starting-level became one important feature of China's economic

---

3. Per capita GNP in the early 1950s were all less than US$100 annually; from 1958 to 1979, China's production output increased by 9.3% (The World Bank, *How to Manage Technological Development, Some Questions for China to Consider*. Beijing, Meteorological Press, 1984); GDP in South Korea and Taiwan province increased by an annual rate of 8.9% and 9.3%, respectively, from 1961 to 1970, and by 8.7% and 9.7%, from 1971 to 1980 (Asia Development Bank, *Asia Development Outlook 1990*. Manila: Asian Development Bank, 1991).
4. The World Bank estimated it to be US$220 (The World Bank, *World Table, 1992*. Baltimore: Johns Hopkins University Press, 1992, p. 184).
5. The United Nations Industrial Development Organization defined those developing counties with an average per capita GNP of less than US$265 to be low-income developing nations in 1980 (UN Industrial Development Organization, *Basics and Trends of Industrialization in World Countries and Regions*. Beijing: China Foreign Translation Publishing Co., 1980, p. 49).

development. Obviously, the lower the initial level, the easier it is to achieve a higher growth rate.[6] And given the same growth rate, an economy with a lower initial level will enjoy less impressive economic consequences. From the growth rate changes in various development stages in Table 3.1, we can see that with the enlargement of the base figure of Chinese economy, the growth rate gradually fell. The figures for industrial growth show this trend even more clearly. During the years of economic recovery from 1949 to 1952, the average annual growth rate was recorded as 34.8%. In the First Five-year Plan period it was 18%. After a sharp drop in early 1960s, it rose to 17.8% between 1963 and 1965. Then it gradually fell to 10% from 1965 to 1980.

Second, China's economic growth varied greatly from industry to industry. Because heavy-industry sectors were the beneficiaries of preferential investment and protection policies, heavy industry developed significantly faster than agriculture or tertiary industry. For example, from 1951 to 1980, industrial growth averaged an annual 11.0%, whereas agricultural growth and commercial growth only stood at 3.2% and 4.2%, respectively.[7] Among the various industrial sectors, heavy industry recorded the highest annual growth rate — 15.3% from 1949 to 1981. This rate propped up national economic growth and raised the share of manufacturing in the national economy. However, since the growth depended lopsidedly on the growth of heavy industry, it could not produce the effect of a coordinated growth. Therefore, a high growth rate of this type does not necessarily mean a substantive economic development.

Third, the high accumulation rate was accompanied with a slow improvement in people's living standards. Resource allocation through government planning could surely increase the savings ratio in the national income by curtailing the consumption ratio. The capital accumulation rate in this way could reach a level that would have been impossible at this development stage in a market economy.

6. See Zheng Youjing and Fang Hanzhong, "A Study on the Trend of Economic Growth", *Economic Research*, No. 2 (1992).

7. The growth rate for commerce was the annual average from 1952 to 1980.

Table 3.1 shows that China had a very high accumulation rate in each historical period. The rate was not only higher than that of the world average but also higher than that of most developing economies, which successfully achieved rapid economic growth. The high rate of accumulation, achieved through the state planning and control, could undoubtedly help to create the high growth rate figures. However, because of the bias in the distribution of national income, personal income and people's living standard were persistently suppressed at a low level. Moreover, because the industrial structure was biased toward the capital-goods industries, the supply of consumer goods was deficient and the living standard improved slowly. One important aspect of economic development was thus neglected under the superficially high rate of economic growth.

Lastly, the growth rate was achieved with extremely low efficiency. Section 3.3 of this chapter explores in detail the efficiency problem in traditional economic system.

3.2 Distorted Structures Under the Traditional Economic Strategy

The adoption of the heavy-industry-oriented development strategy was intended to circumvent the constraints of capital shortage so that national economy could quickly overcome the adverse effect of a weak heavy industry. It was hoped that in this way the economy could grow quickly, and surpass advanced economies in the shortest possible period of time. Through the distortion of product and production factor prices, the cost of developing heavy industries was reduced and more funds were accumulated. A corresponding planned resource-allocation system was also established to ensure that resources flew into heavy industries. In this way, China was indeed able to make heavy industry grow faster than other sectors. The leading coefficient of the growth in heavy industry will clearly illustrate this point. The coefficient is defined as the ratio of the average annual growth rate of heavy industry to that of light industry. It was 1.47 for the period between 1953–79. In the sub-periods, the coefficient was 1.68 for the recovery period, 1.97 for the First Five-year Plan period, 6.0 for the Second Five-year Plan period, 0.7 for 1963–65 due to a structural adjustment prompted by the disaster of the Great Leap Forward Movement, and 1.75 and 1.32, respectively, for the Third and Fourth Five-year Plan periods.

The implementation of this strategy led to huge distortions in China's industrial structure. Table 3.2 shows that the investment ratio of heavy industry to light industry was 5.7 during the First Five-year Plan period. It rose to 8.4 in 1976–78. China's failure to make full use of its comparative advantage in labour and to avoid its comparative disadvantage of insufficient capital led to a series of consequences which can be summed up in two aspects.

First, the share of the manufacturing sector in the industrial structure was extraordinarily high, while that of the service sectors was extremely low. From Tables 3.3 and 3.4, we can see that during the 27 years before the onset of reform, the proportion of agriculture

Table 3.2 Changes in Investment Structure, 1952–78 (According to Current Prices)

Year	Total fixed-asset investment (100 mn.)	Total infrastructure investment (100 mn.)	The structure of infrastructure investment (%)			
			Agriculture	Light industries	Heavy industries	Other sectors
First Five-year Plan period	611.58	587.71	7.1	6.4	36.2	50.3
Second Five-year Plan period	1,307.00	1,206.09	11.3	6.4	54.0	28.3
1963–65	499.45	421.89	17.6	3.9	45.9	32.6
Third Five-year Plan period	1,209.09	976.03	10.7	4.4	51.1	33.8
Fourth Five-year Plan period	2,276.37	1,763.95	9.8	5.8	49.6	34.8
1976–78	1,740.96	1,259.80	10.8	5.9	49.6	33.7

Source: National Bureau of Statistics of China, *China Statistical Yearbook, 1992.* Beijing: China Statistics Press, 1992, pp. 149–58; National Bureau of Statistics of China, *The Statistical Data of Fixed Asset Investment in China, 1950–1985.* Beijing: China Statistics Press, 1987, p. 97.

Table 3.3 Sectoral Composition of National Income 1952–78 (Current Prices)

	1952	1957	1962	1965	1970	1975	1978
Agriculture	57.72	46.81	48.05	46.21	40.39	37.79	32.76
Industry	19.52	28.3	32.79	36.41	40.97	46.02	49.4
Other sectors	22.75	24.5	19.15	17.37	18.64	16.18	17.84

Source: National Bureau of Statistics of China, *China Statistical Yearbook, 1992*. Beijing: China Statistics Press, 1992, p. 35.

Table 3.4 Changes in Employment Structure, 1952–78

Year	Total labour employed (10,000 Persons)				Percentage of labour employed (%)				
	Total	Agri-culture	Industry	Other sectors	Agri-culture	Industry			Other sectors
						Total	Light industry	Heavy industry	
1952	20729	17317	1246	2166	83.5	6.0	4.2	1.8	10.5
1957	23771	19310	1401	3060	81.2	5.9	3.6	2.3	12.9
1965	28670	23398	1828	3444	81.6	6.4	3.0	3.4	12.0
1978	40152	29429	5008	5715	73.3	12.5	4.6	7.9	14.2

Source: Ma Hong and Sun Shangqing, eds., *China's Economic Structural Problems*. Beijing: People's Press, 1981, p. 104; National Bureau of Statistics of China, *China Statistical Yearbook*, 1992. Beijing: China Statistics Press, 1992, p. 97.

in the national income declined steadily, while that of industry increased constantly. That of the other industries (construction, transportation, and commerce) fell or remained stagnant after a brief increase from 22.75% in 1952 to 24.5% in 1957. In 1978, it was 6.7 percentage points lower than it had been in 1957. While the share of industry in the national income rose from 19.52% in 1952 to 49.4% in 1978, employment in the industrial sector rose only from 6.0% in 1952 to 12.5% in 1978. By 1978, 73.3% of the labour force still remained in the agricultural sector. Obviously, such an industrial and labour employment structure was not consistent with the laws of economic development.

Second, coarse processing represented a much greater proportion of the manufacturing sector than did refined processing. Owing to the lopsided pursuit of in-kind indicators and their quantitative growth rates, the capacity of coarse processing far exceeded that of refined processing. For example, in the iron and steel industries, steel smelting (which belonged to the category of coarse processing) grew quickly, while steel rolling (part of refined processing) grew rather slowly. This resulted in the pile-up of steel ingots on the one hand and a large volume of imported refined steel materials on the other.

The Chenery Large Country Model can help to illustrate the distortion in China's industrial structure. The model was based on the historical changes in the industrial structure of various countries.[8] It provides the "typical" economic structures of large low-income countries (with a per capita income of no more than US$300), large lower-middle income countries (with a per capita income of more than US$300 but less than US$600), and large middle-income countries (with a per capita income of more than US$1,200). In 1981, China's per capita GNP was estimated to be US$300 or US$350.[9] The comparison of the economic structures are illustrated in Figure 3.1. It shows that with its low per capita income, China had an exceptionally high proportion of manufacturing industries. Correspondingly, tertiary industries were extremely underdeveloped, accounting for only a very small percentage of the GDP.

This type of industrial structure was inconsistent with China's comparative advantages determined by its factor endowments,[10] and

8. Wang Huijiong and Yang Guanghui, eds., *Possibility and Options for China's Economic Structural Changes and Growth.* Beijing: Meteorological Press, 1984, pp. 67–68.
9. Based on dimensions comparable to other developing nations, the conclusion was made after adjusting to the US$300 level.
10. Compared with heavy industry, which made intensive use of capital, light industry is labour intensive. China is comparatively rich in labour resources, so if the macro-policy environment had not been distorted, light industry should have had a much larger share than heavy industry in the overall economy.

Figure 3.1 GDP structure in 1981

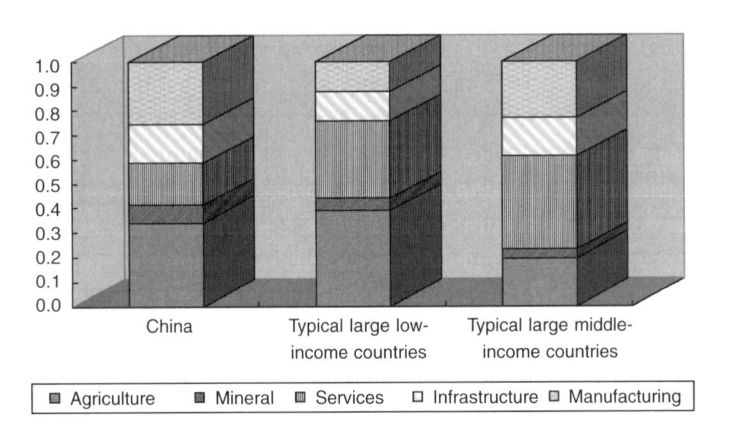

consequently impeded the development of Chinese economy and the improvement of people's living standards. This was also a major drawback of the traditional economic strategy. In order to analyze the problem in a clearer and more direct manner, we shall not consider for the time being the efficiency loss in the traditional economic system (this will be the theme for the next section), and shall assume that through its planning, the government could effectively achieve the goal of developing its priority sectors. We shall only summarize the economic consequences of the distortion in industrial structure.

1. The economic growth rate was depressed. At China's development stage, capital was scarce, while labour resources were abundant. If the market were allowed to function, labour costs would have been low. The comparative cost of labour-intensive products would naturally have been lower than the cost of capital-intensive products, and the former would have been more competitive than the latter in domestic and international markets. Driven by profit, manufacturers would have invested resources in labour-intensive industries and would have made every effort to employ technology that used less capital and more labour.

In Figure 3.2, when the industrial structure in line with comparative advantage is reflected in the PPF, the appropriate production mix

Figure 3.2 Development strategy and production efficiency

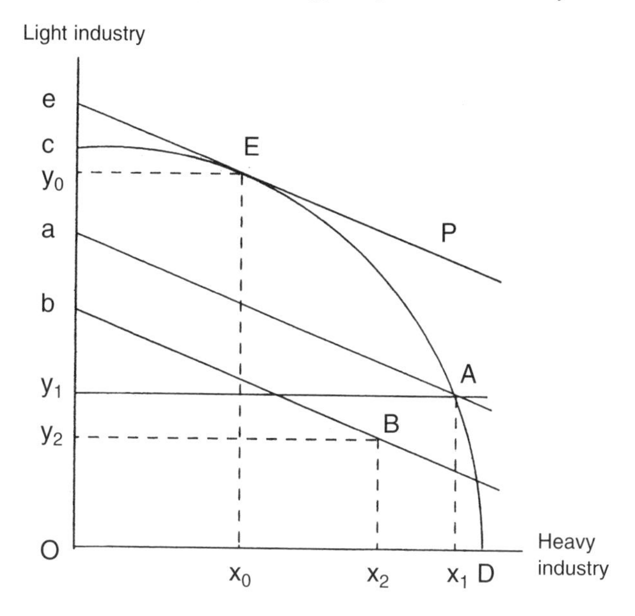

will be point E, where the distortion-free relative-price line touches the production possibility frontier. OY_0 refers to the produced labour-intensive (light-industry) products and OX_0 the capital-intensive (heavy-industry) products. When heavy industry was regarded as the priority, factor prices were distorted, and capital became a relatively cheaper factor. When the government allocated capital to heavy-industry sectors through planning, the development of light-industry sectors was depressed. This depression is shown by the Y_1 A line. As a result, the actual PPF shrank from CEAD to Y_1 AD. The resultant production mix is at point A, and, correspondingly, the output of labour-intensive product is OY_1, while that of the capital-intensive product is OX_1.

As illustrated in Figure 3.2, the static result of suppressing the comparative advantage sector is an absolute loss of ***ea*** or a relative loss of ***ea/eo*** in GNP, calculated on the constant prices. The loss in the GNP implies a reduction in the economic surplus that could be used for investment. Assume that a fixed portion of the GNP is used for investment. On the one hand, the reduction in initial investment will lead to a greater reduction in the total investment for the multiplier effect. (This multiplier is the reciprocal of the social marginal propensity to save). On the other hand, if we assume that the faster development of heavy industry is achieved through a constant investment ratio between the labour-intensive and the capital-intensive sectors, the production in every new period will continue to suffer a relative loss of *ea/eo* and an absolute loss larger than *ea*. Because of the multiplier effect, the total social investment will suffer a far larger reduction. This will significantly suppress the overall economic growth rate. In other words, the fast growth of heavy industries is achieved at the expense of the entire economy's potential for growth. We can thus conclude that, given the savings rate, the heavy-industry-oriented development strategy causes the economy to grow at a lower rate than its potential. Instead of stimulating economic growth, the leap-forward strategy has stunted the growth.

2. The transfer of labour from agricultural to non-agricultural sectors was slowed down, which consequently led to a low level of urbanization. Statistics show that every RMB 100 million investment in China's heavy industry provides only 5,000 employment opportunities which is only one-third of the number provided by light industry. Investing the same amount in SOEs will only create 10,000 employment opportunities, comprising merely one-fifth of the number created by the non-state-owned sectors. However, in this period, employment in heavy industry grew 4.1 times as much as employment in light industry, and the number of SOE employees increased 3.1 times as much as the number in non-state sectors.[11] From this analysis, we can see that because of the heavy industry-oriented development strategy, economic growth has failed to provide as many employment opportunities in non-agricultural industries as it was possible. It has also retarded the shift of labour from agricultural industry, which would normally have accompanied

11. Feng Ruilan and Zhao Lukuan, *China Urban Employment and Salary*. Beijing: People's Press, 1982, p. 10.

economic development. This is the key reason for the inconsistent changes in the employment structure and the industrial structure. In the 27-year pre-reform period, China's agricultural output share dropped from 57.72% to 32.76%, a decrease of about 25 percentage points, while the percentage of labour force in agriculture dropped from 83.5% to 73.3%, a decrease of only 10.2 percentage points. In other words, changes in employment structure lagged far behind the changes in industrial structure (see Tables 3.3 and 3.4).

As China adopted a segregation development policy for urban and rural areas, industries were concentrated in large and medium-sized cities. These industries did not need the complementary industries in surrounding areas, neither could they accelerate the development of related industries in the surrounding areas. In both small and large cities, the urban industrial structure was relatively comprehensive, and the normal urbanization process was obstructed. In 1980, China's urbanization rate was only 19.4%, just 6.9 percentage points higher than the 1952 level. This differs greatly from the general development experience and is a unique characteristic of China's urbanization process. Chenery et al. provided the average urbanization level at different levels of development in a normal development process (see Table 3.5). Using this as a comparison, we can see that China is lagged far behind in urbanization. Calculated at 1964 constant prices in U.S. dollars, China's per capita GNP was around US$154 in 1980.[12] If we

Table 3.5 Predicted Level of Urbanization at Different Income (GNP) Levels

GNP per capita (in U.S. dollars)	100	200	300	400	500	800	1,000
Percentage of urban population	22	36.2	43.9	49	52.7	60.1	63.4

Source: Hollis B. Chenery, et al., *Patterns of Development, 1950–1970*. Beijing: Economic Science Press, 1988, pp. 62, 63 and 69.

12. Cai Fang, "The New Stage in China's Urbanization", *Future and Development*, No. 5 (1990).

compare it with the predicted urbanization level at a GNP per capita of US$100 or US$200 in the table, China's urbanization level was not only much lower than the urbanization level at US$200 but was also lower than the urbanization level at US$100. Low urbanization depressed the development of tertiary industries, and their share in the overall economic structure remained much lower than the normal level.

3. People's living standards improved little over more than 20 years. Maximum resources were allocated, to the maximum possible extent, to the production of capital products, while the production of consumer goods was severely restricted. Moreover, in order to accelerate the growth of heavy industries, the limited available foreign exchange was generally not used for importing consumption goods. Therefore, the economy did not have the required material resources to improve people's living standard. In urban areas, people faced the policy of low wages and wage freeze. Their income and consumption level were in a state of slow growth or even stagnation (see Figure 2.1 and Table 3.6). In rural areas, because of the urban and rural segregation policy, people sufferred from insufficient employment and lacked incentive for agricultural production. Per capita production growth was slow. Income increases and improvements in living standards were hardly possible. The underdevelopment of consumer goods industries and the undersupply of

Table 3.6 Changes in the Level of Consumption for Urban and Rural Residents

Year	National income index	Consumption index of all citizens	Consumption index of rural residents	Consumption index of urban residents
1952	100	100	100	100
1957	153	122.9	117	126.3
1978	453.4	177	157.6	212.6

Note: The national income index and consumption index are calculated on comparable prices basis.

Source: National Bureau of Statistics of China, *China Statistical Yearbook, 1993*. Beijing: China Statistics Press, 1993, pp. 34 and 281.

agricultural products resulted in a perpetual shortage in the supply of daily consumable goods and foodstuffs. Most basic living necessities had to be supplied through a coupon system.

Under such an industrial structure, even if the government wanted to increase the production of consumer goods, it lacked the required resources. People would not work hard because harder work would not bring them a higher income. Therefore, one of the major reasons that people could not improve their living standard was the distortion in the industrial structure.

4. The inward-looking nature of the economy was reinforced by the deviation of economic structure from the pattern based on the economy's comparative advantage. Resources were directed towards the production of capital-intensive goods, which was contrary to China's comparative advantage. Gradually, the proportion of capital goods that China had to acquire from the international market decreased. At the same time, labour-intensive industries, which were consistent with China's comparative advantage, could not fully develop for the lack of sufficient resources allocated to them. Consequently, the amount of labour-intensive products that China could export to the international market decreased. The decline in imports and exports indicated that the economy became increasing inward looking. Table 3.7 shows that the share of import and export value declined from 8.16 percent in 1952–54 to 5.89 percent in 1976–78, a drop of 2.27 percentage points.

Table 3.7 Changes in International Trade, 1952–78

Year	Total output value of agriculture and industry (RMB 100 million)	Total value of import and export (RMB 100 million)	Share of the value of import and export in the total output value of agriculture and industry (%)
1952–54	2,820	230.2	8.16
1976–78	15,148	891.6	5.89

Source: National Bureau of Statistics of China, *China Statistical Yearbook, 1993*. Beijing: China Statistics Press, 1993, pp. 57–58 and 633.

3.3 Lack of Incentives and Low Efficiency

In addition to the distorted industrial structure described above, the low efficiency of the traditional economic system was also a result of the inefficient resource allocation, lack of competition, and poor incentives.

Planned allocation led to inefficient resource allocation. To allocate scarce resources according to plans and to supervise its implementation, a vertical sector management system and a horizontal administrative management system was established, whose functions were partially overlapped. The input and output relationship among various sectors and regions was replaced by competition for investment and other resources. In fact, the planners were unable to obtain all the information required for planning. As a result, planning often became an ex-post adjustment. Meanwhile, when economic structure deviated from the strategic goals, the planners did not resort to the price mechanism. Instead, they further distorted prices, used various direct and indirect subsidies (soft budget constraints) and quantitative adjustment methods to adjust national economic structure.[13] Therefore, all sectors were actually operating under two different sets of constraints.

As shown in Figure 3.3, one type of sector produces (Figure 3.3 (a)) at a calculating price (or accounting price) above the equilibrium level,[14] and the other type produces at a calculating price below the equilibrium level (Figure 3.3 (b)). In the former scenario, as the production sector produces at a higher than equilibrium price, it leads to a surplus of Q_0Q_1.[15] Note that the supply curve SS for the sector is

13. We assume that the equilibrium condition to be that the policy targets are met.
14. The accounting price is defined as an accounting index used by a sector or an enterprise to calculate its actual profit or loss. Under the traditional system, owing to soft budget constraints, such an index refers not only to the planned price but also to the planned supply of capital, raw materials, and so forth, as well as to encouraging or depressing policies that affect the profitability of production.
15. Here, consumer price (P_0) was not consistent with the manufacturer's accounting price (P_1), so the surplus is Q_0Q_1, rather than being higher. This also explains the difference in the case of product shortage.

Figure 3.3 Production under two calculating prices

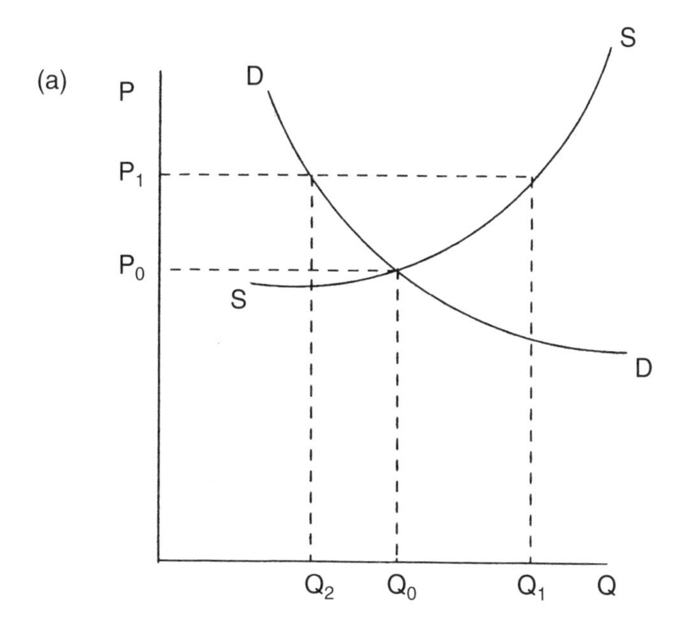

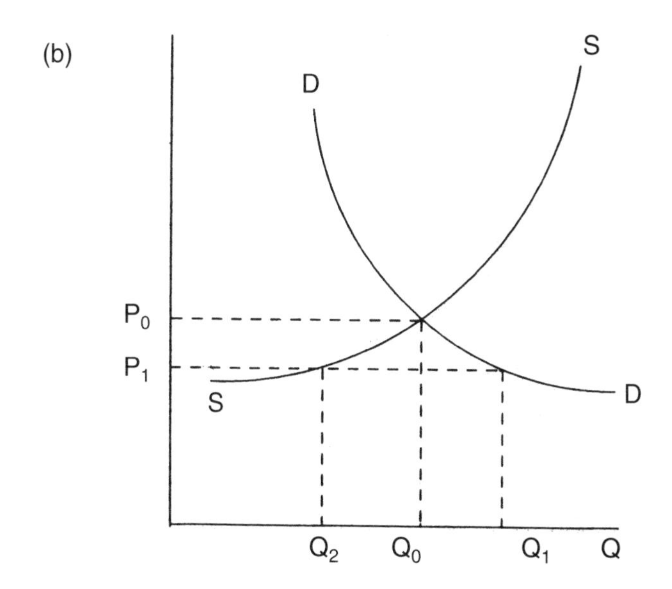

actually its marginal cost curve, so a higher accounting price leads the sector to produce excessive products at a higher marginal cost. In the latter scenario, the accounting price received by the sector is lower than the equilibrium price, and the products will be short of supply by Q_0Q_2.

Which sectors were given favourable prices and which were given unfavourable ones? The answer to this question was determined in two ways. In one case, the prices given to a sector depended on its bargaining power, that is, its relative importance in state plans. The more important sectors received favourable prices more frequently. The output or services of the agriculture, energy and transportation sectors were treated as inputs of the heavy industries, and their prices were frequently given unfavourable prices. This explains why they were bottlenecks for the national economy for a long time. In the other case, sectors, which had similar production characteristics, were in general equally likely to be assigned favourable or unfavourable prices. Their actual prices, however, depended on the planner's judgment of the economic conditions in the previous period. The production capacity in these sectors was constructed according to the state plan, which was based on the perceived long-term equilibrium level. When the calculating price of a sector is favourable, the sector would produce at a high marginal cost. When the calculating price was unfavourable, it would underutilize its capacity. Both created an efficiency loss.

A lack of competition also contributed to the low production efficiency. Giving priority to the development of heavy industry implied simultaneous implementation of primary and secondary import substitution (the former for daily necessities and the latter for machines and equipment). At that time, China's technological level was very low. Moreover, the strategy did not allow the economy to utilize its own comparative advantage. Therefore, the cost of domestic products was high and they were not competitive in the international market. In order to independently develop its own industrial system, China had to protect domestic industries at the expense of efficiency. On the one hand, the cost for domestically produced products was much higher than the foreign exchange that could be saved or earned by their domestic production. On the other hand, persistent protection slowed down the improvement in productivity, and incurred more dynamic losses to the national economy. The limited size of the domestic market made it impossible for certain industries to exploit their economies of scale, and the protected sector and enterprises had little incentive to innovate, due to the lack of international competition and the elimination of domestic competition as a result of entry barriers. In particular, when all resources were allocated according to state plans, all products were sold to and marketed by the state, and all production was carried out according to compulsory plans, enterprises had no incentive to improve their efficiency and improve the quality of their products.

The third shortfall of China's development strategy was the lower incentive to work. With distorted prices and a lack of competition, the profitability of an enterprise was not determined by its performance. If the enterprise were given autonomy, managers and workers would inevitably prey upon its profit and assets. To avoid the erosion of profits and state assets, the state had to deprive enterprises of autonomy. Without autonomy, workers' income level cannot be set in accordance with their performance. Thus, they had little incentive to work hard. Since incentive to work is proportional to the rewards gained from working, to enhance workers' incentive, managers must adopt a system whereby hard work is rewarded. However, under the traditional economic system, a business could neither choose nor fire its workers. Moreover, urban employees were paid a fixed wage, irrespective of their performance. The incentive to work was thus suppressed.[16]

The low incentives in the agricultural sector was somewhat different. Although a production brigade had some power to allocate its surplus, it was usually prohibitively costly to supervise individual performance, since agricultural production was carried out in a large area, and required a long production cycle. As a result, labourers

16. Justin Yifu Lin, Cai Fang, and Li Zhou, *State-owned Enterprise Reform in China*. Hong Kong: Chinese University Press, 2001.

could not be paid according to their work performance. In reality, the production brigades created an identical work-point standard (wage rate) for all members of the same gender and age group. According to this practice, those who worked harder received the same pay as those who shirked their duties, and the under-performance of the latter was borne by the entire group. The result was widespread free riding and a lack of incentive to work.[17]

When we discussed the distortion in the industrial structure created by the traditional economic system, we assumed that there existed no efficiency loss. The economic production was at a point on the production possibility frontier, such as point A in Figure 3.2. But, in fact, the efficiency loss created by the poor incentive mechanism was particularly serious. An international comparison of the efficiency in the use of resources will help to illustrate this point.

Through international comparison on the use of resources and the total factor productivity, we can see that China paid an extremely high price for its economic growth. Tables 3.8, 3.9, and 3.10 show that China's economic development had been highly inefficient. For the production of per unit GDP, the consumption of energy, steel, and transportation in China were, respectively, 63.8–229.5%, 11.9–122.9%, and 85.6–559.6% higher than that of other developing countries. As for the production of per-unit value of its main industrial products, China's situation was quite similar to the above case (except that India had a higher level of steel consumption than China). The differences were even larger when we compare China with developed countries. In the composition of total assets, China's working capital accounted for the largest share, 4.8–25.7 percentage points higher than other economies. This meant that inventory of input and output goods was much larger and kept much longer in China than in other countries. The most telling indicator was the slow

17. Justin Yifu Lin, "The Household Responsibility System in China's Agricultural Reform: A Theoretical and Empirical Study", *Economic Development and Cultural Change*, Vol. 36, No. 3 (April 1988) (Supplement), pp. S199–S224. Also see Justin Yifu Lin, "Supervision, Peer Pressure, and Incentive in a Labor-managed Firm", *China Economic Review*, No. 2 (October 1991), pp. 213–29.

Table 3.8 Material Consumption Rate for Per Unit of GDP: An International Comparison (in 1980 U.S. dollars)

Country	Consumption for per-unit GDP			Consumption for per-unit output of major industrial products		
	Energy (kg standard coal/U.S. dollar)	Steel (ton/ million U.S. dollar)	Quantity transported (ton km/ U.S. dollar)	Energy (kg standard coal/U.S. dollar)	Steel (ton/ million U.S. dollar)	Quantity transported (ton km/ U.S. dollar)
China	2.90	127.3	3.10	1.06	353	6.74
India	1.77	98.4	1.67	0.99	379	6.43
South Korea	1.12	113.8	0.47	0.48	291	1.22
Brazil	0.88	57.1	1.40	0.32	103	4.12
Japan	0.51	63.0	0.41	0.30	146	1.00
France	0.45	30.9	—	0.30	88	—
United States	1.05	44.8	1.80	0.47	132	5.32
Britain	0.57	30.0	—	0.23	91	
Germany	0.49	43.7	—	0.26	95	—

Source: The World Bank 1984 Ecomomic Study Tour, "China: Economic Structure in International Perspective", in *China: Long-term Issues and Options*, Annex 5. Beijing: China Finance and Economic Press, 1987, p. 23.

Table 3.9 Share of Working Capital in Total Assets: An International Comparison (%)

	Year	Working Capital in total assets
China	1981	32.7
India	1979	27.9
South Korea	1963	7.0
Japan	1953	19.9
Britain	1970	12.6
Soviet Union	1972	29.5

Source: The World Bank 1984 Ecomomic Study Tour, "China: Economic Structure in International Perspective", in *China: Long-term Issues and Options*, Annex 5. Beijing: China Finance and Economic Press, 1987, p. 23.

Table 3.10 Growth of Total Factor Productivity: An International Comparison

Country	Period	Annual growth of total factor productivity	Share of total factor productivity growth rate in GNP growth	Country	Period	Annual growth of total factor productivity	Share of total factor productivity growth rate in GNP growth
China*	1952–81	0.53 (–1.0)	8 (–17)	Japan	1952–71	3.8	38
	1952–75	0.3 (–1.1)	5 (–18)		1952–64	5.1	53
	1975–81	1.0 (–0.3)	17 (–5)		1953–71	5.9	58
					1955–71	2.9	25
Brazil	1950–60	3.7	54		1955–70	5.6	55
	1955–70	2.1	34		1966–73	4.5	41
	1966–74	1.6	22				
				United States	1947–60	1.4	38
Korea	1955–60	2.0	47		1960–73	1.3	30
	1955–70	5.0	57				
	1960–73	4.1	42	Soviet Union	1950–60	1.9	32
					1960–70	1.5	29
Average of 19 developing countries		2.0	31		1960–75	1.5	29
					1970–75	0.1	3
Average of 12 market economies		2.7	49	Spain	1959–65	5.0	44

Note: Figures outside the parenthesis are calculated as capital 0.6 and labour 0.4; figures inside the parenthesis are calculated as capital 0.4 and labour 0.6.

Source: The World Bank 1984 Ecomomic Study Tour, "China: Economic Structure in International Perspective", in *China: Long-term Issues and Options*, Annex 5. Beijing: China Finance and Economic Press, 1987, p. 23.

growth of total factor productivity (TFP). Even using the most favourable assumptions, China's TFP, on average, increased by only 0.5% annually from 1952 to 1981. This growth rate in TFP was the smallest figure of all the countries listed in Table 3.10. According to the estimation of the World Bank, between 1957 to 1982 the TFP in China's state-owned sector was in a state of stagnation or even negative growth.[18]

The above analysis of the efficiency loss in the traditional economic system shows that China's economic production was, in fact, in the interior of the production possibility set, say point B in Figure 3.2. This implies that the society had suffered a loss. In light of this efficiency cost, the suppression of economic growth under the traditional economic system must have been much more severe.

3.4 Leap-forward Strategies: An International Comparison

From the 1950s to the late 1970s, although China successfully fed 22% of the world population and established a relatively comprehensive industrial system, it had not achieved its leap-forward objectives. China's economic growth in those years suggests that the heavy-industry-oriented development strategy and the corresponding trinity in the traditional economic system had given rise to two major problems: the distortion in the industrial structure and the ineffective incentive mechanism. In this section, we will examine the economic performance in other developing countries that adopted similar strategies.

The success of the four Little Dragons and the current transition of socialist economies might lead to the conclusion that the economic system is the crucial determining factor for economic performance. However, this is an over-simplification, which has neglected the differences in their development strategy, macro-policy environment,

18. The World Bank 1984 Economic Study Tour, *China: Long-term Issues and Options*. Beijing: China Finance and Economic Press, 1987, p. 145.

resource allocation system and the micro-management system. First, if the success of the four Little Dragons was due to the capitalist system, why did other capitalist developing countries and regions fail to develop as quickly? Second, if socialist economies are doomed to stagnate, why, in the past 22 years, has China's economy become so robust? And third, if socialism causes slow economic growth in socialist countries, why are the former Soviet Union and formerly socialist Eastern European countries still facing so many major difficulties?

All the countries that implemented a leap-forward strategy achieved little economic growth and development. This applies not only to China, the former Soviet Union, and some Eastern European socialist countries, but also to capitalist developing countries that adopted leap-forward strategies or import-substitution strategies. For example, at the end of the 19th century, Argentina, Uruguay, Chile, and Bolivia had a per capita income similar to that of Germany. Now, after a century's development, these countries are still plagued by economic difficulties. Wealth is disproportionately controlled by a small number of elite, and living standards of their people have remained at a low level. The Philippines, which was regarded in 1960s as the rising star in Asia and second only to Japan, is now practically in a state of chaos and stagnation.

In a nutshell, the development strategy chosen by the above countries resulted in the following consequences: First, the economic growth rate was far from satisfactory and the per capita income remained at a relatively low level. From the average annual growth rate of the GDP in 1960–81, we see that the growth rate was 3.5% for India, 5–6% for the Philippines, and 5.4% for Brazil in the first 10 years, and 8.4% in the next 11 years. The growth rate of Argentina's GDP dropped sharply from 4.3% in the first 10 years to 1.9% in the next 11 years. Uruguay's figures were 1.2% and 3.1% in these two periods. These levels of economic growth were not high enough to enable these countries to catch up with, let alone forge ahead of, developed ones. In particular, if we compare these growth rates with those of several other economies that adopted an alternative development strategy, we can see that the growth rates in former countries were much lower.[19] Brazil is an exception. From 1970 to 1981, its economy grew fast due to its highly protective measures and subsidies to stimulate export expansion. However, as export expansion was still fueled by government interventions, the rapid growth rate did not change other important economic and social characteristics of the leap-forward strategy. Griffin points out that Brazil's export expansion during this period was powered by foreign capital and government subsidies, while domestic enterprises contributed little. In fact, after 1981, Brazil's economic growth rate fell sharply. From 1980 to 1991, Brazil's GDP grew by an average annual rate of only 2.5%.[20] From 1960 to 1981, the annual growth rate per capita GNP was 1.4% in India, 2.8% in the Philippines, 5.1% in Brazil, 1.9% in Argentina, and 1.6% in Uruguay. Except for Brazil, all the figures were lower than the average growth rates in their respective income group. The leap-forward strategy was a clear-cut failure.

Second, the chosen strategies led to distorted economic and social structures, which deteriorated income distribution. Because capital-intensive industries were given priority, they comprised a disproportionate share of overall industry. The capacity to absorb employment was therefore limited. For example, from 1963 to 1969, the manufacturing industrial output increased by an average annual rate of 5.9%, 6.1%, and 6.5% in India, the Philippines, and Brazil, respectively. During the same period, the average annual growth rate

19. The World Bank, *World Development Report, 1983*. Beijing: China Finance and Economics Press, 1983, pp. 150–51.

20. During the implementation of the heavy-industry-oriented development strategy, it is easy for a government to stimulate fast economic growth at certain stages, especially in initial development stages. But such a rapid growth rate is achieved by mobilizing resources to the maximum extent. Once domestic resources that can be mobilized are exhausted and foreign capital flow stops, the growth rate slows down abruptly. Therefore, the fast growth from 1970 to 1980 in Brazil was understandable under the heavy-industry-oriented development strategy, and the subsequent slow growth was inevitable. For Brazil's growth rates from 1980 to 1991, see the World Bank, *World Development Report, 1993*. New York: Oxford University Press, 1993, pp. 241, 281.

of employment in the manufacturing industry was only 5.3%, 4.8%, and 1.1%, respectively.[21] This slow growth resulted in high unemployment rates. The existence of a large low-income population means that unequal income distribution did not improve with economic development. Taking Brazil as an example, the richest 5% of the population owned 27.7% of total income in 1960 and 39% in 1976. During the same period, the total income owned by the poorest 50% of the population dropped from 17.7% to 11.8%. That is to say, the per capita income of the richest 5% was 33 times that of the poorest 50%. The Gini coefficient was 0.50 in 1960, which increased to 0.56 in 1970, and 0.60 in 1976.[22]

Third, the traditional economic system led to low efficiency and loss of welfare. When these governments adopted a leap-forward strategy, they exercised highly protective measures. Many industries and enterprises were placed in a monopoly position. As a result, they lacked the incentive to innovate and to improve operations and management, and inefficiency problems followed, for example, from 1955 to 1975, the TFP of Indian manufacturing was negative.[23] In such economies, there was pervasive rent-seeking behaviour. Because the government introduced various kinds of discriminating treatment, such as permit, quotas, low interest loans, price intervention, and so on, once enterprises became the recipients of such preferential treatment of subsidies, they could make an easy profit. Therefore, private entrepreneurs invested a large amount of time, material and money in seeking such institutional rent. Rent-seeking not only corrupted government officials, but discredited the government's reputation as well. According to a study, if the loss in GNP due to resource misallocation brought about by protection was 1% in Brazil in 1967, the loss caused by rent-seeking was estimated

21. Michael P. Todaro, *Economic Development of the Third World*, Part 1. Beijing: China People's University Press, 1988, p. 317.
22. Keith Griffin, *The Alternative Strategies for Economic Development*. Beijing: Economic Science Press, 1992, p. 153.
23. Keith Griffin, *The Alternative Strategies for Economic Development*. Beijing, Economic Science Press, 1992, p. 157.

to be 7–9%.[24] Unfortunately, the leap forward strategy inevitably requires a long-term intensive protection for the manufacturing industries.

Fourth, the traditional economic system led to the deterioration of the fiscal condition and inflation. In the attempt to by-pass a necessary stage of their development, these countries established and developed the capital-intensive industries by way of government subsidies and direct public investment, which placed a heavy burden on public finance and created a large deficit. To fill the gap in capital, governments had to resort to foreign debt. For example, in the late 1970s and the early 1980s, countries such as Brazil and Mexico, in order to pursue high growth rates and expand investments, borrowed heavily from abroad and finally found themselves mired in a debt crisis. Growth rates dropped abruptly, and their economies suffered a period of negative growth. People's living standards fell to the level seen 10 years before. Inflation was also a common disease in many countries that implemented the leap-forward strategy. To support the economic growth, a series of macroeconomic policies were adopted to encourage investment and to expand infrastructure construction. Because the industrial structure was unbalanced, fast growth gave rises to one bottleneck after another. The insufficient supply of products and production factors propelled price hikes, leading to serious inflation. For example, the average annual inflation rate in Brazil was 46.1% in the 1960s and 42.1% in the 1970s; in Argentina, it was 21.4% in the 1960s and 134.2% in the 1970s.[25]

The above analyses indicate that the reason for the failure of these economies to catch up with developed countries, lies in their adoption of the leap-forward strategy and the establishment of corresponding macro-policy environment and the management system characterized by government interventions.

---

24. Keith Griffin, *The Alternative Strategies for Economics Development*. Beijing, Economic Science Press, 1992, p. 153.
25. The World Bank, *World Development Report, 1983*. Beijing: China Finance and Economics Press, 1983, pp. 148–49.

Table 3.11 Structure of Output Value in China and India (%)

	China (1952)	India (1950–51)
Total	100	100
Primary industry	58	60
Secondary industry	23	14
Tertiary industry	19	26

Note: China's output value structure is calculated from national income.
Source: National Bureau of Statistics of China, *China Statistical Yearbook, 1993*. Beijing: China Statistics Press, 1993, p. 33; Sun Peijun, ed., *A Comparative Study on China's and India's Economic Development*. Beijing: Peking University Press, 1991, p. 57.

A detailed comparison between China and India will prove to be illuminating. Why India? First, China and India are large neighbouring countries in Asia, with the two largest populations in the world. Second, both are developing countries, and both became political independent at around the same time. They also adopted similar economic development strategies.[26] Third, the comparative advantages of both countries are in labour resources. As for agriculture, precipitation in both countries varies from season to season and from region to region. And fourth, they were at a similar stance when they began their economic development. In the early 1950s, the two countries had very similar economic structures. In 1952, agriculture accounted for 57.7% of China's national income, and the rural population accounted for 87.5% of the national total; in

26. Jawaharlal Nihru advocated that India gives priority to heavy industry. He stressed that "development of heavy industry is equal to industrialization", and that "the most important sector for the realization of industrialization is the heavy industry that makes machines." P.C. Mahalanubis, followed the strategy and explained in India's Second-Five-Year-Plan outline, which stated that "industrialization speed and national economic growth depend upon the universal development of coal, electricity, iron and steel, heavy machinery, heavy chemical production.... Therefore we should spare no efforts to develop heavy industry." (Quoted from Sun Peijun, ed., *A Comparative Study on China's and India's Economic Development*. Beijing: Peking University Press, 1991, pp. 51–55.)

1950 to 1951, the two indicators for India were 59% and 82.7%, respectively. Generally speaking, China had a larger manufacturing industry and India a larger tertiary industry. However, the differences were not significant.

From the 1950s to 1970s, the greatest difference between China and India lay in their management institution at the micro level of agricultural development. China implemented the highly centralized People's Commune System, whereas by the early 1980s India had just over 9,000 farming communes with 250,000 commune members on 375,000 hectares of farmland (i.e., a mere 0.34% of the total farmlands). However, as both countries implemented a strategy that gave priority to the development of heavy industry, both faced a distorted macro-policy environment. This led to similar agricultural growth rates. From the 1950s to 1980s, grain production in China increased by an average annual rate of 3.00%, and that in India increased by an average annual rate of 3.08%. Table 3.12 shows that the growth of Chinese and Indian agricultural output value was rather similar, if we ignore the fast growth of China after it adopted the reform programme. Table 3.13 shows that, after 30 years, the employment structure of both countries remained identical. This may be one of the reasons that the per capita GNP in both countries remained at a level of just US$100 to US$300.

The leap-forward strategy failed not only in China and other socialist countries but also in India and other developing capitalist countries. This fact suggests that the fundamental reason of China's failure to achieve economic success was its development strategy.

Table 3.12 Growth Index of Agricultural Output Value in China and India (100 for 1950–51)

Years	China	India
1965–66	172.9	138.1
1980–81	326.7	231.1
1985–86	569.5	270.1

Source: Sun Peijun, ed., *A Comparative Study on China's and India's Economic Development*. Beijing: Peking University Press, 1991, p. 131.

Table 3.13 Employment Structure of China and India in 1980 (%)

Industry	China	India
Total	100	100
Primary industry	74	70
Secondary industry	14	13
Tertiary industry	12	17

Source: The World Bank, *World Development Report, 1988*. Beijing: China Finance and Economics Press, 1988, p. 282.

It must be made clear that the leap-forward strategy and philosophy are different from the aspirations of developing countries to catch up with advanced countries. The former refers to the economic school of thought and a policy orientation that distorts the macro-policy environment and institutions, uses administrative intervention, and practices preferential treatment and protection in industry.

The leap-forward school of thought, as an economic belief and policy approach, emerged in the 16th century. The main idea was mercantilism, popular among various European countries, when Adam Smith published *Wealth of Nations* in 1776. After Columbus sailed to the American continent and the circum-navigator Ferdinand Magellan discovered the sea route to the Indian Ocean, European countries vied with each other to see which could expand most rapidly. National economic and military strengths were prerequisites for such expansion. Developing national economies and accumulating national wealth became the major government target in Europe. An early summary of mercantilism notes that all the mercantile measures implemented in the 16th and 17th centuries were "a product of political efforts to direct economic strengths to build a strong and independent country. The goal of mercantilism was to establish an industrial and commercial country in which, through encouragement and constraint of the authorities, private and department interests be subordinated to the efforts to enhance national strength and state independence."[27] This summary reveals the essence of mercantilism in two ways: First, the purpose of mercantilism was to help a country to accumulate wealth and enhance national strength; and second, the mercantilist policy achieved its goals not by the individual's economic interests, but by the authority of the country.

Another theoretical source comes from the German historian school of economics in 1840s. At the time, Germany's economic development level lagged behind that of Britain, France, and other advanced countries. "A natural effort for a country pursuing independence and strengths"[28] was reflected in the emergence of an economic leap-forward theory and the corresponding policy suggested by the historian school. Typically, they denied that there exists a general law of economic development for all countries and held that all countries should implement unique development policies. In view of German industries' backwardness, they opposed free trade advocated by classical economics and promoted protection for Germany's "new and infant industries". Furthermore, they held that even after certain economic development had been achieved, absolute free trade should not be adopted, or countries specializing in exporting primitive products would be at a disadvantage and would became subordinated to others. Naturally, German historian school economists actively advocated the notion that the state should play an important role in its economic life and should promote industrial development by state power.

Development economics emerged after World War II and was popular from the 1950s to the 1970s. With a large number of newly independent countries and the many political leaders eager to catch up economically with advanced countries, the question of how to accomplish this task became a hot issue. At the time, it was of interest not only to developing nations but also to developed countries and

27. R. H. Palgrave, ed., *Dictionary of Political Economy*, Vol. 2. New York: Macmillan, 1896, p. 727.
28. Georg Friedrich List, *The National System of Political Economics*. Beijing: Commercial Press, 1961.

international organizations. Development economists trained at the time inevitably carried with them the inherited leap-forward philosophy. One reason was that these economists had witnessed the sharp contrast between the worldwide crisis in the capitalist economies and the speedy growth of the Soviet economy in the late 1920s and early 1930s. They concluded that planning and state intervention were necessary. A second reason was that Keynesian economics was prevalent at the time. Predictably, the development economics as a new sub-discipline had adopted this popular thinking. A third reason was that some of the earliest development economists reached incorrect conclusions based on short-term observations. For example, theories about the deterioration in the terms of trade and about unequal exchanges between core countries and peripheral countries all suggested that the adoption of import-substitution policies and industrialization process were a necessary stage in economic development.[29]

The fashion among postwar development economics was thus to exaggerate market failures and to propose government intervention. As a consequence, mercantilism's doctrine of state intervention and the German historian school of economics were widely transformed into economic development strategy and government policy. The characteristics of the policies under the leap-forward strategy are summed up below.

First, no matter for what purpose, leap-forward strategies tried to depress trade. Mercantilism did not take into account the theory of comparative advantage. It held mistakenly that selling more and buying less could enrich total national wealth. It advocated exports and curtailed imports. The German historian school advocated protectionism and argued against trade liberalization to protect infant national industry. Theories about "dependency" and "core" versus

---

29. See, for example, John Eatwell, Murray Milgate and Peter Newman, eds., *The New Palgrave: A Dictionary of Economics*, Vol. 3. Beijing: Economic Science Press, 1992, pp. 999–1001; Charles Wilber, *The Political Economy of Development and Underdevelopment*. Beijing: China Social Science Press, 1984.

"peripheral" countries, which developed after World War II, based their arguments on the idea of the political economy of development and under-development. Advocates of these theories assumed that the terms of trade for primary products were deteriorating and that unequal exchanges were being conducted. They held that developing nations should detach themselves from developed countries in economic and trade relations.

Second, it was advocated that the prices of products and production factors should be distorted to suppress trade. The core tenet was to protect nonviable domestic sectors from international competition. When the comparative advantage of domestic factor endowments could not be brought into play, governments had to provide subsidies and maintain the salaries at low levels, depress finance, appreciate domestic currency, and distort prices to lower the cost for the development of these sectors.

Third, to provide preferential terms selectively, governments need to institute a regulation system to grant privileges and monopoly to the priority sectors. Such policies not only led to great losses in the efficiency of resource allocation but also lowered technical efficiency due to the lack of incentives. In addition, such policies led to bribery, rent-seeking, tax evasion, and illegal, underground economic activities.[30]

It is clear that the leap-forward mindset is deeply rooted in some countries, especially among intellectual circles in certain developing nations. The long history of this mindset may help explain the situation. In addition, although classical and neoclassical economics have long served as foils to the leap-forward strategy, and have in fact prevailed over it, they have not produced a comprehensive development strategy to counter it.

The leap-forward strategy is a comparative advantage-defying strategy. In the next chapter, we describe a new economic development strategy — the comparative-advantage-following strategy. On

30. Deepak Lal, *Political Economy and Public Policy* (Occasional Paper No. 9). San Francisco: International Center for Economic Growth, 1990.

the basis of previous economic works, we compare China's situation before and after economic reform. We also compare the development experiences of the four Little Dragons with that of China and of those Latin American economies that also adopted a leap-forward strategy. We present two elements not covered so far in the literature: a clear definition of this strategy and an analysis of the economic development of the four Little Dragons.

CHAPTER 4

The Comparative-advantage-following Strategy

To catch up with and even surpass the economic development level of advanced countries is the aspiration of the political and social elite of almost all backward economies. However, most economies that attempted to do so through the adoption of the leap-forward strategy ignored their own development stages and their comparative advantages in factor endowment. Consequently, instead of achieving their goals, they were overwhelmed by various difficulties. The problems they encountered included increasing poverty in rural and urban areas, persistent high inflation rate, and unbalanced economic structure. If the leap-forward strategy were the only choice, and if there were no instances of a backward economy catching up with a developed one by implementing another strategy, we could not conclude that the leap-forward strategy is an ineffective one. Under those conditions, we could only say that implementing the leap-forward strategy, and suffering the ensuing consequences, was inevitable.

However, some developing countries and regions that did not adopt the leap-forward strategy experienced rapid economic growth. Japan was the first, followed by South Korea, Singapore, Taiwan, and Hong Kong. Although these economies started from the same stance as other developing countries, their performance over the past several decades has been unique. They have become models for high and sustainable economic growth; their achievement have become known as the "East Asian Miracle".[1] What are the differences between the development

1. The World Bank, *The East Asian Miracle: Economic Growth and Public Policy*. New York: Oxford University Press, 1993.

strategies in these economies and the leap-forward strategy? What new knowledge can the performance of these countries contribute to the economic development theory? In this chapter we try to answer these questions.

4.1 Different Interpretations of the East Asian Miracle

Like most other developing economies, after World War II, Japan and the four Little Dragons were at a low level of economic development. In the 1950s, the Little Dragons' industrialization level was very low, and they had almost no capital or foreign reserve. Their per capita GNP was only about US$100. However, over the next 20 to 30 years, these economies experienced fast and sustained growth. They gradually developed their capital- and technology-intensive industries and emerged as newly industrialized economies, ranking among or near advanced economies in terms of per capita income and industrial structure.

It is useful to examine the four Little Dragons' pace of development during their period of economic takeoff[2] and their growth rates in the following decade. From 1965 to 1973, South Korea, Singapore, and Hong Kong recorded an average annual GDP growth of 10.0%, 13.0%, and 7.9%, respectively. During this period, Taiwan's GNP rose by 11.0% per year, but the average annual growth rate was only 5.6% for low-income countries, 6.8% for lower-middle income countries or regions, 7.7% for upper-middle income countries, 9.0% for high-income oil-exporting countries, and 4.7%

2. Basing his calculations on the economic take-off precondition that the average saving rate is higher than the product of capital output ratio and the population growth rate, Jiang Shuojie estimates that the four Little Dragons' economies all took off in the mid-1960s. See "Economic Take-off of the Four Little Asian Dragons", *Taiwan China Times*, 29 March 1984. Using the "turning point" analysis method of John Fei and Gustav Ranis, we can also estimate the economic growth acceleration or the so-called take-off period (John Fei and Gustav Ranis, *Development of the Labor Surplus Economy: Theory and Policy*. Homewood, III: Richard D. Irwin. Inc, 1964).

for industrialized market economies. In the following 11 years (i.e., from 1973 to 1984) South Korea, Singapore, and Hong Kong recorded an average annual GDP growth rate of 7.2%, 8.2%, and 9.1%, respectively, and Taiwan had a GNP growth rate of 7.8%. During the same period, the average annual growth rate was 5.3% for low-income countries, 4.2% for lower-middle-income countries or regions, 4.5% for upper-middle-income countries or regions, 4.5% for high-income oil-exporting countries, and 2.4% for industrialized market economies.[3] It is worth noting that during the period of rapid development in these countries, the income distribution was relatively equal. At the same time, their economic structures and indices for social welfare improved significantly.

How did Japan and the four Little Dragons achieve such rapid economic development? Scholars have offered a number of different explanations. Some have presented explanations that go beyond economic factors. One such theory explains the phenomenon in a cultural perspective. For example, it holds that Japan and the four Little Dragons are deeply influenced by Confucianism. Since Confucianism stresses hard work and thrift, it has contributed to economic success in these countries.[4] If this were the case, why is it that these countries and regions, which have been under the influence of Confucianism for thousands of years, had not led the world in modernization and economic development since the 16th or 17th century? Moreover, why have some countries influenced by Confucianism not achieved any economic success to date? At the same time, why have many countries with no connection to Confucianism achieved economic modernization long ago?[5]

---

3. The World Bank, *World Development Report, 1986*. Beijing: China Finance and Economics Press, 1986, p.183; Fu Zhengluo, et al., *The Four Little Asian Dragons and the Export-oriented Economy*. Beijing: China Foreign Trade Press, 1990, pp. 34–35.
4. An example is: Jin Yaoji, "An Explanation of the East Asian Economic Development from a Cultural Perspective", *Information Newspaper Finance and Economy Monthly*, No. 11 (1987).
5. China is the country most deeply influenced by Confucian culture. But the fact that China has had a backward economy since 1840 shows that China's economic development was not benefited by such a cultural tradition. In fact,

Some scholars offer a different explanation from the geo-political perspective. They hold that during the Cold War, the United States and other Western countries invested heavily in and provided financial assistance to Japan and the four Little Dragons to offset the influence of socialist nations. During this period, the United States was willing to transfer knowledge and skills and open its market to Japan and the four Little Dragons.[6] However, the West patronized many economies during the Cold War, not just the Little Dragons. If the geo-political scholars' explanation were correct, it should follow that the Philippines and a good number of Latin American countries would be economically successful by now. On the contrary, these countries are clear-cut failures in terms of their economic development. It is therefore safe to conclude that political factors resulting from the Cold War were at most auxiliary contributors to Japan's and the Little Dragons' economic success.

Explaining these countries' success from an economics perspective has attracted the attention of many economists. We can organize their viewpoints into three categories. The first is represented by the World Bank economists.[7] They hold that the economic success in these countries can be directly attributed to their free market economy, smaller price distortions, and the proper and efficient allocation of resources. However, this explanation focuses on the

---

some cultural extremists, ashamed of China's backwardness and history of being bullied, have demanded that Confucianism be eradicated. So it is clear that Confucian culture can neither explain the Joseph Needham Puzzle nor answer the question of how the East Asian miracle occurred, just as this interpretation is invalid in the case in which Max Weber explained the well-known "Weber's Conjecture" in his work *The Protestant Ethic and the Spirit of Capitalism* (London: Harper, 1991).

6. For example, S. Haggard, "The Politics of Industrialization in the Republic of Korea and Taiwan", in H. Hughes, ed., *Achieving Industrialization in Asia,* Cambridge: Cambridge University Press, 1988, p. 265; J. E. Woo, *Race to the Swift: State and Finance in Korean Industrialization.* New York: Columbia University Press, 1991, p. 45.
7. The World Bank, *The East Asian Miracle: Economic Growth and Public Policy.* New York: Oxford University Press, 1993; William E. James, Seiji Naya, and Gerald M. Meier, *Asian Development: Economic Success and Policy Lessons.* San Francisco: ICS Press, 1987.

ideal while ignoring deviations from it. Serious observers will notice that government interventions as well as barriers to competition and even price distortions and trade protectionism exist in these economies. For example, authorities in Taiwan, South Korea, and Japan have all adopted import quotas and licenses, credit subsidies, tax concessions, and state ownership to cultivate and protect their infant industries.

Alice Amsden of the Massachusetts Institute of Technology and Robert Wade of the London School of Economics and Politics represent a different perspective. Both hold that the success of Japan and the four Little Dragons should be attributed to their governments' interventions that deliberately distorted prices, limited the role of the market, and implemented policies that support strategic industries.[8] It is true that such interventions do exist in these countries. However, although some countries with government interventions and price distortions have succeeded, many more have failed. As we have already shown, the economic failure of countries that adopted the leap-forward strategy shows that this explanation is not convincing.

Another hypothesis attributes the success of Japan and the four Little Dragons to their export-oriented development policy. With such a policy in place, a country or region must be internationally competitive and thus efficient.[9] According to this view, international trade is crucial to successful economic development. However, it is questionable whether the outward economy is the consequence or the cause of economic development.[10] If it is the cause, a country should

8. Alice H. Amsden, *Asian's Next Giant: South Korea and Late Industrialization*. Oxford: Oxford University Press, 1989; C. Johnson, *MITI and the Japanese Miracle*. Stanford: Stanford University Press, 1982; Robert Wade, *Governing the Market: Economic Theory and the Role of Government in East Asian Industrialization*. Princeton: Princeton University Press, 1990.
9. Anne O. Kruger, *Economic Policy Reform in Developing Countries*. Oxford: Basil Blackwell, 1992.
10. Francisco Rodriguez, and D. Rodrik, "Trade Policy and Economic Growth: A Skeptic's Guide to the Cross-national Evidence", in B. Bernanke and K. Rogoff, *NBER Macroeconomics Annual 2000*. Cambridge, MA: MIT Press, 2000.

implement a development policy that encourages export at any cost, so as to raise the proportion of foreign trade in the economy. In fact, many countries that adopted a leap-forward strategy viewed an export-stimulating policy as necessary at a certain stage of development. However, because they had distorted prices and foreign exchange rates and used direct subsidies to encourage export, the resources were misallocated and their economies ran into serious problems. Recent economic research also finds no significant connection between the proportion of exports and the increase in an economy's total factor productivity.[11]

4.2 An Alternative Development Strategy

Any effective theory must be on the one hand logically coherent and on the other able to withstand empirical tests. The explanations presented above undoubtedly touch on some aspects of the success in Japan and the four Little Dragons, but they fail to reveal its essence. In addition, they are contradictory in nature, and their strengths are offset in the contradiction. Therefore, we offer here a theory that attempts to encompass all the aforementioned explanations.

The experiences of Japan and the four Little Dragons indicate that economic development is a gradual process. One distinct difference between their process and that of the leap-forward strategy is that, during every stage of economic development, the former make good use of their comparative advantages, determined by their factor endowments. Table 4.1 shows that at different development stages, because of different endowment structures, their key industries changed. In all of them, however, it held true that with economic development, capital accumulation and per capita capital availability increased, and the endowment structure improved. The leading industries then shifted from labour-intensive to capital-intensive

11. Robert Z. Lawrence and David E. Weinstein, "Trade and Growth: Import-led or Export-led? Evidence from Japan and Korea", in Joseph E. Stiglitz and Shahid Yusuf, eds., *Rethinking the East Asia Miracle*. Oxford: Oxford University Press, 2001; D. Rodrik, *The New Global Economy and Developing Countries: Making Openness Work*. Washington, DC: Overseas Development Council, 1999.

and technology-intensive, and finally became more information-intensive.

Neither Japan nor any of the four Little Dragons have ever articulated a development strategy. However, with the exception of Hong Kong, all these economies attempted to implement an import-substitution strategy or emphasized heavy and chemical industries during the early periods of their development. If they had continued along that path, the East Asian Miracle may never have occurred. However, these economies were different from other developing countries and regions. Early on, the former became aware of the heavy costs incurred by the leap-forward strategy, and abandoned it accordingly. They developed labour-intensive industries based on their comparative advantages in factor endowment which fully explored their comparative advantage and resulted in the increasing export and outwardness of the economy. Since the key industries, at every stage of their economic development, were consistent with their comparative advantages at the time, we call this "comparative-advantage-following strategy".

Why were Japan and the Little Dragons able to give up the leap-forward strategy early on? Economists have come up with various answers to this question. Compared with other economies that retained the leap-forward strategy, the per capita natural resources of Japan and the Little Dragons were very limited and their populations relatively small. The leap-forward strategy is highly inefficient and costly. Two factors determine how long an economy can sustain a leap-forward strategy: the amount of per capita natural resources and the population size. The extent to which natural resources can be exploited at little costs determines how long an economy can sustain an inefficient development strategy. The population size determines the average amount of costs that need to be shared per person. A relatively small population cannot sustain the waste of resources for long.

The leap-forward strategy in the early period of their development brought Japan and the four Little Dragons face to face with an increasing fiscal deficit, an imbalance in foreign trade, and high inflation. Because of these, the governments were forced to give up

Table 4.1 Key Industries in Different Development Stages of Japan and the Four Little Dragons

	Japan	South Korea	Taiwan	Hong Kong	Singapore
Textile	1900–30s, 1950s		1960s and 1970s	Early 1950s	Early 1960s and 1970s
Garment	1950s		1960s	1950s and 1960s	
Toy, watch, shoe			1960s and 1970s	1960s and 1970s	
Refinery		Early 1960s (promoted)			
Iron and steel	1950s and 1960s	Late 1960s and early 1970s (promoted)			
Chemicals	1960s and 1970s	late 1960s and 1970s			
Ship building	1960s and 1970s	1970s			
Electronics	1970s	Late 1970s and 1980s	1980s		1970s
Automobile	1970s and 1980s	1980s			
Computer and semi-conductor	1980s	Late 1980s			
Bank and financing				Late 1970s and 1980s	1980s

Data source: Takatoshi Ito, "Japanese Economic Development: Are Its Features Idiosyncratic or Universal?" Paper presented at the XIth Congress of the International Economic Association at Tunis, 17–22 December 1995.

the intervention policy, and enterprises were allowed to develop spontaneously. Enterprises, to achieve maximum profits, chose the technology and industries that were consistent with the comparative advantages of their economies. These economies did not deliberately select the comparative-advantage-following strategy as a policy guideline; rather, it developed on its own after the leap-forward strategy had failed. Other economies that still adhere to the leap-forward strategy will surely benefit from this experience.

The early Mercantilism School, the German historian school of economies, the Hoffman Law School, the advocators of development strategy after the World War II, and practitioners of the leap-forward strategy[12] — all viewed differences in industrial structure and technological structure as the fundamental difference between advanced and backward economies. Upgrading the industrial and technological structures of an economy was viewed as equivalent to economic development.[13] Therefore, in the eyes of those who believed in the Big Push Theory or the Core-Periphery Theory, in the heavy-industry-oriented strategy or the import-substitution strategy, such upgrades were seen as equating economic development and as being the key to overtaking advanced economies. To upgrade their industrial and technological structures, these countries or regions mobilized their limited resources to support the development of one or two capital-intensive industries.

The problem is that the upgrade of industrial and technological

---

12. In the 1980s, the World Bank invited those economists and critics that had been famous for their economic development theories and policy suggestions to review the implementation result of their theories. The review was published under the title: G. M. Meier and D. Seers, *Pioneers of the Development Economics* (Beijing: Economic Science Press, 1988).
13. The followings are the typical remarks: "The inevitable prerequisite of development is industrialization" by E. A. Preobrazhensky, quoted in John Eatwell, Murray Milgate and Peter Newman, eds., *The New Palgrave: A Dictionary of Economics*, Vol. 3. Beijing: Economic Science Press, 1992, p. 1001; and "The development of heavy industry is the synonym of industrialization" by Jawaharlal Nehru, quoted in Sun Peijun, ed., *The Comparative Research on the China's and India's Economic Development*. Beijing: Beijing University Press, 1991, p. 51.

structures is an endogenous variable in the economic development process. In other words, it is only the outcome of development or the result of change in an economy's factor endowment structure. The factor endowment structure refers to an economy's relative abundance in natural resources, labour, and capital. Natural resource endowment is usually fixed, and the increase in the labour endowment is determined by population growth, with small differences (usually 1–3%) from country to country. The only factor endowment that can vary greatly is capital. Some countries on the average enjoy an annual growth rate of 20–30% in capital accumulation, while others see an average of 10% or even less. If these differences remain for a long period, say for a century, the impact will be enormous. Hence, when we speak of upgrading the factor endowment structure we are referring to the increase of relative capital abundance.

Severe lack of capital characterizes an economy's early stage of development. When the development of heavy industries was promoted by price distortion and other administrative measures, limited capital could be channeled to a few industries. At the same time, however the development of other industries had to be suppressed. Several problems arise as a result.

First, the development of a few industries at the cost of overall economic performance cannot help to upgrade the factor endowment structure or improve the overall economy. Protected industries, which are not viable in a competitive market, produce little economic surplus, while suppressed industries lack sufficient capital to develop and thus cannot produce the necessary surplus for capital accumulation. Under such circumstances, the factor endowment structure cannot be upgraded. The former Soviet Union, for example, mobilized resources through mandatory planned measures to develop its military industry and space industry so that it could compete with those in the United States. Soviet industrial output value was also high compared with that of advanced economies. However, the former Soviet Union's per capita GNP, which indicates a country's overall strength and factor endowment structure, lagged behind the per capita GNPs of the United States and other advanced capitalist countries. More importantly, the former Soviet Union also lagged far behind in industries for consumer goods. Living standards have remained at a low level for a long period.

Second, industries supported by the leap-forward strategy could survive only when prices were distorted and the state policy remained protective. They could grow only in a noncompetitive environment and could show positive changes in industrial structure only from a statistical perspective. They were doomed to be inefficient and noncompetitive. The difficulties currently faced by China's SOEs, especially those in capital-intensive industries, illustrate this point.

Third, under the leap-forward strategy, the distorted industrial structure ran against China's comparative advantage of abundant labour resources. This distorted industrial structure suppressed the absorption of the labour force; thus most people could not enjoy the benefits of economic development on an equal basis. Consequently, a large number of people remained in poverty.

Fourth, the leap-forward strategy often focuses on the gap in frontier technologies between developing and advanced economies, aiming at reaching advanced countries' technological level. However, as the factor endowment structure cannot be changed, a high concentration of capital in some industries can lead only to less capital in others, so the overall gap between developing and advanced economies in the areas of capital and technology cannot be narrowed under such a strategy.

To sum up, true economic development does not mean isolated growth in certain heavy industries but rather the increase of the overall strength of a state. A backward economy should focus on upgrading its factor endowment structure or on increasing per capita availability of capital. Industrial structural transformation, improvement in technology, and the increase of per capita income are the spontaneous outcomes of the economic development process.

Because Japan and the four Little Dragons were restrained by their per capita natural resources and population sizes, they were not able to sustain the development of a few industries at the heavy cost of most other industries. Therefore, they gave up the leap-forward strategy very early. Their enterprises then developed labour-intensive industries based on their comparative advantage of abundant labour endowment. This in turn enhanced the factor endowment structure. Greater per capita availability of capital sped up the improvement of the industrial and technological structure, thus placing Japan and the four Little Dragons among the advanced economies. The principle of comparative advantage is suitable not only for economies with abundant labour but also for those rich in natural resources.

It is very instructive to compare Australia and New Zealand with Argentina and Uruguay. In the late 19th and early 20th centuries, these countries shared the same level of economic development. In Australia and New Zealand, which took advantage of their comparative advantages in rich natural resources, manufacturing accounted for only 15% and 18% of the GNP, respectively, in 1991 — which were much lower than those of the other developed countries. Nevertheless, the countries' high per capita GNPs, US$17,050 and US$12,350 respectively, ranked them among developed countries. On the contrary, Argentina and Uruguay, which followed the leap-forward strategy, enthusiastically developed their manufacturing industries (35% and 25% in proportion to their respective economies). Their per capita GNP, however, stood at only US$2,790 and US$2,840, respectively, in 1991.[14]

The experiences of Japan and the four Little Dragons show that the comparative-advantage-following strategy is the key to economic success for developing economies. Understanding how this strategy works can help us understand these countries' experiences and thus understand the reason for the failure of the leap-forward strategy.

14. Argentina's manufacturing's proportion is a 1984 figure. All other figures are 1991 figures. (The World Bank, *World Development Report, 1993*. New York: Oxford University Press, 1993, p. 243; The World Bank, *World Development Report, 1989*. New York: Oxford University Press, 1989, p. 209.)

4.3 Comparative Advantage and Upgrading the Factor-endowment Structure

Economic development requires a change in the factor endowment structure (i.e., an increase in the relative abundance of capital in the factor endowment). Capital comes from accumulation, and the accumulation of capital is determined by the scale of economic surplus, which in turn depends on the performance and the characteristics of production activity. If the industrial and technological structures of an economy can make full use of its comparative advantage in existing factor endowment, the economy will enjoy low production costs and become highly competitive. It will also accumulate more capital. There are two types of production activities: social production activity and private production activity. Social production activity can increase the total products or services available in society, while private production activity can increase personal incomes but not necessarily the products and services of the society. One of the main reasons for the inconsistency is rent-seeking. For example, if the government sets a production quota on a product, the domestic manufacturers will gain higher profits from this product. Manufacturers will thus take various measures to persuade government officials to set up and implement such production control. These types of activities consume social resources to effect personal gains without adding to social output. They are beneficial to individuals but detrimental to society. If each individual's private production activity is equivalent to his or her social production activity, there will be more social output and more accumulated surplus. In this section we try to show that if an economy can tap the full potential of its comparative advantage, private and social production activity will be in agreement.

In addition, the accumulation level is determined by saving propensity. The higher the saving propensity, the greater the increase of capital, and the faster the factor endowment structure is upgraded. If a developing economy can make full use of its comparative advantage, the marginal return to capital will be high and the saving propensity will be high as well. The traditional economic growth theories also emphasized the importance of capital accumulation, even to the extent that the savings rate and the investment rate are the key determinants of economic development.[15] An important issue that the traditional economic growth theory failed to address is that of how to increase total social surplus, make all activities productive and competitive from a social viewpoint, and raise savings rate.

Theoretically, how can a country fully exploit its comparative advantage? According to the Heckhel-Ohlin Model,[16] if a country enjoys abundant labour resources, then its comparative advantage lies in labour-intensive industries. Taking this advantage into account, it will make an effort to develop light industries, or labour-intensive industries. Since the production process in such industries requires cheap labour, such industries will become competitive and profitable, and the amount of surplus that can be used for accumulation will be large.

To induce correct responses to the economy's comparative advantage in production, it is necessary to have a factor-price structure that can fully reflect the relative abundance of each factor in the endowment structure. That is, when labour is relatively abundant, labour should be relatively inexpensive; whereas if capital is relatively abundant, capital should be relatively inexpensive. If the factor price structure of an economy can fully reflect the relative scarcity of all the factors, enterprises will automatically adjust so that they can use as many cheap productive factors as possible. Relative scarcity is accurately reflected as a result of market competition, not of government intervention or of a planned mechanism. It is thus reasonable that World Bank economists attributed the economic success of the four Little Dragons to the role of the market.

---

15. See Roy F. Harrold, "An Essay in Dynamic Theory", *Economic Journal,* Vol. 49, No. 193 (March 1939), pp. 14–33; Evsey Domar, "Capital Expansion, Rate of Growth, and Employment", *Econometrica,* Vol. 14, No. 2 (April 1946), pp. 137–47. Robert M. Solow, *Growth Theory: An Exposition*. Oxford: Oxford University Press, 1988.
16. Bertil Ohlin, *Interregional and International Trade*. Cambridge, MA: Harvard University Press, 1968.

Japan and the four Little Dragons are market economies, and, as previously mentioned, their governments abandoned the leap-forward strategy at an early stage. The prices of products and factors in these countries are basically determined by market supply and demand and thus reflect the relative scarcity of various factors. In its product and technology choice, an enterprise will thus take into consideration the economy's comparative advantages at each development stage. In addition, the prices, determined by market competition instead of government, can reduce rent-seeking in the society. Therefore, enterprises and individuals can increase their revenues and incomes only through the improvement of technology and management. Hence, private productive activity is in line with social productive activity. Meanwhile, in developing countries, capital is a scarce factor. The price of capital, or the interest rate, will be high if it is determined by market competition. At the same time, the interest rate is the relative price of current consumption and future consumption. A higher interest rate means a relatively high price for current consumption and a lower price for future consumption, so naturally current consumption will be curbed, and saving propensity will be enhanced.

A competitive market system requires a flexible and effective financial market. In the early stages of development, capital is the scarcest factor, so market interest rate should be relatively high. This encourages saving and conserves the use of capital. Only efficient and profitable enterprises (i.e., those that make the best use of the comparative advantage) can afford to pay such a high price of capital. Therefore, in an economy in which labour is plentiful and capital is scarce, a flexible and effective capital market can guarantee that capital is allocated to labour-intensive enterprises and industries so as to exploit the comparative advantages to the greatest extent.

A competitive market system also requires a competitive labour market. As labour is a relatively abundant production factor in the early stage of development, compared with interest rate, the wage rates for labour should be relatively low. So that enterprises choose to use cheap labour instead of expensive capital, which also helps realize maximum employment of the large workforce.

Finally, a competitive market system requires a competitive and well-developed product market. Dwight Perkins has identified five conditions for the market mechanism to function well:[17] (1) prices are stable, so manufacturers depend on production and sales for profits instead of on speculation; (2) products are distributed through market channels and not by government agencies; (3) prices should reflect relative scarcity in the economy; (4) competition exists, and manufacturers are price takers; and (5) production decision-makers act according to market rules, they make profits by reducing costs and increasing sales, and not by subsidy or monopoly. The major reason that the comparative-advantage-following strategy can speed up economic development also depends on the above aspects of the market mechanism.

Because prices for products and production factors are determined by competition, they can reflect supply, demand, and relative scarcity. Enterprises, based on such prices, can understand the demand and supply situation and the relative scarcity of products and factors, take corresponding measures, and choose product mix and technology based on market demand and resource endowment. From the viewpoint of the whole society, the result of such product and technology choice leads to the industrial and technology structures that are in line with the specific factor endowment.

In a free competitive economy where prices for products and factors are not distorted, an enterprise has to look for cheaper input, new markets, to improve operation and management, and to apply proper technology and other methods to bring about technological innovations in its pursuit of survival and development. Therefore, the enterprise must pay close attention to market conditions, to take advantage of appropriate technologies in production. At the same time, it must do research and forecast future market trends and

17. Dwight H. Perkins, "China's Gradual Approach to Market Reform". Paper presented at the "Conference on Comparative Experience of Economics Reform and Post-Socialist Transformation", EL Escorial, Spain, 6–8 July 1992.

predict where the economy's future comparative advantage lies. Making use of the existing comparative advantages can speed up economic development. Capital can accumulate much faster than the increase of labour and natural resources. Therefore, capital becomes relatively abundant, and its price becomes relatively low. In addition, to be competitive, enterprises must adjust their industrial and technological structures based on the changes of relative prices; thus dynamic comparative advantages can be achieved.

For an economy with relatively abundant labour endowment, implementing a comparative-advantage-following strategy enables it not only to achieve efficient growth through the utilization of static and dynamic comparative advantages but also to realize full employment. With economic growth, labour becomes relatively scarce, and wages increase steadily. The work force can continue to benefit from economic growth. As long as the leap-forward strategy is in place, priority is given to capital-intensive industries, the employment level falls, and wages remain suppressed for long periods. The work force cannot share the benefits of growth. Therefore, the comparative-advantage-following strategy is preferable to the leap-forward strategy because the former enables an economy to achieve equity and efficiency at the same time.

In a fully competitive market system, a manufacturer's profits or losses are determined solely by whether or not it can quickly and accurately react to market signals. According to research, direct efficiency losses in resource allocation caused by distorted prices are not the only social welfare losses caused by the policy environment, because rent-seeking can cause an even more severe indirect efficiency loss. In a macro-policy environment where prices are determined by the market, there is no opportunity for rent-seeking; hence the waste of social resources and related institutional problems are avoided.

In such an institutional environment, every enterprise and even the whole economic structure can make full use of the economy's comparative advantage. The international and domestic competitiveness of products will be high. Meanwhile, the comparative-advantage-following strategy will make it easier for the economy to discover and realize their comparative advantage through foreign trade and to improve the competitiveness of domestic industries and enterprises accordingly. Therefore, the economy will be outward oriented. We can see that the export-oriented aspect of Japan and the four Little Dragons is an important factor in their economic success. However, it is actually the consequence of the development that follows comparative-advantage-following strategy rather than the cause of the success.

4.4 The Government's Role in Economic Development

The government's role in economic development is also part of the comparative-advantage-following strategy. What role the government can play in economic development and how it can help boost such development has long been a topic of discussion in economic and political circles.

The economic success of Japan and the four Little Dragons can be used to support neoclassical economic theories, which stress the market and the individual contribution of entrepreneurs and oppose government intervention. However, these countries' success can also be used to highlight the effectiveness of government intervention — in the form of industrial policy. Arthur Lewis' comments show both sides of the point. "No country has made economic progress without positive stimulus from intelligent government, … On the other hand, there are so many examples of the mischief done to economic life by government that it is easy to fill one's pages with warnings against government participation in economic life." To be more exact, "the failure of government might be that it does not do enough of what it should do or that it does too much of what it should not."[18]

The comparative-advantage-following strategy can help us understand that government does have a role to play in economic development. At the same time, the strategy can help us identify the

18. Arthur Lewis, *The Theories of Economic Growth*. Shanghai: Shanghai Sanlian Bookstore and Shanghai People's Press, 1994, pp. 475–576.

proper boundaries of government's functions. We can see the government's roles in the comparative-advantage-following strategy by comparing this strategy with the leap-forward strategy. For a government to adopt the leap-forward strategy, it must intervene in the economy and distort price signals and the function of market to support the development of non-viable industries. Thus, such governments' inappropriate interventions hamper economic development, usually with disastrous results.

Under the comparative-advantage-following strategy, a government must ensure that the market is given full play and that price signals are correct. Therefore, the role of government is, first of all, to maintain the competitive nature and rules of the market. The government's economic functions should include the following:

(1) Formulating market rules and implementing anti-monopoly laws. This is crucial to guarantee that market mechanism is given full play in resource allocation. When the market is monopolized, price signals and comparative-advantage information is distorted, and the enterprise cannot make investment decisions according to comparative advantage. In this sense, the government's function lies in protecting rather than eliminating market competition and protecting rather than eliminating the operation of price mechanism. In this way, the price mechanism can fully play its role in resource allocation.

(2) Adopting independent monetary policy and fiscal policy to reduce the adverse impact of economic fluctuation. When price mechanisms adjust production and consumption, economic fluctuations are inevitable, and manufacturers will suffer. When such cyclic fluctuations occur, information about market demands will be in disarray and the enterprises will be hard to digest the information and respond appropriately. The government thus could adopt anti-cyclic fiscal and monetary policies. Obviously, such policies would not deny the role of market competition and of the price mechanism.

(3) Investing in some industries with externalities. These include industries that require large-scale initial investments and that take a long time to build, and those with positive externalities, such as infrastructure, education, health care, transportation, and energy. Such participation helps build the infrastructure necessary for social and economic activities, reduces transaction costs for economic activities, and smoothes the operation of the market mechanism.

At the early stages of economic development, a country's comparative advantages usually lie in land and labour-intensive products, such as agricultural products. As capital accumulates and labour increases, land becomes relatively scarce. Labour-intensive farming (e.g., farming of flowers, fruits, vegetables) and some manufacturing industries (e.g., the textile industry, the shoe-making industry, the electrical-home-appliances-assembly industry) gain a comparative advantage. With further economic growth, labour becomes relatively scarce, and its cost increases steadily, while capital become relatively abundant and cheap. Capital- and technology-intensive industries become the economy's comparative advantage. The more effectively an economy exploits its comparative advantage, the faster economic growth and capital accumulation takes place, and the faster comparative advantage shifts to capital-intensive industries.

Therefore, if a country takes advantage of its comparative advantages, the bottlenecks caused by scarce resources will ease. This will lead to more rapid upgrading of the endowment structure. As a result, speedy changes in industrial and technological structures will take place. The fact that adopting the comparative-advantage-following strategy can speed up the upgrading of industrial and technological structures makes government's roles more complicated. In addition to the maintenance of law and order in the market, the government has a lot more to do, especially in the formulation and implementation of its industrial policy. The following is a summary of the nature and content of industrial policies under a comparative-advantage-following strategy, and of the difference between these policies and the industrial policies in a planned economy with the leap-forward strategy in place.

First, as the endowment structure of a country changes, so do the industrial and technological structures. In order to upgrade the industrial structure, both entrepreneurs and the government need information about the technology and sectors that can make full use of the economy's new comparative advantages, about the market potential of a new product, and about the economy's possible competitors. However, most information is a quasi-public good. Although the enterprise has to spend some resources to acquire the information, once the information is obtained, the cost of sharing it with other enterprises is almost zero. The best solution is thus for the government to make the information known to all enterprises. In addition, information gathering, processing, and distribution display economies of scale. The government should thus gather, process, and make the information available to enterprises in the form of an industrial policy so that enterprises can use the information as a reference in their technology and industrial selection. The main distinguishing feature of industrial policy under the comparative-advantage-following strategy is that the policy provides enterprises with options rather than telling them what to do and how to do it.

Second, the government should act to improve social infrastructure and coordination. When the endowment structure upgrades, industrial structure also need to be upgraded; the latter usually requires investments in many related activities. Because of limited capital and because of the existence of risks and externalities, individual enterprises cannot invest in all activities. Uncoordinated investment activities may miss the optimal social investment opportunities. For example, when the agriculture-dominated industrial structure upgrades to a light-industry-dominated structure, education, transportation, commerce, the distribution network, and import and export facilities need to be adjusted accordingly. When the light-industry-dominated industrial structure upgrades to a capital- and technology-intensive structure, adjustments should be made accordingly in education, scientific research, and capital markets. An individual enterprise cannot do all these. The government's role is to decide on the direction of the efforts and to provide information on the steps to be taken. The government should also assist individual enterprises and coordinate the investment activities of various enterprises. Since government guidance is coordination according to the changes in endowment structure, rather than being mandatory or distorted, serious policy mistakes will not ensue.

Finally, the government should provide a certain amount of financial support to compensate for the externalities faced by enterprises when they upgrade their technology and industry. The upgrading of technology and industry is a type of innovation. Just like any innovation, enterprises that follow the government's industrial policy and make technology and industry upgrading face externalities. That is, as the government is not always right, enterprises following the government's industrial policy can either succeed or fail. If they succeed, other enterprises will follow suit, and the above-normal profits will soon disappear. If they fail, other enterprises will take care to avoid similar mistakes. The costs that innovating enterprises pay thus benefit all other enterprises. Whether the innovative enterprises succeed or fail, their experience are valuable to society. If the government does not compensate such enterprises, the overall amount of innovation will be less than the optimal level. Thus, governments should encourage innovative investment through tax reductions, exemptions, or interest subsidies.

Similarly, such government interventions are implemented with changes in the endowment structure. The supported industries are viable. Subsidies are used to compensate for the externalities of innovation efforts, and the scope and size of subsidies are limited. Therefore, these subsidies are different from those under the leap-forward strategy, where subsidized enterprises are not viable.

If the government is limited to activities tied to economies of scale (such as sharing information) and providing subsidies for externalities in innovation, it is necessary and effective. Those that attribute the success of Japan and the four Little Dragons to government intervention are partially correct. However, they fail to consider that such government interventions were intended to compensate for the externalities — quite a different scenario from the one in which intervention were implemented under the leap-forward strategy.

In sum, the success of industrial policy depends on two things: first, the policy should provide information about the changing trends in comparative advantage, and second, the policy's target should not be too far away from existing comparative advantages. In the late 19th century, Germany overtook Great Britain and France with its "Blood and Iron" policy. This is often cited as an argument to support government intervention. It is worth pointing out, however, that Germany made the move when its factor endowment, comparative advantages, and level of economic development were similar to those of Britain and France.[19] In the 1950s, when Japan formulated a strategy to develop its heavy industries, its per capita GNP had reached one-fourth that of the United States.[20] Japan began with relatively labour-intensive type of heavy industries, such as ship building and steel. The experiences of Japan and the four Little Dragons, along with the lessons of socialist and Latin American countries, show that the target of government industrial policy should be to encourage the development of industries consistent with the economy's comparative advantages in the short run. If the objective is too lofty, relative prices of production factors have to be distorted. When the objective is relatively short-term and foreseeable, the government's role will be market conforming instead of market distorting.

Focusing on short-term comparative advantages can save the government from spending too much on the intervention itself. The government has limited administrative resources. If it is mired in direct intervention and in making decisions for enterprises, other areas of policy will suffer. The focus on short-term comparative

---

19. In 1870, per capita GDP in Germany was 60% of that in Britain and a bit higher than that in France. See Augus Maddison, *Monitoring the World Economy, 1820–1992*. Paris: OECD, 1995, pp. 194, 196.
20. Augus Maddison, *Monitoring the World Economy, 1820–1992*. Paris: OECD, 1995, p. 197.

advantages will help to properly define the government functions, and government's influence on industry will result primarily from an exchange of information. This is the watershed between the industrial policies of East Asian economies and the leap-forward strategy of socialist and Latin American economies.

During Japan's and the four Little Dragons' economic development process, these countries' governments were characterized by two important features. First, the governments were small. The extent of government intervention can be judged by the proportion of central government expenditure in the GNP. In 1980 and 1992, the proportions were 18.4% and 15.8% in Japan, respectively, 20.8% and 22.7% in Singapore, and 17.9% and 17.6% in South Korea. In Latin American economies, the proportions were much higher; they were 29.1% and 22.1% in Chile, 20.9% and 25.6% in Brazil, and 29.0% and 22.5% in Bolivia.[21]

Second, the industrial policy implemented by Japan and the four Little Dragons was market-oriented and was implemented within a price-mechanism framework. The government did not intervene in enterprises' decision-making process but rather used informal persuasion techniques to effect change.[22] The development of heavy industry in Japan is a good example. It is true that the Japanese government became too involved in the economic process for a period of time during the economic recovery after World War II.[23]

21. The World Bank, *World Development Report, 1994*. New York: Oxford University Press, 1994.
22. Yujiro Hayami, "A Commentary on the 'East Asian Miracle': Are There Lessons to Be Learned — Review Essay", *Journal of the Japanese and International Economies*, Vol. 10, No. 3 (September 1996), pp. 318–25.
23. Nevertheless, the government had not distorted the market during this stage. In fact, in the 1950s, Japanese industrial development was based on comparative advantage. For instance, the textile, garment, and ship-building industries made full use of the country's rich labour resources. As a matter of fact, Japan's most successful industrial policy and development examples were not in the areas of iron, steel, or automobiles, as is commonly thought, but in ship building, and ship building was the industry that used rich labour resources in the 1950s, thereby aligning itself with Japan's comparative advantage in those years. (See M. Shinohara, *Industrial Growth, Trade, and Dynamic Patterns in the Japanese Economy*. Tokyo: University of Tokyo Press, 1982.)

However, in the early 1960s, Japan's industrial policy began to shift from direct intervention to guidance and indirect influence. The industrial planning of 1963, when heavy and chemical industries were selected as the keys to development, was a product of this shift.[24] In the early 1960s, Japan's per capita GDP was already more than one-third that of the United States. It had already passed the stage of insufficient capital, and was no longer at a comparative advantage for non-skilled labour-intensive industry. Under these conditions, Japan speeded up the development of its energy-intensive and material-intensive heavy and chemical industries in the 1960s. In the late 1960s, investments in factories and equipment increased by an annual average rate of more than 20%. Japan's industrial policy was thus formulated pragmatically. The government, industry and experts from the fields of science and technology worked together to create a dynamic vision of Japan's visible comparative advantages.

4.5 The Comparative-advantage-following Strategy and the Asian Financial Crisis

When people were still talking about Japan's and the four Little Dragons' miraculous economic ascent, the Asian financial crisis erupted, affecting all these economies. People may well ask whether a link exists between the financial crisis and the development strategies of Japan and the four Little Dragons. The answer begins with an explanation of the cause and progression of a financial crisis.

Financial crises are often directly linked to cross-border capital flow. It makes sense that money flows to areas that yield the greatest returns. When the economy is growing fast and projections are positive, investments and credit activities are naturally active. If an economy is healthy, investments can be reclaimed by increased production. Cross-border capital flow will not lead to a financial crisis. However, in Southeast Asia, Japan, and South Korea, there was a high non-performing loans ratio, which was the direct occasion

24. C. Freeman, *Technology Policy and Economic Performance: Lessons from Japan*. London and New York: Pinter Publishers, 1987.

for the financial crisis, and the high NPL ratio was mainly caused by the rupturing of the bubble economy and the wrong industrial development policies.

Economic bubbles usually take shape when continuous price increases are accompanied by optimistic market expectations. These two factors will encourage active purchases and create speculative opportunities. When people are too involved in the speculative purchases and sales, and are not at all concerned about real economic performance, the bubble economy forms.[25] Economic bubbles can be categorized as real estate bubbles or stock market bubbles. Real estate bubbles were prevalent in Japan, South Korea, and other Southeast Asian countries and regions prior to the onset of the financial crisis.

The emergence of bubble economies is easily characterized. Generally speaking, the population density of Asian countries and regions is relatively high, and land resources are relatively scarce. Under normal conditions, land prices are relatively high. More importantly, in the course of economic development, the price of factors with low supply elasticity shoots up. With the increasing demand for land from the real estate sector, along with the over-concentration of economic activities in a few regions, land becomes the factor that is least flexible in supply. When an economy is developing quickly, people expect land prices will rise. Hence, they invest in real estate to gain capital returns, which in turn stimulates the continued increase of land prices.

Another factor contributing to the creation of a bubble economy is a price hike in the stock market. Much like what happens in the real estate market, in the short term, the supply elasticity of stocks is low. When the economy is growing, people see stock prices rising. They thus invest a great deal of capital in the stock market, fueling further price hikes.

Bubble economies burst as frequently as they appear. Their

---

25. John Eatwell, Murray Milgate and Peter Newman, eds., *The New Palgrave: A Dictionary of Economics*, Vol. 1. Beijing: Economic Science Press, 1992, p. 306.

sustainability is determined by two factors: the amount of capital in an economy that can be invested, and people's anticipation of economic growth. From a static point of view, when no more money can be mobilized, prices for real estate and stocks stop rising. Since there are risks and opportunity costs associated with funds, some people will then begin to sell; this results in falling prices, which in turn lead to more selling orders. From a dynamic point of view, when prices rise quickly, too much capital is invested in real estate development, and less is invested for production purposes. This leads to economic stagnation. In turn, expectations of rising prices in real estate and of stocks with a low elasticity of supply are less optimistic and may even become pessimistic. Meanwhile, an increased supply of real estate brings prices down quickly. In due time, the bubble bursts.

However, the existence of a bubble economy does not in itself necessarily lead to financial crisis. If all the capital used for speculation in the bubble economy belongs to individual investors, then the rupture of the bubble may not lead to a banking crisis. Unfortunately, when investors see that the prices of real estate and stocks continue to rise, they will take out loans to speculate further, using their real estate and stocks as pledge to apply for more collateral loans. Such self-enforcing expectations prompt banks and other financial institutions to grant loans and even to invest directly in real estate and stock markets. When the bubble bursts, prices for real estate and stocks fall sharply, and the price of collateral falls below its hypothecary value. Investors cannot recoup their investments, banks cannot call in their loans, and many bad debts result.

At such a juncture, whether a banking crisis will break out depends on the proportion of capital self-owned by investors in each loan and on the overall structure of bank assets. Therefore, the bank asset structure and banking supervision system are also involved. If there are no restrictions on loans that use real estate and stocks as collateral, or if there are no restrictions on the proportion of funds that can use real estate and stocks as collateral, or if supervision is weak in spite of the existence of certain restrictions, when the bubble increases, investors will choose to borrow money from banks to make speculative investments. Banks and other financial institutions then have to bear the moral hazard.[26] A great deal of bank capital will be used in speculation. When economic growth slows, the economic bubble bursts, and bad loans become bad debts. A banking crisis thus occurs.

If only domestic savings are invested in bubble industries, when the bubble bursts, a banking crisis will not turn into a currency crisis of the type that erupted across East Asia. However, if foreign investment in addition to domestic savings is channelled into speculation either directly, or indirectly through financial institutions, the bubble will grow even bigger. When economic growth slows and expectations change — or, for example, if the government cannot save the economy from a series of investment failures — investors' confidence diminishes. If the currency is freely convertible so that capital can flow freely, capital withdrawal and bank run will occur. If capital has a high liquidity, fast capital outflow will speed up the collapse of the financial system. If exchange rates are fixed, the central bank has to intervene, which may give international financial speculators opportunities to make profits. For instance, speculators may borrow in local currency from a domestic bank, and then sell the currency on the international money market. The government has to use its foreign reserve to maintain the exchange rate in the monetary market. However, when domestic savers have noticed the potential crisis in domestic financial institutions, exacerbated by the attacks from foreign speculators, they may lose

26. Paul Krugman summed up the financial system's problem as moral hazard in financial intermediates' behaviours, that is, because financial institutions enjoy the government's explicit or implicit credit guarantees, they lack the incentives to supervise the borrower' uses of funds. Financial intermediates actually manage the savings of depositors. Their thinking might go as follows: "If I make money, it's mine; if I lose money, it's the depositors' money." Therefore, in the selection of investment projects, the intermediates would not choose risk-neutral projects, rather, they choose projects with the highest potential returns which generally involve the greatest risks. See Paul Krugman, "What Happened to Asia?" at http://web.mit.edlu/krugman/www/DISINTER.html, January 1998.

confidence and sell domestic currency just as the international financial speculators do. As noted in a recent *Economist* article, when East Asia experienced the financial crisis, those who sold the most domestic currency were not speculators but local enterprises that wanted to avoid loss and needed U.S. dollars to repay their debts.[27] When the central bank has exhausted its limited foreign reserves and can do nothing more to support the local currency in the monetary market, the exchange rate falls sharply. This is how the currency and payment crises occurred during the Asian financial crisis.

An excessively high proportion of non-performing loans is another outcome of poor industrial policy. If the government chooses to support the development of nonviable industries, it will have to suppress the interest rate and instruct banks to provide loans to support the expansion of such projects. As such projects are unable to accumulate much capital on their own, investors will turn to foreign lending institutions when the limited capital of domestic banks is exhausted. However, East Asia's comparative advantage does not lie in capital- and technology-intensive projects. With government support, such industries can be established, but production cost will be so high compared with that in developed countries that every sale of the product will generate an amount of loss. As a result, enterprises investing in such projects cannot repay loans and interest, which then become the NPLs in domestic and international banks.

As a result, lendable funds in financial institutions shrink, bank capital tightens, and interest rates rise. The number of enterprises that cannot repay bank loans increases. Lendable funds decrease further as interest rates continue to rise, and NPLs quickly accumulate. Meanwhile, when the increase in NPLs shakes the public confidence in a bank, a bank run occurs, causing the bank to collapse. The collapse of one or two banks can lead to the collapse of many. A financial crisis follows. On the other hand, if an economy has real estate and stock bubbles, when lendable funds shrink, interest rates

27. "Keeping the Hot Money Out", *The Economist*, 24 January 1998, p. 71.

rise, demand for investment and consumption drops, and economic growth slows down, and lead to the burst of bubbles which then may result in the financial crisis.

If the overall investment of an economy is based on comparative advantage, there will be no serious flaws in the industrial structure. Enterprises will make profits, products will be competitive, capital accumulates quickly, and enterprises are less reliant on foreign loans. The economy's credit rating will be high, and it will have sufficient capacity to pay debts. Its growth will be sustainable, and real estate and stock bubbles may not burst. Even if they do burst and a banking crisis occurs, the economy as a whole is still competitive, foreign trade will continue to grow, and currency and payment crises will not occur. During the Asian financial crisis, this is what happened in Japan and Taiwan.

The countries hit by the East Asian financial crisis, such as Thailand, Malaysia, Indonesia, and South Korea, fell victim to the crisis due both to the bubbles and to an inappropriate industrial policy. Real estate bubbles were pervasive in Japan, South Korea, Thailand, Malaysia, and Indonesia. In addition, bank loans were provided to inefficient industries and enterprises.

The governments of these countries had almost no regulation on the development of financial institutions or on the amount of loans. They also lacked supervision over the banking system. Sometimes political loans were combined with family-based management in the enterprises, which led to rampant corruption. As a result, many loans flew into real estate sector. Once a confidence crisis occurred, or when foreign speculators attacked, a large number of financial institutions went bankrupt, and the amount of NPLs rose sharply. It was estimated that, by the end of 1997, the average NPL ratio in Thailand, Malaysia, Indonesia, and Singapore had reached at least 15%, which accounted for 13% of the GDP. In Malaysia, NPLs amounted to 20% of the GDP in 1998. Excessive foreign debts in these countries exceeded what economic growth and export growth could support. With the exception of Malaysia, Southeast Asian countries had to pay a large part of their export earnings to repay foreign debts, the proportion were the internationally accepted dangerous line of 25%.[28] Meanwhile, these countries also liberalized their financial system, made their currencies fully convertible, allowed the capital to flow freely and adopted a fixed exchange rate system. Therefore, when the economic growth slowed down in these countries, bubbles burst, bank, currency and payment crises occurred and a financial storm took place.

The above analysis shows that the implementation of a comparative-advantage-following strategy does not necessary lead to a financial crises. First, a bubble economy can appear in any fast-growing economy. As the comparative-advantage-following strategy can speed up economic growth, it may lead to the creation of a bubble in such an economy. Second, the comparative-advantage-following strategy does not necessarily lead to the bursting of the bubble. On the contrary, if an economy keeps on making use of its comparative advantage, it will enjoy a strong and a more sustainable growth, and thus postpone the rupture. Third, in a financial crisis there are two key linkages in converting a burst of bubble to a bank crisis and a bank crisis to a currency crisis. If bank supervision can be strengthened, bank loans flowing to real estate and stock markets can be reduced, the burst of a bubble will not lead to a bank crisis and to a currency crisis. The comparative-advantage-following strategy can also help stave off the financial crisis. Competitive industries can make a profit. Even if they take out bank loans, such loans probably will not become NPLs. Second, under such a strategy, the capital intensity of the industries is in line with the economy's endowment structure, and necessary capital come mainly from domestic savings, which minimizes the reliance on foreign debt. Thus, the currency and payment crises can be avoided.

Therefore, the comparative-advantage-following strategy does not in itself lead to financial crisis, nor does it increase the possibility of financial crisis. On the contrary, it can guard against financial crisis. The East Asian financial crisis provides us with two important

---

28. Chen Wenhong, et al., *Where Should the East Asian Economies Head For—A Review and Outlook of '97 East Asian Financial Storms*. Beijing: Economic Management Press, 1998, pp. 62–63.

pieces of information about the comparative-advantage-following strategy and the East Asian Miracle.

First, the comparative-advantage-following strategy can help limit government intervention, but this does not mean a financial crisis will never occur. Financial risk exists in all economic development. Therefore, a sound banking supervision system is a must.

Second, Japan and the four Little Dragons each adopted a comparative-advantage-following strategy. However, even within the same country or region, the strategy was abided to different extents at different development stages.[29] As a result, differences do exist among these economies in terms of their economic performance, the healthiness of their economic structure, and their ability to prevent financial crises.

Insufficient banking supervision is most often seen in South Korea and Japan. For example, Japan's main bank system allowed banks to hold shares of enterprises. In a bubble economy, the increase in asset prices enhanced banks' ability to lend, so they would invest more in bubble industries such as real estate. When the bubble ruptured, the stocks and real estate held by banks and financial institutions depreciated quickly, and their assets shrank dramatically. Most real estate loans become NPLs. In South Korea, the government focused on supporting super-large conglomerates and imposed no limit on loans to these conglomerates. Under its industrial policy, the top 30 conglomerates had a 350% debt/asset ratio in 1996. However, their products were not competitive, and the enterprises performed poorly. In light of their soft budget constraints, the solvency of these conglomerates was very low.

The later development approaches of Taiwan and South Korea are significantly different from one another. Both countries are Little Dragons, and both have enjoyed fast economic growth since the

29. Japanese industrial policies sometimes deviated away from its comparative advantages and were opposed and failed. For examples of such incidents, see Takatoshi Ito, *The Japanese Economy*. Cambridge, MA: The MIT Press, 1982, p. 202.

1960s. Before the 1970s, both had labour-intensive industries. But after that, the two adopted different development strategies, and their economic systems differed greatly. The South Korean government put a great deal of effort into developing capital-intensive industries by supporting super-large enterprise groups. Researchers have found that in the early 1980s the concentration ratio of Korean enterprises was much higher than that of Taiwan and even higher than that of Japan.[30] At present, South Korea's four largest conglomerates (Hyundai, Samsang, Daewoo and LG) account for one-third of the national sales volume and over half of the national exports. In contrast to South Korea, many Taiwanese enterprises chose to supply accessories to U.S. and Japanese enterprises instead of creating their own brands.

Take the auto industry as an example. South Korea manufactures and exports cars, while Taiwan manufactures and exports parts and components. In the personal computer industry, South Korea makes chips, while Taiwan produces mice, keyboards, mother boards, monitors, non-brand computers, assembly computers, and out-sourced chips for brand manufacturers. However, the cars and chips made in South Korea, which could not compete with products from Europe, the United States, or Japan, were exported at below-cost prices, while Taiwan's exports of vehicle parts and computer products returned tremendous profits. As Taiwan's industries enjoyed high profitability, they accumulated a large surplus, allowing the economy to upgrade their industries rapidly. New investment projects in Taiwan usually do not exceed the capital size that its capital market can mobilize, and its foreign debt is small. All these features reduced financial risk in Taiwan. Therefore, although Taiwan had traces of a bubble economy,[31] its economy and export

30. The World Bank, *East Asian Miracle*. Beijing, China Finance Press, 1995, p. 66.

31. According to estimates of Merrill Lynch Taiwan Branch Co., 40% of Taiwan's bank loans are used for real estate investment. This percentage is similar to the percentages of Southeast Asian economies when they were hit by the financial crisis; two-thirds of all financial loans in Taiwan use land as collateral, twice the proportion of Japan.

could still grow at a reasonable rate. Its real estate and stock bubbles did not burst under the influence of the Southeast Asian financial crisis. Even if Taiwan's economy grows as much as Japan's economy did in history, moving from fast development to slower growth as its gap of technologies with the developed countries narrows, the burst of bubble may not throw Taiwan immediately into currency and payment crises, as what happened in Thailand, Korea, and Indonesia.

CHAPTER 5

Economic Reform in China

The inefficiency of China's traditional economic system was first recognized in the 1960s. Attempts to solve this problem can be traced back to that period. However, fundamental changes did not take place until the Third Plenary Session of the 11th Chinese Communist Party Congress in December 1978. Before that, economic reforms existed only in the form of a re-delineation of economic and administrative functions among sectoral and regional governments, and in a corresponding cyclical increase or decrease in the number of administrative authorities. The basic trinity of the traditional economic system remained intact.

Unlike the reforms preceding it, the one put in place in 1978 had two distinct features. First, the reform was not done through the assignment of administrative functions to different government agents. Instead, enterprises and farmers were given more production and management autonomy. Second, as the reform proceeded, the reformed micro-management institutions often ran into conflicts with the planned resource-allocation mechanism and the distorted macro-policy environment. Despite the fact that institutional regression occurred several times, overall, there was no retreat to the traditional system. Rather, the reform became further reaching, beginning with the micro-management institution and continuing into the areas of the resource-allocation system and macro-policy environment. The reform of the resource-allocation system and the macro-policy environment, in return, helped to solve the remained problems in the reform of micro-management institutions.

This chapter examines the economic reform that started in late 1978. We will categorize the reforms into those of the micro-management institution, the resource-allocation system and the macro-policy environment, and discuss them accordingly. We will use major reforms to analyze the evolution process of the reform and to illustrate the intrinsic logic behind this process.

5.1 Differences between Pre-1978 and Post-1978 Reforms

Until 1978, there were no major changes made in the basic framework of China's traditional economic system. After 1978, however, reform gradually breaks the internal integrity of the traditional economic system.

Before 1978, the economic trinity was regarded as the formal realization of socialism. Therefore, reforms had not touched on the basic framework of the traditional economic system. Major measures of the pre-1978 reforms included (1) eliminating the central government's over-concentration of power by decentralizing administrative authority and responsibility and (2) eliminating unequal distribution of earnings among regions and sectors by adjusting their administrative authority and responsibility.

However, these changes only altered the ability of the local and sectoral authorities to allocate resources. The traditional development strategy, and accordingly the distorted macro-policy environment, the planned resource-allocation mechanism, and the puppet-like micro-management institution were left intact. Since their vested interests were lost through administrative adjustment, local and sectoral authorities would naturally try to regain the interests in the new round of adjustments. Economic reforms were thus caught in the cycle of decentralizing and re-centralizing administrative power and in the corresponding repetitious cycle of expansion and reduction in administrative organizations (see Table 5.1). For several decades, to implement the heavy-industry-oriented development strategy, China and many other countries relied on the trinity of the traditional economic system. None of them succeeded in achieving economic development. This taught China's leaders that the prevailing economic theories and practices could not solve China's problems.

Table 5.1 Pre-reform Decentralization and Re-centralization Cycle

	1953	1957	1958 (year-end)	1963	1971–73
Number of SOEs under direct control of the central government	2,800	9,300	1,200	10,000	2,000
Number of materials allocated by state commissions and ministries	227	532	132	500	217

Source: Yu Guangyuan, ed., *China's Socialist Modernization*. Beijing: Foreign Languages Press, 1984, p. 76.

To develop the economy, the traditional economic system had to be fundamentally reformed.

The economic reform that began in 1978 signified Chinese leaders' search for a new path toward the realization of socialism. The basic framework of traditional economic system was no longer off limits, this enabled reform to penetrate all levels of the economic system. Thanks to the thorough and increasingly powerful reforms, compulsory plans were gradually replaced by indicative plans, and the planned allocation mechanism was replaced by a market mechanism. The new economic system gradually took shape as a result of the survival-of-the-fittest process.

There are several reasons behind China's decision to implement a new type of reform. First, the heavy-industry-oriented development strategy had not achieved the intended goals. Rather than enabling China to surpass developed economies, this strategy enlarged the gap between China and developed countries. The income levels of urban and rural households remained stagnant. There was a serious shortage of daily necessities, and several hundred million peasants still lived under the threat of starvation. The national economy was on the verge of collapse after 10 years of turmoil during the Cultural Revolution, which lasted from 1966 to 1976. These factors stimulated Chinese leaders' re-evaluation of the traditional economic system.

Second, during the same period, while China was pursuing the leap-forward strategy, neighbouring countries and regions, especially the four Little Dragons who were originally at the same footing with China in terms of economic conditions, developed rapidly and emerged as newly industrialized economies. The gap between China and these economies widened, exerting great pressure on China's leaders to institute reforms.

Third, the micro-management units (i.e., SOEs and the People's Communes) suffered from low economic efficiency and insufficient production incentives. When the new leadership resumed power after the Cultural Revolution, the death of Chairman Mao, and the purge of the ultra-left Gang of Four, they hoped to strengthen their legitimacy by using reform measures to speed up economic growth and improve people's living standards.

Moreover, shortfalls deriving from the leap-forward strategy became more apparent over time. As people's living standards failed to improve decade after decade, the opportunity cost of discarding the traditional economic system fell. This lowered cost also played a major role in pushing China to reform its economic system.

5.2 Reform of the Micro-management Institution

As discussed in Chapter 2, the adoption of the heavy-industry-oriented development strategy resulted endogenously in the formation of the price-distorted macro-policy environment, a highly centralized planned resource-allocation mechanism, and puppet-like micro-management institutions. The distortion in the prices of production factors and products was the key component in the trinity. Their underlying connections can be described as follows: (1) a macro-policy environment with depressed interest rates, exchange rates, and prices for scarce goods was seen as the prerequisite for developing nonviable heavy industry; (2) the planned resource-allocation mechanism was implemented in response to a distorted macro-policy environment in which total demand exceeded total supply, so as to guarantee that resources go to heavy industries; and (3) puppet-like micro-management institution was adopted to prevent SOEs from corroding profits and state assets by abusing their autonomous power. In rural areas, the People's Commune system was created to guarantee that the state monopolize the purchasing and marketing of agricultural products.

Both the distorted macro-policy environment and the highly centralized planned resource-allocation mechanism were inherently problematic but not so intuitively clear. The relation between production inefficiency and the lack of incentive for workers and peasants was, however, highly evident. This explains why the post-1978 reforms began with the micro-management institution. In rural areas, a household responsibility system was initiated. In cities, a series of comprehensive and specific reforms was carried out to address the management of SOEs, which were focused, at the time, on decentralization and profit sharing. These two aspects of the reform are elaborated upon below.

1. The Household Responsibility System

From the collectivization movement in the 1950s to the introduction of the household responsibility system in the late 1970s, the production team system was the basic farming institution in China. Under the production team system, each labourer received a *gongfen* (work point) each day for their work. At the end of the year, the net income of the production team — after state taxes and allocations for public accumulation funds and public welfare funds were deducted — was allotted to each individual according to his or her *gongfen*. The nature of agricultural work makes good supervision exceedingly costly. The linkage between work points earned by a worker and the contribution done by the worker was extremely weak. Because the work point system could not accurately reflect the quantity and quality of the work done, it severely dampened labour incentives. The fact that workers were forbidden to exit the commune (an important mechanism to prevent free riding) further reduced their incentive to work.[1] The outcome was that an absolute shortage of agricultural products became a persistent, unsolvable problem. In order to improve labour incentives in agricultural production, the household responsibility system was introduced in the late 1970s.

The development of the household responsibility system itself can be roughly divided into three phases: the work-quota contract phase, the output-quota contract phase, and the responsibility contract phase. Every phase experienced the same evolution process from the contract with a group of workers, to the contract with each individual worker, and finally to the contract with a household. The three major modes in this evolution process were the group work-quota contract, the household output-quota contract, and the household responsibility contract.

Under the group work-quota contract, the production team assigned a certain work quota with pre-specified requirements for time, quantity, and quality to a group of workers and then rewarded or punished the whole group according to its performance. With quantity, quality, time limit, and compensations for their work clearly defined, work teams would be formed voluntarily, labour supervision costs would fall, and free rides would be avoided. All this would create a stronger incentive to work.

Under the household output-quota contract, a specific output quota and plot of land were assigned to a household. The household was responsible for delivering to the production team a pre-determined quantity of output. Output exceeding the quota would be given to the household or shared between the household and the production team. There are two differences between the household output-quota contract and the group work-quota contract. First, under the household output-quota contract, contracts were extended from one stage of the production process to the entire process, thereby

1. Justin Yifu Lin, "The Household Responsibility System in China's Agricultural Reform: The Theoretical and Empirical Study", *Economic Development and Cultural Change,* Vol. 36, No. 3 (April 1988) (Supplement), pp. S199–S224; Justin Yifu Lin, "Collectivization and China's Agricultural Crisis in 1959–1961", *Journal of Political Economy,* Vol. 98, No. 6 (December 1990), pp. 1228–52.

eliminating the difficult task of assessing intermediate performance in agricultural production. Second, the unit of the contractor changed from work groups to households, thereby eliminating the difficult task of labour supervision and the problem of free riding.

Under the household responsibility system, land was assigned to each household according to the number of its members or according to the number of both its members and workers. Households were required by the contract to pay state taxes, fulfil contracted procurement quotas, and submit certain amount of produce to the production team as public accumulation funds and public welfare funds. After these obligations had been fulfilled, all remaining output belonged to the household. The most significant difference between the household output-quota contract and the household responsibility system was the cancellation of unified income allocation by the production team in the latter.

The household responsibility system evolved from being absolutely illegal, to being partially legal, to eventually being promoted by the government. During the years of the People's Communes, production teams adopted certain responsibility contracts with households whenever agriculture ran into difficulty. This was effective in the short term, but, since it did not match socialist ideology, it was abolished repeatedly.[2] As early as the 1950s, when the People's Commune system had just been established, the household responsibility system emerged and then faded from view. During the late 1970s, when the national economy was on the verge of collapse, the system revived. Fortunately, this time it was tolerated as an exception rather than being condemned outright as a return to capitalism.

In September 1979, the Central Committee of the Chinese Communist Party passed *The Decision on Certain Issues Concerning*

2. Because agriculture does not display many characteristics of a scale economy, and because supervising and measuring agricultural work is difficult, agriculture is suitable for household operations. The fact that household-based agriculture could prosper in market economies in developed economies suggests that household operation is not an institutional barrier for the modernization of agriculture.

the Acceleration of Agriculture Development. This document stipulated that — with the exception of the special needs of some sideline productions and isolated households in remote areas — production contract with household was not allowed. This was the first official indication that production contract with household could exist as an exception. In the late 1980, as the household responsibility system had significantly helped to address the issue of food and clothing, the government further relaxed its policies. Meeting minutes issued by the Central Committee of the Chinese Communist Party, titled "Issues Regarding Further Accelerating and Perfecting the Agricultural Production Responsibility System" in Autumn 1980, stated that "in the remote and poor areas, production should be contracted to households, in the form of household output-quota system or the household responsibility system, if the team members wanted to do so."

Under this more lenient government policy, the proportion of production teams adopting the household output-quota contract system or the household responsibility system soared from 1.1% at the beginning of 1980 to about 20% at the end of 1980. By that time, the poorest production teams had all adopted the household output-quota contract system or the household responsibility system. The new policy greatly improved rural workers' production incentive. Wherever the household contract system was adopted, agricultural output increased substantially. Given the success of the household contract system, the government further relaxed its policy in 1981, and in 1982 it eliminated all restrictions, which respectively enabled 30% of lower-middle income production teams and 30% of higher-middle income production teams to implement the new practice. In 1983, an ideological justification was provided for such a micro-foundation reform. The household responsibility system was explicitly accepted as an integrated operational mode combining individual management and unified operation in the socialist collective economy, which was regarded different in nature from the small private economy. As such, the system was "in line with the current stage of development, where agricultural work is pre-dominant manual, and the characteristics of agricultural production. The system is also conformed to the needs of productivity improvement in the modernization process." Thus, another 15% of the teams, those with high incomes, were added to the list. In 1984, the government promulgated new methods and measures by which to strengthen and improve the household responsibility system. The measures brought the remaining 4% of the best production teams into the system, which marked the completion of the reform of the system in rural areas.

Statistical data reveals that total agricultural growth and average annual growth from 1978 to 1984, when the household responsibility system became predominant, stood at 42.23% and 6.05%, respectively, after price adjustment. Such growth had not been seen since the founding of the People's Republic of China in 1949. The household responsibility system was the main reason for the high growth rate. An econometric study shows that 46.89% of the total output increase in the period can be attributed to the household responsibility system. Although other factors, such as the increases in the procurement prices of agricultural products and the decreases in the prices of agricultural inputs, also contributed to growth, none had made as significant a contribution as the household responsibility system did.[3]

The reason that the household responsibility system could be the major contributor to agricultural development was because under the system, households were permitted to keep anything they produced after they had fulfilled state quotas. This makes farmers become the residual claimants and stimulated farmers' initiative to increase their production.[4] Thus, China's comparative advantage in agriculture — abundant labour — could be fully exploited.

3. Justin Yifu Lin, "Rural Reforms and Agricultural Growth in China", *American Economic Review,* Vol. 82, No. 1 (March 1992), pp. 34–51.
4. The rural reform in China did not change rural land ownership. The household responsibility system can be regarded as a kind of leasing system. Under the household responsibility system, farmers can keep all residuals after fulfilling their quota obligations. Therefore, the system is quite similar to the fixed-rent leasing system. The household responsibility system can link an individual worker's effort and his/her reward much better than the work-point system in the production team and a share tenancy system. Therefore, the household responsibility system can effectively bring the farmers' initiative into full pay.

An important endeavour that further improved the household responsibility system was establishing and improving the dual-level operation system in agriculture. In the early stages, the collective level in the cooperative economy was largely unable to provide various services necessary to the household level. Thus, the dual-level system was nominal. Agriculture infrastructure, the supply of production factors, and the sale of agricultural products are all characterized by economies of scale. In order to benefit all farmers from these externalities and economies of scale, collective cooperation had to be promoted to serve the needs of rural households. Statistics show that in recent years the cooperative operation has gradually expanded in scope. It has helped promote farming technology and has improved crop variety and animal breeding. The construction of water conservancy works has developed much more quickly in recent years than in the early stage of the rural reform. Sales of staple agricultural products have also enjoyed a strong rising momentum. As a whole, there is still much to be done at the cooperative level, including expanding marketing services to reduce transaction costs and organizing farmers to participate in the construction of public utilities. For example, the constructions of irrigation projects through the system of compulsory labour services could be launched to allow farmers to benefit from external economies of scale.

Meanwhile, grassroots economic organizations are reformed. Under the People's Communes, grassroots organizations had been set up to serve the leap-forward strategy. Community organizations were needed to serve several functions. First, they helped control rural production resources so that such resources could not flow out of the agricultural sector and could be used in the production sectors required by the state. For example, community organizations had to ensure that rural labour forces would not be transferred out of the agricultural sector and to guarantee that the surplus and accumulation of rural production would be controlled by the state. Second, these organizations helped control the sale of agricultural products and levy agricultural taxes. Their most important function was to ensure that major agricultural and sideline products were sold at fixed prices to state commercial institutions, where the state could levy a hidden tax from the price scissors between the agricultural and the industrial products. Third, the organizations exerted control over almost all aspects of social, political, and economic life in rural communities. Family planning (population reproduction) is such an example.

The grassroots organizations set up to fulfill these functions were the product of the government's institutional arrangement rather than the choice of the community. This mandatory institutional arrangement ruled out any "exit" options. As long as their mandate to serve the state's industrialization strategy remained unchanged, these organizations would remain mandatory, and no exit would be permitted.

Almost simultaneously, and with the same enthusiasm with which they discarded the People's Communes, rural residents began looking for another kind of cooperative organization. If the People's Communes were a comprehensive community organization covering industrial, agricultural, military, educational and business functions, the organizations that rural residents sought should cover a wide range of fields as well. Such organizations as agricultural technology associations, farmers' economic associations, specialized technique associations (technical services and sales cooperatives associations), and rural cooperative funds drew attention from the media as well as from scholars and policy researchers. At the same time, there remained a tiny proportion of communities that maintained the form of collective farming. In the 1980s, rural industry became the leading force behind rural economic development; 60% to 70% of rural output value was produced by township and village enterprises (TVEs). Cooperative organizations were voluntary. Farmers could exit when government intervention or the high cost of free riding damaged work incentives. By solving the incentive problem, the cooperatives created economies of scale that rural residents recognized as desirable.

We can divide rural community organizations into two types — the voluntarily-formed cooperatives for pursuing certain benefits and the mandatory community organizations imposed by the government to effectively reduce taxation costs. The basic difference between the two lies in the compatibility of incentives between the organization and its members. In the former case, the farmers encounter economies of scale, or an external economy, in the community's economic activities, such as production, marketing, and credit. They may choose a mutually acceptable cooperative organization and may exit whenever necessary. This ensures that everyone can benefit. In the latter case, the state imposes an organization on rural residents, aiming to lower taxation costs. The main consideration in forming such an organization is the state's benefits rather than the farmers' benefits. Farmers cannot withdraw from these organizations. Once the right to exit is denied, free riding will occur, leading to the failure of the organization.

As discussed above, the People's Commune system came into being to serve industrialization by effecting a mandatory drain on rural surplus. Taxation was carried out through the control of basic rural production factors, the monopoly in the circulation of agricultural products, and especially the price scissors between industrial and agricultural products. Chinese economists have assessed the total value drained from agriculture through scissor pricing from the 1950s to 1980s. Because they used different definitions and data processing, their results differ. But most scholars agree that there was a net unilateral outflow of agricultural resources to other sectors. For example, in the mid-1980s a group of economists at the Development Research Institute estimated that rural workers contributed at least RMB 800 billion to industrialization by scissor pricing in the three decades. Li Wei asserted that from 1955 to 1985, the government drained a total of RMB 543 billion via the scissors gap. If we add the total amount from the three arenas — public taxes, price scissors, and the deposit net outflow — this figure reaches RMB 692.6 billion. Zhou Qiren made a similar estimate: The state gained RMB 612.7 billion through agricultural taxation, unfair exchange, and net deposit outflow from 1952 to 1982.[5]

China's former rural economic system had some incurable defects in respect to the incentive mechanism. The resultant production inefficiency became so serious a problem that the system could no longer provide the government with sufficient agricultural surplus. When farmers began to discard it in the late 1970s and early 1980s, the government acquiesced. However, capital accumulation through taxation, price distortion and through the financial drainage mechanism in the banking system was not discarded completely. As long as the state continued to rely on unfair exchanges in order to divert agriculture resources for industrialization, it would maintain control over community organizations to serve the goal. Neither the grassroots government organizations (governments at town or township levels) nor the farmers' autonomous organizations (village) could possibly evade the obligation. Farmers' attitude towards economic organizations presented itself as a unique phenomenon from abandoning to re-seeking. During different stages of development in agriculture and the national economy, the functions of rural community organizations may change. When it became unnecessary to rely purely on community organizations to levy taxes against farmers, they were able to gradually transform themselves so farmers could benefit from economies of scale and the external economy. Under these circumstances, the exit right is protected. Rural organizations will help to bolster the incentive to work. Therefore, the cooperative economy is no longer destined to fail again.

2. *State-owned Enterprise Reform*

The reform of China's SOEs took place at about the same time as the rural reform, and the former has gone through three phases. The first phase (1979–84) focused on granting SOEs a certain amount of autonomy in exchange for higher efficiency. Unlike the previous

5. Please refer to: Development Research Institute, *Reform Facing Institutional Challenges*. Shanghai: Shanghai Sanlian Bookstore, 1988; Li Wei, *Rural Surplus and Industrial Capital Accumulation*. Kunming City: Yuannan People's Press, 1993; Qiren Zhou, "China's Rural Reform: The Changes in the Country and the Relationship of Ownership — A Retrospect into the Vicissitudes of Economic Institutions", in Unirule Institute, ed., *China Economics, 1994*. Shanghai: Shanghai People's Press, 1995.

approach, this time the reform was mainly done through the sharing of management power and profit between government and SOEs. It was hoped that in pursuit of their share in the newly created profit, managers and workers would put in more effort in production and make a more efficient use of resources, so that in the end, both the social welfare and individual income would increase accordingly. In October 1978, pilot reform programmes delegating more powers to SOEs were applied to six SOEs in Sichuan Province. In May 1979, the State Economic Commission, the Ministry of Finance, and four other ministries decided to apply such pilot programmes to eight SOEs in Beijing, Tianjin, and Shanghai, the three municipalities under direct control of the central government. These pilot programmes evoked strong positive responses in workers in many SOEs. A large number of regions and departments followed suit and worked out their own pilot programmes.

The major measures taken in the experiments were aimed to expand the management autonomous power at the local and micro level and enhance their concern for economic efficiency. The measures included pay raises, bonuses, and retention of profits in enterprises so as to stimulate the work incentives of workers and managers, and the decentralization of fiscal authority and resource-allocation autonomy to the local government and concerned ministries so as to make them more concerned about the economic performance of enterprises. For many years, worker's income was linked only to seniority rather than performance. All SOE expenditures were reimbursed by the state. All profits were turned over to the state. The above-mentioned changes produced remarkable results. In the autumn of 1980, given the successes of the experiment, the central government introduced the reforms to more than 6,000 industrial SOEs, which accounted for 16% of all SOEs in number, 60% of all SOEs in terms of output value, and 70% of all SOEs in terms of economic returns for the whole country.

Profit retention indeed had a positive effect on incentive. However, because of the unchanged distorted macro-policy environment under which SOEs' losses or profits did not accurately reflect their management, power delegated to SOEs also made it possible for some managers to embezzle funds from SOEs' returns. Enhanced working incentive did not guarantee complete fulfilment of state financial quotas. To solve the problem, Shandong Province took the lead by changing the profit-retention system to a profit-quota system in the early 1980s. Under the profit-quota system, SOEs had to turn over some profits to the state, while all or part of what remained was at their own disposal or was divided between SOEs and the state. Soon the so-called "industrial economic responsibility system" was approved by the state, and it spread rapidly throughout the country. By the end of August 1981, 65% of SOEs at or above the county level in the country had adopted the industrial economic responsibility system. In the eastern provinces and municipalities, which bore much of the state revenues, as many as 80% of SOEs had adopted the system.

Although the reforms of the period had some positive effects, the success was limited because of the loopholes in the dual-track price system, the possibility of rent-seeking, and the lack of clearly defined boundary of SOEs' autonomy. Some SOEs even changed the goals set in the state plan, failed to fulfil the product and profit quota obligations, and competed with each other in giving bonuses to workers.

In phase two (1984–86) of the SOE reform, efforts focused on enhancing SOE vitality. The major measures put into place were to "simplify administrative control and decentralize authority", to reform taxation and introduce a manager-responsibility system. These reforms were to some extent a response to pressure exerted by emerging nonstate enterprises (i.e., township and village enterprises). Unlike SOEs, non-SOEs could not get cheap resources within the state plan. The only way they could survive and develop was to gain the upper hand in fierce market competition. However, the hard constraints turned out to be a blessing for non-SOEs. Because of the constraints, they achieved a higher degree of economic efficiency and could afford to buy resources at higher prices. Resources in short supply thus flowed to the non-state-owned sector. Competition for scarce resources became a strong impetus for the state to enact reforms that aimed to revitalize SOEs.

The second-round reform replaced profit remittance with corporate taxes, changed direct fiscal appropriation to indirect bank loans, and adopted the responsibility system and the shareholding system. All these measures were taken to deal with competitive pressure. Two reform measures were taken to invigorate the management of the SOEs. First, the government gradually reduced the SOE quota obligations. By 1990, the number of products under state mandatory plan had decreased to 58 (it was 120 in 1979). The proportion of these products in total industrial output value decreased from 40% to 16%. Important materials and merchandise allocated by the State Planning Commission fell in number from 256 and 65 to 19 and 20, respectively; exclusive state exports decreased in number from 900 to 27, and their proportion in the total value of export fell to around 20%.

In addition, a series of administrative regulations were promulgated to expand SOEs' decision-making power. Such power included the ability to control sales and marketing, set prices, select factors of production, use corporate funds, distribute salaries and bonuses, cooperatively manage ventures, and direct technical progress. In September 1985, the State Planning Commission made this policy more explicit in *Temporary Regulations on the Many Problems of Invigorating the Large and Medium-sized SOEs*. With the prerequisite of fulfilling the state quotas, the document stated that SOEs could diversify their products and operations based on market demand and their own advantages. These reform measures were in effect encouraging SOEs to make full use of their comparative advantages.

In order to smooth the relationship between enterprises and the government, in the mid-1980s, China began to replace the profit remittance system with the corporate tax system. This reform was carried out in two steps. Its main objectives were to delineate the boundary between the government fiscal income and the disposable revenue of an enterprise, and to establish a mechanism by which the government fiscal income was linked to tax revenue and enterprise's income was linked to its profits. As the first step, profit remittance was replaced by taxes beginning on 1 January 1983, and the collection of taxes began on 1 June of the same year. More specifically, 55% of corporate income tax was levied on all SOEs, except for small ones that had adopted the contract responsibility system. In essence, the new system changed the original remitted profit (which was 55% of its total profit) into corporate taxes. The after-tax profit was to be divided between the state and enterprises. The state's share varied according to each enterprise's specific situation. The possibilities included: submitting an increasing amount of profit each year, submitting a fixed proportion of profit, submitting a fixed amount of profit, and paying an adjustment tax. The rule for each enterprise would remain unchanged for three years once it was determined.

The first step of the "profit to tax" reform was designed primarily to end the traditional practice of obscuring taxes with profits. To tackle the remaining problems, a second step was taken in September 1984, when a uniform tax-levying system was introduced. The new system made improvement to the income taxes and adjustment taxes which were introduced during the first step. It also introduced more taxes, such as those for fund-raising, city maintenance and construction, real estate, land use, and vehicle ownership, as well as the product tax, value-added tax, sales tax, and salt tax. The new system was effected on 1 June 1985. The second step produced satisfactory results at the beginning. However, with the economic accounting and auditing system yet to be strengthened, SOEs could increase their income and reduce the tax burden through various flexible methods, for example, by dispatching labour forces to build flats for workers while the material expenses were added to production costs. It followed that government tax revenue did not increase and the SOEs that were reluctant to use these flexible means bore an excessive tax burden. The government had to roll out the tax contract system for SOEs.

There was no need to separate profit and taxes as long as the old economic system was in place. Under the old system, the state exercised direct control over SOE activities, and price did not signal resource allocation. However, in an economic environment in which price fluctuation guides resource allocation, taxes and profit must be separated. Separating the two is thus inherent to market-oriented reform. The major purpose of market-oriented reform is to create an environment in which competition is fair. The two-step reforms failed to put into place a tax system capable of establishing a proper relationship between the central government and local governments and between the government and SOEs. Indeed, what worked in reality was the tax-responsibility system. Nevertheless, tax system reform could not have been skipped. The first two steps were a positive beginning, and they led to a system that included 20 types of taxes. This helped to pave the way for the later implementation of the tax-sharing system.

In 1988, the government launched another pilot reform programme of SOEs. The programme was called "separating taxes from profit, paying taxes before repaying bank loans and contracting for after-tax profits." The new pilot programme included the following mandates: (1) Relieved the tax burden. The adjustment tax was cancelled, and income tax rates were reduced in all SOEs. (2) For after-tax profit, set up a profit turnover base or fees for using state property. According to Shanghai's practice, the use fees of liquid assets and fixed assets were the interest rates of corresponding loans, respectively. (3) Changed the policy of paying taxes after repaying loans to one of paying tax before repaying loans, and cancelled the stipulation that SOEs drew welfare funds and bonus funds according to loan repayment.

In 1987, the SOE reform entered its third phase. In this phase, the reform focused on the reconstruction of the SOE management mechanism. The basic measure through the reform was the implementation of management-responsibility system, including the contract system in the large- and medium-sized SOEs, leasing in small SOEs, and experiments on the shareholding system. The dominant form before 1991 was the contract system. According to primary statistics from 28 provinces, municipalities, autonomous regions, and the seven fiscal-planning-independent cities (cities which were granted the same status as provinces in the central government's fiscal plan) throughout China, by the second quarter of 1987, 33,312 SOEs, whose revenues were included in the government's budgets, adopted the asset contract responsibility system. The number made up 90% of the total number of enterprises in that category.[6] Since 1992, the dominant view has been that SOEs' non-competitiveness was caused by ambiguities in property rights and that the shareholding system was the best cure for the problem. Indeed, the shareholding system has become widespread. However, in reality, the system was used mainly by large SOEs as a means of raising funds. At least so far, the shareholding system has not proven successful in transforming the SOE management mechanism. Only about 1200 large SOEs have been allowed to issue shares for trading on stock markets by 2000. However, the listed SOEs' corporate governance and efficiency have not shown much improvement.

The major remaining problem was the absence of competitive markets for products, production factors, and managerial personnel. While the first two factors raised information costs for managerial supervision, the third made it hard to reward managerial talents or punish managerial ineptitude. Without autonomy, managers lack the incentive to perform well; if SOEs are granted autonomy, the infringement of managerial rights upon propriety rights occurs. All in all, the development of competitive product, factor, and managerial personnel markets constitutes the basic condition necessary for the shareholding system to work. If these markets are not developed, the scale and effectiveness of the shareholding system will be very limited. Given the under-development of the three markets, the obscurity of property rights will be more serious and the shareholding system will only bring about more managerial discretion, to say nothing of eliminating infringement of managerial power upon property rights. The shareholding system is no better than the contract system in this regard. It will only aggravate the situation. Therefore, to the SOEs with a leap-forward strategic mission, the solution was more complicated than introducing a shareholding system.

6. State Commission for the Restructuring of the Economic System, ed., *China's Economic Restructuring Yearbook, 1992*. Beijing: Reform Press, 1992, p. 167.

The reform of SOEs was mainly a reform of those that manufactured non-public goods. It focused on fulfilling three functions: improving the competitiveness of asset management, increasing the liquidity of assets, and enhancing the state's supervision of asset management. In chronological order it was implemented in the following sequence: "adjusting the interest relationship between the state and SOEs", "giving SOEs more decision-making power", and "establishing an enterprise system under a market economy". Just as the reform goals gradually developed as the reform proceeded, so did the goals of the SOE reform. The reform was first designed to solve the problem of inefficiency in SOEs. However, as the reform deepened, the goal was adjusted to transforming the SOE managerial mechanisms and pushing SOEs into the market.

It can be observed that, as the reform continued, the degree of SOEs' involvement in the market and their capacity to optimize resource allocation was gradually enhanced. However, so far, SOE reform has not taken a crucial step, and management is still in a dire state. Thirty-five percent of the domestic industrial SOEs within the state budget are losing a total of RMB 48.259 billion yuan in 1994.[7] The figure reflects only explicit losses. A much-quoted view is that one-third of the country's SOEs incur explicit losses, one-third incur implicit losses, and only the remaining one-third are making a profit. The year 1997 even saw that in certain industries all the SOEs were losing money. All these show that the Chinese reform of SOEs is far from complete.

5.3 Reform of the Planned Resource-allocation System

SOEs began to reap the benefits of their own profits and to produce their own products under the reform of the micro-management institution. To use the retained profits for investment, it is necessary to find more channels through which they could purchase equipments

7. National Bureau of Statistics of China, *China Statistical Yearbook, 1995*. Beijing: China Statistics Press, 1995, p. 403; Xie Ping, "Analysis of China's Financial Capital Structure", *Economics Research*, No. 11 (1992), p. 34.

and inputs. To maximize returns from sales of new products, it is necessary to find more channels through which they could sell the products, outside the state's plan. All these changes exerted a strong impact on the highly centralized planned resource-allocation system. To create the necessary conditions for the SOE reform, the state carried out a series of reforms in the management of materials, foreign trade, and finance. The reform of material management has been the most thorough and successful, while financial reform has proceeded most slowly.

We first discuss the reform of the materials management system. After 1978, the materials management reform was implemented with the aim to "revitalize SOEs, promote material circulation, and foster market development". It has gone through two stages. The first phase (1979–84) of reform emphasized the relaxation of state control over resource allocation in order to realize SOEs decision-making power and disposal power over their retained profit.

The major measures implemented in this period included the following: (1) The expansion of enterprises' right to sell their products. After they fulfilled the state plan and the supply contract, with the exception of special stipulations, SOEs could sell products through their own channels. Products they could sell included those made with their own materials, newly developed, trial products, and products beyond the state plan. By 1984, steel that SOEs could sell on the market accounted for 9.6% of total output, and cement produced by large and medium-sized cement SOEs that they could sell accounted for 8.8% of total output. The proportions for mechanical and electrical products were even higher. (2) Lifting restrictions on the sales of some planned allocation materials. Since 1980, among the 77 types of mechanical and electrical products and 83 nonferrous metals, only 7 were still allocated according to state plan; restrictions on all others had been lifted. (3) Adopting flexible supply methods. These mainly included supply according to fixed locations and quantity, supply according to needs after verification, supply based on a complete set of contracts, and supply according to coupons. (4) Setting up markets for production factors. During this period, related departments established many production factor markets in Sichuan, Shanghai, and elsewhere. Because transaction activities could be carried out regardless of administrative regions, department, and enterprise ownership, consumers could choose what they wanted. These measures greatly improved resource circulation. (5) Using cities as props to rationally organize material circulation in different economic zones and to develop a network to reduce transaction costs.

The emphasis of the second phase of reform (1985–present) was on the reduction of the variety, quantity, and scope of planned allocation materials and the establishment of production factor markets of various forms and different scales. Four main measures have been implemented during this period. First, since 1985, except for production in some key construction programmes, planned allocations have remained at 1984 levels to meet general needs. The number of materials under the unified state distribution system decreased from 256 in 1980 to 27 in 1988. The number of materials allocated under the mandatory plans of corresponding departments in the State Council decreased from 316 to 45. The number of material under state contract have decreased to 93, and the number of materials linking production and demand have decreased to 209. The number of materials that can be bought and sold freely increased to 149. Second, in order to raise the price of production factors, beginning in 1984, the state has been raising the prices of coal, timber, pig iron, steel, cement, caustic soda, sulfuric acid, and tires by means of making proper adjustments within the state plan and gradually liberalizing prices outside the plan. Third, the state has further explored the possibility of adopting indicative plan in material circulation. Fourth, the development of the market was fostered. In 1985, given the lifting of restrictions over material prices outside the plan, the city of Shijiazhuang unified the sales price of plan and non-plan materials and gave the price difference to suppliers or buyers, thus combining price liberalization with necessary subsidies in order to expand the market. By 1988, about 90 large and medium-sized cities had followed suit. Price liberalization also expanded to 16 products, including timber, cement, and pig iron. Steel that was originally within the state plan but later turned to market pricing accounted for 60% of the total. In 1990, the types of state-allocated production factors decreased to 19. In 1992, with the number of types unchanged, the proportion of unified distribution decreased substantially. In 1994, the number was 11. By 1997, the State Planning Commission was exercising allocation plans over only crude oil, processed oil, natural gas, less than 40% of coal, and less than 3% of cars. To promote market development, in 1998 the mandatory allocation plans for steel and cement was changed into plans to match supplies with demand.

It is also important to discuss the reform in foreign-trade regime. The reform can be divided into three phases. The first phase (late 1978–86) had five goals: (1) To expand the foreign trade power of SOEs and the regional and sectoral authorities. The government introduced a foreign-trade responsibility system and delegated supervisory and approval authority over trading companies to provinces, municipalities, and autonomous regions. (2) To reform the planned foreign-trade regime by gradually reducing the number and scope of goods in the mandatory plan, increasing the variety and widening the scope of goods in the indicative plan, and drastically reducing the variety and scale of exports and imports under direct central government control. Since 1985, the responsible departments under the central government have not drawn up or assigned any mandatory plans for the procurement and allotment of exports. (3) To adjust the foreign trade financial system. The finances of industrial and state trading companies and companies under responsible departments were linked to the central government budget. SOEs with foreign trade operation rights can be made financially independent. As for the locally-arranged foreign trade, in principle, the local government should take sole responsibility for economic performance. (4) To reform the foreign trade operations. The formerly state-monopolized foreign trade enterprises were diversified and a single-commodity based operation system was changed to a manufacture-cum-trade or technology-cum-trade operation system. At the same time, foreign trade enterprises were allowed to conduct the import-export business independently, and the agency system were introduced into the trade for several commodities. (5) To encourage regions, SOEs, and departments to become actively involved in foreign trade. To this end, a foreign exchange retention system was carried out in 1979. Although foreign exchange was under centralized management, and the central government gave priority to some key projects, some proportion of foreign exchange retention was left to foreign-exchange-earning units. The foreign-exchange-earning units had some decision-making power over the use of the retained foreign exchange. They could also participate in the swap of foreign exchange so that foreign exchange entitlement could go to other enterprises that needed it.

The second phase (1987–90) of reform focused on promoting the foreign-trade responsibility system. After a pilot programme was carried out in 1987, this reform was formally launched in 1988. Its main points included the following: (1) Adopting a state-region contract system regarding the regions' responsibility for foreign exchange quotas through exports, foreign exchange turnover quotas, and profit quotas. The base quota should remain valid for three years, from 1988 through 1990. Regions should in turn carry through these quotas to local trading companies. Most of the foreign exchange earnings within the quota would be turned over to the state, a small part would be left to local governments and foreign trade enterprises. As for the foreign exchange exceeding the quota, local governments and foreign trade enterprises would receive most of it. (2) Making the state trading companies responsible for their performance. This policy was first implemented for light industries, handicrafts, and garment industries. The major measures taken were to leave most earned foreign exchange to state trading companies, manufacturing SOEs, and local governments. Only a small part of the foreign exchange earned was turned over to the state. (3) Further the reform of the foreign-trade planning regime. Except for the 21 types of export goods of unified and joint management that remained under the dual-track export plans, all export goods were switched to a single-export plan, with local governments directly responsible to the state. (4) Further the reform of the foreign-trade financial regime. State trading companies should contract the profit quota with the state. Export tax concessions should be implemented according to international practice. Branches of specialized local trading companies would be financially linked to local government budgets and de-linked from the central budget. (5) Further the reform of the foreign-trade operational system so as to delineate the division of management and trade activities. Only a few staple-type resource products were handled by specific foreign trade enterprises. A few other products, which were more sensitive in the international market, were handled in a decentralized manner by enterprises with the right to export. All the other products were open for competition. (6) Increasing local governments' proportion of foreign exchange retention, cancelling the foreign exchange quota, opening the foreign exchange swap markets, and allowing trading and manufacturing companies to dispose freely of their retained foreign exchange.

During the third phase (1991–present) of the reform, a management and operation mechanism of uniform policy, fair competition, and autonomous management was established, manufacturing and trade were integrated, an agency system was introduced, and a united position on trade issues was established. The government took concrete measures to end foreign trade enterprises' long-time reliance on subsidies and to push them into international markets. First, export subsidies were severed, while the proportion of foreign exchange retention was increased, so as to harden their budget constraints. Second, the practice of giving different regions different foreign exchange retention ratios was changed to the practice of establishing a uniform retention ratio nationwide for each category of commodities. The change gave the enterprises exporting the same category of commodities an equal basis for competition. Third, the central government contracted with each province, autonomous region, fiscal-plan-independent city, and specialized foreign trade company as well as other foreign trade enterprise. The contracts specified export quotas, foreign exchange earning quotas, and foreign exchange turnovers (including foreign exchange purchases) to the central government. The quotas were to be examined and approved annually. Fourth, the coordination and management function of specialized companies and the import-export associations were strengthened. Fifth, the responsibility system in foreign trade companies was further refined. Sixth, the foreign exchange swap market was further liberalized. No ministry or bureau was allowed to use administrative measures to interfere with the circulation of foreign exchange.

The foreign-trade regime reform was originally intended to encourage export and earn foreign exchange for the import of advanced technological equipment. All the above-mentioned measures, including the reduction on the scope of mandatory plans on foreign trade, the expansion of local government's autonomy in foreign trade, and the introduction of the foreign exchange retention system, were intended to serve this purpose. In the process, the reform also greatly boosted the development and expansion of foreign trade sectors. China's total imports and exports increased in value from US$20.64 billion in 1978 to US$474.3 billion in 2000, with a growth rate about 5 percentage points higher than that of the GNP. Calculated in terms of RMB, the total value of imports and exports accounted for 44.5% of the GNP in 2000, more than twice that of India, Brazil, the United States, and Japan. This made China the most open economy of all the large countries in the world.

We also need to explore the financial reform in China. Capital, labour, and natural resources are indispensable for effective production. For a developing country like China, capital is the scarcest of the three factors, and has constantly been the bottleneck for economic development. Its allocation efficiency thus has the most significant impact on economic growth. Two decades of consecutive economic growth has led to the continuous deepening of financial reform, and the increase in the importance of financial sectors. Statistics shows that in 2000, the household savings deposits reached RMB 6,433.2 billion, 304.2 times more than the 1978 amount. The total amount of credit loans reached RMB 9,937.1 billion, 52.4 times more than the 1978 amount. Economic growth's dependence on finance[8] was 52.1% in 1979, and about 100% in 2000. It is clear that financial organizations have changed from being government

8. The dependence rate of economic growth on finance equals to the GNP divided by the surplus of credit loans of the banks,

accounting units to a key sector that dominates economic operations. The reform of the banking system proceeds in the following respects:

(1) The single banking system was reformed, and a more diversified financial system was roughly established, in which specialized banks was the mainstay under the direction of the central bank and other financial institutions were allowed. Before the Third Session of the 11th Central Committee of the Communist Party of China, China's banking system had been unified and consolidated. The People's Bank of China was the only bank.[9] It issued currency and conducted business via commercial loans and insurance. The first step of the banking reform was thus to establish a banking system. In 1979, the government re-opened the Agricultural Bank of China. The Bank of China was also set up as a specialized bank to conduct foreign exchange business and foreign exchange loans. In 1984, the Industrial and Commercial Bank of China and the China People's Insurance Company were set up separately. The former was put in charge of deposits, loans, and account settlement of industrial and commercial enterprises, and the saving services in cities and towns. The latter was independent in its operation and had its own operation system. In November 1985, the People's Construction Bank of China was made independent of the Ministry of Finance. All

9. Nominally, there were the People's Construction Bank of China, the Bank of China, and the Agricultural Bank of China. The People's Construction Bank of China was set up in 1954. Under the administration of the Ministry of Finance, its major order of business was to conduct relevant infrastructure construction funds allocation and settlement. In 1970, it was put under the administration of the People's Bank of China. In 1972, it broke away from the People's Bank of China and was again put under the adminsitration of the Ministry of Finance. The Bank of China was domestically known as the administrative bureau of foreign business of the People's Bank of China. The Agricultural Bank of China was domestically known only as the rural financial administrative bureau. It later merged with the People's Bank of China twice and conducted business independently for only four years. From 1969 to 1978, the name of the Head Office of the People's Bank of China was reserved; however, all its staff and business were merged into the Ministry of Finance, and its branches were merged into corresponding financial bureaus at different levels of government.

its capital was merged into the comprehensive credit plan of the People's Bank of China and its operations also came under the leadership and supervision of the People's Bank of China. After legal tender issuance, industrial and commercial credit services, and savings services were clearly separated, the People's Bank of China became the central bank.

From 1986 onwards, the market mechanism was introduced into the financial system on an experimental basis. A horizontal capital-flow network using key cities as props evolved into interbank loan markets. Market mechanism was used to ease capital shortages. After several years, a banking system under the leadership of the People's Bank emerged, complementing the specialized banks and comprehensive banks with insurance and trust funds. Securities organizations and rural and urban cooperatives were also gradually instated.

(2) The credit management system was reformed. Under the old system, all deposits were submitted to the state, all loans were approved by the state, and all profits were remitted to the state. The income of bank employees was not related to deposits, loans, or profit the bank handled or made. Neither was there any competition pressure among different banks or different branches within the same bank. In the reform, this system was replaced by one in which credit planning was unified by the state, funds were independent between banks, issuance of loans in a bank depended on the bank's deposits, and inter-bank loans were permitted. For the management of credit funds, the former policy was changed to one in which the government only controlled the difference between planned credit, and the bank's actual credit depended on its actual deposit. The system thus allowed vertical supervision and horizontal competition to exist. On this basis, banks were allowed to take part in different lines of business. The strict business division between specialized banks was abolished. The Industrial and Commercial Bank of China could extend its business to rural areas, the Agricultural Bank could extend its business to urban areas, the Bank of China could do domestic business, and the Construction Bank could be involved in non-construction business. Banks no longer specialized in and

monopolized certain businesses. The reform led to a new two-way selection mechanism in which banks chose enterprises and enterprises chose banks.[10]

(3) The interest rate management system was reformed. The reform adjusted the interest level of deposits and loans, the categories of interest rates, and the management authority on the interest rate. The policy of differential interest rates, floating interest rates, prime rates and penalty rates was introduced to enterprise loans. These measures transformed the interest rate into a powerful device that could more effectively adjust the capital supply and demand, and direct the rational flow of capital. Moreover, these measures helped to foster a kind of financial mechanism that could attract more savings and convert them more effectively to investment. In April 1993, China gave up its particular way of calculating the interest of time deposits and adopted the standard practice in the world. This suggests that through its financial reform, China was attempting to approach standard world practices.[11]

(4) The credit system was reformed. The government partially liberalized its controls over state, commercial, and consumer credits, gave up the policy that all credit be centralized in the banks. This reform provided opportunities for the development of nonbank

10. The banks' business specializations were as follows: The Industrial and Commercial Bank mainly did business within industrial and commercial circles, and the Agricultural Bank usually conducted business in rural areas. The Bank of China mainly conducted foreign business, and the Construction Bank dealt with infrastructure construction.

11. China used to calculate the interest rate of the term deposit in the following way: When a depositor wanted to withdraw money, if the date exceeded the deposit certificate date, the days exceeded should be calculated according to the due term deposit rate. If the depositor wanted to withdraw the money before the maturing date, interest should be calculated according to the rate of the nearest term deposit. For example, let us suppose that a depositor has opened a two-year term deposit account. If he withdrew the money two and a half years later, the interest of the exceeded six months should be calculated according to the two-year term rate. If he wanted to withdraw it one and a half years later, if the nearest term deposit rate was a one-year rate, then the interest should be calculated according to the one-year interest rate.

financial institutions and for the adoption of various financial instruments. For example, the credit system reform led to the significant development of trust and investment companies, insurance companies, leasing companies, securities companies, securities exchanges, and nonbanking institutions such as rural and urban credit cooperatives. The reform also leads to the increasing roles of government and corporate bonds and stocks in the economy. Some traditional business, such as term bills, promissory notes, and bills of exchanges also gradually developed.

(5) Financial markets were fostered. The increase of financial institutions and the adoption of various financial instruments accelerated the development of financial markets. To date, the interbank lending market, the deposit certificate market, government bonds, the security bond market, the corporate bond market, and the stock market play an increasingly important role in the country's financial system.[12]

Here, we look more closely at the development of the securities market. After the founding of the People's Republic of China, the government issued the People's Victory Index Bonds and National Economic Construction Bonds a few times to stabilize prices and expedite economic construction. These bonds were non-circulating and were paid off by early 1968. After the Third Plenary Session of the 11th Central Committee of the Communist Party of China, the state launched a series of large-scale construction, which resulted in a budget deficit. The deficit in 1979 and 1980 was RMB 13.5 billion

12. Since 1987, in addition to treasury bonds, the Ministry of Finance also issued a series of other bonds, such as the State Key Project Construction Bond, State Construction Bond, the Infrastructure Construction Bond, the Inflation-indexed Public Bond, and special national bonds. As the scale of the bonds expanded, in 1985, the four state banks were also allowed to issue bonds, and other banks, such as the Bank of Communications and, some trust and investment companies were given the same right later. In additon, some SOEs were allowed to issue corporate bonds and stocks. These developments and the expansion of business demanded that the financial market be established quickly. At the same time, they also indirectly created conditions for its development.

and RMB 6.9 billion, respectively. To overcome financial difficulties and raise funds for construction, in 1981 the Ministry of Finance reissued treasury bonds to make up for its deficit after its borrowing and overdrafting from the central bank. From 1994 onwards, the state has not been allowed to borrow or overdraft from the central bank, and it has to make up the deficit by bond issuance. The scale of treasury bonds issuance has thus been loomingly large. By late 1997, the total amount of domestic government bonds reached RMB 910 billion. Corporate bonds reached RMB 260 billion. The proportion of treasury bonds in financial expenditures for the same fiscal year increased from 4.3% in 1981 to 26.7% in 1997 (see Table 5.2).

Table 5.2. The Scale of Government Bonds and Its Proportion in Government Expenditures

Year	Expenditures		
	Public debt volume (RMB 100 million)	Fiscal expenditures (RMB 100 million)	Proportion in fiscal expenditures (%)
1981	48.7	1138.41	4.3
1982	43.8	1229.98	3.6
1983	41.6	1409.52	3.0
1984	42.5	1701.02	2.5
1985	60.6	2004.25	3.0
1986	62.5	2204.91	2.8
1987	63.1	2262.18	2.8
1988	63.1	2491.21	2.5
1989	132.2	2823.78	4.7
1990	138.9	3083.59	4.5
1991	197.2	3386.62	5.8
1992	281.3	3742.20	7.5
1993	460.8	4642.30	9.9
1994	381.3	5792.62	6.6
1995	1028.6	6823.72	15.1
1996	1847.8	7937.55	23.3
1997	2467.8	9233.56	26.7

Source: National Bureau of Statistics of China, *20 Years of Magnificent Achievement*. Beijing: China Statistics Press, 1998, pp. 320, 367.

In addition, it is also important to look more closely at the development of the stock market. Small collective enterprises were the origins of the shareholding system. In order to ease capital shortages, they adopted methods of voluntary share purchasing by managers and workers or selling shares in public and transforming themselves into shareholding enterprises. In August 1980, the Fushun City Bank in Liaoning Province, a subsidiary of the People's Bank of China, issued RMB 2.11 million stocks for an enterprise. This was regarded as the banking system's first involvement in stock transactions. In September 1984, Tianqiao Department Store Joint Stock Company Ltd. was set up in Beijing, marking the first instance in which an SOE had turned into a shareholding company. Afterwards, pilot programmes of the stock system were carried out in Shanghai, Guangzhou, and Shenyang.

As stock companies developed and the number of stocks increased, it became necessary to establish secondary markets for stock transfer. The circulation of stocks was put on the agenda. In January 1986, in cities where pilot programmes had been carried out, such as Shengyang, Wuhan, Guangzhou, Chongqing, and Changzhou, the government allowed the financial institutions to conduct business on stock issuance and transfer. In August 1986, the Shenyang Trust and Investment Company started to handle over-the-counter transactions. In September of that year, the Shanghai Industrial and Commercial Bank in the Jing'an District set up security transaction counters — the Jing'an Securities Operation Department, the first of its kind in the country. It also created the Shanghai stock exchange market, where Feile stock and Yanzhong stock were listed.

In 1988, stocks of the Shenzhen Development Bank were formally listed in the Shenzhen Security Company, which marked the beginning of the Shenzhen stock exchange. Although the Shenzhen stock exchange started late, the transaction volume increased enormously. In 1990, the annual transaction volume reached RMB 1,765 million, 30 times more than Shanghai's 49.63 million. China's stock exchange market embarked on a rule-based stage, marked by the establishment of the Shanghai Stock Exchange

Table 5.3 Development of the Stock Market in Mainland China since the 1990s

Year	Number of listed company	Annual transaction volume (RMB 100 million)	Market value (RMB 100 million)
1991	14	43	109
1992	53	681	1048
1993	183	3667	3541
1994	291	8127	3691
1995	323	4396	3474
1996	530	21331	9842
1997	745	30720	17529

Source: National Bureau of Statistics of China, *20 Years of Magnificent Achievement*. Beijing: China Statistics Press, 1998, p. 330.

on 26 November 1990, and the Shenzhen Stock Exchange on 3 July 1991. By late April 1998, 784 companies were listed. The total market value of domestic stocks was more than RMB 2,000 billion yuan (see Table 5.3). At the same time, investment fund markets were beginning to take hold.

China's financial reform centred on three tasks: (1) to establish and improve a financial system under the leadership of the central bank in which banking finance and non-banking finance could co-exist, with specialized banks as the mainstay; (2) to promote the transformation of specialized banks into commercial banks and to develop financial markets; and (3) to establish and improve the macro-financial regulatory framework. At present, the first task of reforms is almost complete. However, much work remains to be done regarding the second and the third tasks. The major problem is that the return of financial assets are still not linked to their risks. For example, national bonds issued by the government as primary bonds usually bear little risk. Usually, their rate would be lower than the bank interest rate. However, unlike rates in other market economies, their rates in China have always been 1% to 2% higher than the deposit rate. In fact, some high-risk financial assets have not enjoyed a higher rate than have national bonds. The reason for this is that under the present system, the risks of various financial assets are still not quite transparent. The interest rate thus becomes the financial institutions' sole means in attracting financial resources. In 1993, the government proposed a banking system reform that attempted to separate commercial banks from policy banks, establish a vertical management mechanism under the People's Bank and put an end to local government interventions. This reform is still in progress.

If we examine the budgetary appropriation and finance jointly, we find that as financial reform grew further reaching, the role of finance in investment became increasingly important, whereas the role of budgetary appropriation shrunk. Statistics show that, from 1981 to 1997, the amount of budgetary investment on fixed asset increased from RMB 26.98 billion to RMB 69.67 billion, or an increase of 158.3%. The fixed asset investment financed by bank loans increased from RMB 8.34 billion to RMB 1,546.87 billion,[13] or an increase of 184.5 times.[14] As for the total investments in fixed assets by both the public finance and bank loans, the former decreased from 76.4% in 1981 to 4.3% in 1997, while the latter increased from 23.6% to 95.7%. This change clearly shows that the enterprises' dependence on the budgetary appropriation for fixed asset investment decreased, while their dependence on banks increased. This trend reflects the market economy-oriented feature of China's reform. Because banks are more concerned with efficiency than the government, this change will induce enterprises to exploit the comparative advantage of the economy in their investment decisions.

---

13. According to the balance sheet of monetary institutions in: National Bureau of Statistics of China, *China Statistics Yearbook, 1998*, long-term and mid-term loans had substituted loans in the form of fixed assets.
14. National Bureau of Statistics of China, *The Statistical Data of Fixed Asset Investment in China, 1950–1985*. Beijing: China Statistics Press, 1987, p. 8; National Bureau of Statistics of China, *China Statistical Yearbook, 1987*. Beijing: China Statistics Press, 1987, p. 639; National Bureau of Statistics of China, *China Statistical Yearbook, 1998*. Beijing: China Statistics Press, 1998, pp. 187, 668.

5.4 The Reform of the Macro-policy Environment

Reforming the micro-management institution and the resource-allocation mechanism while maintaining the traditional macro-policy environment improved the external environment for profit-seeking enterprises. However, it also caused complications, such as unfair competition and rent-seeking due to the dual-track price system. To solve these problems, the reform expanded to the macro-policy environment. In a broad sense, the reform is a price reform, covering the prices of inputs (i.e., raw materials, materials, intermediate inputs, fuels) and outputs (i.e., finished products and services), interest rates (i.e., the prices of capital), exchange rates (i.e., the price of foreign exchange) and wages (i.e., the price of labour). Among these, input and output price reform, interest rate reform, and exchange rate reform are the most important.

Price Policy Reform

China's price reform initially adopted a dual-track price system. Some scholars posited that a dual-track system could not succeed, since market forces could not break the bounds set by the powerful planned economy at the time. However, over the past 22 years, the role of market prices in resource allocation has been enhanced, while the role of planned prices has diminished.

The price reform targeted at consumer goods, intermediate inputs, and production factors. So far, it has gone through two stages. During the first stage, from 1978 to 1984, while relative price was adjusted, the reform did not involve the creation of a market pricing mechanism. In other words, the government raised the price of goods in shortage and reduce the price of goods in surplus, thus narrowed the differences between planned prices and market equilibrium prices.

From 1985 onward, the price reform entered its second period with the introduction of market mechanism into price formation. One major measure implemented during this period was the dual-track price system, under which prices of goods or products within the state plan were set by the government, while prices of goods or products outside the state plan were determined by the market. The dual-track price system was achieved gradually. With the rapid expansion of production and circulation outside the planned system and the increasing importance of the non-state economy, the weight of the market-price track increased while that of the planned-price track decreased. By 1996, 93% of all retail goods, 79% of all agricultural products, and 81% of the total sales volume of production factors were priced solely by the market (see Table 5.4).

Table 5.4 Changes in Price Controls (%)

	Price forms	1990	1992	1994	1996
Total volume of retailing merchandise	Government fixed price	29.8	5.9	7.2	6.3
	Government guidance price	17.2	1.1	2.4	1.2
	Market regulatory price	53.0	93.0	90.4	92.5
Total purchase volume of agricultural products	Government fixed price	25.0	12.5	16.6	16.9
	Government guidance price	23.4	5.7	4.1	4.1
	Market regulatory price	51.6	81.8	79.3	79.0
Total sales volume of the means of production	Government fixed price	44.6	18.7	14.7	14.0
	Government guidance price	19.0	7.5	5.3	4.9
	Market regulatory price	36.4	73.8	80.0	81.1

Source: State Planning Commission, Price Administration Bureau; "The Weights and Changes of Three Patterns of Prices", *Price in China*, No. 12 (1997).

In industry, the proportion of goods determined by mandatory prices decreased in total output value from 70% in 1979 to 5% in 2000. Market pricing is now the key force exerting pressure on enterprises to change their operational mechanisms.

Exchange Rate Policy Reform

Under the old policy, the foreign exchange revenues and expenditures of trade and non-trade were settled according to a single official rate. Under the leap-forward strategy, the exchange rate was distorted, which suppressed China's foreign exchange earning capacity. To increase foreign exchange revenue, the government carried out a series of reforms on the exchange rate. In August 1979, the State Council issued a regulation that provided guidelines on how to develop foreign trade and increase foreign exchange revenue. The regulation was significant because it allowed the foreign-trade sector to enjoy the "internal settlement exchange rate" after 1981. Although the department responsible explained the internal settlement rate as a price that balanced internally the imports and exports, it is actually a kind of exchange rate. Thus, two exchange rates came into being. Of the two, the externally announced official rate was linked with price fluctuations of consumer goods at home and abroad. It is used in settlements of remittances from overseas Chinese and in converting currencies for non-trade activities, like those from tourism, foreign embassies in China, foreign organizations in China, Chinese institutions abroad, and Chinese officials sent abroad. The internal settlement exchange rate was linked with the average cost of earning foreign exchange inside China plus an appropriate markup for profit.[15] It was used in the settlement of trade balance. The internal rate was kept constant, while the official rate was adjusted several times, which narrowed the gap between the two. In 1985 the internal settlement exchange rate was abolished. Meanwhile, changes in the national average cost of earning foreign exchange became the basis for adjusting the official rate. All the adjustments to the exchange rate after 1985 were closely linked to the average cost to earn foreign exchange in China.

Prior to the adoption of the internal settlement rate in 1979, in order to stimulate trading companies' initiative to earn foreign exchange, a foreign exchange retention system was adopted. The result was that some trading companies retained more foreign exchange than they could use, while others retained less than they wanted. As a sub-system of the retention system, a swap system was introduced to adjust the unbalanced foreign exchange surplus among

15. The internal settlement exchange rate in 1981 was 1:2.8 (which equals the average cost of RMB 2.53 for one U.S. dollar in 1978 plus a 10% profit).

different trading companies. In October 1980, the Bank of China provided the swap business in its branches in 12 cities, including Beijing, Shanghai, Tianjin, Guangzhou, Qingdao, and Dalian and so on. However, the scope and exchange rate were strictly restricted, which made it in effect a non-market transaction. In 1988, to promote a comprehensive foreign-trade-contract-responsibility system, the State Council decided to set up the foreign exchange swap market, and it enacted several decisions pertaining to the foreign-exchange-retention regulation. The State Council clearly stipulated the adoption of a managed floating rate in the swap market, and the exchange rate should be determined by demand and supply. It also delineated regulations on the sources and uses of foreign exchange that could engage in the swap market, the procedures for application, registration, transaction, and transfer of foreign exchange, and the responsibilities of the authorities in charge of the foreign exchange swap markets.

The exchange rate on the swap market could more accurately reflect the real price of RMB relative to foreign currencies. As the economic reform grew further reaching, it played an increasingly important role in international trade. On 1 January 1994, as an effort to expedite the development of the market system and to create favourable conditions for the early resumption of the General Agreement on Trade and Tariffs (GATT) membership, the government introduced a single managed floating exchange rate that reflected changes in market demand and supply, and interbank foreign exchange transactions were allowed. This, in essence, merged the dual-track exchange rate into one single-market exchange rate. It was a prelude to the introduction of convertible RMB, which will have a profound and persistent effect on China's adoption of the comparative-advantage-following strategy and on the overall development of a market economic system.

To countries pursuing a leap-forward strategy, it is no easy task to transform the seriously distorted planned exchange rates into market rates. There are two reasons that China's reform proceeded smoothly in this respect. First, the market-adjusted exchange rate played an increasingly important role. By 1993, 80% of foreign trade was settled according to the market-adjusted exchange rate. Second, the market swap rate served as a reference point for adjusting the state-planned exchange rate and the degree of distortion was reduced. Thus the distortion in foreign exchange rates had a gradually decreasing impact on the economy. When the two tracks were merged into a single market track, the impact of the change was very slight.

The exchange rate reform underwent three stages. In the first stage, the state-planned single exchange rate system was made into a multiple exchange rate system (which encompassed the official rate, the internal settlement rate, and the swap rate). But the major operating rates were the first two that belonged to the planned system and aimed at stimulating exports and, to a reasonable extent, restricting imports. In the second stage, the multiple exchange rate system was reformed into a dual exchange rate system. The official exchange rate and the swap exchange rate belonged, respectively, to the planning system and the market system. The aim at this stage was to gradually make enterprises compete on the international market. In the third stage, the dual exchange rates were merged into a single market exchange rate in order to establish the market economic system.

The exchange rate reform was successful on a number of fronts. For example, foreign exchange certificates started disappearing from circulation on 1 January 1995. In July 1996, the state loosened its control over residents' private use of foreign exchange. Free conversion of RMB under current accounts was realized in December 1996, three years ahead of the government's deadline. In September 1996, the People's Bank became a full member of the International Settlement Bank, and it permitted foreign banks to conduct trial RMB business in the Pudong district of Shanghai.

Interest Rate Policy Reform

Lowering the price of capital, i.e., interest rates, was a basic measure adopted to pursue the leap-forward strategy under severe capital shortages. However, this measure resulted in various problems such as the severe shortage of capital and inefficient capital allocation. These problems severely impeded the steady economic growth and led to a widening of the gap between China and the rest of the world. To solve such problems, the government must allow the interest rate to reflect the supply and demand conditions for capital. Only then will it be able to guide the efficient use of capital and promote capital-saving technology innovations. This is actually the goal of the interest rate reform.

The measure adopted in China's interest rate reform was the adjustment of interest rates. In 1979, the first adjustment restored interest rates to pre-Cultural Revolution levels. From 1980 to 1989, financial institutions took steps to correct distorted rates by raising the deposit and credit rate on nine occasions. In September 1988, interest rates for time deposits longer than three years were temporarily pegged to the inflation rate. This was called the "value-guaranteed savings deposit". The years 1990 to 1992 saw setbacks. During this period, financial institutions lowered the interest rate of deposit and credit loans three times. The interest rate reform was in stagnation or even in regression. Owing to the under-development of non-state financial market, the lowering of interest rate did not have a significant impact on savings deposits. After 1992, non-state financial markets, such as corporate bonds and stocks markets, began to develop rapidly. Their high returns made them attractive. This triggered a deposit shift that had a considerable impact on state banks and forced the government to launch another round of the interest rate reform. The government raised interest rates in May and July 1993 and restored the value-guaranteed savings deposit which, as expected, stopped the shift of deposit from the state banks. After the mid-1990s, in order to stimulate the macro economy, the government again lowered the interest rate several times. It is clear that the government has continued its regulation of interest rate and has taken it as an important macroeconomic lever.

China's interest rate reform lagged far behind the reforms in material prices and foreign exchange rate.[16] This is extremely

---

16. The price reform of production factors in China adopted the "adjust first and liberalize control later" method. This meant that the price was first adjusted toward market equilibrium price and then followed by the

inconsistent with the important role that the interest rate plays in the economy. It is no exaggeration to say that if the problem of interest rate is not properly handled, investment-driven economic overheating and inflation will continue, non-state financial instruments will not develop normally, the public will not have stable expectations of the value of their financial assets, and as a result, the economy will fail to enjoy a stable growth. The difficulty of reforming interest rate policy lies mainly in the constraints of the leap-forward strategy and the overlapping of state banks' commercial and policy functions, which makes the commercialization of state banks impossible. We shall discuss this issue further in Chapters 7 and 8.

5.5. The Economic Logic of "Crossing the River by Groping the Stones" — China's Approach to Reform

When China began its reform, the government did not have a well worked out reform blueprint. The adopted reform measures were intended to solve conspicuous economic problems the government encountered at that moment. The intensity of the reform depended on the government's judgment of the utmost socially acceptable intensity. These features were best characterized as "crossing the river by groping underwater stones in the way". In other words, reform proceeded step by step, moving forward at the rate the government deemed appropriate at any given time. Our analysis shows that although there have been ups and downs in the reform process, the main thrust of the reform has remained clear, and overall it is following the predictions of economic theory.

The starting point of reform was the micro-management institution reform that gave autonomy to micro-management units

liberalization of prices, which meant that market demand and supply would determine prices. After 15 years of reform, the pricing systems of both resources and foreign exchange changed from adjustment systems to a market system. However, interest rate still lingered in the adjustment stage.

and allowed them to share profits. As intended, the reform improved production incentives and created a stream of additional resources. With the help of the reform in the resource-allocation systems, part of the new stream of resources was allocated to sectors, which had been suppressed under the traditional economic system. Thus the preliminary goals of accelerating economic growth and adjusting the industrial structure were achieved. Moreover, the reform was a Pareto-improvement. The whole society benefited from decentralization and profit sharing. As the reform proceeded, conflicts between the traditional macro-policy environment and the reformed micro-management institution, and those between the traditional macro-policy environment and the reformed resource-allocation mechanism arose. The conflicts resulted in an internal inconsistency within the economic system. The government often chose the traditional method of administrative re-centralization to forcefully bring the reformed micro-management institution and reformed resource allocation mechanism in line with the traditional macro-policy environment. However, such an approach did not have the support of managers, workers, and peasants, who had enjoyed the fruits of decentralization reform. It also put the government in financial straits. Consequently, the government had no other choice but to extend the reform to the macro-policy environment so as to make it adapt to the reformed micro-management institution and resource-allocation mechanism.

This is how China's incremental reform has proceeded. The reform is irreversible because it started with a change in the micro-management institution. Power and benefits given to enterprises, workers, and farmers cannot be taken away again. Therefore, when the inconsistency within the trinity of economic system began to cause serious economic problems, the reform was eventually carried out in such a way that the resource allocation mechanism and the macro-policy environment were made to adapt to the liberalized micro-management institutions in spite of government reluctance. Reform has proceeded in a logically consistent manner, despite ups and downs. This is because the root of every economic problem that the reform attempted to solve possessed an economic logic of its own. After thoroughly analyzing and summarizing China's reform process, we were surprised to discover a splendid blueprint underneath China's incremental transition to a market economy. The reform and development of TVEs is the best illustration of the gradual approach to reform. In the 1980s, three conditions led TVEs to expand significantly. First, they enjoyed cheap production factors, which facilitated the primitive accumulation. For example, their startup capital came from the collective's accumulation, banks, and credit cooperatives. Because China was so populous and migration to cities was restricted, a huge labour surplus existed in rural areas. Cheap labour forces became a major advantage for TVE development. Rural collectives had jurisdiction over land use. This was the case before and after the household responsibility system was implemented. TVEs did not have to pay for land use and had an almost unlimited land supply.

Second, as soon as they took off, TVEs began to enjoy relatively abundant market opportunities. Since the First Five-year Plan, SOEs had been developed primarily to serve the goal of heavy-industry-oriented development strategy. Before 1978, almost half of the investment in fixed assets had been spent on heavy industries and less than six 6% on light industries. This caused a severe shortage of light industrial products. Relying on their advantages in abundant labour, TVEs invested in the under-developed sectors to meet the market shortages, made quick profits, and accumulated capital. The TVEs' take-off stage happened to coincide with the period that people's incomes were rapidly increasing while their demands had not upgraded to higher quality products, TVEs' cheap products catered to market needs. TVEs, still fragile in the 1980s, benefited from the fact that the reform of SOEs came only later.

Last, but nevertheless the most importantly, TVEs faced fierce market competition from the very beginning. TVEs were not products of a planned economy. Their major supply of energy and raw materials came from outside the state allocation plan, and their products were sold outside planned channels. In the early 1980s, the reform in micro-management institution gave partial autonomy and a portion of profits to SOEs. At the same time, the dual-track system of resource allocation and price mechanism emerged, with the market track began to grow. This allowed TVEs to enter markets and develop. On the other hand, there was also more market pressure on TVEs than there was on SOEs. More seriously restricted by their own budgets, TVEs have an inherent ability to adapt to market competition.

Any institutional arrangement has to be formed under a specific institutional structure. The change of institutional structure in general has to go through the process from quantitative changes to qualitative ones. At the initial stage of TVE development, there were political and ideological restrictions regarding private ownership. Most TVEs thus adopted a mode of collective ownership. Not until the 1990s did TVEs, facing new challenges, begin to reform their ownership structure, mainly through developing a joint-stock cooperative system. This reform, which came about spontaneously, addressed a series of problems faced by TVEs, like the ownership ambiguity, confusion about business and government function, asset stripping, and the closed nature of the enterprise. The joint-stock cooperative system started in the Zhoucun District of Shandong Province and the Baoan District of Guangdong Province and then rapidly spread throughout the nation during the 1990s.

The reform of the joint-stock cooperative system in TVEs primarily addressed the problem of how the local government can stimulate and supervise managerial personnel in collectively-owned enterprises. Early on, this problem was easy to solve via community ownership, since the number of TVEs in each community was limited, and there was no serious information asymmetry between township leaders and managerial personnel. That is, community leaders could know as much as TVE managers to guarantee supervision effectiveness. In addition, since job options were limited, salary levels and community status were enough to stimulate TVE managers to work hard. In fact, ambiguous ownership and the overlapping of business and government functions was an effective institutional arrangement at the time.

With the development of the rural economy and various forms of ownership, institutional arrangements began to change. Most importantly, the original supervision and incentive mechanism became ineffective. TVE managers were not government officials. Their job mobility was limited and they had not much chance to be promoted. Long-term management over the same TVEs enabled them to accumulate private information. At the same time, non-collective enterprises mushroomed, providing job opportunities for those who were good managers. Lastly, the increased number of TVEs and their expansion in scale made it impossible for community governments to obtain full and detailed information about TVEs' operation. Hence, direct supervision became ineffective.

Compared with SOEs, TVEs had two advantages. First, township governments and rural collectives were relatively dependent on TVE development. Community residents were also more concerned about TVEs. The nature of TVE ownership was tangible and real. Second, TVEs never had to bear any burdens imposed by government policies and could therefore carry out reforms without many restrictions. Under such circumstances, the joint-stock cooperative system, which provided managerial personnel with a desirable share of capital, became an effective incentive under the new environment. At the same time, the non-separation of business and government function gave township and village government the right to control TVE's surplus. This control of TVE's surplus became difficult when the information asymmetry between local officials and TVE managers grew serious. The local authorities then needed a stable institutional arrangement to gain a comparatively stable share of surplus from TVE's profits. The worsening of information asymmetry made a new form of supervision necessary. The result was a rapid diffusion of the joint-stock cooperative system.

Since the TVEs faced various problems, and because they differed from each other in terms of their scale, technological level, management, and history, the reform also had to be flexible. Along with the typical joint-stock cooperative system, many other forms have recently come into being, like limited-liability companies, shareholding companies, leasing, selling, merging, asset-value-adding contracts, conglomerates, foreign joint ventures, and privatization.[17] If the development of non-SOEs represented by TVEs injected vitality into the overall economy in the 1980s, the diversity in the evolution of TVEs' ownership and governance in the 1990s has surely changed the fundamentals of China's rural economy.

17. Lu Wen, "The Development of the Property Right System Reform in the TVEs", *Rural Economy in China*, No. 11 (1997).

CHAPTER 6

Success of the Economic Reform

In Chapter 4, we conclude that the key to the economic success of the four Little Dragons lies in their exploitation of their comparative advantages at every stage of development. The Little Dragons adopted this development approach unintentionally. Since every country has its own comparative advantages, and since its implications for the necessary policy environment and government actions are well defined, a country can thus intentionally exploit its comparative advantages in their economic development. We can call such an intentional action by a government as adopting a comparative-advantage-following strategy, or simply the comparative-advantage strategy. The economic sizes of the four Little Dragons were rather small. It is true that the development approach suitable for small economies may not be appropriate for large economies. To determine whether the comparative-advantage strategy has universal implications, we need to answer whether this strategy is appropriate for large countries, whether socialist countries can develop according to this strategy, and whether large socialist countries can successfully rely on it. This chapter will answer these questions from the perspective of the experiences of China's reform.

The conclusions of this chapter are as follows: Since the late 1970s, reforms in China have been aimed at overcoming the constraints of insufficient capital under the leap-forward strategy in the traditional economic system. With the reform of the micro-management institutions, workers' and farmers' incentive improved. A great potential for production was unleashed, and productivity increased. However, the rapid growth has also benefited from a better exploitation of China's comparative advantages during this period.

Especially in coastal areas, where the development follows closely their comparative advantages, the growth performance far exceeded that of the four Little Dragons. This indicates that the comparative-advantage strategy can be effective not only in small capitalist countries but also in large socialist countries. Thus, we can conclude that China should shift further from the traditional leap-forward strategy to the comparative-advantage strategy and take more initiative to implement the latter. This is the key to the country's economic prosperity.

6.1 Improvement of Incentives and Efficiency

In Chapter 1, we have discussed China's remarkable economic growth and the improvement in its people's living standards since the reform started in 1979. Improvement in economic incentives and efficiency were the two major contributing factors for this rapid economic growth. The economic incentive mechanism of non-SOEs was markedly superior to that of SOEs — one important reasons for the higher growth rate of the non-state-owned sector. Furthermore, the incentive improvement triggered by the reform of the micro-management institution and the efficiency improvement in resource-allocation resulted from a better utilization of China's comparative-advantages were key contributors to the higher economic growth rates and better sustainability in development during the reform period.

Before proceeding further, let us first discuss the improvement of economic incentives in China after the reform. Prior to 1978, state sectors were predominately in urban areas and rural areas were primarily under collective economy. There was a lack of economic incentive in both state and collective sectors. This accounted not only for the poor performance of urban and rural economies but also for the rural areas' limited contribution to economic growth, even though rural areas held a comparative advantage in terms of their abundant and cheap labour force. Since 1978, a series of changes have taken place in China. In particular, the collective system was replaced by a household responsibility system. This change stimulated peasants' incentive to produce. Between 1978 and 1984, rural production increased annually by an average of 7.6% — more than twice the average annual growth rate between 1952 and 1978 (which was 2.9%). According to econometric studies, the productivity of household farms was about 20% higher than that of collective teams at that time. Between 1978 and 1984, half of all the agricultural growth could be attributed to improved incentives, an improvement that was stimulated by the change from the collective team system to the household responsibility system.[1] The reform of the micro-management institutions, which had been characterized by decentralization and profit sharing, and the reform of the resource-allocation system also improved SOEs' incentive mechanism, thereby improved management efficiency. According to the estimation of the economist Yang Jianbai, during the 25 years prior to the reform (1953–78), China's total factor productivity on average was in negative growth (the total factor productivity in 1953–57 was 0.77%, and the rate of contribution to economic growth was 8.7%).[2] In 1979–89, China's total factor productivity and its rate of contribution to economic growth were 2.48% and 28.5%, respectively.[3] The total factor productivity rose from being negative in the period before the reform to nearly 2.5%, accounting for 50% of economic growth since the reform. Research by the World Bank has yielded similar results (see Table 6.1).

On the other hand, the relaxation of state control over economy created favourable conditions for non-state sector development, including city and township collective economies, TVEs, and urban and rural private (individual) enterprises. These enterprises did not

1. Justin Yifu Lin, "Rural Reform and Agricultural Growth in China", *American Economic Review,* Vol. 82, No. 1 (March 1992), pp. 34–52.
2. The total factor productivity is the productivity induced by technological progress and improvement in organizational and institutional arrangements. Between 1957 and 1978, China made steady technological progress. The main reason for the negative growth of the total factor productivity was the lack of efficiency in organizational and institutional arrangements.
3. Yang Jianbai, "Speed, Structure and Efficiency", *Economic Research,* No. 9 (1991), p. 43.

Table 6.1 Output Growth Rate and Total Factor Productivity (%)

	1980–88	1980–84	1984–88
State sector output	8.49	6.77	10.22
Total factor productivity	2.40	1.80	3.01
Collective sector output	16.94	14.03	19.86
Total factor productivity	4.63	3.45	5.86

Source: The World Bank, *Reform and the Role of Planning in the 1990s.* Washington, DC: The World Bank, 1992.

receive any special treatment from the government, and their workers and staff were not allowed any government subsidies. Indeed, the pressure from market competition provided these enterprises with the motivation to optimize their resource allocation. What's more, a distribution system that matched worker remuneration with actual contribution stimulated each worker's incentives considerably. Consequently, the market competition mechanism and the incentive mechanism according to individual performance enabled the non-state sector to grow rapidly.

As indicated in Tables 6.2 and 6.3, since 1978 the proportion of non-state-sector products has been continuously increasing both in the industrial output value and in the total retail volume of social commodities. The proportion of the non-state sector in total industrial output value grew from 22.4% in 1978 to 74.5% in 1997, an increase of 52.1 percentage points. The proportion of the non-state sector in the total retail volume of commodities rose from 45.4% to 75.5%, an increase of 30.1 percentage points. It should be noted that the growth rates in state industry and commerce did not decline during this period (see Figure 6.1). The increase in the proportion of the non-state sector during this period was due to its higher growth rate than that of the state sector. The above-mentioned data show that the rapid national economic growth since the reform was characterized by the development of the new, non-state sector.

The "survival of the fittest" competition mechanism and the incentive mechanism of remuneration according to work performance were also effective for the state-owned sector of the economy. The main reason for its less remarkable performance is that many

SOEs established under the planned economic system were not viable in a market economy.[4] With the economy still in transition, the government had to support the nonviable SOEs; this support made it unnecessary for them to adjust their choice of industries and technologies according to the comparative advantages of the economy, which were reflected in the relative prices in the competitive market. As a result, on one hand, the government was required to provide them with low-cost production factors and price protection as well as with employee income subsidies that were unrelated to economic performance, and sometimes even subsidies to

Table 6.2 Changes in the Structure of Industrial Output Value

(Unit: RMB 100 million, %)

Year	Total industrial output value	SOEs		City and township collective economies, TVEs		Urban and rural private (individual) enterprises		Other enterprises	
		Output value	%	Output value	%	Output value	%	Output value	%
1978	4,237	3,289	77.63	948	22.37	0	0.00	0	0.00
1980	5,154	3,916	75.98	1,213	23.53	1	0.02	24	0.47
1985	9,716	6,302	64.86	3,117	32.08	180	1.85	117	1.21
1990	23,924	13,064	54.61	8,523	35.62	1,290	5.39	1,047	4.38
1995	91,894	31,220	33.97	33,623	36.59	11,821	12.86	15,231	16.58
1997	113,733	29,028	25.52	43,347	38.11	20,376	17.92	20,982	18.45

Note: a. In this table, the total national industrial output value includes the industrial output value of TVEs at the village level and below.

b. The state industrial output value in 1994 does not include RMB 460 billion of output value from enterprises of which the state is the majority stock holder.

Source: National Bureau of Statistics of China, *20 Years of Magnificent Achievement*. Beijing: China Statistics Press, 1998, p. 388.

4. A normally managed firm will not be viable if its choices of industry and/or technology are not consistent with the pattern endogenously determined by the endowment structure of the economy. See the discussion in Chapter 4 of this book and Justin Yifu Lin, "Development Strategy, Viability, and Economic Convergence" (Inaugural D. Gale Johnson Lecture, Department of Economics, the University of Chicago, 14 May 2001).

Table 6.3 Changes in the Structure of the Total Retail Sales of Commodity

(Unit: RMB 100 million, %)

Year	Total value	SOEs		City and township collective economies, TVEs		Urban and rural private (individual) enterprises		Other enterprises	
		Output value	%	Output value	%	Output value	%	Output value	%
1978	1,558.6	851.0	54.6	674.4	43.3	2.1	0.1	31.1	2.0
1980	2,139.6	1,100.7	51.4	954.9	44.6	15.0	0.7	69.0	3.2
1985	4,292.3	1,740.0	40.5	1,600.3	37.3	661.0	15.4	291.0	6.8
1990	8,259.8	3,285.9	39.8	2,631.0	31.9	1,569.6	19.0	773.3	9.4
1995	20,546.8	6,154.1	30.0	3,981.6	19.4	6,253.8	30.4	4,157.3	20.2
1997	26,699.4	6,533.2	24.5	4,887.6	18.3	8,955.8	33.5	6,322.8	23.7

Source: National Bureau of Statistics of China, *China Development Report, 1998.* Beijing: China Statistics Press, 1998, p. 69.

Figure 6.1 Annual growth rate of state industries and commerce and their shares in total output value and total volume of retail sales

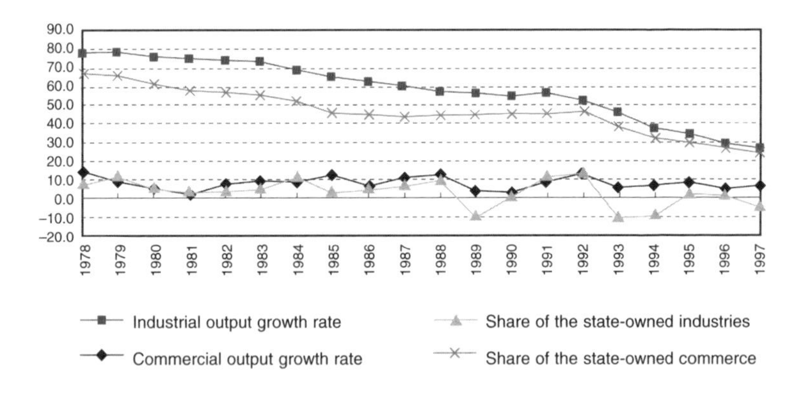

Source: National Bureau of Statistics of China, *China Statistical Yearbook, 1993.* Beijing: China Statistics Press, 1993, pp. 413–14.

cover their losses; and on the other hand the SOEs lack incentives to improve production and productivity due to the policy supports and soft-budget constraints.[5]

With pressure from the rapid development of the non-state sector, the cost of subsidizing the nonviable SOEs has become much higher, while the opportunity cost of completely transforming the state-owned sector and abandoning the traditional development strategy has decreased significantly. It is time for China to shift from the leap-forward strategy to the comparative-advantage strategy. Only when China has completely realized this transition, will the distorted macro-policy environment, the planned resource-allocation mechanism and the corresponding micro-management institution (which were endogenously determined by the leap-forward strategy) cease to exist. The nonviable SOEs will withdraw from production. The viable SOEs will get rid of policy burdens, and will not receive any special treatment from the government. They will face the same market competition as enterprises with other types of ownership structures. In this way, China will realize sustainable, rapid, and healthy economic growth.

In the decades that China followed the heavy-industry-oriented development strategy, both rural and urban areas failed to develop. The rapid development of TVEs in the last 20 years shows that when government stops the artificial distortion of factors and product prices — including artificially suppressed or raised prices (or providing subsidies) — enterprises will have incentives to make full use of the economy's comparative advantages. When there are rich labour resources, labour-intensive production, especially skill-intensive production, will be enhanced, and the production factor in relative

---

5. See Justin Yifu Lin, Fang Cai, and Zhou Li, *State-owned Enterprise Reform in China*. Hong Kong: Chinese University Press, 2001; Justin Yifu Lin, Fang Cai, and Zhou Li, "Competition, Policy Burdens and State-owned Enterprises Reform", *American Economic Review*, Vol. 88, No. 2 (May 1998), pp. 422–27; Justin Yifu Lin and Guofu Tan, "Policy Burdens, Accountability and Soft-budget Constraint", *American Economic Review*, Vol. 89, No. 2 (May 1999), pp. 426–31.

scarcity will be substituted by labour. Moreover, it will lead to a more efficient use of the resource in scarcity. As the comparative advantage changes with economic development, profit motives will stimulate enterprises to adjust their products and technological structure in order to exploit the new comparative advantages. As a result, China's industrialization and modernization will make further progress.

6.2. Correction of the Industrial Structure

The distorted industrial structure has been corrected in the reform process. In a distortion-free economy, the industrial structure is determined by the economy's comparative advantage that lies in the endowment structure. As the comparative advantage changes, the industrial structure will change accordingly. The adoption of the leap-forward strategy before the reform caused China's industrial structure to deviate from the optimum pattern determined by the country's comparative advantage, and resulted in a series of problems. For example, the overall industrial structure was too capital-intensive; and the proportion of construction, transportation and service industries in the national income remained at a low level, or even in a declining state. This distorted industrial structure ran contrary to the general laws of economic development, and has led to negative economic growth on several occasions. Since the 1978 reform, however, the bias against labour-intensive industries has been gradually alleviated and the distortion in industrial structure has been gradually corrected.

As calculated using comparable prices, between 1952 and 1978, heavy industry and light industry grew by 2779.5% and 905.2%, respectively. Between 1978 and 1997, the two industries grew by 1195.8% and 1349.3%, respectively. Agriculture has undergone a similar change in structure after 1978. There has been a reduction in the sown areas of grain crops, which requires low labour input and has relative low yield, while there has been rapid growth in cash crops, which requires high labour input and has relatively high yield (see Figure 6.2). With resources flowing to more efficient sectors, the

Figure 6.2 Changes in the sown areas of major agricultural crops

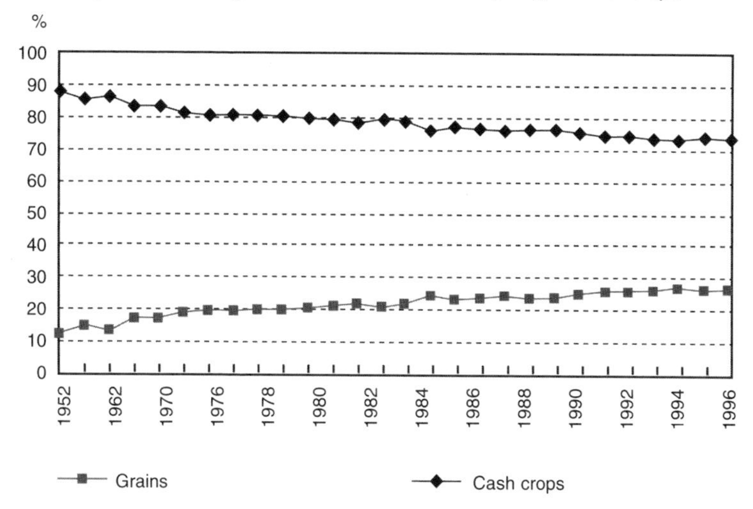

Source: National Bureau of Statistics of China, *China Statistical Yearbook, 1997.* Beijing: China Statistics Press, 1997.

sector proportions of construction, transportation, and commerce in the national income have all risen. The old, distorted industrial structure has been to a large degree corrected.

The employment structure, whose change lagged far behind that of the output structure before 1978, has also been corrected. Before the reform, the People's Communes and the household registration system fettered peasants to rural regions and to agriculture. Although there were policies to improve peasants' opportunities directly (through state work recruitment efforts) or indirectly (through military conscription), in reality these options were unavailable to most peasants. The government tried on several occasions to address this problem, but failed, either because of economic recessions or because of financial constraints. For example, from 1958 to 1960, in order to realize the Great Leap Forward, the government mobilized 28 million peasants to come to the cities to work, but it then had to force them back as a result of the ensuing economic disaster brought out by the Leap.

After reform had been launched, the government changed the dual control over the peasants' job and residence location into a single household registration control. In the past, peasants had to stay in rural areas, their households were registered as "rural", and their sole choice of profession was agricultural production. Such controls were abolished. When hundreds of millions of peasants gained the right to choose job freely, they moved into non-agricultural industries. This job migration contributed inestimably to solving the problem that had perplexed the government for several decades (i.e., how to match the employment structure with the output value structure). Between 1978 and 1997, the number of labourers that were employed in TVEs rose by 102.2 million.[6] This alone accounted for 41.4% of the increase in the number of non-agricultural labourers (246.71 million) nationally. If peasants engaging in non-agricultural activities in other industries (e.g., going into the cities on an individual basis as contract labourers, temporary workers, domestic workers, and business people) are accounted for, the percentage is even higher. According to calculations based on a large sample survey by the Chinese Association of Township and Village Enterprises, non-agricultural work already accounted for 40% of the total work of peasants in 1992.

The rapid development of collective and individual economies in cities also created many employment opportunities. Between 1978 and 1997, the number of labourers in collective and individual economies in cities and towns increased from 20.6 million to 54.9 million, an increase of 165.9%. This accounted for 13.9% of the labour increase in non-agricultural industries. The change also contributed significantly to reducing the temporary urban unemployment rate. Moreover, SOEs also made important contributions to the increase of non-agricultural employment opportunities.

With the rapid development of the manufacturing industry and tertiary industries, the proportion of primary industry labour in the total labour force decreased from 70.5% in 1978 to 50% in 2000. At

6. According to data in: National Bureau of Statistics of China, *China Statistical Yearbook, 1998*. Beijing: China Statistics Press, 1998, p. 420.

the same time, the proportion of non-agricultural labour in total labour increased from 29.5% in 1978 to 50% in 2000, an increase of 20.5 percentage points.[7] The mismatch of employment structure and output value structure has been alleviated substantially.

Moreover, the inward-looking economic structure has been corrected. One of the most remarkable changes has been China's move from a closed to an open economy. During the past two decades, China has increasingly opened its economy to the outside world. In 1979, the central government decided that Guangdong and Fujian Provinces should take the lead in practicing flexible policies. In 1980, the government opened up Shenzhen, Zhuhai, Shantou, and Xiamen cities as special economic zones (SEZs). In the spring of 1984, fourteen port cities along the coast, as well as Hainan Island, were opened up. In the spring of 1985, the government decided to open up the Yangtze River Delta, the Pearl River Delta, and the Triangular Region of Southern Fujing Province. In 1986, the Shandong Peninsula and the Eastern Peninsula of Liaoning Province opened up consecutively. In the spring of 1988, the central government turned Hainan Island into a province and made it the largest SEZ. In addition, large areas in Guangdong and Fujian Provinces were made experimental zones for reform and opening up. In 1991, it decided to extend the open door policy to coastal and border areas and areas along the rivers, thus opening the country at all levels and in all domains. In 1992, the Pudong district in Shanghai was opened for foreign investment. The government hoped that this could strongly stimulate the opening and development of provinces along the Yangtze River.

In light of a series of measures implemented by the government, the Chinese economy witnessed two major changes: the rapid increase of foreign trade and the dramatic inflow of foreign capital. Regarding foreign trade, from 1978 to 2000, the total volume of import and export increased from US$20.64 billion to US$474.29

7. National Bureau of Statistics of China, *China Statistical Yearbook, 2001*. Beijing: China Statistics Press, 2001, p. 108.

billion, an average annual increase of 15.3%. The total volume of export increased from US$9.75 billion to US$249.2 billion, an annual increase of 15.9%. The total volume of import increased from US$10.89 billion to US$225.09 billion, with an annual increase of 15.2%.[8] Both growth rates exceeded the annual growth rate of the GDP. The Chinese dependence rate on foreign trade increased from 9.8% in 1978 to 43.9% in 2000 (see Table 6.4).

Statistics also show that the inflow of foreign capital increased greatly. Between 1979 and 1983, the contract value and used value of foreign capital averaged at an annual level of US$4.8 billion and US$2.9 billion respectively. Whereas between 1996 and 2000, the corresponding figures increased respectively to US$85.3 billion and US$58.0 billion, which increased by 17.8 times and 20 times, respectively. Between 1979 and 2000, the utilization of foreign capital in terms of total contract value and used value reached US$840.3 billion and US$518.9 billion, respectively.[10] These changes mark the increasing integration of the Chinese economy into the world economy and also indicate that since the onset of reform, the nature of the economy has been gradually growing more outward looking.

Finally, the investment structure, which once relied solely on state accumulation, has been adjusted. With rural development and income increases for urban and rural residents, household savings grew dramatically and played an increasingly important role in capital accumulation. For total capital investment, the proportion from state financial appropriations has dropped from 75% to less than 20% in recent years, while the proportion from bank loans and fund-raising from the financial market has increased to over 80%

8. National Bureau of Statistics of China, *China Statistical Yearbook, 2001*. Beijing: China Statistics Press, 2001, p. 586.
9. Here, the trade dependence ratio was calculated according to the official GNP. Apparently, if it was calculated by GNP estimated using various purchasing power parity measurements, China's trade dependence ratio would be much lower.
10. National Bureau of Statistics of China, *China Statistical Yearbook, 2001*. Beijing: China Statistics Press, 2001, p. 602.

Table 6.4 Changes in the Chinese Economy's Trade Dependence Ratio[9]

(Unit: RMB 100 million, %)

Year	GNP	Total value of import and export		Total value of export		Total value of import	
		Value	Share in GNP	Value	Share in GNP	Value	Share in GNP
1978	3,624.1	355.0	9.80	167.6	4.62	187.4	5.17
1979	4,038.2	454.6	11.26	211.7	5.24	242.9	6.02
1980	4,517.8	570.0	12.62	271.2	6.00	298.8	6.61
1981	4,860.3	735.3	15.13	367.6	7.56	367.7	7.57
1982	5,301.8	771.3	14.55	413.8	7.80	357.5	6.74
1983	5,957.1	860.1	14.44	438.3	7.36	421.8	7.08
1984	7,206.7	1,201.0	16.67	580.5	8.06	620.5	8.61
1985	8,989.1	2,066.7	22.99	808.9	9.00	1,257.8	13.99
1986	10,201.4	2,580.4	25.29	1,082.1	10.61	1,498.3	14.69
1987	11,954.5	3,084.2	25.80	1,470.0	12.30	1,614.2	13.50
1988	14,922.3	3,821.8	25.61	1,766.7	11.84	2,055.1	13.77
1989	16,917.8	4,155.9	24.57	1,956.0	11.56	2,199.9	13.00
1990	18,598.4	5,560.1	29.90	2,985.8	16.05	2,574.3	13.84
1991	21,662.5	7,225.8	33.36	3,827.1	17.67	3,398.7	15.69
1992	26,651.9	9,119.6	34.22	4,676.3	17.55	4,443.3	16.67
1993	34,560.5	11,271.0	32.61	5,284.8	15.29	5,986.2	17.32
1994	46,670.0	20,381.9	43.67	10,421.8	22.33	9,960.1	21.34
1995	57,494.9	23,499.9	40.87	12,451.8	21.66	11,048.1	19.22
1996	66,850.5	24,133.8	36.10	12,576.4	18.81	11,557.4	17.29
1997	73,452.5	26,958.6	36.70	15,152.8	20.63	11,805.8	16.07

Source: National Bureau of Statistics of China, *China Statistical Yearbook, 2001*. Beijing: China Statistics Press, 2001, p. 586.

(see Tables 6.5 and 6.6). With household savings as the main source of investment, an investment structure consisting of government, enterprises, and households has replaced the one that relied solely on the state.

Table 6.5 Total Investment in Fixed Assets by Source of Funds and Its Changes

(Unit: RMB 100 million, %)

Year	Total invest-ment	State budgetary appropriation		Domestic loans		Foreign investment		Fundraising and others	
		Value	Share	Value	Share	Value	Share	Value	Share
1981	961.01	269.76	28.07	122.00	12.69	36.36	3.78	532.89	55.45
1985	2,543.19	407.80	16.04	510.27	20.06	91.48	3.60	1,533.64	60.30
1990	4,517.50	393.03	8.70	885.45	19.60	284.61	6.30	2,954.41	65.40
1995	20,524.86	621.05	3.02	4,198.73	20.46	2,295.89	11.19	13,409.19	65.33
1997	25,259.67	696.74	2.76	4,782.55	18.93	2,683.89	10.63	17,096.49	67.68

Note: National Bureau of Statistics of China, *China Statistical Yearbook, 2001*. Beijing: China Statistics Press, 2001, p. 159.

Table 6.6 Total Investment in Fixed Assets by Ownership and Its Changes

(Unit: RMB 100 million, %)

Year	Total invest-ment	State-owned units		Collective-owned units		Individuals economy		Other types of ownership	
		Value	Share	Value	Share	Value	Share	Value	Share
1981	961.0	667.5	69.46	115.2	11.99	178.3	18.55		
1985	2,543.2	1,680.5	66.08	327.5	12.88	535.2	21.04		
1990	4,517.6	2,986.9	66.12	529.5	11.72	1,001.2	22.16		
1991	5,594.6	3,713.9	66.39	697.8	12.47	1,182.9	21.14		
1992	8,080.1	5,498.7	68.05	1,359.4	16.83	1,222.0	15.12		
1993	13,072.3	7,925.9	60.63	2,317.3	17.73	1,476.2	11.29	1,352.9	10.35
1994	17,042.1	9,615.0	56.42	2,758.9	16.19	1,970.6	11.56	2,697.6	15.83
1995	20,019.3	10,898.2	54.44	3,289.4	16.43	2,560.2	12.79	3,271.5	16.34
1996	22,974.0	12,056.2	52.48	3,660.6	15.93	3,211.2	13.98	4,046.0	17.61
1997	25,300.1	13,418.6	53.04	3,873.5	15.31	3,426.8	13.54	4,581.2	18.11

Source: National Bureau of Statistics of China, *China Statistical Yearbook, 2001*. Beijing: China Statistics Press, 2001, p. 158.

6.3 Exploitating Comparative Advantage

The problems in pre-reform China were inadequate incentives and low efficiency. Therefore, the reform was initiated from the micro-management institutions. However, since the traditional economic system was an organic whole, its drawbacks were also intrinsically related to one another. The traditional economic system evolved endogenously from the conflict between the heavy-industry oriented development strategy and the capital-scarce, labour-abundant endowment structure. Therefore, no matter where the reform started and how the reform was carried out, the reform will affect the traditional development strategy. The changes usually began with the incremental resources created in the economic growth and the reallocation of these resources to new sectors. The impact of new incremental resources on the heavy-industry-oriented development strategy has typically affected the non-state-owned sector. For example, the ratio of the non-state-owned sector in total industrial output value increased from 22.4% in 1978 to 76.5% in 2000. At the same time, the ratio of urban employment in the non-state-owned sector increased from 21.7% in 1978 to 48.9% in 2000.

The development of the non-state-owned sector, which came about as a result of resource redistribution, signified that the whole reform and development process was actually a process that the role of the market mechanism was brought into play and China's comparative advantage was utilized. For example, the previously suppressed light industries were boosted by the development of the non-state-owned industrial sector. In 1997, while heavy industries' output value still accounted for 71.7% of the total industrial output value of SOEs, it only accounted for 44.2% of the total industrial output value of the foreign-funded enterprises. The non-state-owned sector accounted for a relatively large proportion of labour-intensive industries. In addition, the non-state-owned sector was inclined toward using labour-intensive and capital-saving technologies. As a result, their capital organic composition was much lower than that of SOEs. For example, in 1997, one unit of industrial-added value produced by the SOEs required 2.67 units of net value of fixed asset.

In comparison, one such unit required 1.04 units by collectively-owned enterprises, 1.85 units by shareholding enterprises, 1.82 units by foreign-invested enterprises, and 1.98 units by Hong Kong-, Macao-, or Taiwan-invested enterprises.[11]

The process of resource redistribution promoted the development of product and factor markets, improved domestic investment structure, and attracted foreign investments. It also led to the expansion of foreign trade and to a series of institutional changes. Some scholars attribute China's economic growth to four sources: the flow of labour forces, efficiency brought about by market growth, foreign trade and the introduction of technology, and domestic investment and the introduction of foreign capital (see Table 6.7). These four sources describe the effects of market development brought about by the reform and by exploitation of China's comparative advantage since the reforms of 1978.

TVEs provide the most appropriate example for our analysis of the impact of comparative advantage. The most widely acknowledged achievements in Chinese economic reform were: first, the adoption of the household responsibility system, which resulted in

Table 6.7 The Composition of China's Economic Growth Rate (Percentage Points, %)

Sources of growth	Contribution
(1) Labour migration	1.50 (16.30)
(2) Market growth	0.38 (4.13)
(3) Foreign trade and the introduction of technology	0.50 (5.43)
(4) Domestic investment and the introduction of foreign capital	6.82 (74.13)
Total	9.20 (100)

Source: Francis A. Lees, *China Superpower: Requisites for High Growth*. New York: St. Martin's Press, 1997, p. 66.

11. National Bureau of Statistics of China, *China Statistical Yearbook, 1998*. Beijing: China Statistics Press, pp. 444–45.

the termination of chronic shortages in agricultural product and laid a solid foundation for economic prosperity and political stability, and second, the vigorous development of TVEs, which thoroughly reversed the history of long-term stagnation in the rural employment structure, drastically accelerated the process of rural industrialization, and began to bring prosperity to rural areas.

TVEs had an increasingly positive effect on China's economy. First, they had already become the major source of increases in state tax revenue since mid-1980s. Between 1985 and 1990, state tax revenue registered a net increase of RMB 77.32 billion, of which RMB 16.69 billion was from TVEs, making up 21.6% of the total. Between 1990 and 1994, state tax revenue increased by RMB 204.21 billion, of which RMB 80.359 billion was from TVEs, making up 39.3% of the total.[12] Official statistical data does not reflect TVEs' real contribution. In fact, TVEs constitute one of the major sources of government off-budget revenue in China. According to some investigations, one-third to two-thirds of off-budget revenue has come from TVEs.[13] TVEs must also purchase inputs according to the market prices. They cannot obtain low-interest loans from the state. Therefore, their gross increase of tax was equivalent to the net increase of tax revenue to the state, whereas the net increase of tax revenue from SOEs was calculated after deducting government subsidies and discounted loan interest.

Second, TVEs have become the major source for new jobs and the major force for the adjustment of China's employment structure. Under the traditional economic system, rural labourers were tied to agricultural sector and economic growth did not bring out changes in employment structure and urbanization. However, after about 20 years of reform, over 120 million peasants have moved into TVEs.

12. National Bureau of Statistics of China, *China Statistical Yearbook, 1993*. Beijing: China Statistics Press, 1993, p. 396; National Bureau of Statistics of China, *China Statistical Yearbook, 1995*. Beijing: China Statistics Press, 1995, pp. 218, 366.
13. Sun Tanzhen and Zhu Gang, "Analysis on China's Finance Outside of the System in the Towns and Villages", *Economic Research*, No. 9 (1993), pp. 38–44.

This is one of the most remarkable changes that have occurred since the reform.[14]

Third, TVEs have become the major force in the growth of rural areas as well as of overall national economic growth. It took the TVEs only 7 years to raise their output value from RMB 100 billion to RMB 1,000 billion, while it took the national economy 31 years to do so. At present, TVEs' output value constitutes the major component of the total output value in rural areas, and its share is still rising. Moreover, the growth of TVEs has also become the major contributing factor to the growth of national economy and its share is also enlarging. From 1985 to 1990, the increase of the GNP in manufacturing and tertiary industries was RMB 709.1 billion, of which RMB 213.4 billion was contributed by TVEs, making up 30.1% of the total. From 1990 to 1994, these two figures were RMB 2,205.1 billion and RMB 1,186.4 billion, respectively, with the TVEs' share standing at 53.8%.[15] This indicates that the TVE has become an increasingly important force in national economic growth. In recent years, the interregional disparity in China has mainly been manifested in the disparity within the rural areas, while the disparity in rural areas arises mainly from the disparity in TVE development. The development of TVEs has thus become crucially important for the income increases of rural people and for the narrowing down of the interregional disparities.

The most crucial point behind TVE development has been TVEs' ability to exploit China's comparative advantage in rich labour forces. Let TVEs' share in the output value of a certain industry divided by that industry's share in total industrial output value, and

14. The number of workers and staff in the TVEs in 1978 was 28.266 million. This number rose to 130.504 million in 1994, a net increase of 102.238 million (see National Bureau of Statistics of China, *China Statistical Yearbook, 1998*, p. 420).

15. In the calculations, the comparative value of the total social output value against its corresponding GDP was used to adjust the output value of the TVEs to the GDP (see National Bureau of Statistics of China, *China Statistical Yearbook, 1993*, p. 50; *China Statistical Yearbook, 1995*, pp. 32, 365).

name the quotient the "leading coefficient of TVEs". With this coefficient, we carry out a correlation analysis with the TVEs' net value of fixed-asset per capita in the corresponding industries. The correlation coefficient is –0.3, while rank correlation is –0.53. This indicates that the TVEs have followed the comparative advantage of the economy, and are inclined to use relatively cheap labour forces while selecting an industry. The correlation analysis of TVE labour distribution and the capital intensity in various industries also reveals a negative relationship, showing that TVEs were concentrated in labour-intensive industries. In addition, in the same industry, the net value of fixed-asset per capita in TVEs was lower than that of SOEs, indicating that TVEs tend to use more labour-intensive technologies. In 1986, for example, the average net value of fixed-asset per capita for the nation's industrial enterprises was RMB 7,510, while that for TVEs was only RMB 1,709, less than one-fourth of the national average.[16]

16. National Bureau of Statistics of China, *China's Industrial Economic Statistical Data*. Beijing: China Statistics Press, 1987, p. 3; National Bureau of Statistics of China, *China Statistical Yearbook, 1987*. Beijing: China Statistics Press, 1987, p. 205.

CHAPTER 7

Problems with China's Reform

In the past two decades, China's economy has sustained an annual growth rate of about 9.6% on average. This is unprecedented in human economic history. No other populous country has ever sustained such a rapid economic growth for so long a period of time. In this regard, China has doubtlessly created a miracle. However, in the process of development, there are also various latent problems that remained unsolved. This is manifested in the fluctuations of economic growth, which in essence reflects the development cycles in the economy and the ups and downs of the reform. Now, the main problems still in front of Chinese economic reform are: (1) rampant rent-seeking and corruption, (2) the comparatively slow progress in the reform of the financial system, (3) a lack of significant progress in the SOE reform, (4) the widening gap in income levels and regional development, (5) China's potential for grain production. All these problems have accompanied the economic development ever since the initiation of reform, and they tend to aggravate and become recalcitrant. China has to address these problems properly if it does not want them to hinder further economic development and reform.

This chapter and Chapter 8 illustrate the causes of these problems. We shall show that these problems have their roots in the institutional incompatibility arising from the piecemeal, gradual transition approach from a planned economy to market economy. We shall also show that the transition to a well-functioning market economy has not been accomplished because the SOEs are still nonviable and their survival still relies on the distorted traditional institutional arrangements. Therefore, a successful SOE reform is the key to the successful solution of the problems mentioned above.

7.1 The Cyclic Nature of Reform and Development

China's economy has been developing rapidly since 1978, with the average annual GDP growth rate reaching 9.8% between 1978 and 1997.[1] At the same time, people's living standards have been raised considerably and the industrial structure has been adjusted. However, a closer look shows that the rapid economic growth of the past twenty years has been marked by cyclical fluctuations. The annual GDP growth rate reached 13–15% in the peak years, but it was only at 3–4% when development slowed down. Four cycles have occurred since the end of 1978, with one every four to five years (see Figure 7.1).

There is no doubt that the national economy has to pay a great deal for cyclical fluctuations in economic growth. The costs may be tolerable if cyclical fluctuations are mild or gentle. Unfortunately, fluctuations have been becoming increasingly drastic. It is not without reason to fear that one day the national economy might suddenly collapse. Should this happen, China cannot possibly realize

Figure 7.1 Cyclical fluctuations in economic growth and inflation

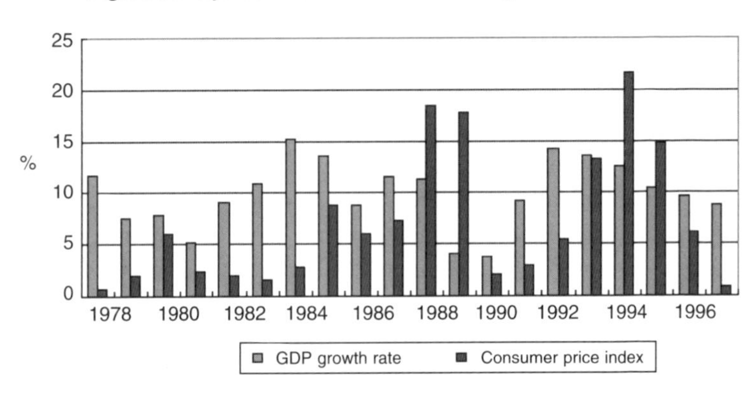

Source: National Bureau of Statistics of China, *China Statistical Yearbook, 1998.* Beijing: China Statistics Press, 1998, pp. 57–301.

1. A new deflationary phenomenon started to appear in the Chinese economy in 1998. The causes of the deflation and the policy options for dealing with the deflation will be discussed in Chapter 9.

its current expectations of becoming the largest economy in the world by the mid-twenty-first century.

In fact, the manifestation of the cyclicity in Chinese economy is not only limited to growth fluctuation, but also in hesitant steps of economic restructuring and a series of serious social problems. The cycle is self-propelling: vigour leads to disorder; disorder leads to retrenchment; retrenchment leads to stagnation; stagnation leads to decentralization. The "decentralization leads to disorder" phase occurs when the economy becomes overheated, resulting in the "speed constrained by bottleneck". With the reform of micro management, enterprises began to have independent interests with a strong motive to pursue profits. When capital prices were kept at an artificially low level, enterprises enthusiastically obtained loans for expansion as soon as the government relaxed restrictions on credit and investment. A "bottleneck" then formed due to a short supply of energy, transportation, and raw and processed materials. At this point, the government had to take measures to restrict the blind expansion of investments.

Theoretically speaking, the pace of economic development, like that of physical competition, depends on the basic supporting conditions and the soundness of movement. There should be no such a thing as an absolute restriction on speed. Conditions permitting, it should be the case that the faster, the better. There is no need to set artificially a so-called "appropriate speed". The main factors that have restricted growth since the reform have been the insufficient supply in basic industries, plus the lack of market pricing for energy, raw and processed materials, and transportation. As a result, the allocation of such resources and services was not determined by competitiveness. High-speed growth was not accompanied by an improvement in efficiency. To the contrary, the rapid growth rate was achieved on an unsound basis.

The second phase of the cycle, "vigour leads to disorder", manifested itself in hidden inflation pressures and cyclical inflation. Although there has been inflation over the past twenty years, the rates have been low compared with those in some other countries. However, because there had been almost no inflation during the pre-reform decades, post-reform inflation seriously affected China's citizens.

The first serious bout of inflation occurred in 1985. As noted above, the reform featured by deregulation in credit system took a step forward in the year, while there was only slight changes of interest rate. For example, on 1 April 1985, the average annual interest rate on loans was readjusted to 7.3% for state-owned agricultural, industrial, and commercial enterprises, township collective enterprises, and urban and rural individual enterprises. It was only 0.78 percentage point higher than that before the readjustment. Moreover, the major changes were in the interest rates for loans to self-employed businesses in both urban and rural areas. These interest rates increased from 8.6% to 9.4–11.5%. At that time, the interest rates for one-year term deposits were only 6.8%. The relaxation of credit control under conditions of low interest rate gave rise to a grave expansion in investment in 1984 and 1985.

Compared with the situation in 1983, net investment in fixed assets in 1984 saw an increase of 37.6% with an increase of 120% in circulating funds. In 1985 the increases were 94.4% and 110% respectively. However, interest rates were not increased accordingly. As a result, there was no increase in total bank savings. The formerly restrained demand for loans was now met through the loosening of credit control, which resulted in the widening of the gap between deposits and loans and could only be made up by issuing additional currency. As the total currency issued went out of control, prices were skyrocketed. In 1984, the currency in circulation increased by 49.5%, which led to the high inflation in 1985. In the same year, the total national retail price index went up to 108.8, and the index of living expenses reached 111.9, an increases of 6 percentage points and 9.2 percentage points respectively compared with those in 1984.

If the first serious bout of inflation since the reform was a direct result of the policy of maintaining the low interest rate and the loosening of credit, the inflation of 1988 was directly caused by the low interest rate policy and the general expectation of high inflation. The inflation of 1993 was related to the low interest rate policy, the decentralization of credit management, and multiple-channel fund-raising.

The third phase of the cycle manifested itself in the recurring cycles of reform. During the reform, much attention was paid to micro management, the reform of which gave impetus to the restructuring of the resource allocation system. The initiative given to enterprise management and the decentralization of resource allocation led to the economic prosperity. This process was called "decentralization leading to vigour".

When the bottleneck constraint and inflation reached a serious level, normal economic growth was impeded and disorder appeared, which caused discontent and a loss of confidence in the reform. In accordance with the traditional logic of economic development, the government stepped in. Under the precondition of maintaining the old price distortions, the readjustment measures included:

(1) Strictly controlled prices. The first thing the government did was to stabilize prices of consumer goods and production materials, interest rates, and exchange rate by resorting to state power. Price reforms had to be stopped at this time.
(2) Recall management power. In order to restrain enterprise behaviour and correct investment deviation from the old strategic goal, the government often strengthened centralized control by recalling some of the management powers that had been ceded to enterprises or resource allocation departments. The readjustment in the micro management mechanism and resource allocation system after the reforms tended to revert to the traditional development strategy.
(3) Strengthen the control on credit scale. Due to its rigidity, the interest rate does not regulate fund demand and supply. Restraint on investment and its direction can depend only on strict control of the credit scale. There is no mechanism that can distinguish efficient enterprises from inefficient ones. As a result, all enterprises had to be treated in the same way.
(4) Suppress the development of non-state sector. The government deliberately adopted discriminating policies concern-

ing resource allocation against non-state-owned enterprises, since it saw that the strong rent-seeking behaviour of the latter tended to contradict its strategic goal. At the same time, under the conditions of less resources and greater government power, the government always gave preferential treatment to the large and medium-sized SOEs. This policy was crippling so far as resource allocation to the non-state-owned sector was concerned.

In sum, the basic methods used by the government in major and minor readjustments and the so-called "strengthening macro regulation and control" were all carried out through strict administrative means, which were typical of the "disorder leads to retrenchment" phase. The government's policies were a double-edged sword. On the one hand, strict control of investment size and inflation helped cool down the overheated economic growth and check inflation. Strict administrative measures also effectively restrained rent-seeking while increasing economic order. On the other hand, planned resource allocation was strengthened again and price reforms had to be stopped. Once again, the traditional economic system was revitalized. Resources flowed from the efficient non-state-owned economy to inefficient state-owned departments. The cycle moved toward the phase of "retrenchment leads to stagnation".

Once the economy ran into such a situation, enterprises began to incur serious losses. Prices played no role in product and factor markets. Resource allocation was inefficient and growth rates went down by a large margin. Government finance was in deficit. Calls for decentralization then became louder. The non-state-owned sector strengthened its competition for resources. Finally, new reforms took place. This describes the "stagnation leads to decentralization" phase of the cycle. Without a thorough transition in economic strategy, a new cycle then began.

During the 1990s, the Chinese economy once again experienced such a readjustment. At that time, the central government took a series of macro control measures, in particular enacting a moderately tight monetary policy to restrain investment and growth. The government acted when it saw an overheated economy or a bubble economy with overheated real estate, overheated development zones, and excessive investment. Within a few years, inflation was brought down to a relatively low level, while the economy retained a more or less satisfactory growth rate — a phenomenon often described as a "soft landing".

However, the situation has changed. While the government practiced macro-control and a sustained, moderately tight money policy, China's economy went through the heated investment period of 1993–96, left behind long-term shortage and entered a period of over-production. With the farewell to shortage, speculation opportunities no longer existed. At the same time, banks strengthened their control. Therefore, in the mid-1990s the traditional pattern did not emerge. On the contrary, although monetary policy moved toward investment promotion and a series of financial measures were taken, demand did not grow as rapidly as in previous cycles. Moreover, affected by the financial crisis in Southeast Asia, China's foreign trade and foreign capital inflow slowed down.

The emergence of this new phenomenon did not mean that the traditional cycle had come to an end. It is still the case that without a thorough transformation, economic development strategy will not fit the micro reform. Compared with the large and medium-sized state-owned enterprises built under the traditional economic system, small and medium-sized enterprises have the merit of quick accumulation and response, and they can enjoy a rapid rate of development and sound investment cycles. In fact, the newly rising economic sectors represented by the non-state-owned enterprises accounted for an increasingly important proportion in the national economy. However, without a thorough reform in the financial system, a sound development environment will not be created. The fundamental solutions are to accelerate financial reform, realize market interest rates, commercialize the banking system, and regulate investment, consumption and bank deposit via interest rates, which will enable efficient enterprises to attract investments. The main hurdle for financial reform lies in SOE protection, because at present the survival of many SOEs still depends on the support of cheap bank loans. The reform of the state-owned enterprises has thus become the key to develop the economy and quit the traditional cycle.

7.2 Rent-seeking and Corruption

Whenever prices are suppressed and monopolies are created, enterprises have strong incentives to pursue the rents created by the price distortions or monopoly. Under the traditional macro-policy environment, the prices of outputs and inputs are distorted; any enterprise will profit once it has obtained investment, foreign exchange, and materials in short supply from the planning authorities. The amount of the profit will be the difference between the market price and the planned price multiplied by the amount of resources the enterprise has obtained.

In Figure 7.2, when the price of a certain product or production factor is determined on the market, let the price be P_0, the corresponding supply and demand will both be Ob. The market clears. If price is determined by a state plan and is kept below equilibrium level, such as P_1, the market supply will be Oa, far less than the demand. At such a price, market demand can drive the market price (or the price in the black market) to P_2. Therefore, if an enterprise can obtain materials through planned allocation at price P_1, it will at once earn the profit in the shaded area if the resource is assessed with the price P_2. This extra income originates from the macro policy of suppressing prices and from the corresponding institutional arrangement. The enterprises that are able to obtain such cheap-in-price resources are also selected according to the development policy. We term this kind of income as "institutional rent". Rent-seeking activities involve illicit activities (including "back-door" activities, bribery of officials, and various kinds of lobbying by interest groups) so as to obtain resources at low prices and to earn this institutional rent.

Institutional rent and rent-seeking were the inevitable outcomes of the macro-policy environment distorting relative prices. They came into being in the traditional economic system. However, before the reform, because it was difficult to realize these institutional rents,

Figure 7.2 Price control and rent-seeking

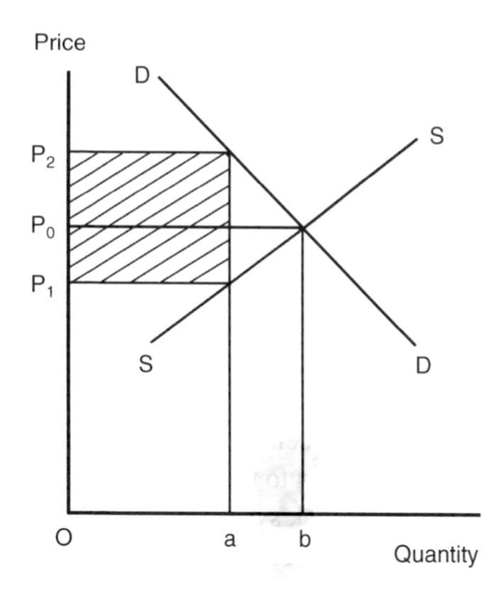

the motivation for rent-seeking activities was weak, and rent-seeking was uncommon. Theoretically, the macro-policy environment that was in place before 1979, with suppressed interest rates, exchange rates, and materials and product prices, had already created the gap between planned prices and market prices, in other words, it had created the institutional rent. Only when individuals or enterprises can actually benefit from rent-seeking activities will the institutional rent be so attractive that rent-seeking becomes so common a phenomenon.

During the years of highly centralized economic management, enterprises were under an accounting system of unified revenue and unified appropriation, where gains from rent-seeking activities could not be translated into private income. Rent-seeking of enterprises were only intended to expand their business. Therefore, there was little incentive to engage in rent-seeking activities. As for officials in charge of resource allocation, their income sources and consumption styles were simple and transparent. Taking bribes would evidently increase their income and consumption levels, which were easily supervised. Besides, the punishment was severe. Therefore, although the institutional rent existed at the time, the motivation for rent-seeking activities were too weak. What did exist at the time were only the activities to acquire resources through personal relations.[2]

Since 1979, the gradual deregulation in the management system and the lag in the reform of the policy environment have increased the appeal of rent-seeking. In addition, owing to the softening of institutional restraints, cash transactions are now more common. The sources of personal income and ways of consumption have diversified. All these have made it possible for rent-seeking activities to surface and become a prevalent phenomenon.

Firstly, the development of the dual-track system gave rise to increased opportunities for rent-seeking. Motivation for rent-seeking is proportional to the gap between the planned price and the market price, and inversely proportional to the probability that penalties will be incurred. Under the dual-track system, more resources entered the market and helped to lower the price gap as well as the rent value for every unit of resource. In this way, this system indeed weakened the motive for rent-seeking activities. But the demarcation line between the planned allocation of resources and market transactions also became blurred. As a result, supervision costs increased, and merely shifting resources from the planned track to the market track could create huge profits for the involved persons. Thus, obtaining under-priced resources allocated by the state became a low-risk but high-gain activity. "*Guandao*" (arbitrage by officials) and "*sidao*" (arbitrage by private individuals) became shortcuts to fortune.

According to the estimates of some scholars, institutional rent created by gaps in the prices, interest rates and foreign exchange rates

2. Some scholars have noted that rent under the dual-track system is less than that under the planned economy. They are therefore of the opinion that rent-seeking behaviour under the dual-track system is not necessarily more severe than that under the planned economy. See Liew Leong, *The Chinese Economy in Transition: From Plan to Market*. Cheltenham, UK and Brookfield, USA: Edward Elgar, 1997, pp. 67–77. However, this analysis overlooks the differences in motivation under the dual-track system and that under the planned economy. Such motivation is not necessarily related to the intensity of the government management function.

amounted to RMB 200 billion in 1987 and RMB 350 billion in 1988, accounting for 20–25% of the GNP.[3] As a result, large quantities of resources leaked from the planned track. Some resources that should have been allocated according to the plan were priced but were unavailable for enterprises, while some had only market prices but no planned price. Every regulatory and distributional department became the target for rent-seekers, as long as they were in charge of either capital, or foreign exchange, or other materials in short supply. Even if they were not in charge of the allocation of resources, so long as they could influence those in charge, they became the targets for bribers.

Secondly, while the gradual reform in the traditional resource allocation system was taking place, control over the circulation system relaxed. In order to seek the institutional rent, various types of companies and business entities rushed into the allocation system of productive factors and the circulation system of products. At the time, some administrative companies were established to serve the special interest of particular departments. These companies significantly facilitated the "official arbitrage". Since they were subsidiary institutions to those departments, some of them directly got control over the resources in the planned track. When these companies sold the resources on the market, they immediately got a huge amount of profit in hand. Because of this huge rent, some of the officials in charge of the companies could not resist the temptation of briberies. All this gave rise to corruption. To limit operating units' huge illegal profits, the government at times restricted the range of the added prices in distribution. But it only resulted in the extension of the rent-seeking chain and made rent-seeking activities more diversified and complicated. After the rent had been shared on every link in the distribution and circulation system, producers would still buy the resource although the price had become relatively higher.

Under the dual-track economic system, resources ran through

---

3. Hu Heli, "Three Measures for a Clean Government", in *Corruption: Trading of Power for Money*. Beijing: China Outlook Press, 1989, pp. 36–43.

numerous phases and were allocated through various channels. Although this distributional mode did help the non-state-owned sector to obtain resources at competitive prices, it had incurred enormous social cost. Firstly, when resources were obtained by more competitive non-state-owned businesses, the state had to meet the demands of large and medium-sized enterprises by issuing more currency. This practice led to inflation and an unbalanced distribution of resources, which finally resulted in an overheated economy. Secondly, to obtain necessary materials, some SOEs had to pay much higher prices, or they themselves joined rent-seekers by offering bribes to officials, which in turn increased their production costs. Hard bargaining followed in determining the profit sharing ratio between the state and the SOEs while they were signing the contracts. With their bargaining power, these SOEs transferred the cost to the government. When the government found that it could no longer bear the burden fiscally, it tended to restrain the development of non-SOEs by administrative measures. Thirdly, the wide spread of rent-seeking and bribery activities corrupted government officials and poisoned the social atmosphere. It had also impaired people's confidence in the reform. Therefore, the losses caused by rent-seeking activities were too costly to be measured by money.

Finally, the diversified sources of income and various ways of consumption enhanced the chances for people to increase their income and consumption. At the same time, the policy that allowed certain individuals to become wealthy before others, made it possible for proceeds from rent-seeking activities to mingle with legal income. Illegal proceeds of rent seekers and bribe takers could thus be sheltered in the legal income. The costs of supervision and detection thereby increased. Lastly, the high income-level of the non-state-owned enterprise managers and those rent-seekers and bribery takers reduced the relative income level of other government officials and workers in SOEs. In this way, the gap in income levels widened, and those who became rich illegally without being punished had obviously some demonstrative effects on others. All these inspired the motivation for personal gains, and created a lot of new rent-seekers and bribery takers.

7.3 Difficulties in the Reform of State-owned Enterprises

China's SOEs were established to accomplish the government's goal of pursuing a heavy-industry-oriented development strategy. The government consistently regarded SOEs, especially large and medium-sized ones, as the basic means to achieve its goals under the traditional development strategy. While small SOEs and non-SOEs entered the market and adapted themselves to the market environment, the reform of large and medium-sized SOEs were tied down by the objectives of traditional development strategy. As a result, the reform in this area has so far failed to make a substantial break through. This section will focus on the problems in the reform of large and medium-sized SOEs. Later, when we use the word "SOEs", we actually refer to the large and medium-sized SOEs.

Since the onset of economic reform, SOEs have been the focus of the reform. In general, the process has tarried around the line of expanding SOEs' autonomy and increasing SOEs' retained profit. The adoption of this approach is intended to counteract the inefficiency and lifelessness of traditional economic system, which was characterized by ultimate state control in the economic planning, accounting, purchasing and marketing. Indeed, the measures were successful in certain aspects. When SOEs were permitted to retain a larger share of their profits, their incentives for profit earning, technological innovation, and market-oriented production increased. These measures accelerated the reform in the resource-allocation system and, to a certain extent, promoted the reform in the macro-policy environment. In addition, as profits were used independently for enterprise development and to increase workers' welfare and bonuses, the incentives of workers and managers increased further, and efficiency improved. An unexpected result is that: some enterprises put part of their profits into sectors that had been depressed under the old development strategy; hence, the efficiency in resource allocation improved and more economic resources were created for incremental reform.

Up to now, the reform in SOEs has two effects. As we look into the incentive mechanism and the efficiency of enterprises, it is evident that the reform has brought about positive effects. For example, an investigation of SOEs shows that the profit sharing rate, the degree of market participation and the index of "marketization" rose synchronously in the late 1980s.[4] However, as we view the reform from the point of view of the owner, the reform has had a negative effect on state equity, which has been increasingly encroached upon in the process of the reform by way of profit retention and decentralization, and later in the reform of enterprise ownership.

SOEs and their management structures are products of the traditional development strategy. Before the reform, in order to develop strategic industries that were not viable under the market economy, the government distorted prices of products and factors to subsidize firms in those industries. Since there was no competitive market, there was no such thing as normal profit level in the industry that could be used as a criterion to assess the performance of individual enterprise. The profit level of a particular enterprise therefore could not fully reflect the functioning of the enterprise and thus could not be used as an indicator for its management efficiency. It was too costly for the owner to obtain relevant information, such as whether there were problems in the expenditures and profit of the firm and whether owners' interests were carefully protected.

Because of this information asymmetry between managers and owners, the incompatibility of incentives between them became an insurmountable problem. Under the traditional system, there were great discrepancies in the returns for factors among enterprises and industries. If SOEs could make independent investment decisions, they could allocate resources to the place with highest marginal returns.[5] Such marginal adjustments would obviously upset the

4. Du Haiyan, et al., "Decision-making Power of the State-owned Enterprise, Market Structure and the Bonus System", *Economic Research*, No. 1 (1990).
5. The results achieved in the reform of SOEs in the early 1980s can be used as evidence for the occurrence of this possibility. When an SOE obtains some management power it would allocate its available resources to industries of high marginal payment.

implementation of the heavy-industry-oriented development strategy and the functioning of the planned economic system. Moreover, with the help of information asymmetry, managers could make managerial and distributional decisions in favour of themselves at the expense of the state.

Since the survival of SOEs depends on the absence of competitive market, and the establishment of SOEs was intended to get control over production surplus of the enterprise, SOEs should not of course have any decision-making power. This was an implicit prerequisite for a successful implementation of the old development strategy. In other words, the only practical way to prevent encroachment upon state-owned assets was to deprive the enterprise of its right to make managerial decisions. Under these conditions, the government allocated investments and other productive factors free of charge, whereas the specification, quantity, allocation, and marketing of products were all decided in the government plan. Financial accounting existed under a system of unified revenue and unified appropriation, with the state taking all the profits and writing off all the losses. In such a distorted macro-policy environment and highly centralized allocation system, the kind of institutional setup mentioned above was actually the one with the lowest supervision cost. In fact, the institutional setups in the management of SOEs did follow the same logic. As a result, although the traditional system experienced several rounds of decentralization and centralization reform, management rights were never truly delegated to enterprises.

Since 1979, the reform in areas of micro efficiency and incentive mechanisms have indeed made some substantial progress, but there has been no fundamental changes in the old development strategy. In order to support the SOEs in heavy industry, the reform in the macro-policy environment was retarded, and was left far behind by reforms in other areas. On the other hand, the reform in the institutional setups of enterprise management and the allocation system of economic resources has made a much more rapid and thorough progress. Consequently, the overall institutional setups of economy becomes disharmonious, which leads to a series of problems.

Because of these mal-coordinated reform policies, SOEs have to bear a series of policy burdens and consequently they cannot have an equal competition with non-state-owned enterprises. In other words, the heavy-industry-oriented development strategy has not been changed fundamentally. Because of this, while non-state-owned sectors were making adjustment to the distorted industrial structure, the SOEs were put in the position to carry on with the traditional strategy. This is illustrated by the three major policy burdens laid on the SOEs.

Firstly, in light of the capital scarcity situation in China, many large SOEs are too capital-intensive, and therefore lack viability in a competitive market economy. With the help of non-state-owned sectors, the resources newly created through micro-reform flowed into industries with comparative advantages. In this way, the distorted industrial structure was adjusted incrementally. Since the old economic development strategy had not been discarded completely, in order to maintain a certain proportion of heavy industries and realize the development strategy, most of the strategic burdens fall on the shoulders of SOEs.

From the public data, we can have the share of the NFAV (net fixed asset value) of industrial enterprises by ownership in the overall NFAV of all industrial sectors. The corresponding share of the value-added of industry by ownership is also available. We use the quotient of these two shares to denote the relative capital intensities of enterprises with different ownership. In 1995, the relative capital intensity in SOEs was 1.22, while that for collective-owned enterprises was 0.57, for shareholding enterprises was 0.96, for foreign-funded enterprises was 0.83, and for Hong Kong-, Taiwan-, and Macau-funded enterprises was 1.03. The capital intensity in SOEs was still comparatively too high. SOEs would have found it difficult to survive if they had been required to pay interest rates at the market level. It would also be too difficult for them to compete with domestic labour-intensive non-SOEs and foreign capital-intensive enterprises, because the latter two both follow their economies' comparative advantages.

Secondly, SOEs had to pay the pensions, staff welfare

expenditures, subsidies for laid-off workers and support redundant personnel. The SOE accounting system before reform was one of unified revenue and unified appropriation. Expenditures were all paid by the state. Therefore the above expenditures were no serious burdens for SOEs. After reform, SOEs had to pay the wages and pensions themselves. This was difficult for them, because on the one hand they had not accumulated sufficient funds to cover pensions, on the other hand they had to absorb a large amount of redundant workers. Even under this condition, the government still demanded that they provide subsidies for laid-off workers. The financial burden on SOEs had thus become extremely heavy.

According to conservative estimates, redundant staff in SOEs in general account for one-third of the total number of SOE employees. As for the number of retired workers and staff, it was 25.15 million in 1996, half of whom left work or retired before 1988. Those who left work or retired before 1985 constituted about one-third, and those who left work or retired before 1978 constituted less than 6%. In late 1990s, the ratio between on-the-job employees and retirees is about 5.9 to 1, which means that SOEs would have paid 46% less in wages if they had not been obliged to absorb redundant employees and pay the pensions.

The problem of urban unemployment has become increasingly severe since the mid-1990s. There are two sources of unemployment in China. The first is workers leaving their jobs, thereby lose their income as an employee. The registered unemployment rate in cities and towns was only 3.1% in 1997. However, many surveys have shown that the actual rate might have reached 6–8% or higher. Those who register as unemployed usually receive unemployment allowance from the state. The second source of unemployment is layoffs. Laid-off workers leave their jobs but maintain their employment relationship with their former employer. Their former employer continues to ensure that they have basic life necessities. Enterprises thus take on some of the responsibilities of the social security system to provide assistance to laid-off workers. In this situation, they have only two options: to absorb the redundant workers and practice a work-sharing system, or to take on the burden of subsidizing the unemployed, thereby in effect continue the practice of a revenue-sharing system.

Thirdly, some product prices of SOEs are still distorted. Distortion in prices of energy, transportation, raw materials and other public services is an indispensable condition for the implementation of heavy-industry-oriented development strategy, or else the implementation of this strategy would be too costly. Inflation caused by price adjustments in upper-stream industries has continued to be of great concern for the government. For these reasons, most price control and regulations exist in areas, in which large and medium-sized SOEs operate. By the end of 1996, in the total sale of production materials, 14% of the prices were set by the government, and another 5% were set under government guidance. Most of these price regulations are meant to suppress the prices of products and services mentioned above. Under these conditions, SOEs found it difficult to compete with non-SOEs, not to mention international enterprises.

These problems have three consequences. First, they lead to serious financial losses. In 1996, about one-third of SOEs enjoyed profits, one-third suffered explicit losses, and the other one-third suffered hidden losses. In 1997, there emerged a new phenomenon, i.e., certain industry as a whole suffered losses. Second, there is the serious losses in state-owned assets. Based on the 1994 investigation of the assets and capital of 124,000 SOEs conducted by the Ministry of Finance, it is calculated that among the 80,000 small SOEs, the loss of state equity (including net losses in asset value, operational losses, and implicit losses in accounts) accounted for 82.8% of total net value of the state equity. The percentage for medium-sized SOEs was 59.4%, while for large SOEs the percentage was 15.2%.[6] Third, the asset-liability ratio of SOEs is too high. Since government appropriations were replaced by loans, this ratio has increased significantly. It was 30% in 1980, 40% in 1985, 60% in 1990, and jumped to 75% in 1994.

6. Lu Zhongyuan, "Actively Push Forward the Reform of the Small State-owned Enterprises", *China Industrial Economy*, No. 4 (1996), pp. 30–32.

7.4 Non-performing Loans and Malpractice in the Financial System

SOEs' high asset-liability ratio is obviously not caused by the reform in enterprise financing from government appropriation to bank loans. The intention of this reform was to harden SOEs' soft budget constraints and to enable the SOEs to become independent micro-economic units. However, owing to the above-mentioned policy burdens, SOEs were in no position to compete with non-SOEs in the competitive market. Because these policy burdens were imposed on them by the government against their will, the SOEs could continue to ask for government subsidies under this pretext. Consequently, while explicit financial subsidies for SOEs were gradually reduced, hidden subsidies through bank loans increased.

Hidden subsidies through state-owned banks took two forms. One was the low-interest-rate loan. In 1985, of the total subsidies obtained by SOEs, only 24.2% came through financial channels, with the rest coming through fiscal channels. In 1994, the proportion of subsidies given to SOEs through financial channels rose to 43.6%, while the share through fiscal channels decreased.[7] The other form of subsidies was actually obtained through the delays of loan payments. Because SOEs could deny their responsibilities for poor management under the pretext of various policy burdens, and because they ensured large-scale employment and in effect provide security services for their employees, the government would often continue to provide them with loans for their operation and maintenance, even if they were losing money. As a result, their liabilities to banks increased gradually, and the liabilities gradually became too large for them to pay off either the principal or the interest on these loans. Then most of the loans became non-performing loans or bad debts. It was estimated that in the late 1990s non-performing loans made up 20–25% of the total loans of the four major state-owned specialized

7. The World Bank, *The Chinese Economy: Fighting Inflation, Deepening Reforms*, Vol. I (Report No. 15288-CNA, 1996), p. 16.

banks, a rate even higher than Thailand, Malaysia, Indonesia and Korea's debt ratios during the financial crisis.

These problems in the loans of Chinese state-owned banks were caused by SOEs and their policy burdens. They also revealed the existing malpractices in the financial system. In 1993, the Third Plenary Session of the 14th Congress of the Communist Party of China decided to aim financial reform toward "commercialization of banks and marketization of interest rate". Up till now, the interest rate is still under state control and the state-owned banks still enjoy the monopoly power in the financial sector. The goals of financial reform are far from realized.

Firstly, interest rates still fail to reflect the capital scarcity in China. In recent years, in order to deal with price fluctuations and the aggregate demand of the economy, the central bank has begun to regulate interest rates flexibly, so as to control or stimulate aggregate demand. However, the interest rate has never reflected capital scarcity. Whether the interest rate is raised or lowered, it is still distorted. At present, since capital scarcity is still the basic characteristic of the Chinese economic endowment structure, the present interest rate is too low. If competition were introduced into the financial sector with commercial operation and market interest rates, state-owned banks would definitely lose their monopoly.

Secondly, state-owned banks have to undertake the task of implementing state industrial policies. At the same time, in order to maintain social stability, they are obliged to provide loans to SOEs that suffer losses and cannot repay their debts. Although the reform in the banking system has transferred some policy-related operations to policy banks, commercial banks still have to meet many policy-related requirements. This makes it impossible to accurately assess the actual performance of commercial banks. Losses from poor management is often mixed up with losses caused by policy factors, which makes it difficult to operate commercially. Moreover, protective policies for large enterprises are harmful to the development of small and medium-sized enterprises, especially non-SOEs.

Finally, because of the problems in the management system of state-owned banks and the lack of flexibility in their business operations under a non-market interest rate, banks have to rely on their monopolistic power. At present, one important provision included in China's financial regulations is the control of non-state-owned banks and other financial institutions as well as their business operations. The existence and operation of private loans, rural cooperative funds, and foreign financial institutions are all strictly controlled. Even cooperative financial organizations with significant economic scales are banned to participate in banking activities. The resulting lack of competition has given rise to various kinds of malpractice in the management of state-owned banks. It has also given rise to their inability to support the development of non-state-owned sector, an important function they should have been performing.

7.5 The Aggravation of Uneven Regional Development

The reform in the past 20 years has seen growing regional disparities. In the late 1970s, China's central region played a major role in the reform. For instance, the household responsibility system and the experiment of delegating power to SOEs were both started from there. When pricing and financial reforms took hold, the eastern regions began to outperform other parts of the country. The first special economic zones and development zones were located in the east. Especially after the mid-1980s, TVEs with a solid foundation in the eastern areas played an important role in economic development. At the same time, a number of special policies were applied to the coastal areas. These made the eastern regions the center of reform and development, leaving the central and western regions in a disadvantageous position.

This pattern of reform and development had doubtlessly led to the unevenness in economic development and in the per capita income level among regions. The disparities were most apparent in rural development, rural income levels, and the widening gap between rural and urban areas. According to the relevant data, the changes in the ratio of rural income and expenditure to urban income and expenditure took on a U-shape, with 1985 being the turning point. Below is an analysis of the changes in the income disparities between rural and urban areas and that among different regions.

The first issue to be explored is the widening gap between rural and urban per capita income. The narrowing down of this gap is a fundamental benchmark of economic and social development. However, the reality is that, in China, the once-narrowing gap is widening again. Firstly, this can be seen in the relative decrease in rural household income. Since the beginning of the reform, the annual net income per capita in rural areas, calculated in current prices, had increased 16.9 times by the end of 2000, from the RMB 133.6 in 1978 to RMB 2,253.4 in 2000. If price factors were deducted, it had increased 3.84 times. This is in sharp contrast to the pre-1978 situation, when per capita rural income saw little increase over several decades. However, in comparison with per capita income in cities and towns, rural per capita income had decreased relatively. Based on current prices, the ratio of per capita income in cities and towns to that in rural areas in 1978 was 2.36:1, the former being nearly 140% higher than the latter. In 1984, the ratio decreased to 1.7:1, but it increased to 2.71:1 in 1995. Although it decreased somewhat in 2000, to 2.69:1, it was still higher than that of 1978.

Secondly, compared with the consumption of city and town residents, rural consumption decreased relatively. Urban people can spend their entire income on living expenditures, but rural residents must spend part of their net income on production. Therefore, it is more useful to compare their consumption levels. According to the statistics, the ratio of urban per capita annual living expenditures to that of rural areas was 2.9:1 in 1978; that is, consumption level in urban areas was 190% higher than that in rural areas. In 1985, it decreased to 2.2:1. This ratio increased after 1989. It reached 3.5:1. in 1994. Although it went down to 3.1:1 in 1997, but went up again to 3.5:1 in 2000.

The second issue to be explored is the widening regional income disparities (RID). This is shown in the following aspects: (1) the widening income disparities between coastal and inland areas, (2) the widening income disparities between eastern and western regions,[8] and (3) the widening income disparities between the eastern rural and central and western rural areas.

In 1978, the per capita income ratio between the eastern and central regions was 1.15:1, and the ratio between the eastern and western regions was 1.26:1. These ratios increased to 1.47:1 and 1.77:1, respectively, in 1997. There was basically no change in per capita income in the eastern, central and western urban areas from 1978 to 1984, but some changes did occur thereafter. Comparatively speaking, the changes in Inter-RID (inter-regional income disparities) in urban areas were small. The ratio of per capita income in the urban areas of the eastern region to that of the central region was 1.13:1 in 1978; while the ratio of per capita income in the urban areas of the eastern region to that of the western region was 1.14:1. In 1997, they rose to 1.44:1 and 1.36:1, respectively. In short, there were only small changes in the Inter-RID in urban areas. According to some analyses, this was caused by the small inter-regional differences in the reform of SOE distributional system, and because most of the urban labour was employed in SOEs.

The Inter-RID in per capita terms was most significant in rural areas. In 1978, the ratio of per capita income in the rural areas of the eastern region to that of the central region was 1.15:1, and the ratio of per capita income in the rural areas of the eastern region to that of the western region was 1.19:1. In 1997, the figures increased to 1.43:1 and 1.79:1, respectively. The ratio of the eastern and western rural areas was significantly higher than the corresponding ratio in urban areas. If we compare the figures of the most developed provinces with that of ordinary provinces, the disparity is more striking. For example, in 1997, the per capita annual income of rural inhabitants of

8. The eastern region includes Beijing, Tianjin, Hebei, Liaoning, Shanghai, Jiangsu, Zhejiang, Fujian, Shandong, Guangdong, Guangxi and Hainan, a total of 12 provinces and municipalities. The central region includes Shanxi, Inner Mongolia, Jilin, Heilongjiang, Anhui, Jiangxi, Henan, Hubei, and Hunan, a total of 9 provinces. The western region includes Sichuan, Guizhou, Yunnan, Tibet, Shaanxi, Gansu, Qinghai, Ningxia and Xinjiang, a total of 9 provinces.

Shanghai was RMB 5,277.02 and that of rural inhabitants of Sichuan Province was only RMB 1,298.54; the ratio of the two figures was 4.06:1 — more than two times larger than the average regional difference.

To illustrate the changes in the development gap among regions, we have calculated income and consumption Gini coefficients of rural and urban residents from 1978 to 1997, based on the data at province level (including municipalities directly under the central government's administration and autonomous regions) (see Table 7.1). It illustrates that in both urban and rural areas, changes in income disparity followed a U-shape. This indicates that income disparity decreased in the initial stages of the reform but increased after the mid-1980s.

To determine the origins of the differences, we adopted the Theil entropy method. We separated the total disparity of per capita income into Intra-RID (or internal disparity) of the eastern region, the central

Table 7.1 Changes in the Gini Coefficient of Per Capita Income and Consumption in Urban and Rural Areas* (1978–97)

Year	Urban income Gini coefficient	Rural income Gini coefficient	Urban consumption Gini coefficient	Rural consumption Gini coefficient
1978	0.0766	0.1000	0.0849	0.1276
1980	0.0692	0.1136	0.0751	0.0916
1982	0.0661	0.1304	0.0696	0.1014
1984	0.0710	0.1127	0.0790	0.1029
1986	0.0786	0.1194	0.0743	0.1088
1988	0.0949	0.1545	0.0816	0.1204
1990	0.1035	0.1279	0.0743	0.1264
1991	0.1109	0.1582	0.0729	0.1269
1992	0.1314	0.1651	0.0785	0.1282
1993	0.1499	0.1810	0.0902	0.1299
1994	0.1578	0.1876	0.0999	0.1348
1995	0.1509	0.2080	0.1263	0.1325
1996	0.1354	0.3384	0.1557	0.1680
1997	0.1365	0.1900	0.1160	0.1665

* Regional disparities based on data at province-level

Source: National Bureau of Statistics of China, *China Statistical Yearbook*, various issues.

region, and the western region, and Inter-RID. The results indicate that, among the overall regional disparities in per capita income (i.e., RID), the Inter-RID (i.e., the regional income disparity among the three regions) was most important (see Table 7.2). The contribution of this Inter-RID amounted to 50% of the total, while the Intra-RID of the eastern region had the second largest effect, which constituted a little more than 20%. The contribution of the Intra-RID of the central and western regions were about the same, both constituted about 15%. As for the changes in the relative importance, the contribution of the Intra-RID of the eastern and central regions had decreased, while that of the western region had increased. None of these changes were significant.

Table 7.2 The Contribution of Intra- and Inter-RID to the Overall RID in the Per Capita Income (%)

Year	Intra-RID of the east	Intra-RID of the central	Intra-RID of the west	Inter-RID
1978	21.52	14.95	14.57	48.95
1979	21.21	14.78	14.67	49.34
1980	21.12	14.72	14.76	49.40
1981	20.79	14.75	14.87	49.59
1982	20.67	14.77	14.91	49.66
1983	20.61	14.81	14.95	49.64
1984	20.71	14.74	14.95	49.60
1985	20.74	14.73	14.92	49.62
1986	20.76	14.69	14.91	49.64
1987	20.73	14.66	14.85	49.76
1988	20.74	14.65	14.87	49.75
1989	20.84	14.62	14.81	49.73
1990	20.78	14.70	14.78	49.74
1991	20.77	14.61	14.66	49.96
1992	20.80	14.57	14.67	49.96
1993	20.99	14.43	14.61	49.96
1994	21.09	14.36	14.68	49.87
1995	20.88	14.39	14.58	50.15

Source: Justin Yifu Lin, Cai Fang, and Li Zhou, "Consequences des Reformes Economicques sur les Disparites Regionales en Chine", *Revue d'Economie du Development*, Vol. 1, No. 2 (1999), pp. 7–32.

Using the same method, we have also decomposed the overall regional per capita income disparity into the following three categories: (1) Rural-RID (i.e., income disparity within rural areas), (2) Urban-RID (i.e., income disparity within cities and towns), and (3) UR-RID (i.e., income disparity between the rural and urban areas). Their individual contributions (in percentage) to the overall regional income disparity (RID) are presented in Table 7.3. The table shows that UR-RID had the greatest contribution (which moved around 50%). The overall contribution of Rural-RID and Urban-RID also amounted to about 50%. The contribution of Rural-RID was a bit larger than that of Urban-RID. As for the changes in the relative importance, the contribution of Rural-RID increased most rapidly, from 23.82% in 1978 to 27.02% in 1995. The contribution of Urban-RID also increased, but it was less significant than that of Rural-RID;

Table 7.3 Contribution of of Rural-, Urban- and UR-RID to the Overall RID (%)

Year	Rural-RID	Urban-RID	UR-RID
1978	23.82	22.82	53.36
1979	24.16	23.21	52.63
1980	24.45	23.63	51.92
1981	24.72	23.95	51.33
1982	25.04	24.2	50.76
1983	25.33	24.43	50.24
1984	25.73	24.37	49.89
1985	25.17	24.36	50.47
1986	25.06	23.93	51.01
1987	25.23	23.98	50.79
1988	25.36	24.05	50.58
1989	25.38	23.77	50.85
1990	26.12	23.86	50.02
1991	26.27	23.65	50.08
1992	26.15	23.56	50.29
1993	26.10	23.4	50.50
1994	26.42	23.37	50.20
1995	27.02	23.47	49.51

Source: Justin Yifu Lin, Cai Fang, and Li Zhou, "Consequences des Reformes Economicques sur les Disparites Regionales en Chine", *Revue d'Economie du Development*, Vol. 1, No. 2 (1999), pp. 7–32.

In the same period, it only increased from 22.82% to 23.47%. We have identified an interesting phenomenon: although UR-RID made important contributions to overall RID, its contributions had decreased from 53.36% to 49.51% and showed a tendency to decrease further. People often noticed the widening UR-RID but fail to recognize that its contribution to the overall regional disparity tended to diminish.

Province-level data have one shortcoming: they have covered up internal disparities within provinces. For this reason, we re-calculated the disparity of the country as a whole and the disparities within provinces. The 1992 county-level data was used in the calculation (see Table 7.4). The results of our calculation indicate that the Gini coefficients of the national per capita income, the national per capita income of the rural population, and the national per capita income of the urban population were, as expected, higher than those based on province-level data. In most provinces, based on the county-level data of per capita income, the Gini coefficient of a particular province was smaller than that of the country as a whole. This indicates that the income was more evenly distributed within most of the provinces than that in the whole country, except for Guangdong, Yunnan, Gansu, and Ningxia Provinces. The per capita income disparity in Beijing, Tianjin, and Shanghai was the smallest.

In recent year, UR-RID and Inter-RID are widening. This is mainly due to the slow increase in the income of rural households. Their consumption levels have seen a relative decline. Various forms of funds retained by the rural collectives have become heavy burdens for rural residents in many areas. Although rural development is faster than urban development, UR-RID is still widening, this is abnormal. If this problem is put aside for too long, it will not only disturb grassroot political stability but may also eventually give rise to political disturbances. The widening regional income gap, especially the excessive income disparity[9] between rural residents

9. A relevant survey indicates that the income of the latter is only 23.6% of the former.

Table 7.4 Gini Coefficient Calculated on the Basis of County-level Data, 1992

	Per capita income	Rural per capita income	Urban per capita income
Nationwide (Province-level data)	0.1484	0.1437	0.0910
Nationwide (County-level data)	0.3519	0.2003	0.1448
Beijing	0.0446	0.1330	
Tianjin	0.1434	0.0251	
Hebei	0.2996	0.1741	0.0616
Shanxi	0.3158	0.1460	0.0951
Inner Mongolia	0.2331	0.1328	0.0691
Liaoning	0.2408	0.1475	0.0631
Jilin	0.1991	0.0491	0.0505
Heilongjiang	0.2142	0.1240	0.0991
Shannghai	0.1171	0.0893	
Jiangsu	0.2991	0.1575	0.0813
Zhejiang	0.3134	0.2258	0.0498
Anhui	0.2593	0.1258	0.0533
Fujian	0.2375	0.1006	0.1229
Jiangxi	0.2154	0.1578	0.0289
Shandong	0.3118	0.1336	0.0586
Henan	0.2470	0.1301	0.0798
Hubei	0.3122	0.1554	0.0572
Hunan	0.2272	0.1181	0.0700
Guangdong	0.3969	0,1239	0.1194
Guangxi	0.2455	0.1710	0.0475
Hainan	0.2949	0.0818	
Sichuan	0.3038	0.1752	0.0445
Guizhou	0.3385	0.1770	0.0386
Yunnan	0.3886	0.2515	0.0499
Tibet	0.1644	0.1644	
Shaanxi	0.2954	0.1320	0.0652
Gansu	0.3803	0.2362	0.0706
Qinghai	0.3069	0.1510	
Ningxia	0.4259	0.3026	
Xinjiang	0.3141	0.1524	0.1048

Note: No Gini coefficient is calculated for provinces with less than three city samples.

Source: Justin Yifu Lin, Cai Fang, and Li Zhou, "Consequences des Reformes Economicques sur les Disparites Regionales en Chine", *Revue d'Economie du Development*, Vol. 1, No. 2 (1999), pp. 7–32.

remaining in rural areas and those moving to cities, may lead to blind migration. Without relevant reforms in the household registration system and the construction of relevant urban infrastructure, those rural residents working in cities would often be inappropriately forced to return home. As a result, they would not expect stability and would thus be more likely to take short-term activities. This constitutes a hidden danger to social fabric, which may lead to social disturbances.

7.6 The Potential of Grain Supply

In the past few decades, China, although short of arable land, has successfully managed to feed 21% of the world population. However, before 1979, there had been in effect no real remarkable achievement in agricultural production. Real changes began in the late 1970s. The production team system was replaced by the household responsibility system. Markets for rural products and production factors were re-opened. Meanwhile, restrictions on prices were relaxed for agricultural products except for grain and cotton. Then, we saw the Chinese miracle in grain production. However, since the mid-1980s, China has seen repeated fluctuations in its annual output of grains. At the same time, in light of its continuous population growth, its natural resources conditions, the changes in its comparative advantages and its possible influence on the international grain market, China's grain productions has been a constant concern of the international community, of Chinese policy-makers, and of Chinese and foreign scholars.

Let's do the demand and supply analysis as usual. As for the demand side: first, China's present per capita nutritional level is above the world average. However, it is still much lower than that of developed countries, especially in view of the low dietary intake from animal products (see Table 7.5). Of course, food consumption patterns are not determined solely by income level; they are also affected by economic and cultural factors. But if the experiences of Hong Kong, South Korea, and Japan are of any indication, China's demand for animal products will grow proportionally by a large

Table 7.5 Per Capita Daily Nutrition and Its Source (1995)

	Chinese Mainland		Developed countries		Hong Kong		Korea		Japan	
	Total	Animal	Total	Animal	Total	Animal	Total	Animal	Total	Animal
Energy (Kcal.)	2741	506	3191	861	3285	1048	3268	511	2887	596
Protein (g.)	72	24	98	55	109	78	85	35	96	53
Fat (g)	69	44	114	63	137	72	82	38	80	36

Source: Food and Agriculture Organization (FAO), "FAOSTAT", at http://www.fao.org.

margin with the increase of per capita income. This means that a decrease in direct per capita grain consumption due to an income increase will be offset by an increase in indirect grain consumption through an increase in the consumption of animal products. In addition, population growth will add to direct grain consumption. China's population of 1999 stood at 1.28 billion, and it will have increased by 30–40% by the year 2030. As a result, the demand for grain will be much greater, even if grain consumption per capita remained stable since 1999.

Secondly, with the increase in per capita income, there will be a greater demand for vegetables and fruits, which will take up part of China's limited arable farmland for grain production. During the past 20 years, as household income has increased in China, the agricultural structure has changed considerably to accommodate changing consumption patterns. In the total sown area, the proportion of sown area of grain crops decreased from 80.3% in 1978 to 73.8% in 1996, whereas that of vegetables and fruits increased from 2.5% to 7.7% during the same period. A greater demand for freshwater aquatic products will similarly decrease the amount of farmland devoted to grain production or other farm crops. In addition, a higher per capita income will give rise to a rapid development of Chinese liquor production industry, which will result in more consumption of grains.

As for the supply side, whether the output increase of grains could be maintained and whether the food security of China could be ensured, all depend on the potential of scientific and technical progress as well as on the appropriateness of policy. Since the great agricultural crisis of 1959–61, due to the strenuous research efforts, China has taken the lead in the world in many areas of the grain-production-related scientific research. In 1966, the International Rice Research Institute located in the Philippines developed semi-dwarf rice varieties, which marked the beginning of the Green Revolution. As early as 1964, China had already developed and popularized a similar strain of rice. In 1976, hybrid-rice was popularized. Until 1990s, China remained to be the only country that produced hybrid-rice in large scale. In recent years, Professor Yuan Longping, "father of hybrid-rice", has been working on the transition of interbred rice from the three-line approach to a two-line approach. According to a survey, the highest yield obtained in China's experimental plots is roughly 1.5–3.5 times as large as that of the unit yield of regular grain farmland. There is thus a great potential for future increase of grain production in China.[10]

Increasing grain production through scientific and technological progress requires the support of appropriate policies. At present, however, a number of policies tend to have unfavourable effects on the sustained growth of grain production. Firstly, the price of grains is kept intentionally too low. Accurate price signals are one of the most important guaranties for the protection of grain-crops producers and their enthusiasm in production. Due to the reform in the last two decades, the prices of most farm crops are now determined by supply and demand on the market. At present, the prices of about 80% of agricultural products are determined on the market (see Table 7.6), but grain remains one of the few agricultural products whose price is still under control. The relative prices for grain fluctuate with the government's perception of the grain production. As a result, grain output has fluctuated, and new technology applications have been

10. Justin Yifu Lin, Shen Minggao and Zhou Hao, *Agricultural Research Priorities: An Demand and Supply Analysis of Grain Technology in China.* Beijing: Agriculture Press, 1996.

Table 7.6 Proportions in the Total Purchase of Agricultural Products under Different Price-setting Mechanisms

	1990	1992	1994	1996
Price set by government	25.0	12.5	16.6	16.9
Price set by government guidance	23.4	5.7	4.1	4.1
Price set by the market	51.6	81.8	79.3	79.0

Source: State Planning Commission, Price Administration Bureau, "The Weights and Changes of Three Patterns of Prices", *Price in China*, No. 12 (1997).

impeded. Moreover, as the per capita income increases, the comparative advantages also changes. In agricultural sector, grain production needs more farmland and less labour, which contradicts the comparative advantage of China's agricultural resources. Therefore, maintaining an excessively high level of self-sufficiency in grain production will increase production costs, and dampen farmers' enthusiasm in grain production and in the adoption of new technologies.

Secondly, the current level of government investment in agricultural studies is inadequate. The reform of the fund-raising policy for agricultural research in the 1990s constitutes part of the overall market-oriented reform. The government has decreased financial appropriations for agricultural research. Financing shifted from a pattern of fixed payments to financing with competition. Commercialized research is encouraged, and part of the revenue from technology innovation is used to subsidize research activities. Although income from commercial technology has grown, the proportion used to subsidize research activities is quite low, much lower than needed to make up for the decrease in financial appropriations. Because research into new agricultural technology such as genetic engineering requires large investments, decreasing government appropriations will in the long run hinder the progress of agricultural research in China. A related problem is the low salaries of agricultural researchers, scientists, and technology extension staff, which have resulted in serious brain drain. The wage of a highly trained seed-breeding personnel is about the same as that of an unskilled labourer. This distribution system has hindered talented young graduates from taking up agricultural research projects and has prevented many outstanding agricultural scientists who have received degrees in agriculture in foreign countries from returning to China. As market reforms are further intensified, these negative effects will increase. In fact, China began losing agricultural scientists in huge numbers as early as the mid-1980s. From 1986 to 1996, the total number of government-employed agricultural scientists, excluding university professors, decreased from 233,000 to 197,000, a reduction of more than 15%.

Finally, investments in agricultural infrastructure construction are decreasing. The population of Mainland China makes up 21% of the world population and 38% of that in under-developed countries. Per capita arable land in China is 0.1 ha., only about 40% of the world average. Moreover, China is one of the most arid countries, and its rainfall is extremely unevenly distributed. The volume of water runoff is lower than the world average, and exploitable resources constitute only one-third of the total runoff. With the growth of economy and population, per capita farmland and fresh water for agriculture will decrease. In particular, the amount of available farmland will decrease year by year owing to the construction of houses, roads, industrial establishments, and infrastructure. At the same time, population pressures will lead to environmental deterioration, and due to this deterioration, the total amount of arable land will also decrease. It is therefore extremely important to protect the reserve of natural resources against erosion, floods, and droughts, and to improve soil fertility. In the pre-reform period, Chinese government was famous for its ability to mobilize the labour force to build basic agricultural infrastructures. Its ability to do this has weakened since the adoption of the household responsibility system. Therefore, the government itself should play an increasingly important role in constructing agricultural infrastructure for the purpose of preserving and improving the agricultural resource base.

Since the 1980s, there has been no significant increase in the proportion of government expenditure on agriculture and in the share of the national budget for investment in agricultural infrastructure. The proportions have fluctuated with changes in grain output. Because of ecological pressures and because of the decrease in the government's investment in agricultural infrastructure, the capacity of China's agricultural industry to resist natural disasters has been impaired, resulting in a considerable increase in the frequency of disaster occurrence and in the significance of subsequent losses. If the government fails to increase its investment in this area, it will be difficult for China to maintain sustained and stable growth in per-unit yield and total output of grains.

CHAPTER 8

The Internal and External Environment for Economic Reform and Sustainable Development

Today, the Chinese economy is at a crossroad. Further internal reform and development is needed to overcome the problems discussed in Chapter 7. In addition, the economy faces challenges stemming from the external economic environment, such as the Asian financial crisis and globalization. How can China deal with these internal and external restrictive factors appropriately, and maintain a sustainable growth under such economic conditions? The solution to this question will be the key to retaining the gains that China has made in economic reform and development over the past two decades. It will also be the key to the realization of the ultimate goals for its reform and development.

The traditional economic system under reform is a complicated entanglement of a series of institutional setups. Every part of this system is logically and historically related to the others. In order to achieve an ultimate success of reform and maintain a sustainable, rapid and sound growth, it is necessary to establish a new macro-policy environment, a resource-allocation system, and a micro-management system based on market principles. However, the accomplishment of all these relies on the ultimate success of the SOE reform and of the transition to a new development strategy. In this chapter, we seek to further analyze the institutional roots of the problems discussed in Chapter 7, to explain the relationships between the problems, and to offer proposals for further reform.

8.1 Coordination of the State-owned Enterprise Reform and the Reform in Economic System

As discussed in previous chapters, the development of the traditional economic system was a logically endogenous process. The starting point was the adoption of a heavy-industry-oriented development strategy, which is inconsistent with China's comparative advantages at the time. To implement this strategy and support the development of nonviable "strategic industries", the government had to create a macro-policy environment that distorted the prices of products and production factors. Resources were allocated through a highly-centralized planning system. To get the control over the surplus generated during the economic development process, so that this surplus could be used to further the development of heavy industry, a state-owned industrial economy and agricultural collectivization were introduced. This constituted the micro-operational system in the traditional economic system. Thus a trinity structure was constructed. This trinity structure is exactly what we call the traditional economic system. Although the three elements were coordinated, the defects of the traditional economic system were most evidently manifested in the micro-management system, especially in the lack of incentives and efficiency

So far, the reform has striven to improve the incentive mechanism so as to improve economic efficiency. The reform began with the micro-management system. The basic strategy was to decentralize power and to give up part of the profits to microeconomic agent. The result of these measures is the so called "decentralization leads to vigour". The increase in decision-making power at the micro-management level, along with the increase in self-disposable products and in retained profit, required corresponding changes in the resource-allocation system and the macro-policy environment. This pushed the reform to a deeper level. Nevertheless, the reform has not been thorough enough. This is because the government still needs to protect the large and medium-sized SOEs that were established under the traditional system and to help the newly-formed SOEs when there is no fundamental change in the country's development strategy.

There are two reasons for protecting SOEs. Firstly, the old development strategy left behind a legacy of social burdens. This adds to SOEs' operational costs (e.g., pensions and wages to redundant workers). Secondly, a number of large SOEs still need to follow the state's development strategy. Although these enterprises were in industries that China has no comparative advantages, the enterprises are not allowed to withdraw and shift into other industries which are in line with China's comparative advatnages. Such an obligation to stay in the non-comparative advantage industry can be regarded as the SOE's strategic burden. Social burdens and strategic burdens constitute the SOEs' policy burdens.

Because of these two restrictive conditions, a fair competition market has not been established. Owing to the existence of policy burdens, SOEs' profits cannot be used as a sufficient indicator for the managers' performances. The problems of incentive incompatibility and information asymmetry between SOE owners and managers remain. Without effective rewards and penalties, managers will not endeavor to increase revenues in line with state interests. Instead, they may strive to increase their retained share of profits and to encroach upon state-owned assets to maximize their personal income. As the decentralization and profit-sharing reform goes on, the conflict of interest between owners and managers intensifies, and it becomes less likely that managers are about to refrain from such behaviour. As a result, the returns to the state assets decline and the stripping of state assets continues.

Since the government is responsible for SOEs' policy burdens, SOEs can turn to the government for various preferential policies. Furthermore, even when SOEs suffer losses, they have an excuse to ask the government for more subsidies. Because the government lacks adequate information, it cannot tell policy-induced losses from operational losses. SOEs tend to attribute all losses as policy-induced, so the government must bear the brunt of all their losses. As a result, SOEs' budget constraints are softened, and managers have a lower incentive to improve business operation and management.[1]

The existence of policy burdens on SOEs, meanwhile, serves as

1. Justin Yifu Lin, Cai Fang and Li Zhou, "Competition, Policy Burdens, and State-owned Enterprise Reform", *American Economic Review*, Vol. 88, No. 2 (May 1998), pp. 422–27; Justin Yifu Lin, Cai Fang and Li Zhou, *State-owned Enterprise Reform in China*. Hong Kong: Chinese University Press, 2001.

an obstacle to the reform of the financial system. The marketization of interest rate should be the heart core of this reform. The reform should also include the diversification of financial institutions and the commercialization of banks. However, since China is still short of capital, relaxing interest rate controls will inevitably result in the increases of interest rate. In 1983, state subsidies of cost-free fiscal appropriation were replaced with low interest-rate loans from state-owned banks. The government has thus been hesitant to completely liberalize the interest rates.[2]

As long as the low interest-rate policy continues, so will its effects. Competition among financial institutions will be impossible, and bank commercialization will remain nominal. If competition exists amongst financial institutions, since non-state-owned banks usually have a higher efficiency and better services, they will probably attract savings away from state-owned banks. This will limit the state-owned banks' ability to give subsidies to SOEs with low interest loans. In addition, if the low interest-rate policy is maintained, demand for bank loans and credits will continue to exceed supply; credit loans will still have to be allocated through administrative measures, and any real commercialization of banks will be a mission impossible.

In fact, TVEs and other non-SOEs have taken an interest rate close to the market level for a long time. These sectors still enjoy a much higher growth rate than state-owned sectors; thus, they make up an increasingly larger part of the national economy. This means that it is imperative to reform the financial sector in order to provide a better service to the non-state-owned sectors. The slow progress of the financial sector reform is the result of the policy burdens on SOEs. What is more, because of the inefficiency of SOEs, many loans and credits become non-performing loans and bad loans, which could result in a crisis in the operation of state-owned commercial banks.

---

2. China's price reform for production factors lags behind that of product. Many economists have noticed this phenomenon. See Nicholas R. Lardy, *China in the World Economy*. Washington, DC: Institute for International Economics, 1994, pp. 8–14.

Under the low interest-rate policy, capital supply cannot keep up with capital demand. Under the traditional economic system, although enterprises had a strong demand for investment and loans, inflation usually did not occur, since credit quotas and allocations were strictly controlled by the central government. Because currency issuance was basically maintained within the aggregate target range, inflation did not occur. However, a long-term imbalance between aggregate demand and aggregate supply will eventually lead to inflation. China's economy has been in a state of depressed inflation for several decades. The reform of the micro-management system and of the resource-allocation system beginning in the early 1980s has led to a decentralization of power in the financial system. With economic reform in full flow in cities by 1984, the authority of credit examination and approval and the authority to allocate loans were transferred to lower-level banks in 1985. The state-monopolized revenue and expenditure system, in which each specialized bank had to report to the central bank and each local bank to its headquarters, was dismantled. Each specialized bank and local bank can now lend more when it has more deposits and can keep a balance of capital. Most mandatory plans for detailed items have been removed, and indicative plans for aggregate control have been adopted. However, since the macro-policy environment of low interest-rates has not changed accordingly, inflation will become explicit. Because non-state-owned economic sectors obtain some credit by rent-seeking, to protect SOEs the state has to issue more currency to make up for fund shortages. As a result, a potentially serious inflation is emerging.

All the inflations after 1978 were actually caused by the lack of coordination among economic reforms. That is, the reform of the macro-policy environment lags far behind the reforms of the micro-management system and the resource-allocation system. The common reason for inflation is as follows. Within the fund-circulation system, the total fund demand exceeds fund supply, and and the administrative system can no longer ration funds effectively. Therefore it has to ask a currency administration outside the fund-circulation system to issue additional currency to make up for the fund shortage. This is the natural result of the low interest-rate policy and the imperfect adjustment mechanism. Hence, we call the inflation since reform "endogenous inflation".

Figure 8.1 illustrates the formation of the endogenous inflation in China since the reform began. In the figure, P_0 is the rate generated on the market, an equilibrium interest rate reflecting the demand and supply of funds. The demand and supply of funds corresponding to this interest rate are equal, so fluctuation in the market rate can adjust the demand and supply, and the money supply becomes a macro variable that can be exogenously controlled. In the macro-policy environment of low interest-rates, the interest rate is purposely kept at a level lower than that decided by the market, such as P_1. At this interest rate level, the volume of funds demanded (Od) and supplied (Ob) are no longer equal; thus, fund shortage (bd) is created. Under the strict planning system, planning departments and financial administration departments could allocate funds (Ob) among all fund-demanding enterprises; Ob is the amount that could be put into

Figure 8.1 Mechanism of the endogenous inflation

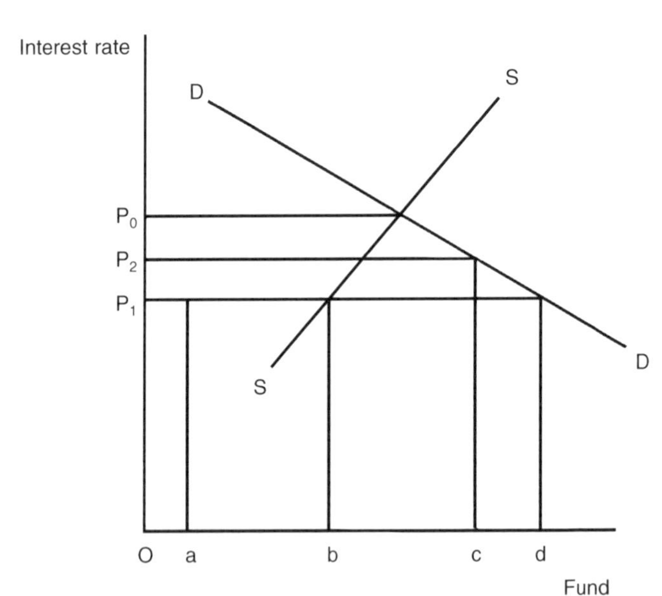

circulation through the plan. This practice not only fulfilled the state's strategic goals but also checked the over-issuance of money. Looking first at SOEs, we can assume that the total loans (Ob) obtained by SOEs all come from savings. After the reform was carried out in the micro-management system and the financial administration system, non-state-owned sectors emerged. Enterprises within this sector have a more flexible operational mechanism than those in the state-owned sector, and they can pay a higher nominal interest rate or provide bribes to obtain loans at a real interest rate (e.g., P_2) higher than P_1. This competition for loans is possible because the authority over loan administration has been transferred to lower levels, and because financial institutions now have stronger incentives to earn more profits. To make the model simpler, we suppose that the non-state-owned sectors receive part (bc) of the total fund (Ob) transformed from savings, while SOEs, because of incompetence, receive the smaller part Oa (namely, Ob minus bc). However, since the state has not entirely abandoned the heavy-industry-oriented development strategy, and since non-state-owned sectors cannot carry out the strategy, large and medium-sized SOEs' demand for funds must still be met. Suppose that their demand volume is still Ob. To fill the fund gap ab, more money has to be issued. Hence, endogenous inflation is generated. As long as the low interest-rate policy has not been reformed, once we increase financial institutions' decision-making power and loose control over credit and investment, there will emerge a new round of investment-led fast economic growth supported by credit expansion. This phenomenon is characterized as "decentralization leads to vigour". The subsequent increase in money supply leads to inflation, and thus the "vigour leads to disorder" phenomenon emerges.[3]

With no fundamental changes in the low-interest-rate policy, in

---

3. For an analysis of the inflation in China in the 1980s and early 1990s, see Justin Yifu Lin and Cai Fang, "On China's Inflation, Its Prevention and Control", *Newsletter on Development Research*, No. 2 (1989); Justin Yifu Lin, Cai Fang, Li Zhou and Shen Gaoming, "The Major Problems in the Current Economic Reform and Development and Their Solutions", *Study Materials for Economists*, No. 23 (1993).

order to resume economic order, the government has to reduce loans, cut off investment, and strengthen state control. Such actions mark a return to the traditional economic system and drive resource allocation toward less efficient state-owned economic sectors. The "centralization leads to stagnation" phenomenon is the natural outcome of this regression to the traditional economic system. At this point, demand for efficiency and a higher growth rate is again voiced, and control is lifted once again. At the same time, rent-seeking occurs under a dual-price system. Once the economy becomes overheated, production resources are in short supply. The gap between planning prices and market prices enlarges, and rent-seeking becomes more prevalent. Thus within the vigour/chaos cycle, rent-seeking, rampant corruption, bottleneck constraints, and inflation are synchronous. At this particular moment, they all become prominent, marking an economic bust in the cycle.

All the same, the non-market prices of basic agricultural products and mining products also prevent regions from making the most of their comparative advantages, and thus give rise to the widening regional income disparities. The government has made it clear that the goal of economic reform is to establish a market economy. However, the prices of certain products, such as energy, raw materials, transportation, cotton and grains, are still strictly controlled. This is connected to the fact that the viability of SOEs have not been completely transformed.

The price formation of products or services provided by energy, raw materials and transportation sectors differs from that of products and services provided by the other sectors. Firstly, the former products or services have low price elasticity of demand (i.e., price changes have a small effect on demand). This is because these products and services are produced mainly to meet the basic needs of other economic sectors. This demand is mainly determined by the economic development itself, and is thus a relatively fixed amount. The influence of price changes on the demand is little. In addition, it is difficult to find substitutes for these products and services. Therefore, when price changes, the change in demand through substitution is insignificant.

Secondly, these products or services have a relatively low price elasticity of supply (i.e., supply is relatively unaffected by price changes). This is because an increase in their production capacity requires heavy investment and a relatively long period of time to realize, and is strictly constrained by the resources available. Thus, there is an inelastic supply in the short run.

Generally speaking, neither the supply nor the demand of a product is fixed. Usually, as the economy grows, demand increases, which raises the price and in turn boosts supply. Then price falls. During this process, different products adjust differently. Figure 8.2 compares the differences between basic and common products in this process toward equilibrium. In Figure 8.2, the left-hand graph illustrates the case of basic products from infrastructure sectors. The low price elasticity of supply and demand is illustrated in the steep supply and demand curve. The right-hand graph illustrates the case of common products. Its high price elasticity is represented by the relatively flatness of the demand and supply curves.

The comparison of two graphs illustrate that: given the same amount of increase in demand, if we try to clear the market through price changes, the price of products and services in the infrastructure sectors has to rise more than that of the common goods. Its practical

Figure 8.2 Price effect and elasticities of supply and demand

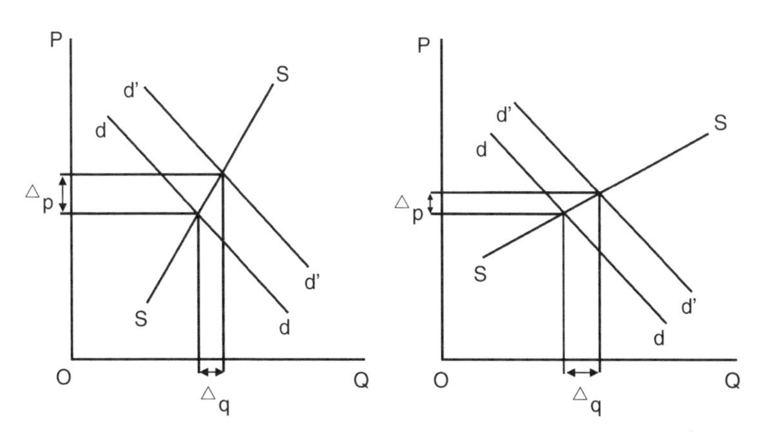

implication is that: infrastructure industries are slow in response to an increase in demand. In other words, it is relatively hard for these industries to form new production capacities, and overcome the bottleneck constraints for economic development if there is no sharp price increase.

However, the yet-to-be-reformed SOEs can only survive in the market when they are guaranteed an adequate supply of low-priced energy and raw materials and a secure supply of funds and foreign exchange. These infrastructure industries are in the upper stream of the industrial chain that their price changes may affect extensively. To maintain production conditions for large and medium-sized SOEs, the government has only cautiously made some minor adjustment in the prices, let alone a thorough liberalization in the price system in these industries.

The incomplete price reform has prevented the price to fully adjust to market conditions, thus could not provide the supply side with a large enough impetus to increase their supply and break the bottleneck constraint. At the same time, this incomplete price reform also resulted in the regression of prices to its original relative level. Every time the prices of products and services from infrastructure sectors are adjusted, SOEs are allowed to adjust prices accordingly, and a *de facto* price-adjusting chain forms as a result. Sectors and enterprises that have already been in the dual-price system also adjust prices by changing the relative range between the planning track and the market track (i.e., by raising market prices). As we know, what really matters for production activities is the relative prices, rather than the absolute price level. Since market mechanism is absent from these industries, prices cannot automatically adjust to the equilibrium level. The actual price adjustment is conducted by government, which is not only slow in response but also too minor in range. As a result, these adjustments have never achieved the expected results. Instead, they lead to a series of subsequent price increases, which quickly return to the original relative level. Since relative prices of basic products and services are always lower than the other products, the output always falls short. The national economic growth is severely curtailed by the bottleneck. What is more, as we have discussed in Chapter 7, since these infrastructure sectors are operated mainly by SOEs, the SOEs themselves are unfavourably affected by this incomplete price reform.

The traditional macro-policy environment is also the primary reason for the widening UR-RID (urban-rural income disparity) and RID (regional income disparity). Because of the distortion in the factor and product prices, the comparative advantage of the local economy formed on the basis of the distorted price system is different from the comparative advantage based on the local factor endowment structure. For instance, the primary reason for the decrease in farmers' income is the government policy that prevents them from realizing their comparative advantages. In 1989 and 1990, the government ordered farmers to grow grain crops and to shut down most TVEs. This resulted in an 8.4% decrease in the per capita net income of rural households in 1989 and a minor increase of 1.5% in 1990. When inflation is deducted, the per capita net income of those two years was lower than that of 1985. In addition, after the household responsibility system had fully released the suppressed productivity, rural people could not detect the new comparative advantages because of the distortion in prices. As a result, the growth of rural income was seriously hindered.

In recent years, development in the central and western parts of the country has followed a course quite different from that in the eastern regions. In coastal rural areas, comparative advantages in abundant labour have been exploited effectively. Labour-intensive TVEs were developed, which resulted in a rapid growth of the local economy. On the other hand, in the central and western rural areas, the comparative advantages lie in land-intensive products such as grains, cotton, and minerals. The issue here is that the prices of these products are artificially suppressed, so is the functioning of the market system. As a result, the more eastern areas develop, the more produce and minerals they buy from central and western areas. The poor central and western areas are in effect subsidizing the relatively developed eastern areas. Therefore, the central and western areas are unable to boost their economic development by exploiting their comparative advantages.

Under such a macro-policy environment, development in the eastern areas cannot stimulate development in the central and western areas, and the widening income disparities between eastern areas and central and western areas is inevitable. In order to narrow the gap, the macro-policy environment must be changed and an integrated national market must be established. Only after such changes will the regional comparative advantages formed on basis of price system be consistent with those based on regional factor endowment. In such an integrated market, there is no artificial price intervention. Factors and products can flow freely. Their relative scarcity will be accurately reflected by the fluctuations of market demand and supply. This accurate information can thus be used as the guidance of regional economic development, so that people of different regions can develop industries or choose product mixes that are consistent with their comparative advantages. In this way, regional economic development will be accelerated. Meanwhile, if all the regions follow their comparative advantages, as they upgrade their industry and product mix, they are also creating demand for the products of other regions. For instance, when eastern areas develop their economy and upgrade their industrial structure, demand for farming products and minerals will increase, and prices will rise. Development in the central and western areas will be accelerated. The inter-regional income gap will thus narrow gradually as a result of economic development.

Quantitative analysis by Simon Kuznetz on statistical data from multiple countries shows that economic development yields an inverted U-curve in income distribution, i.e. disparity will widen up first and then narrow down gradually.[4] In Taiwan, however, the income disparity decreased with economic development, indicating that the inverted U-curve in income distribution does not necessarily always hold true. Taiwan is not the only counter-example. Other economies that have followed their comparative advantages more

4. Simon Kuznetz, *Economic Growth of Nations: Total Output and Production Structure*. Cambridge, MA: Harvard University Press, 1971.

closely, such as South Korea, have shown similar results.[5] Therefore, we can conclude that the widening income disparities in economic development is connected with particular conditions. If those conditions are eliminated, a widening income disparities can be avoided. Below we explore ways to create conditions conducive to preventing a widening income gap during economic development.

Taiwan's experience shows that, in places with abundant labour forces, if there is a macro-policy environment that can fully exploit this comparative advantage, priority can be given to the development of labour-intensive industries, which could absorb more labour with a given amount of fund. In this way, wages will constitute a greater share in income distribution among production factors, which may prevent the widening of income gap during economic development. As economy develops, labour will become relatively scarce, the absolute level of wages will rise and the share of wages in the national income will increase too. In this process, the resource endowment structure gradually changes. If the capital-intensive industries are developed gradually in accordance with this change in endowment structure, the income disparity will not increase.

Some political leaders and economists in China believe that the large income disparity is mainly caused by the inadequate support for central and western region and for rural areas. If more favourable policies were adopted for these areas, this problem might readily be solved. Among all their suggestions, four are of particular influence: (1) Take protective measures for the agricultural industry, like price support for farm crops. In this way, it hopes to eliminate the "price scissors" between farm and industrial products and ease the income disparity between urban and rural areas. (2) Direct a larger share of the total national economic investment into the central and western areas, hence reduce the difference in capital endowment across regions and ease the problem of unbalanced inter-regional development. (3) Establish a complete industrial chain in central and western

5. G. M. Meier, *Leading Issues in Economic Development*. New York: Oxford University Press, 1998, p. 16.

areas, which fully exploits their comparative advantages in natural resources. The chain should include all the related industrial branches from the mining and quarrying industry to the one that produce the finished products. It hopes that this could narrow the inter-regional gap of the value-added rate and solve the problem of unbalanced development. (4) Exchanging low-priced primary products with low-priced finished products at the local government level, and try to narrow the profit margin in inter-regional exchange, hence solve the problem of unbalanced development.

However, each of these suggestions has shortcomings. If we followed the first suggestion, it would create too heavy a burden for the national economy, which would not only impede national economic development, but also the development in rural areas and central and western regions. The second suggestion is actually preventing the capital to flow into eastern regions where the capital could have a higher return. The third may lead to a dramatic decrease in macro-economic efficiency, because eastern areas would not be able to fully exploit their existing production capacity owing to their lack of raw materials, while central and western areas would not be able to produce high-quality products owing to their lack of technology. The fourth plan asks the government to interfere with business operations, which is sure to be an obstacle to market development. In short, although these four proposals have different starting points, they all use administrative adjustment and regulation instead of market means and thus all lead to inefficiency, which will never result in a fair income distribution.

Take agricultural protection as an example. Agricultural protection is to maintain the prices of agricultural products above market level through administrative means. It leads to two problems. The first is a surplus of agricultural products. At the market equilibrium price, supply equals demand. If the supported price is higher than the market price, supply will exceed demand. The second problem is production at too high a cost (as compared to market equilibrium). Equilibrium in resource distribution implies that marginal cost equals marginal revenue. If the supported price is higher than the market price, the marginal revenue is thus higher, and some products will be produced at too high a cost. Hence, the real effect of supported prices is that farmers are encouraged to produce surplus in costly ways. If the government is obliged to buy up all this surplus, it will eventually be too much for the government finance. If the government does not take up this responsibility, prices will fall as production increases, and farmers will eventually suffer greater losses.

The only way to solve the grain problem is to allow the market to function smoothly. After resource distribution for grain production has become a function of market mechanism, less government interference in the grain market is needed. This reduces the financial burdens for government. The government can then provide a stronger financial support for agro-scientific research and technology extension. China can become self-sufficient in grains if the market is allowed to play its role and scientific and technical achievement is made. At the same time, in line with the changes in its comparative advantage, China should make full use of international market to solve the food problem at a lower cost.

It is evident that all the problems associated with China's economic life and the difficulties of its economic reforms originate from uncoordinated reform. The reason for this uncoordinated reform is that the reform of SOEs lags behind other reforms. Therefore, further economic reform and the elimination of the vigour/chaos cycle and other problems will depend on SOEs reforms. As illustrated in the beginning part of this section, the reform of SOEs should begin with an elimination of policy burdens to establish a fair competition environment, under which adequate information can be collected to fully reflect business operations. Gradually, an internal governance structure suitable for enterprises will be set up, which may minimize manager opportunism and create compatible incentives between owners and managers. Once the SOE reform succeeds, it will not be necessary for the state to maintain a low interest rate and low prices for major primary products. Reforms of the financial system and the interest rate regime will proceed smoothly. The inter-regional gap and the grain problem can both be settled through the market mechanism. Moreover, corruption will lose its institutional breeding ground.

8.2 Further Reform and Prevention of Financial Crises

In Chapter 4 we discussed the causes, mechanism, and results of the Asian financial crisis. Below we draw lessons from China's development experiences, so as to understand better the development strategy, economic structure, industrial organization system, economic development layout and financial regimes. In this way, we hope to find ways to prevent a similar calamity from befalling on China in the future.

Firstly, industrial development should fully exploit comparative advantages. The lesson of Korea's failure to support its large conglomerates illustrates that an industrial policy attempting to support industries bypassing its development stage can only impair the competitiveness of domestic industries and their capacity to accumulate capital. Enterprise expansion that relies on domestic and foreign debts will increase financial risks. As for China, abundant labour force will remain to be its comparative advantage in endowment for a relatively long period. Enterprises that are established on the basis of this comparative advantage will be competitive and profitable. They will have the ability to accumulate financial resources rapidly. Such enterprises are usually not large in size, which means they can fully rely on domestic funds and avoid excessive dependence on foreign capital. Countries with their industrial structure and organizations based on the comparative advantage of factor endowments are usually strongly competitive, enjoy high rates of return, and have good solvency. As the economy develops, capital will accumulate and its scarcity reduces, and labour will become relatively scarce. As this upgrading process of the factor endowment structure is taking place, both industrial and technological structure will upgrade accordingly. Such a development strategy will help the national economy embark on a road toward fast, stable, and sustainable development.

Secondly, at China's current stage of development, as it attracts foreign investment, the focus should be laid on the direct foreign investment. Foreign enterprises should be encouraged to set up in relatively capital- and technology-intensive industries with good market potential, and various forms of cooperation with foreign companies should be encouraged. In this way, we shall not only make up for domestic capital shortages but also introduce advanced technologies to China through the introduction of foreign capital and technologies. Investment risks involved will be undertaken by foreign investors. In particular, an overheated or slumping domestic economy will be avoided because the foreign direct investment is largely unaffected by factors such as psychology and short-term expectations. As for the opening-up of the capital market, China should take a prudent approach, especially in the following two areas: (1) allowing foreign investors to speculate in highly liquid domestic stocks or bonds and (2) allowing domestic enterprises to borrow short-term foreign loans. Before the opening-up of the capital market, the domestic financial and banking systems should have a thorough reform toward the "commercialization of banks and the marketization of interest rate", so that banks are independent in their business operations and fully responsible for their own performances.

Thirdly, China should reduce administrative intervention in investment. The reform of the financial system should be combined with a change in industrial policy. For a few SOEs in industries that are essential for national defense, the state can continue its support through direct investment and fiscal subsidies. In all the other industries, the state should withdraw from the regular investment activities and cease to oblige banks to give loans to enterprises in non-comparative advantage industries. At the same time, the government should liberalize interest rates and ease the financial suppression. Then when the government looses its control on credit quotas, it will not necessarily lead to overheated investment and duplicated construction. Thus, it can prevent the construction of redundant production capacity and can reduce non-performing loans.

Finally, China should foster a more balanced urbanization pattern, a more efficient financial system (based mainly on indirect finance), and a more effective financial supervision and regulation system, so that it can guard against the formation of a bubble economy caused by overheated real estate development and stock market speculation. In a period of fast economic development, development in real estate and stock markets can easily become overheated. In Asian countries and regions with limited land, the price of real estate is expected to rise quickly because of a low elasticity of supply, which in turn leads to heavy speculation and economic bubbles. The experience of Asian countries shows that a low elasticity of land supply is especially pronounced in Japan, South Korea, Thailand, and the Philippines, where economies are concentrated in metropolitan areas, such as Tokyo, Osaka, Seoul, Bangkok, and Manila. China can reduce an overheated real estate development to some extent by preventing economic activities from over-concentrating in a few big cities and by encouraging a reasonable development pattern among cities to ensure an efficient supply of land.

At the present stage, China still has a comparative advantage in labour-intensive industries, since there is still an abundant labour force but only limited capital. Compared with the enterprises in capital- and technology-intensive industries, the enterprises in labour-intensive industries are relatively small in size, their capital comes mainly from self-accumulation and indirect bank financing. To cope with the development of the labour-intensive industries, the banking sector should be highly commercial and liberalized, and banks should be free to compete. However, loans with securities and real estate as collateral should be strictly regulated and controlled so as to prevent the formation of economic bubbles and reduce financial risks.

8.3 Exploiting Comparative Advantages to Realize Sustainable Economic Development

At present, China's comparative advantages lie in the labour-intensive, relatively low-technology industries. However, following the comparative advantage development strategy will not trap China permanently at a low industrial level. On the contrary, following such a strategy is the quickest way to accumulate capital and to upgrade the endowment structure. As this change in factor endowment goes on, the industrial structure can be upgraded continuously through introducing advanced foreign technologies that are in line with the changed factor endowment. The economy will maintain fast growth in the long term due to continuous low-cost technological innovations. This will lead to sustainable development, and the economy will be able to catch up with the advanced economies more quickly.

To support the development of labour-intensive small and medium-sized enterprises, sound policies regarding capital and technology supply must be formulated. In fact, the Chinese government has begun to set up special lending departments for this purpose in the top four specialized banks. However, the operation of the four banks is in line with the financing mechanism under the traditional economic system, which is to finance prioritized development items. In addition, large banks tend to grant loans to large enterprises and projects. They are reluctant to serve small and medium-sized firms. Large enterprises usually apply for large loans since their credit and debt-repayment ability are easily monitored and because their average banking costs are relatively low. Small transactions, on the other hand, are relatively more costly. In addition, it is difficult for large banks to investigate the credit and solvency of small and medium-sized enterprises whose locations are scattered.

One way to solve this problem is to develop local small and medium-sized banks to serve small and medium-sized enterprises. What is more, transaction costs can be reduced because small and medium-sized banks can easily exchange information with small and medium-sized enterprises. Of course, setting up small and medium-sized banks right away is not feasible, because of the lack of relevant laws, regulations, financial system reform, and financial supervision.

One alternative is to grant lending authority to lower levels within the current banking system. Currently, lending authority is highly centralized. The authority for small and medium-sized loans can be delegated to branch offices at the county level. Small and medium-sized enterprises will then have a much better chance at obtaining loans, since branch offices at the county level have a relatively close relationship with local small and medium-sized enterprises. It is easy for them to collect information about the credit and solvency of such enterprises. In addition, the life-time responsibility system for lending, introduced after mid-1990s, should be further amended to allow for a reasonable failure ratio so that reluctance to lend can be avoided. Because investment always bears some risks and so does loans, putting all the responsibility on banking staffs is unreasonable.

Another important issue in developing small and medium-sized enterprises is technology supply. At present, the Chinese economy is in relative over-production, with markets close to the saturation point.[6] New products should be developed, and product quality should be improved to open up new markets. The development of small and medium-sized labour-intensive enterprises also needs technology, especially advanced technology. Any enterprise with backward technologies is non-competitive. There are plenty of off-the-shelf technologies available on the international market, which are suitable for China's small and medium-sized enterprises. To make these technologies accessible to such enterprises, ties to the rest of the world should be strengthened. Foreign small and medium-sized enterprises should be encouraged to invest in China in the form of foreign ventures or joint ventures. In addition, information about new products and technologies should be issued through newspapers, magazines, websites, and other means. At the same time, China's small and medium-sized enterprises should be free to enter the world market to exchange information, personnel, and products.

Based on our analysis in Chapter 1, China is well equipped to maintain its high level of economic growth in the coming decades, as long as economic reform proceeds in the right direction. Future reforms must eliminate policy burdens on SOEs to realize the transition to the new development strategy and to put an end to the vigour/chaos cycle. If China's economic reform follows this path, such growth potential will be realized, and China will surpass the United States as the world's largest economy by the mid-21st century.

---

6. For further discussion on the surplus in supply and the resultant deflation, please refer to the next chapter.

CHAPTER 9

Deflation in China since 1998[1]

As discussed in Chapter 7, the Chinese economy had a pattern of cyclic fluctuation in growth after the reform started in 1979. The latest cycle started with signs of overheating in the spring of 1993. As a counter-measure, in July 1993 the Chinese government began to implement a retrenchment programme, which lasted until 1997. The economic growth rate did not drop sharply because the programme resulted in a "soft-landing". The rate of economic growth began a gradual slow-down in 1995 but has been maintained at a relatively high level. After the Fifteenth Party Congress in September 1997, the Chinese government switched its policy orientation, adopting a new package of policies to stimulate economic growth. However, unlike the previous vigour/chaos cycles, which were heavily influenced by government's policies, the efforts that the government has exerted through many channels so far have not yielded the expected results. Investment and consumption demand have shown no signs of a strong increase and the gross domestic product (GDP) growth rate reached only 7.8 % in 1998, 7.1% in 1999, 8.0% in 2000 and 7.3% in 2001, all lower than the average 9.5% of the past 23 years. During the period of "soft-landing", the lowest level that the rate of economic growth reached was 8.8% in 1997.

From September 1997 to the present day, Chinese economy has not shown any sign of warming-up and market demand has declined continuously. From October 1996, the monthly wholesale price index

1. This chapter draws on Jusitn Yifu Lin, "The Current Deflation in China: Causes and Policy Options", *Asian Pacific Journal of Economics and Business*, Vol. 4, No. 2 (December 2000), pp. 4–21.

of production materials, compared to the index in the same period of the previous year, has been falling. The monthly retail price index, compared to the same period of the previous year, has also been falling since October 1997. As for the monthly consumer price index, it has declined since March 1998. In 1998, 1999, and 2000 the yearly retail price index dropped, respectively, by 2.6%, 3.0%, and 15%.[2] Thus, China has been confronted with deflation in recent years.

The slow-down in the current growth rate of non-government investment is particularly alarming. The Chinese economy has never encountered the problem of deflation in its 20 years of reform. In the past two decades, the main feature of the Chinese economy was rapid growth. The old system was reformed in a period of rapid growth so that it was possible for everyone to gain from the reform, and the friction of, and resistance to, reform was reduced. This is the key to China's successful reform of the past 20 years. Keeping the economic growth at a high level is essential to the deepening of reform and the completion of complex social and economic development in China. Therefore, the current economic situation constitutes a severe test for the government.

This chapter examines the causes of the current deflation, looking first at the demand side (in the following section) and then the supply side (the section after that). The chapter then analyses the attempts by the Chinese government to use monetary and fiscal policy to rectify the deflation. In the concluding section, the chapter discusses other policy options available to the Chinese government and concludes that the most effective way to combat the deflation is to invest in rural infrastructure that are complementary to the use of domestic appliances.

9.1 The Demand Side of Deflation

Deflation is an economic phenomenon characterized by continuous

2. National Bureau of Statistics of China, *China Statistical Yearbook, 2001*. Beijing: China Statistics Press, 2001, p. 281.

decline in the price level throughout the economy. Theoretically, a deflation is either due to an overall drop in demand in an economy, or due to a sharp increase in supply. The demand drop could result from credit contraction, which leads to an increase in interest rates, and a decline in investment and current consumption. The decline in investment and consumption may lead, in turn, to enterprises operating below capacity. This would further reduce the investment and labour income. Consumption will thus decline further. Demand decline can also originate from the collapse of financial and real estate bubbles, and lead to shrinkages in national wealth, which will then result in further declines in consumption. At the same time, it will lead to an increase in bad loans and a decrease in credit supply and investment demand. The other cause of deflation, oversupply, can arise from a productivity increase due to technological innovation, or from over-investment, which causes the increase in production capacity to exceed the increase in demand.

Theoretically, all the factors mentioned above can result in deflation. Chinese economists tend to emphasize the demand-side factors in their analyses of current deflation in China.[3] However, the question of what is the main factor of the current deflation can only be answered by empirical analysis.

An examination of the credit supply scenario shows that the Chinese government had reduced interest rates twice — on 1 May and 23 August 1996 — before the announcement of success in achieving the soft-landing in September 1997. Since 1997, the central government has reduced interest rates five more times. By mid-1999, the interest rate for one-year loans was about half of the rate in 1996 and the interest rate for deposit was only a quarter of the 1996 level (see Table 9.1). Theoretically, the reductions in interest rates should have had a large stimulating effect on investment and consumption, especially following the changes that the Central Bank

3. See Yu Yongding, "Breaking the Vicious Cycle of Deflation: A New Challenge to China's Economic Development", *Jingji Yanjiu*, July 1999; Li Xiaoxi, "Deflation, Insufficient Demand and Policy Option", *Caimao Jingji*, August 1999.

Table 9.1 Interest Rate Reductions by the People's Bank of China since 1996

Date	1996		1997	1998			1999
	1 May	23 Aug.	23 Oct.	25 Mar.	1 July	10 Dec.	10 June
Average decrease in annual deposit rate (%)	0.98	1.50	1.10	0.16	0.49	0.50	1.00
Average decrease in annual lending rate (%)	0.75	1.20	1.50	0.60	1.12	0.50	0.75
Annual deposit rate after adjustment (%)	9.18	7.47	5.67	5.22	4.77	3.78	2.25
0.5–1.0 year lending rate after adjustment (%)	10.98	10.08	8.64	7.92	6.93	6.39	5.85

Source: "The Central Bank Lowered the Interest Rates Seven Times", *China Security News*, 12 June 1999.

of China made to the deposit reserve system in March 1998. The 7% reserve for payment requirement was abolished and the reserve against deposit requirement was lowered from 13% down to 8%. These measures led to a 60% reduction in the overall rate of reserve requirement against deposit. According to the common reasoning in a market economy, these measures should have had strong stimulating effects on the national economy. On 25 December 1997, the People's Bank of China (PBOC) decided to abolish the credit rationing of state-owned commercial banks and to implement the asset/liability management and risk management. Since 1998, the PBOC has not given any instructional loan planning, and would give only quarterly indicative loan planning. The commercial banks would have sufficient autonomy over new loans.

To encourage urban households to buy houses and thus stimulate real estate development, the PBOC promulgated the *Administration Measure of Individual Housing Loan* to stimulate loans for housing. The credit supply in China since 1997, therefore, has been relatively loose and the cost of loans is quite low. Investment demand contraction should not be attributed to interest rate increases and credit contraction.

Table 9.2 Money Supply Growth Rate, After Seasonal Adjustment (Compared with the Same Period of the Previous Year)

	1994	1995	1996	1997			1998			1999		
				June	Dec.	Whole year	June	Dec.	Whole year	Mar.	June	Aug.
M0	24.28	8.19	11.60	17.85	17.20	15.63	5.77	10.10	10.09	11.20	11.90	12.50
M1	26.17	16.80	18.90	26.14	22.50	16.45	8.59	11.90	11.58	14.90	14.90	14.40
M2	34.53	29.50	25.30	21.32	19.82	17.32	14.30	15.30	15.34	17.80	17.70	16.00

Sources: People's Bank of China, *Statistical Quarterly*, No. 4 (1998), p. 9; National Bureau of Statistics of China, *China Statistical Yearbook, 1999*, pp. 2, 5, 8, 10; Bank of China, Institute of International Finance, *Analysis of the Current International and Domestic Economic and Financial Situation.* Beijing: Bank of China,1999.

Although the growth rate of M0, M1, and M2 had been falling from 1997 until the first half of 1999, at which point they rose a little, the growth rate of M2 has been above 15%, which was twice the GDP growth rate. The growth rate of M0 and M1 has been above 10%, which is also higher than the GDP growth rate. The M0 growth rate, which was under the control of the central bank, was maintained at the 1995/1996 level. The government also fine-tuned its monetary policy from "relatively tight" to "active and positive" and has kept expansionary monetary supply. Compared to the rapid money supply growth from 1992 to 1995, the current fall in the money supply growth rate is partly due to the abnormal growth in the previous period, which led to high inflation. The previous period should be taken as a reference for comparison. Furthermore, the decline in the money supply growth rate had not constrained investment because the annual money supply increase was even lower than the government target in 1998.[4]

Table 9.3 shows that the velocity of money has decreased since 1996 and the trend has become more serious. Money demand and

4. See Xie Ping and Shen Bingxi, "Deflation and Monetary Policy", *Jingji Yanjiu*, August 1999.

Table 9.3 Money Velocity

	1996	1997	1998	1999	1996–1999
V1	2.33	2.13	2.02	1.86	
V2	0.89	0.82	0.76	0.64	
V1 change (%)	–7.30	–7.90	–7.30	–15.80	–9.60
V2 change (%)	–2.50	–9.70	–5.10	–8.80	–6.50

Notes: 1. V1 is the money circulating velocity of M1; V2 is the money circulating velocity of M2.
2. The 1999 annual data was calculated from the data in the first half of 1999 and the past years.

Source: National Bureau of Statistics of China, Comprehensive Division, "Assessment of Current Money Supply Growth and Policy Recommendations", *Statistical Data*, No. 30 (October 1999).

money circulating velocity work in reverse directions. The drop in money velocity shows a strong social preference for holding currency. Deflation, of course, is a monetary phenomenon, but the deflation since 1997 should be ascribed to the fall in the money velocity instead of the decline in the money supply.[5]

As is well known, the 1929 Great Depression in the United States and the consequent deflation, which continued throughout the Depression, resulted from the collapse of bubbles in the stock market and the break-down of the financial system, leading to a sharp decline in consumption. The recent Japanese deflation also resulted from the 1991 collapse of the bubble in stock and real estate markets. However, the stock and real estate markets are still relatively insignificant in the Chinese economy and these markets work under a special institutional environment. Thus, their effect over the total demand should not be over-estimated.

Although the level of debt and bad loans in China's banking system is very high, a banking crisis has not occurred and the public still has confidence in the banking system. This is quite different from the situation in other East Asian countries. In May 1997 the

5. Bank of China, Institute of International Finance, *Analysis of the Current International and Domestic Economic and Financial Situation*. Beijing: Bank of China, 1999, p. 7.

Chinese stock market experienced a shock, during which the Shanghai Stock Index fell by one-third, transactions decreased significantly and many stockholders suffered severe losses. However, Chinese stock market only came into existence in the early 1990s and was still quite insignificant in the national economy. The percentage of assets in the form of stock was very low in the overall household financial assets. As shown in Table 9.4, the share was only 7.7% in 1997. In addition, stock prices and security prices moved in reverse directions in the markets. In 1997, 11.9% of households' financial assets were held in the form of securities, which was far higher than the share of stock assets. The drop of stock market prices will lead to the increase of security prices, partially offsetting the adverse effects of the drop in stock price.

In fact, stockholders in China know very well the risk of stock market price fluctuations as they have experienced a number of stock market crashes in the past. There is no necessary connection between stock market price fluctuations and the overall economic situation in China. In the economic boom in 1992–94, China experienced a crash in the stock market. Therefore, whilst fluctuations in the stock market may lead to temporary financial losses for stockholders, its impact on the overall wealth of households is not significant. Table 9.5 also shows that direct financing constitutes only a small share of the total financial sources of Chinese enterprises (less than 5%). The

Table 9.4 The Structure of Households' Financial Assets (%)

Year	Currency	Deposit	Security	Stocks	Insurance reserve	Total
1992	19.3	60.6	15.1	3.9	1.2	100
1993	22.4	66.6	5.9	3.9	1.2	100
1994	13.7	79.4	5.6	0.5	0.7	100
1995	5.0	87.1	6.6	0.3	1.0	100
1996	7.1	77.5	11.5	2.8	1.2	100
1997	10.9	67.1	11.9	7.7	2.5	100

Source: Data provided by People's Bank of China and National Bureau of Statistics of China, quoted in Liu Hongru and Li Zhiling, "The Reform of China's Financial System and the Role of the Stock Market", *Jingrong Yanjiu*, August 1999.

Table 9.5 The Structure of Finance in Chinese Enterprises (%)

	1989	1990	1991	1992	1993	1994	1995	1996
Direct finance	3.37	2.35	3.24	6.27	5.82	4.29	3.59	3.53
Indirect finance	96.63	97.65	96.96	93.73	94.18	95.71	96.41	96.47

Source: Li Ming and Yuan Guoliang, "Debt Financing and Sustainable Development for Firms", *Jingrong Yanjiu*, July 1999.

financing of enterprises was not very much dependent on the stock market and the stock market did not have much influence on firms' financial position. Therefore, the stock market fluctuation will not lead to significant changes in the behaviour of firms and households. The proposition that the drop of stock market prices led to the shrinkage of the total demand, which, in turn, caused the current deflation, is not supported by evidence.

In 1992 there was a nationwide "development zone fever" and "real estate fever", in which real estate prices rose sharply and real estate speculation was widespread. In 1993 and 1994 the central government's retrenchment programme led to the collapse of the real estate bubble and a depression in the real estate market. If the collapse of the real estate bubble had affected overall demand, the effect should have appeared in 1995 and 1996; however, the deflation did not appear until 1998. The real estate market in China is quite different from that in other countries. Land is owned by the state instead of households. The rise and fall of real estate prices have very little effect on the wealth of individuals. The real estate developers and the bank which provided loans to the developers were the ones that were mostly affected. With the exception of a few areas, the bust in real estate markets did not lead to a significant drop in real estate prices; instead, it only led to the result that real estate market transactions came to a halt and the banks found it difficult to get loan repayments. Since most investments in real estate came from bank loans and public funds, the pressure of repayment was limited. The providers of loans/funds did not want to sell real estates at discounted prices and see the resultant shrinkage in the book value. It is safe to

Figure 9.1 Annual consumption growth rate

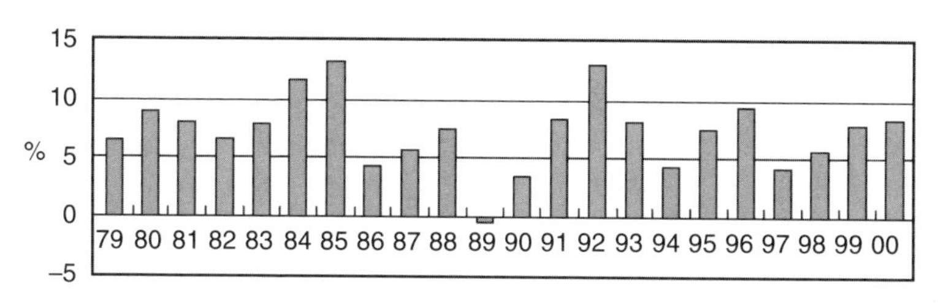

Source: National Bureau of Statistics of China, *China Statistical Abstract, 2001*. Beijing: China Statistics Press, 2001, p. 66.

say that the current bust in the real estate market had a very limited effect on the consumption demand.

It is important to note from Figure 9.1 that consumption demand still grew at 4.2% and 5.6% in the years 1997 and 1998, respectively, when deflation was already very serious. They are not much different from the average rate of 7.1% in the two decades from 1979 to 1998. From Figure 9.1, it can be inferred that current deflation is not caused by the reduction of consumption due to the collapse of bubbles in the stock and real estate market.

9.2 Serious Over-supply Is the Main Cause of Deflation

The analysis in the previous section suggests that the current deflation is not caused by a decline in investment demand due to credit squeezes or by a decline in consumption demand due to the collapse of stock and real estate bubbles. Therefore, the current deflation can only be caused by over-supply. China's annual GDP growth rate averaged 9.7% from 1979 to 1998. The total GDP in 1998 was 6.4 times the GDP in 1978 and the value added in the industrial sectors was 9.4 times that of 1978.[6] The traditional pattern of economic shortage in a socialist economy had come to an end in

6. National Bureau of Statistics of China, *China Statistical Abstract, 1999*. Beijing: China Statistics Press, 1999, p. 4.

China in the early 1990s, which is evident in the abolishing of all kinds of rationing coupons in the early 1990s. Immediately following the end of the shortage era, over-supply and competition prevailed in most markets and production capacity was widely under-utilized. Currently, over-supply has become very common in the economy, as shown clearly in Table 9.6. By 1995, the production capacity utilization rate was only around 50% in many important manufacturing industries; in some cases, the rate was even lower than 40%. If the high inventories are taken into account, the situation is more serious than the figures suggest. It is estimated that, in about half of the industries in China, the production capacity utilization rate is lower than 60% and the lowest is only 10%.[7]

Production capacity increases mainly come from fixed asset investment and technological innovation; the latter is usually embodied in new fixed investment. It is necessary to look at fixed assets to understand the changes in production capacity. Figure 9.2 gives the leading coefficient of fixed asset investment over the household consumption. The leading coefficient is defined as the difference between the index of the fixed asset investment and the index of the average household consumption level. Taking 1980 as the base year, in 1990 the coefficient was 305.2. From 1991 it increased rapidly and the coefficient reached 2206.8 in 1996, and further increased to 2782.9 in 1998. If 1990 is taken as the base year, the coefficient was 342.1 in 1996 and rose to 447.4 in 1998. The increase in the leading coefficient is mainly due to an increase in the growth rate of fixed asset investment, which was only 19.5% and 16.5% per year, respectively, in the Sixth Five-year Plan period (1981–85) and the Seventh Five-year Plan period (1986–90), but jumped to 36.9% in the Eighth Five-year Plan period (1991–95).

As a result, the production capacity in the economy, represented by the net value of fixed assets, quickly exceeded the economy's final consumption. Figure 9.3 depicts the leading coefficient of the net value of fixed assets over the final consumption, which is defined as

7. Mao Zong, "What were Covered by the Over-capacity", *China's National Situation and Power*, No. 4 (1999).

Table 9.6 Utilization Rates of Existing Production Capacity of Major Industrial Products in 1995

Item	Black & white TV set	Colour TV set	Household refrigerator	Washing machine	Popular video tape recorder	Air-conditioner	Video camera	Radio and tape recorder	Printed and dyed fabric
Utilization rate (%)	47.8	46.1	50.4	43.4	40.3	33.5	12.3	57.2	23.6
Item	Machine-processed sugar	Chemical fibre	Liquor	Motor vehicle	Motorcycle	Internal-combustion engine	Rolled-steel	Copper processing	Metal-cutting machine tool
Utilization rate (%)	56.7	76.4	64.9	44.3	61.6	43.9	62	51.4	46.2
Item	Traditional Chinese medicine	Tyre (cover)	Large and medium tractor	Mini-tractor	Aluminium oxide	Cement	Chemical pesticide	Refractory material products	
Utilization rate (%)	34.3	54.7	60.6	65.9	66.3	72.9	41.6	26.2	

Source: National Bureau of Statistics of China, *China Statistical Yearbook, 1997*. Beijing: China Statistics Press, 1997, pp. 454–55.

Figure 9.2 The leading coefficient of fixed asset investment growth over consumption growth

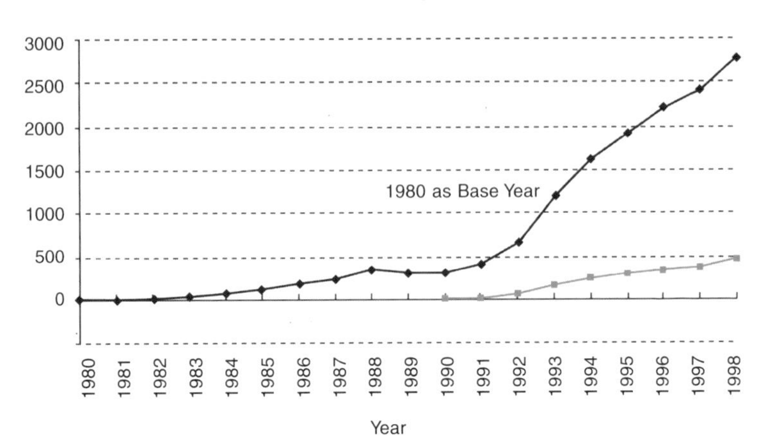

Notes:

1. Since 1997, with the exceptions of real estate, rural collective and individual investment, the statistical starting-point for basic construction, renovation and other forms of fixed asset investment rose from RMB 50,000 to 500,000 yuan.
2. The leading coefficient is defined as the difference between the index of the fixed asset investment and the index of the average household consumption level. Taking 1980 as the base year means that the index of fixed asset investment and the index of household consumption level are both assumed to be 100 in 1980. Taking 1990 as the base year means that the index of fixed asset investment and the index of household consumption level are both set to 100 in 1990.

Source: National Bureau of Statistics of China, *China Statistical Yearbook, 1999.* Beijing: China Statistics Press, 1999, pp. 27–41.

the difference between the index of net value of fixed assets and the index of final consumption. It shows that if 1978 is taken as the base year, then since 1993 the growth in the net value of assets has begun to rapidly surpass the growth of final consumption and the difference is increasing. In 1992 the difference in these two indices was still –6.5. In 1993 it turned positive and reached 45.9; and further increased to 138.6 in 1996; and to 183.3 in 1998. If 1990 is used as the base year, the point can be seen more clearly. If the difference between the index of net value of fixed asset and the index of final consumption in 1990 is assumed to be zero, in 1996 the growth of net value of

Figure 9.3 The leading coefficient of growth of net value of fixed assets over final consumption

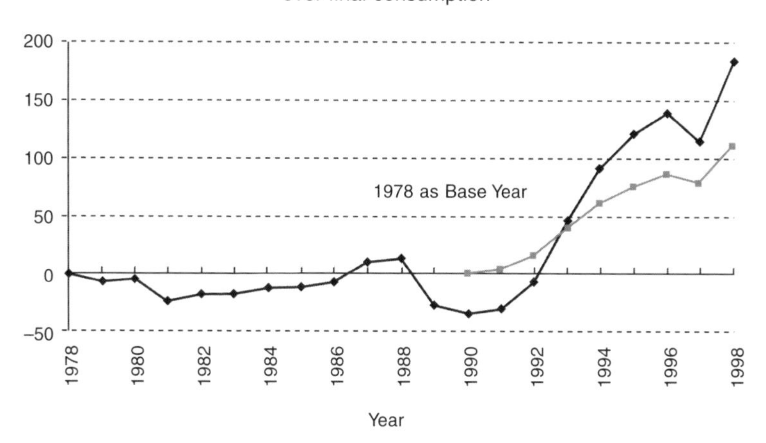

Note: The leading coefficient is defined as the difference between the index of net value of fixed asset and the index of final consumption. Taking 1978 as the base year means that the index of net fixed asset and the index of final consumption are both set to be 100 in 1978. Taking 1990 as the base year means that the index of net value of fixed asset and the index of final consumption are both set to be 100 in 1990.

Source: National Bureau of Statistics of China, *China Statistical Yearbook, 1999.* Beijing: China Statistics Press, 1999, p. 76; National Bureau of Statistics of China, National Economic Accounting Division, *The Gross Domestic Product of China, 1952–1995*. Beijing: Northeast Finance University Press, 1997, pp. 42–76.

fixed asset exceeded the growth of final consumption by 84.4%; and in 1998, by 110.4%. In other words, from 1990 to 1998, the formation of net fixed assets exceeded the growth of final consumption by over 100%.

Taking the state-owned economy as an example, the net value of fixed asset increased from RMB 1,089 billion in 1990 to RMB 2,959 billion in 1995, equivalent to a 273% increase. Since the technological innovation is embodied in the new fixed asset, the production capacity in 1995 is at least 2.7 times that of the capacity in 1990. The non-state-owned economy grew faster than the state-owned economy in the same period. However, the increase in consumption demand was constrained by the increase of income. In the Eighth Five-year Plan period, income growth was only slightly higher than that of the 1980s,[8] thus, the final consumption cannot grow synchronously with the growth of production capacity. In the 1980s, the difference between the production capacity growth and final demand growth was offset by economic shortage that existed long before the reform. By the 1990s the long-existing shortages in the Chinese economy had come to an end, and the difference in the growth of production capacity and the demand led to the situation shown in Table 9.6. Therefore, it is mainly over-investment during the Eighth Five-year Plan period and the resultant growth of production capacity far exceeding the growth of consumption that caused the current difficult situation of excessive production capacity and serious deflation.

In the period from 1992 to 1994, the Chinese economy was overheating and the economy encountered serious inflation. In 1993 and 1994 the retail price index grew at 14.7% and 24.1%, respectively and in 1995 the rate was still 17.1%.[9] The annual growth rate of fixed asset investment was 44.4%, 61.8% and 30.4%, in 1992, 1993 and 1994, respectively, which were the highest since the beginning of reform.[10] The net value of fixed asset also grew annually at 23.9%, 24.8% and 17.7% in these three years, which were also the highest after the beginning of the reform.[11] If no measures had been taken to constrain the over-expansion of fixed asset investment at that time, the situation of over-capacity would have been much more serious than what the Chinese economy has encountered now and the deflation would have been much more severe. If from 1995 to the success of the soft-landing in 1997, the

8. The average annual GDP growth rates for the Sixth, Seventh, and Eighth Five-year Plans were 10.8%, 7.9%, and 11.6%, respectively.
9. National Bureau of Statistics of China, *China Statistical Yearbook, 1997*. Beijing: China Statistics Press, 1997, p. 263.
10. National Bureau of Statistics of China, *China Statistical Yearbook, 1998*. Beijing: China Statistics Press, 1998, p. 41.
11. National Bureau of Statistics of China, National Economic Accounting Division, *The Gross Domestic Product of China, 1952–1995*. Beijing: Northeast Finance University Press, 1997, p. 51.

retrenchment policy had not been implemented thoroughly, the overheating in the Eighth Five-year Plan period would have been prolonged for several more years; and, after that, more serious over-capacity and deflation would have been the result. Therefore, it is wrong to attribute the current deflation to the retrenchment policy. On the contrary, it is the retrenchment measures taken by the government that has prevented the Chinese economy from having a more serious over-capacity and deflation situation, and has enabled the Chinese economy to maintain a reasonably high growth rate in the adverse domestic and international environment.

9.3 The Effects of Excess Capacity and Deflation

When a serious excess capacity exists in the overall economy, the economy will encounter a deflation, i.e. a continuous decline in the price level. Furthermore, the economy will also slip into a vicious cycle and many of the policy instruments which used to be very effective when the economy is basically in equilibrium will suddenly become ineffective.

When excess capacity prevails in the economy, enterprises cannot easily find good investment opportunities. Investment demand in the economy will decline. At the same time, enterprises will run under capacity, equipment utilization will be low and profits will fall. Enterprises will face the possibility of bankruptcy and a worker's risk of unemployment will increase. A worker's permanent income expectation will drop and consumption will decline.[12] As we know, the investment demand of firms and consumption demand of households are the main components of total final demand. Taking China as an example, these two components constituted 84.6% of the 1998 GDP.[13] If the growth rates of both demands drop and, at the same time, the production capacity is still growing at a higher rate

12. In the current situation in China, the decline of consumption is also exacerbated by the reforms in housing, medical cares, education, pension, and social welfare system.
13. National Bureau of Statistics of China, *China Statistical Yearbook, 1999*. Beijing: China Statistics Press, 1999.

than the demand growth, the excess capacity situation will become even more serious. In turn, investment and consumption demand will become even more depressed, and a more serious deflation will follow. A vicious circle will thus emerge if the government takes no effective measures.[14]

Interest is the cost of investment and also the relative price of current and future consumption. Theoretically, the reduction of interest rates will stimulate investment and current consumption. When investment and consumption demand decline, the government often adopts a monetary policy that reduces interest rates in order to stimulate investment and current consumption. The Chinese government began to take this measure in 1996 when it lowered the interest rate. Interest rates were reduced three times in 1998 alone. When the government lowered the rate for the seventh time in June 1999, the one-year lending rate was 5.85%, only half of the rate prevailed in 1996 when the government began to adopt this policy. The interest rate for a one-year term deposit was 2.25%, only a quarter of the rate in 1996 before the policy was adopted.

The frequency of interest cuts has been very high and the extent has been large but these policies have not produced the expected results. The main reason for the ineffectiveness is that the deflation was caused by the existence of serious excess capacity in all sectors. When serious over-capacity exists, firms cannot find good investment opportunities and are reluctant to borrow from banks to make investments, even when the interest rate is very low. In addition, when income growth expectation is pessimistic and the risk of unemployment rises, households will save more, even when the interest rate is reduced. Therefore, the stimulating effect of monetary policy will not be very effective.[15] At the same time, when the

14. China Center for Economic Research (CCER), Macroeconomic Research Group, Peking University, "Take the Deflation Pressure Seriously and Expedite the Micro-mechanism Reform", *Economic Research*, No. 7 (1999).
15. Japanese economy is a good example. The interest rates in Japan are close to zero now. However, due to the same reason of excess capacity, its investment and consumption have not been stimulated by the low interest rates.

investment propensity of firms and the consumption propensity of households decrease, the currency holding propensity of firms and households will increase, and the money velocity drops. The effect of increasing the money supply will be offset by the decrease in the velocity of money. Therefore, the government cannot stop the deflation by the increase in the money supply. For the same reason, the taxation of interest earnings will not be effective in stimulating current consumption when the households' expectation of future income and job security is pessimistic.

When the monetary and taxation policies, which indirectly affect firm investment and household consumption decisions, are not effective, governments in many countries often switch to fiscal policies to stimulate the economy directly. Roosevelt's New Deal is the best known example. In 1998, the Chinese government also began to implement active fiscal policies and issued RMB 100 billion of special bonds to support infrastructure construction.[16] In 1999, 2000, and 2001, another RMB 60 billion, 150 billion, and again 150 billion of bonds were issued respectively. However, so far the expansionary fiscal policy has also failed to stop the deflation. The main reason for this ineffectiveness is that the proportion of state budgetary appropriations in the total fixed asset investment has been falling since the beginning of reform, and by the early 1990s, it has become insignificant. From 1992 to 1997, the proportions were only 4.3%, 3.7%, 3.0%, 3.0%, 2.7% and 2.8%, respectively.[17] In addition, in 1998, the government's total fiscal revenues constituted only 12.4% of GDP, among which the central government only had half of the total revenue. The strength of fiscal policy is limited in a situation like this. In 1998, the public bond for infrastructure investment was RMB 100 billion, which was quite large relative to the RMB 489.2 billion of central government revenue, but it was only 3.5% of the total fixed asset investment in China. With the RMB 100 billion

16. State Planning Council, Research Group on Macroeconomic Situation, "Managing Deflation with All Efforts", *People's Daily*, 28 June 1999 and "Proposal for Stopping Deflation", *People's Daily*, 5 July 1999.
17. National Bureau of Statistics of China, *China Statistical Yearbook, 1998*. Beijing: China Statistics Press, 1998, p. 187.

special bond, the proportion of public investment in total fixed asset investment rose only from 2.8% in 1997 to 4.2% in 1998.

When excess capacity is very serious and firms have little incentive to invest, public investment will not be able to offset the reduction in firm investments. Even if the investment by firms had not declined, the increase in government's infrastructure investment, no matter how large, would not be enough to digest the 30% or more excess capacity in the economy. It is worth mentioning that a common conclusion by scholars with respect to the Great Depression is that the Roosevelt New Deal had no substantial effect in helping the U.S. economy to get out of the Great Depression.[18]

In the same way, constrained by government fiscal power, the income reallocation policy, which included social relief to the poor and an increase in government employees' salary level, will not improve the real income of households by a large margin. The policy's stimulating effect on consumption is limited, even though the policy may help to improve social stability. Take the wage increase policy of September 1999 as an example. It increased the basic wages of government employees by 30%. However, even if all increased income were used for consumption, the total demand in the economy would only increase by 1%.[19]

The total demand in an economy includes firm investment, household consumption, government investment and consumption, and exports. In 1998, the total Chinese exports were US$183.76 billion, 19.1% of the GDP. However, half of the exports depended on imported intermediate goods from foreign countries. A 10% increase in exports can only lead to a 1% increase in total demand. With the adverse effects from the current East Asian financial crisis, the export growth fell from 21% in 1997 to 0.5% in 1998. The export growth is expected to be maintained at a low rate for the near future.

---

18. See Thomas E. Hall and J. David Ferguson, *The Great Depression: An International Disaster of Perverse Economic Policies*. Ann Arbor: The University of Michigan Press, 1998.
19. Of course, increasing the relief for the poor is necessary at the current stage of economic development, whether the economic situation is good or bad.

Even if it is possible to recover to the same dynamic growth of 1997, the increase will not play a big role in digesting the current huge excess capacity in the economy.[20]

The contingent monetary, fiscal, taxation, income redistribution and trade policies detailed in economics textbooks are effective only when the total demand and supply in the economy are relatively balanced. However, with the current 30% or more excess capacity in all major sectors in the Chinese economy, the implementation of any single policy or even the combination of all of the above policies will not be effective in creating a large enough demand to digest the excess capacity. In fact, in Japan when the bubble collapsed in 1991, and resulted in wealth shrinkage, consumption decline, excess capacity and deflation, the Japanese government also took various measures to stimulate the economy, but has not been able to get the economy out of its plight so far. The same happened in the U.S. in the Great Depression of the 1920s and 1930s. The U.S. economy grew out of the Depression only when the U.S. mobilized its economy to engage in World War II in 1941. China must seek another way to solve the problems arising from the current deflation.

9.4 The New Village Movement and Solution to Deflation

In a large economy, where exports constitute a small portion of the GDP, there are only two solutions to the problem of deflation, regardless of whether the deflation is caused by a sharp drop in consumption, as in the case of the Great Depression in the U.S., or by a sharp increase in supply, as in the case of China's current situation. The first solution is to let time dissipate the excess capacity. In this way, the national economy will experience a long-term depression. Inefficient firms will go bankrupt and total supply will decrease. The economy will regain balance at a low capacity level. The merit of this approach is to eliminate inefficient firms through competition and to

20. People's Press, *Xinhua Monthly*, various issues, 1996–99.

improve resource allocation and utilization level, making the economy more competitive when the economy regain its dynamism. However, the Chinese economy needs to create 8 million new jobs annually to meet the urban employment demand. In addition, the Chinese economy needs to find jobs to relocate 20 to 30 million workers released from state-owned enterprises. Without a decent growth rate, it would be hard for the Chinese economy to maintain social stability.

The second solution is to rely on the government to find or create a large enough social demand to consume the excess capacity. In a developed market economy, the opportunity for the government to do so would be limited because most effective demands have been met. Only with a special occasion such as the World War II, was it possible for the U.S. government to create a huge social demand. China is still in its transition from a planned economy to a market economy. Its market is underdeveloped and the condition for consumption is insufficient. In rural areas, In particular, where 69.6% of the population live, there is a huge effective consumption demand which cannot be satisfied due to constraints or a lack of consumption-related infrastructures. Compared to the Great Depression in the 1930s and Japan's deflation in the 1990s, the existence of a huge unsatisfied consumption demand in rural areas is a great advantage for China to solve the deflation problem.

Using the household electrical appliances as an example, urban markets are basically saturated, but in the rural areas, the number of durable consumer goods owned per 100 households like colour TV set, refrigerator, and washing machine were 32.6, 9.3 and 22.8 in 1998, respectively, which were only 30.1%, 12.2% and 25.2% of the corresponding figures in the urban areas (see Table 9.7).

Colour TV set, refrigerator, and washing machine are the hot items of urban demand in late 1980s and early 1990s and contributed a lot to market prosperity. In 1998 the output for these three goods reached 34.97 million, 10.6 million and 120.7 million, respectively, and the capacity utilization rates were only about 50%, as shown in Table 9.6. Currently the total number of rural households is 230 million, more than twice the 110 million in urban areas. A 10%

Table 9.7 Number of Durable Consumer Goods Owned Per 100 Households and the Net Income Per Capita

	1998 urban households	1998 rural households	1991 urban households	1998 rural households in Guangdong
Color TV set	105.4	32.6	68.4	55.4
Refrigerator	76.1	9.3	48.7	11.0
Washing machine	90.6	22.8	80.6	20.3
Radio & tape recorders	57.6	32.6	34.7	49.0
Net income per capita (yuan)	5,425	2,162	2,025	3,527

Source: National Bureau of Statistics of China, *China Statistical Yearbook, 1999.* Beijing: China Statistics Press, 1999, pp. 340, 347–48.

increase in the number of durable consumer goods owned of the three goods in rural areas will be enough to consume the excess capacity of these products.

Early in the late 1980s, many people had already turned their attention to rural markets. The efforts have not borne the expected results. The main constraint for rural household consumption of modern appliances, such as colour TV, refrigerators, and washing machines, is not income level, although the rural income level is lower than the urban level. In 1998, the annual gross income per capita in rural areas reached RMB 3,018. After deducting production costs, tax and fees, the net income was RMB 2,162 per capita, which was slightly higher than the RMB 2,025 urban per capita income level in 1991. In 1991 the number of durable consumer goods owned per 100 households in urban areas for colour TV, refrigerator, and washing machine were respectively 68.4, 48.7, 80.6, which were 1.1, 4.2 and 2.5 times higher than the number in rural areas in 1998. The prices for the above three goods in 1998 were less than half the 1991 prices.

Some people argue that part of the net rural household income is in-kind income and the disposable money income for rural households is less than that of urban households of the same net income level. However, if Guangdong Province is used as an example, the per capita net income for rural households in 1998 was RMB 3,527, 74% higher than that of urban households in 1991. The disposable money income for rural households in Guangdong Province must be higher than that of urban households in 1991. However, in 1998, Guangdong peasants owned much fewer household electrical appliances than did urban households in 1991, as shown in Table 9.7. Therefore, income level is not the main constraint for rural households to consume electrical appliances.

Some people also argue that consumer habits may be the main cause for the low number of household electrical products owned per 100 households in rural areas. For example, they argue that peasants like to spend money on housing. In many rural regions, peasants have built, dismantled and rebuilt houses three times since the reform started, as the argument runs. The expenditure on housing has caused them to ignore other types of consumption. However, the argument is unfounded. If one looks at the number of tape recorders, the number owned per 100 households in rural areas was 32.6 in 1998, which was almost the same as the figure of 34.7 in urban areas in 1991. In the rural areas of Guangdong, the figure was 49, i.e. 41% higher than that in urban areas in 1991, which was consistent with the difference in their income levels.

Why does the number of tape recorders owned differs from that of the colour TV set, refrigerator, and washing machine? That is because the use of tape recorder does not rely so much on other infrastructures. The use of colour TV set, refrigerator and washing machine is dependent on the availability of electricity, television signal and tap water. However, in the countryside, the electricity network is old, the voltage unstable, and the price is very high, usually three, five or even ten times the level in urban areas. In addition, the TV signal is weak in rural areas, and 49.7% of rural households have no tap water. All these factors greatly limit rural household demand for colour TV sets, refrigerators and washing machines. If the quality of electricity network is improved, the price of electricity lowered to the urban level, TV satellite signal receiving stations established in villages, tap water towers constructed and tap water provided, it can be expected that a consumption boom in the household durable appliances will emerge. The excess-capacities in household electrical industries will disappear.

To narrow the urban and rural disparities is a goal of economic development in China. The improvement of infrastructure in rural areas should have been on the government's agenda long ago. To get out of the current deflation trap, the government can launch a nationwide new village movement, in which the provision of consumption-related infrastructures, such as electricity, tap water and road networks, are the core elements.

In the rural areas, the investments in roads, electricity network, tap water, and TV signal transmission and reception require a small amount of funds, take short construction periods, and have quick and beneficial social and economic effects. The government fiscal expenditures on these projects would produce high leverage effects in stimulating consumption demands. In 1998, Guangxi provincial government adopted a new policy of "providing TV service to households in each village" by setting up a ground satellite receiving station in every village. The cost for setting up the system in a village with 200 households was about RMB 5,000. Since then, colour TV sets has become a "hot" sale item in Guangxi. The *Hunan Daily* helped a poor village, which was on the nation's poverty list, to construct a ground TV satellite reception network, and over 180 colour TV sets were then bought in this village of 267 households. China has 740,000 administrative villages. Even constructing satellite reception stations in two-thirds of them at a cost of RMB 10,000 for one station, the total investment would only be RMB 5 billion. According to the current rural income level and the price level of colour TV set, the number owned per 100 households in the countryside could at least reach the 1991 urban level. If the electricity and TV signal problems can be solved, China will not have the problem of excess capacity in colour TV sets. Furthermore, half of the 740,000 villages do not have tap water supply. If the infrastructure construction is to provide tap water, like constructing water towers and related conduits in the 370,000 villages, the total investment would be RMB 74 billion. Once the tap water is supplied, the demands for refrigerators and washing machines will surely increase tremendously. Furthermore, this will start a revolution in kitchen, toilet and other modern living facilities in rural households. All the above activities will create a huge demand and the existing excess capacities in most industries will disappear.

Confronted with the economic problems like excess capacities, weak markets and deflation, the government has to adopt fiscal measures to stimulate the economy. However, to be effective, the fiscal expenditures should be used in areas that will result in high leverage effects in inducing household demand. The "New Village Movement" which gives priorities to the construction of rural roads, and the provision of electricity and tap water, is surely the one that will have the highest leverage effect. These projects can remove the constraints that limit the realization of the great consumption potential in rural areas. In addition, compared to the other large infrastructure projects, these investments have the following merits: they require less funds, create more employment opportunities (due to the labour intensity of the projects), and stimulate more demands (due to the use of more domestic inputs).

Rural infrastructure construction needs to be implemented by local governments and grassroots organizations due to its small scale and scattered nature. The central government and local governments can invest jointly. The central government can allocate special funds and require that the local governments provide a certain supporting fund. The exact way of fund-raising can be explored in practice. It is unreasonable to depend on county, township and village-level governments to finance completely the rural infrastructure projects. If the projects are carried out in that way, the cost of these projects will inevitably fall on rural households. In the past, the government provided funds for the construction of urban infrastructures while rural peasants had to finance the rural infrastructures by themselves. This has been the main reason for the backwardness of rural infrastructure and the existence of unbearable burdens on rural households. To expedite rural infrastructure development, governments at all levels should change both their attitudes and the criteria for assessing government performance, so that the government can really give higher priorities to rural infrastructure investments. In the past, the economic relationship between rural and urban areas was not equal: the former subsidized the latter. It is time to compensate the former by allocating more fiscal investment to the rural areas.

The attempt to expedite the development of rural infrastructure in the New Village Movement does not contradict the attempt to develop small cities and townships in rural areas. Urbanization is a natural process of economic development.[21] Without sufficient non-agricultural employment opportunities, small cities will not be attractive to peasants. It is not practical for agricultural households, which operate small plots of land, to live in a small city that is far away from their land. There is a long way to go for Chinese rural areas to become urbanized. Before that, it is necessary to speed up rural infrastructure development and improve the living environment for peasants. The investment in the rural infrastructure will not be wasted because the investment will generate high enough returns in the near future.

21. See Justin Yifu Lin, "Deepening Market-oriented Reform is the Only Way to Solve the Current Peasant Problem", *Jingji Yanjiu*, November 1998.

CHAPTER 10

WTO Accession and China's Reform[1]

After 15 years of effort, China has finally become a formal member of World Trade Organization (WTO) on 10 December 2001. The basic spirit of the WTO is to lower tariff rates, to eliminate non-tariff barriers, and to allow market entries so that production could be allocate globally according to the principle of comparative advantage. Top Chinese leaders regard the WTO accession as the second most important change in China's economic policy regime, following Deng Xiaoping's reform and opening-door policy in the late 1970s. This change will have undoubtedly profound impacts on the future course of China's economic development. Some analysts are very positive about the accession. They believe that any drawback will be overwhelmed by the efficiency gains, injecting new growth impetus into China's reform and economic development. According to them, China will enter an entirely new development stage. However, China is still a developing country and, at the same time, is in its transition from a planned economy to a market economy. Not surprisingly, in its economy there exist many sectors, which are not competitive. It's expected that the accession to the WTO will bring challenge to the national economy as well. Other

1. This chapter draws heavily on Justin Yifu Lin, "WTO Accession and Financial Market Reform in China", *The Cato Journal*, Vol. 21, No. 1 (Spring/Summer 2001), pp. 13–19; Justin Yifu Lin, "WTO Accession and China's Agriculture", *China Economic Review*, Vol. 11, No. 4 (2000), pp. 405–408; and Justin Yifu Lin, "WTO Accession and China's SOE Reform", in Kyung Tae Lee, Justin Yifu Lin, and Si Joong Kim, eds., *China's Integration with the World Economy: Repercussions of China's Accession to the WTO*. Seoul: Korea Institute for International Economic Policy, 2001.

analysts are worried that China's weak economic base would not be able to sustain the tremendous external shocks brought by the entry to the WTO. They argue that the WTO accession will do more harm than good to the Chinese economy.[2]

Our judgment is that, before the expiration of the grace periods in the bilateral agreements, most sectors in Chinese economy are still protected. However, in anticipation of the opening up of China's domestic markets after the grace period, foreign direct investments from multinational companies will increase substantially immediately after the accession. Therefore, the accession should bring an immediate boost to investments and a spurt to economic growth in Chinese economy in the immediate, short run. In the long run, a membership at the WTO will undoubtedly enable Chinese economy to have a closer integration with the world economy, facilitating a better access to foreign technology, capital and world market. Therefore, the accession will be beneficial to China's overall economic growth in the long run. The real challenge to Chinese economy will be in the intermediate period after the expiration of the grace period and before the completion of Chinese economy's adjustments to the long run equilibrium. The challenges in the intermediate period will certainly be different from one sector to another, depending on the gains and adjustments that the sector needs to make.[3]

Agriculture and financial agreements are two of the most sensitive areas in China's bilateral negotiations. The state-owned enterprises (SOEs) are among the least efficient enterprises in China. A good understanding of the effects of WTO accession on agriculture, financial sector and SOEs will help us comprehend the overall impact of WTO accession on Chinese economy. In this

---

2. See Li Shantong, Wang Zhi, Qu Fan and Wang Lin, *WTO: China and the World*. Beijing: China Development Press, 2000.
3. See Justin Yifu Lin, "What is the Direction of China's Financial Reform?" in Hai Wen and Lu Feng, eds., *China Economic Transition and Economic Policy*. Beijing: Peking University Press, 2000, pp. 296–301; Justin Yifu Lin, and Hu Shudong, "To be a Member of WTO: Challenges and Opportunities for China". Working paper of China Center for Economic Research, Peking University, No. C2000004, March 2000.

chapter, we will discuss the potential impacts of the WTO accession on China's agricultural sector and financial sector, and analyze its impact and implications for the reform on SOEs.

10.1 WTO Accession and China's Agriculture

Agriculture is the most sensitive issue in the WTO negotiations and is the most difficult part in reaching an agreement. This applies also to other WTO member countries. Conflicts and disputes on agricultural problems always result in lengthy negotiations among not only the developed countries themselves but also between developing and developed countries. China is a developing country with the largest population in the world. Most Chinese people still live in the countryside. Many people are worried that Chinese farmers endowed with small plots of land and backward technology cannot compete with the large farmers equipped with modern technology in advanced countries, such as the United States, Canada, and Australia and that WTO accession will have substantial negative impacts on Chinese agriculture. They give as evidence that current prices of grain in Chinese markets are already close to or even exceed world market prices. For example, on March 1999, the price of corn in the domestic market was RMB 1.44/kg on average; however, the average price in the Chicago Futures Market was equivalent to RMB 0.72/kg. Therefore, the anxiety about the agricultural impact of WTO entry is understandable.

In the bilateral agreement between China and the U.S., agricultural trade occupies a premier position. The agricultural agreement with the U.S. is most comprehensive and has received most public attention. The following analysis will base mainly on the agreement between China and the U.S., supplemented with the agreement between China and the European Union (EU) only when it is necessary. The main contents of the China-U.S. agreement cover the following five areas:[4]

4. Sino-U.S. agreement is drawn from the White House Office of Public Liason, *Summary of U.S.-China Bilateral WTO Agreement*, available at the website of U.S.-China Business Council at http://www.uschina.org.

1. Elimination of sanitary and phyto-sanitary barriers on U.S. exports of wheat, citrus and meat, for example, the bans on importing wheat from TCK-affected regions.
2. Elimination of China's subsidies to agricultural exports.
3. Liberalization of state companies' monopoly and allowing private companies to engage in agricultural trade.
4. Adoption of a tariff-rate quota (TRQ) system for grain imports.
5. Reduction of tariffs on agricultural products to well below 20% for major agricultural imports from U.S.[5]

The first item listed above will not have much impact on China's imports because those trade barriers affect only small amounts of agricultural products and are hard to implement. The second item will not have much impact on China's export either, because there are currently few subsidies for Chinese agricultural exports. The third item is beneficial to Chinese farmers and consumers. The state monopoly on agricultural export/import is extremely inefficient. The liberalization of agricultural trade and the consequent competition between private and state traders should be most welcomed by farmers and consumers. Controversy focuses mainly on the fourth and fifth items, namely, agreements on the import of grain and the reduction of import tariffs.

China is a land-scarce economy. Agricultural production requires land input. However, it does not mean that the agriculture sector in China will be decimated when China enters the WTO. The

5. According to the agreement with the U.S., China will also eliminate restrictions on soybean imports, tariff on which will be cut down to 3%. Tariffs on wine will be reduced from 65% to 20%. Tariffs on beef will be reduced from 45% to 12%, on pork will be from 20% to 12%, and on poultry from 20% to 10%. Tariffs on orange will be decreased from 40% to 12%, on grape from 40% to 13%, and on apple from 30% to 10%. Tariffs on apricot will be reduced from 30% to 10%, on cheese from 50% to 12%, and on ice cream from 45% to 10%. China made further concessions to EU and agreed to reduce the tariff on wine to 14%, on all spirits to 10%, butter to 10%, milk powder to 10%, mandarins to 12%, olives to 10%, pasta to 15%, rape oil to 9%, and wheat gluten to 18%. See Arthur Lapres, "The E.U.-China WTO Deal Compared", at www.gyoza.com/lapres.

relatively low price of grain in U.S. is due to multiple factors. Grain, one of the major agricultural products, is land-intensive and the United States is relatively land-rich, giving it a comparative advantage in grain. In addition, the U.S. government subsidized and protected grain farmers for years through technology development, export subsidies and price supports. Such policies deviate from the recent WTO agricultural cooperation agreement. Moreover, the WTO members including the U.S. are encouraging new negotiation on free trade of agricultural products, including grain. Thus, the U.S. will eventually have to give up almost all of its current protective agricultural policies, leading to a greatly diminished price advantage for U. S. grain. Agricultural production in the EU is not much of a threat to Chinese agriculture since for most agricultural products other than wine, spirits, and milk products, European countries do not have comparative advantages.

Given that China has limited land but abundant population, it does not have a comparative advantage in grain production. Importing grain is equivalent to importing land, which is not harmful to Chinese economic development. In addition, a considerable portion of the price of grain in the domestic market does not reflect actual production cost, due to the inefficient monopolized operation of the state grain agency. In accordance with China's commitment to allow the entry of private traders, this situation will be improved after China enters the WTO. Therefore, the market competitiveness of grain production in China will be enhanced.

Moreover, the Sino-U.S. agreement on grain is a tariff-rate quota (TRQ) system. Within the agreed import quota, low tariffs will be implemented; for imports exceeding quota limits, high protective tariff will be imposed. The TRQ is initially 14.4 million tons and will gradually increase to 21.8 million tons.[6] In general, imports will not

---

6. The TRQ for wheat will increase from 7.3 million tons at the time of accession to 9.3 million tons after five years, while the share for private traders will be 10%. The TRQ for corn will increase initially from 4.5 million tons to 7.2 million tons, and the share for private traders will grow from 25% to 40%. The TRQ for rice will increase from 2.6 million tons to 5.3 million

exceed the quota, because the high over-quota tariffs are prohibitive. In addition, even if the TRQ of 21.8 million tons is fully used, the resulting grain imports will only be less than 5% of China's average grain output in the 1990s. The impact on domestic prices, and therefore on farmers' income, will be very limited.[7]

Apart from the land-intensive grains, many other agricultural products, such as animal husbandry, horticulture, aqua culture, and processed agricultural products, are labour intensive. In these commodities, China has a comparative advantage over most other countries.[8] In fact, since reform began in the late 1970s, China's agricultural trade has always been in surplus, soaring from US$57 million in 1980 to US$6.8 billion in 1999.[9] One of the important reasons for this trend is the increase in exports of labour-intensive agricultural products.[10] The reduction of China's import tariffs will not hurt China's net exports of those labour-intensive products at all. Moreover, the past growth of agricultural exports was achieved under high protective tariffs and non-tariff barriers set by the importing

---

tons, and the share for private traders is up to 50%. No TRQ is set for importing barley and its tariff will be reduced to 9%.

7. With the exception of the farmers in the northeast of China. Northeast is the corn and soybean belt of China. Both the price of corn and the price of soybean are higher than international prices. There is no quota on the importation of soybean. The import of corn and soybean is likely to reduce substantially the income of farmers in northeast. It is therefore imperative for the Chinese government to increase research investments in soybean and corn so as to increase corn and soybean productivity in the northeast as a way to mitigate the adverse impact on farmers' income in the region.
8. The exceptions are those commodities that are itemized in the tariff agreements with the U.S. and the EU. However, those commodities comprise only a very small part compared to China's production except for soybean (See D. Gale Johnson, "WTO and Chinese Agriculture". Paper presented in a seminar at the China Center for Economic Research, Peking University, 23 March 2000).
9. National Bureau of Statistics of China, *China Statistical Abstract, 2000*. Beijing: China Statistics Press, 2000, p. 140.
10. Lu Feng, *The Comparative Advantage and the China's Structure of Grain Trade: The Third Choice for Restructuring China's Agriculture Policy* (mimeo). Beijing: China Center for Economic Research, Peking University, 1999.

countries. The agricultural trade interventions by WTO members have been reduced substantially recently, and will diminish further in the near future. After joining the WTO, China will have increased access to foreign agricultural product markets. It is expected that China's exports of labour-intensive agricultural products will increase tremendously.

10.2 Accession's Potential Impacts on Financial Sector

The financial sector is another most sensitive issue in the bilateral negotiations. In a market economy, the primary role of banks and financial institutions is to serve as an intermediary between savers and investors and to facilitate payments between economic units. As discussed in Chapter 2, prior to the economic reform, China had a planned economy with heavy industry as its priority of development. The financial system was an integral part of the planned economy. Regular financial market activities were banned. The People's Bank of China (PBOC) was the only financial institution, serving as the central bank and at the same time providing commercial banking services. After the start of economic reform, those previously banned banks and non-bank financial institutions were gradually re-opened. However, the four big state banks, namely Industrial and Commercial Bank of China, Agricultural Bank of China, Bank of China, and Construction Bank of China, still dominate China's financial sector.[11]

Statistics data shows that by early 2000 foreign banks and financial institutions have already set up 191 representative offices and subsidiaries in China with total assets of US$36 billion in 23 locations, including Shanghai, Beijing, Tianjin and Shenzhen, and Hainan Province. Many foreign banks have been recently allowed to upgrade their representative offices to branches and to conduct local currency business in Pudong and Shenzhen. For insurance, the

11. See Yi Gang, "China's Financial Assets: Structural Analysis and Policy Implications", in Hai Wen, Lu Feng and Ping Xinqiao, eds., *Economic Research on China*. Beijing: Peking University Press, 1999.

Chinese government recently approved four foreign insurance companies to set up new branches or joint ventures.

After the WTO accession, China agrees to remove the geographic and business restrictions by 2005, allowing foreign banks to set up branches in all other cities in China, conduct RMB business, and provide retailing services. Foreign insurance companies will also be allowed to own up to 50% equity of the joint ventures and to operate in more cities.

It is predictable that China's financial sector will become increasingly open to foreign financial institutions after the WTO accession. For a long time, China has treated the financial sector as a special industry. It had been very cautious in liberalizing the sector to foreign competition and had imposed many restrictions on the entry and operation of local financial institutions. After the WTO accession, foreign financial institutions will receive a national treatment. The state-owned banks and insurance companies will lose their existing protections. Therefore, the competition in China's financial market is expected to be very strong.

The financial sector and the state-owned enterprises are the two important and unaccomplished areas of reform in China's transition from a planned economy to a market economy. For a long time, the high ratio of non-performing loans in China's banking sector has aroused great concern.[12] The state banks have heavy burdens of policy-related lending. Meanwhile, the monopolistic nature of the state banks results in low efficiency in their operations. The overall quality of China's banking industry is poor and not competitive. In fact, China did not have a clear direction of financial reform until 1994. Since then, the four state banks have attempted to move their operations towards commercial banking. China has also set up a number of other regional and nationwide banks. In addition, the

12. Lardy estimated that about 50 percent of the outstanding loans of the four big state banks was non-performing loans. However, the most accepted figure among the Chinese banking officials is 25 percent, which is still higher than the levels of non-performing loans in Thailand, Korea, and Indonesia before the financial crisis in 1997. See Nicholas R. Lardy, *China's Unfinished Economic Revolution*. Washington, DC: Brookings Institution Press, 1998.

government issues more licenses to domestic insurance companies. The government has also acquired a better understanding of the equity market and its possible implications for the SOE reforms and for China's economic development.

The WTO accession will eventually deprived the four big state banks of their monopolistic position. The asset value and business volume of these four banks are no larger than other major foreign banks. Their operations and techniques are not as advanced as the overseas banks. Therefore, foreign banks have the ability to bring in a large enough shock to end the monopolistic nature of China's banking industry. Of course, the local banks, especially the four state banks, have developed for yeas a relatively complete service network. Therefore, they still have an advantageous position in this regard. How long this advantage can be maintained depends on whether local banks can learn from foreign banks, improve their services, and become competitive. This advantage, however, has its limitation. China's banking business concentrates in the developed, coastal regions and major cities. Foreign banks can easily open branches in those areas. They will first compete for the high profit, low cost, and less risky business, such as international clearance. Data show that foreign banks have already handled over 40% of China's trade settlements.

Foreign banks and other international financial institutions are very attractive to domestic customers, because of their quality and efficiency of services, complete range of financial products and innovations, and sound financial positions. Therefore, it is inevitable that certain business will shift from domestic banks to foreign banks. Those foreign enterprises in China are even more likely to do so because of their familiarity with foreign banks' operations. In the loan business, foreign banks depend mainly on customers' credit ranking and ability of repayment. Because of the transparency and efficiency of their business operation, good state-owned and private enterprises as well as foreign enterprises are inclined to borrow from foreign banks. Foreign financial institutions also have advantages in other business, including discount of promissory notes, insurance, and security investments.

Another competition in the financial sector will be in the saving deposit business. State banks' financial resources come mainly from domestic households and enterprises' deposits. One frequently raised concern in the domestic discussion of the WTO accession is whether or not the deposits will be relocated in a large amount to the foreign banks. Some fears this would happen because of the concentration of deposits in a small percentage of wealthy depositors. It is argued that they are likely to relocate their deposits to foreign banks because of the better services and sound financial positions of the foreign banks. The state banks' problem of high NPL ratio would be exposed if the relocation occurs. This incidence could lead to bank runs and other crisis. If handled inappropriately, it could in turn accelerate the relocation of deposits and further weaken the state banks. The survival of many SOEs depends on the continuous support of loans from the state banks. If such a scenario occurs, the four state banks will not have the means to support the SOEs. Many of those poorly-performed and inefficient SOEs would go bankrupt. In my judgement, such a doomsday prediction will not occur because of the recent change of policy from an anonymous banking to a real-name banking. The reallocation of deposits from the state banks to foreign banks will reveal those wealthy depositors' identities, an undesirable situation to them. Therefore, the competition among state banks and foreign banks for deposits is likely to be on the new stream of savings instead of those savings already in the state banks.

It is undoubted that the WTO accession will bring competitive pressure to the financial sector in China. Foreign institutions can bring in advanced management skills and business practices. If China's financial institutions can master the advanced business practices, develop new financial products, improve service quality, and cut down operational costs, Chinese financial institutions will be able to compete with their foreign counterparts. They need to do the above reforms in order to survive. Therefore, the pressure from the WTO accession will be beneficial to the development of China's financial sector, enabling the sector to provide more efficient and convenient services to customers, and benefiting China's overall economic growth.

China will relax the entry restriction on the financial sector after the WTO accession, which will not only allow foreign financial institutions to enter China's financial market, but also provide opportunities for other domestic financial institutions to develop. The latter possibility is especially important for China's long-term development. After the WTO accession, the Chinese government will not have enough means to support the nonviable big SOEs. Chinese economy will have to develop more closely along the line of China's comparative advantages, at this stage of economic development, namely, more labour-intensive industries, as argued in this book. Most enterprises in the labour-intensive industries are small and medium in size. The best institution to serve their financial needs is the local, small- and medium-sized banks.[13] In the past, the government suppressed the development of local, small- and medium-sized banks to favour the development of the four big state banks. The financial needs of the small- and medium-sized enterprises were under-served. The WTO accession will provide a better opportunity for the small- and medium-sized banks to develop, which in turn will facilitate the growth of small- and medium-sized enterprises and enhance Chinese economy's competitiveness.

10.3 WTO Accession and SOE Reform

It's evident that the enterprises are the ultimate bearers of the possible shock brought by WTO accession. The SOEs are among the least efficient enterprises in China. In Chapter 8, we argue that the success of the SOE reform is the key to China's successful transition to market economy. There exists the possibility that WTO accession will force SOEs to achieve a successful reform. The question is what are the challenges and how to achieve successful reform within the grace period before the abolishment of protections required by the WTO agreements.

13. Justin Yifu Lin, "What is the Direction of China's Financial Reform?", in Hai Wen and Lu Feng, eds., *China: Economic Transition and Economic Policy*. Beijing: Peking University Press, 2000, pp. 296–301.

1. The Viability Problem and the Challenges

The tradable sectors will be the first to be affected by the WTO accession. China's endowment structure, relatively scarce in capital and natural resource and relatively abundant in labour, will not be changed in the short run. Therefore, China has comparative advantages in labour-intensive industries and in labour-intensive segments of capital-intensive and natural-resource-intensive industries. Meanwhile, China has comparative disadvantages in industrial segments, which are too capital intensive or natural-resource intensive. This is a basic fact that we need to bear in mind when we try to analyze the impact of WTO accession on SOEs' reform.

The analyses in the previous chapters have shown that quite a few large SOEs have such a viability problem, i.e., they cannot survive without a monopoly position in the market or the government's policy support or subsidies. However, the reason that the government is willing to give SOEs protections is because many large SOEs were set up for the purpose of catching up and overtaking the industrial/technological structure of the developed economies. Therefore, the SOEs carry a "strategic burden", i.e., the burden generated from the government's development strategy.[14] To ensure the survival of the nonviable SOEs, the government adopted a planning system.

China's planning system has been reformed substantially since 1978. However, SOEs still receive preferential treatment and subsidies. In essence, it is because the SOEs are still not viable in an open, competitive market. This problem will become more apparent after China enters WTO.

2. Opportunities

The SOEs, especially those in capital-intensive industry, need protection because they violate China's comparative advantages and thus are not viable. The correct resolution for SOE reform in the

14. See Justin Yifu Lin, Cai Fang and Li Zhou, "Competition, Policy Burdens, and State-owned Enterprises Reform", *American Economic Review*, Vol. 88, No. 2 (May 1998), pp. 422–27.

future is to eliminate policy burdens from SOEs so that SOEs have to be solely responsible for their performance in a competitive market. As a result, the problem of soft budget constraint will automatically disappear. In order to meet the challenges from China's WTO accession, and because the specific policy protections for SOEs are not permitted any more, the government has to release SOEs from policy burdens and hence make SOEs viable in a competitive market. It is analyzed in detail as follows:

(1) The emerging competitive markets will provide a better guide for SOEs' development. China's WTO accession will surely help to create a more competitive market, in which factor markets will also become much more competitive. When the domestic market is opened up to the global market, a more flexible price system, which reflects the supply and demand of commodities and relative scarcities of factor endowments in the economy, will gradually come into being. In particular, prices of tradable raw materials and products in domestic market will soon get close to the international level. With the elimination of policy burdens and price distortions, the performance of SOEs will become a "sufficient information index" of its managerial performance.[15] The SOEs will be induced to choose products and production technology according to market demands and factor scarcities. After China enters the WTO, government interventions in the economy will disappear gradually. Meanwhile, a competitive market and flexible pricing system will come into being, constituting a sound basis for the economy to make sustainable growth in accordance with its comparative advantage. Needless to say for SOEs, this is also the sound basis to further their current reforms and achieve future developments.

(2) The inflow of foreign capital and technologies will improve SOEs' viability. For nonviable capital-intensive SOEs, if their products have a large domestic market, the way to make them viable

15. See Justin Yifu Lin, Cai Fang and Li Zhou, *State-owned Enterprise Reform in China*. Hong Kong: Chinese University Press, 2001. Justin Yifu Lin, Cai Fang, Li Zhou, "Competition, Policy Burdens, and State-owned Enterprises Reform", *American Economic Review*, Vol. 88, No. 2 (May 1998), pp. 422–27.

is to get access to foreign capital through joint ventures or listing in foreign capital markets. Since foreign capital has a comparatively lower cost in its home country, to use foreign capital may relieve China's constraints on the adoption of capital-intensive technology or the production of capital-intensive products due to the relative scarcity of capital in China. China's WTO membership will make foreign investors more confident in China's regulatory environment and economic growth, and attract more foreign capital inflow. This is helpful for China to resolve the SOEs' viability problem.[16]

Currently, China has attracted the largest amount of foreign capital among developing countries. Foreign capital inflow in general comes with new technology. After China enters the WTO, China will follow WTO rules. Foreign enterprises will have more confidence in making direct investments in China. It is hence supposed that foreign capital will inflow more rapidly. It will provide more opportunities for SOEs to get access to foreign capital and improve their viability.

(3) The development of labour-intensive industries provides more opportunities for SOEs' restructuring. The WTO accession will bring in not simply domestic competition pressures, but foreign export markets as well. In the markets of other WTO members, China's products will face less prohibitive tariff, or non-tariff trade barriers. All sorts of unfair treatment will be removed. For instance, there will be a better dispute-settling mechanism for trade issues, a much lower tariff and non-tariff trade barriers for China's exports. The Multiple Fiber Agreement (MFA), which restricts China's fiber-product exports to developed countries, will be phased out gradually. That is, industries in line with China's comparative advantage, including textile and garment industry and household electrical appliances industries, will be greatly promoted. A large amount of

16. There are two approaches to import foreign capital. First, foreign capital is directly injected into SOEs. As a result, the proportion of state owned equity shares would correspondingly decrease. The other is to make swaps between foreign capital and state-owned equity shares. Consequently, the state-owned shares decrease with the enterprise's total capital unchanged.

empirical researches and model simulations have shown that after China enters the WTO, China's textile industry will take a larger market share in the international market and provide more employment opportunities.

For SOEs that have limited domestic markets for their products, the only way to become viable is to change their production lines to other products, which have large markets and at the same time are consistent with China's comparative advantage. Since the future of labour-intensive industries is very promising after China enters the WTO, the WTO accession thus provides SOEs with a bright future for shifting their production lines to the labour-intensive industries. In addition, in view that costs of restructuring is unaffordable for the government, it is thus necessary for the government to make use of foreign capital. The WTO membership will also help SOEs to obtain foreign capital in their restructuring.

3. WTO Accession: The Turning Point for Accelerating China's SOE Reform

How seriously will the WTO accession affect China's economy? It depends on whether China will be able to reform its SOEs in the right direction during the grace period before China has to abide by the whole set of WTO rules. Therefore, the government has to accelerate the pace of SOE reform.

(1) Giving up the unrealistic thinking and practice of leap-forward strategy. The harmful results of traditional thinking and practice of the heavy-industry-oriented strategy have been widely recognized in China. However, soon after it becomes clear that China will enter the WTO, the traditional thinking turns to revive in new forms: going after advanced technology and increasing enterprises' scale via non-market measures. The intention to develop economy is good, the practice based on the above ideas is rather bad, however.

A more advanced technology level in some specific industry doesn't necessarily suggest anything about the whole economy's technology level. To catch up with more developed economies in terms of technology level means reaching a comparable technology level on the whole, but not in only one or two specific industries. Meanwhile, since an economy's technology level as a whole is determined by its factor endowment structure, it is of primary importance to upgrade its factor endowment structure. Herein the factor endowment structure refers to the relative scarcities between land (natural resources), labour, and capital. Since land is given, an economy's factor endowment structure primarily depends on the relative scarcity between labour and capital, in other words, capital per capita. Capital accrues in an economy from residuals generated by this economy. The more residuals are generated and saved, the quicker the economy's factor endowment structure will be upgraded. If an economy develops in accordance with its comparative advantage, the whole economy will gain its competitive edge as much as possible both in domestic and international markets, and it will increase its market share and acquire its economic residuals to the greatest possible extent. That is, its factor endowment structure can be upgraded as fast as possible. As a result, a developing economy is able to narrow its gap with developed economies as fast as possible with good use of its existing comparative advantage. When Japan and the four Asian Little Dragons carried out their industry and technology upgrading, they followed closely the dynamic change of their comparative advantages, which were determined by the upgrading of their endowment structures. Chapter 4 has shown that this is the key reason why they had transformed themselves into newly industrialized economies successfully and caught up with other developed countries after World War II. For other economies, including socialist economies, however, they usually ended up suffering from their burdensome economic problems and failed to achieve their development objectives because they had attempted to defy their comparative advantages.

To some extent it can be asserted that it is exactly from their technological gaps with developed economies that the developing economies get their commodious space to make rapid and sustainable economic growth. A case in point is the technological gaps provide a possibility for Japan and newly industrialized economies in East Asia to have a 40–50 year period of rapid economic growth by borrowing technology from the advanced countries. There is no need for less-developed economies to make enormous investments in R&D to have technological innovations. The task for less-developed economies is to import appropriate technologies, which have shown their potential business value and are consistent with their comparative advantages.[17] In the meantime, these technologies to be imported usually have lost their competitive edge in developed economies because they no longer conform to their comparative advantages. When appropriate technologies are introduced and comparative advantages are fully used at each development stage, residuals would be maximized and accumulated. China's growth potential in the following 20–30 years also lies in its technological gap with developed economies. Only when technologies in accordance with China's comparative advantages are introduced at each stage of development, will the maximum amounts of profit be obtained, resulting in quick enough upgrading of China's factor endowment structure to narrow the endowment gap between China and developed economies. With the narrowing of the gap in the factor endowment structure, the gap in terms of overall technological level and industrial level will be reduced, too.

At the same time, the size of a company is not a necessary precondition for competitiveness in the market; instead, the size should be endogenously determined by market competition. An enterprise's competitive edge depends on its cost level, not its size. Furthermore, its cost level is in essence determined by the level of consistency between the capital intensity of its technology and the factor endowment structure in the economy. A large size may be economical or not, depending on the characteristics of the related industries, technologies, and markets. The large size of multinational

17. Justin Yifu Lin, "The Outlook of China's Economy at the New Millennium", in Hai Wen, Lu Feng and Ping Xinqiao, eds., *Economic Research on China*. Beijing: Peking University Press, 1999; Justin Yifu Lin, "Development Strategy, Viability, and Economic Convergence" (Inaugural D. Gale Johnson Lecture, Department of Economics, the University of Chicago, 14 May 2001).

companies is usually an associated result of horizontal integration, vertical integration, and operational diversification. Horizontal integration is aimed at achieving an optimal economic scale for one product. Vertical integration is for the sake of overcoming possible transaction uncertainties between upstream and downstream enterprises. Operational diversification is used by highly capital abundant and large-scale enterprises to create a product portfolio thereby reducing the risk of producing only a single product. In China, most enterprises will be located at labour-intensive industrial segments for quite a long time in the future. For labour-intensive industrial segments, since the optimal scale of an enterprise tends to be relatively small, horizontal integration is not very meaningful in most cases. And, in view of the loose connection between upstream and downstream enterprises, there seems also no apparent necessity for related enterprises to make large-scale investment for the purpose of vertical integration. Finally, the comparatively easiness for enterprises to make product adjustments makes it unnecessary to have product diversification. Conclusively, it is unreasonable to radically enlarge enterprises' scale in China.

Market principles must be respected in the development of advanced technologies and the enlargement of enterprises' scale. That is, it is the enterprises themselves that make the related decisions, after they have considered their operational needs and price signals in the market. Meanwhile, any government attempt to "hasten the growth of the shoots by pulling them upward" will only spoil things. The contrast between South Korea and Taiwan is a good case in point. Before the 1970s, the comparative advantages of both economies lied in labour-intensive industries. In the 1970s and thereafter, the two economies adopted different development strategies. South Korean government decided to take preferential measures to zealously support capital-intensive large-scale conglomerates. In the meantime, it is the relatively labour-intensive industries that were developed in Taiwan. Since Korea's enterprises heavily disregard their comparative advantages, their competitive edges were undermined by their burdensome capital-intensities, resulting in a lower profitability and higher leverage ratio (liability relative to asset). When the Asian financial crisis occurred in 1997, large Korean conglomerates were heavily damaged. On the contrary, in spite of their much smaller scales and relatively higher labour-intensity, enterprises in Taiwan demonstrated a strong competitive edge and better profitability. Not surprisingly, Taiwan's enterprises weathered the crisis in a much better shape.[18]

Take China's auto industry as another example. It is definite that some enterprises will have to close down after China enters the WTO. Does this mean that these enterprises should go all out making new investments for technologies currently applied in developed countries? Or making mergers and acquisitions so as to form giant enterprise groups? Or is there some other way out? A hint may be found considering the contrast between Korea and Taiwan. Korean-made cars have managed to wedge into the U.S. market at the cost of colossal explicit and implicit subsidies from its government. In other words, the Korean government is using its domestic taxpayers' money to subsidize the car consumption in U.S. For Taiwan's auto industry, however, it mainly produces auto parts and obtains considerable profits. Therefore, a large part of China's auto enterprises should produce auto parts for domestic and foreign automakers instead of complete cars.

(2) Promote interest-rate liberalization and reform existing financial system. In spite of the remarkable development of the market system, China's capital market, especially its indirect financing institutions, have still failed to make substantial progress. Credit extension and interest rates have not been liberalized. The underlying reason, as analyzed before, is to protect SOEs. However, here is a self-enforcing vicious feedback: the lower the SOEs' competitiveness and viability, the more protections they will need; furthermore, the more protections they get, the less incentives they will have to improve their competitiveness and viability. Since China is capital scarce, the implications of interest rate liberalization in

18. See Justin Yifu Lin, "What is the Direction of China's Financial Reform?" in Hai Wen and Lu Feng, eds., *China Economic Transition and Economic Policy*. Beijing: Peking University Press, 2000, pp. 296–301.

China is self-evident: it will not only affect the survival of the state-owned financial sector, but will also affect the long-run economic growth and the success of the comparative-advantage-following strategy. Therefore, interest rate liberalization is a must. As for SOEs' viability problem, it has to be resolved with other measures.

Specific industrial structure requires a corresponding financial system.[19] In developed economies, the dominated enterprises are capital-intensive and technology-advanced large-scale ones. Correspondingly, there are highly developed financial systems composed of stock market, corporate-bond market and big commercial banks. In China, however, the dominated enterprises are labour-intensive small and medium ones, which correspondingly requires a financial system mainly composed of small and medium commercial banks. In view of China's current financial system dominated by the four big state-owned commercial banks, it is not suitable for the development of labour-intensive industries. For small and medium enterprises, on the one hand, the cost to get listed in stock market is prohibitively high; on the other hand, big commercial banks have an inherent discrimination against small and medium enterprises. In spite of the establishment of related credit departments for small and medium enterprises at the four big state-owned banks, it is still difficult for small and medium enterprises to get loans from these banks. After China enters the WTO, the government should reduce its intervention in the domestic banking industry and encourage the development of small and medium commercial banks for the sake of the development of labour-intensive small and medium enterprises, which are consistent with China's comparative advantages.

(3) Adjust the industrial and regional distribution of SOEs in accordance with comparative advantages. The key for SOEs' to improve their viability is to adjust their production according to market signals and China's comparative advantages. For the

19. See Justin Yifu Lin, "What is the Direction of China's Financial Reform?", in Hai Wen and Lu Feng, eds., *China: Economic Transition and Economic Policy*. Beijing: Peking University Press, 2000, pp. 296–301.

government, the tasks in the first place are to offload SOEs' policy burdens and to put the pricing system in order. Accordingly, preconditions will be created for SOEs to adjust their industrial and regional allocations so as to improve their viability and competitive edge.

For the few enterprises essential to national defense, their high-level capital-intensity is necessary for production and it is impossible for them to become joint ventures or to list in foreign capital markets. The policy burden derived from their high-level capital-intensity needs continuously to be fiscally subsidized. Except for these few enterprises, other SOEs can be divided into three categories and be reformed separately: (1) Changing production lines. For SOEs without a large domestic market for their products, they ought to change into industries, which have large domestic market demand and at the same time are consistent with China's comparative advantages. (2) Regional restructuring. Regionally, coastal provinces are more developed and more capital abundant than hinterland provinces. Therefore, in China, a sound regional industrial structure in accordance with comparative advantage is that: the capital-intensity of enterprises in coastal regions should be higher than that of enterprises in hinterland regions. Specifically, after China enters the WTO, coastal regions should continue to absorb new applicable foreign technologies. In the meantime, because of economic development, the upgrading of factor endowment and the increase of labour cost, some enterprises of labour-intensive industries, including textile industry and other light industries, become nonviable in coastal regions and need to be relocated to hinterland regions for the sake of being viable again. With further economic development and capital accumulation, factor endowment structures in both coastal regions and hinterland regions will be further upgraded. In this process, coastal regions will introduce new higher-level technology-based industries while transferring industries, which have become comparative disadvantages due to the upgrading of factor endowment structure, to hinterland regions. This layered industrial distribution is the basic way for China to develop its economy in inland areas as proposed by the Central Committee of the

Chinese Communist Party. That is to say, for labour-intensive industries that have lost comparative advantages in coastal regions, they should be transferred to hinterland regions in order to make use of their sufficient labour supply and comparatively lower labour costs. (3) Using foreign capital. For industries and enterprises, which have promising domestic market demands but are not viable due to its over capital intensity, one solution is to form joint ventures with foreign enterprises or to list in foreign capital markets. Consequently, their viability could be improved.

(4) An appropriate policy that guides the inflow of foreign investment. Capital is currently the scarcest production factor in China. In the past 20 years, a large amount of foreign capital inflow has greatly expedited China's economic growth. After China enters the WTO, foreign capital inflow is anticipated to increase further. However, it should be recognized in the wake of the 1997 Asian financial crisis that proper regulation is more than necessary. The key issue is still how to regulate the inflow of foreign capital and its structure according to the principle of comparative advantage.

First of all, the inflow of foreign capital should mainly be long-term FDI. Industries that are apt to produce exceptional bubbles during economic growth include real estate and security markets, which are characterized by their comparatively inelastic supply and strong appeal for hot money. With the magnifying effect of the large amount of short-term hot money flowing into (or out of) these sectors, the economy tends to be excessively prosperous (or depressive) during the corresponding economic boom (or bust) stages. Therefore, proper regulations should be imposed on short-term foreign capital inflows into enterprises, including SOEs, in domestic real estate and security markets. Instead, long-term FDI usually introduce not only capital, but also technology, management and market as well. Long-term FDI has significant effects on the economy. At the same time, it is not so easy to incur abrupt reversion of capital inflow and outflow. As a result, FDI should be the main form of foreign capital inflow.

Secondly, foreign capital should be channelled to fill the gap between the capital intensity in SOEs and China's factor endowment structure. Currently, some government departments and local governments are craving for enterprises with extraordinary large-scale and advanced technology. Korea's experiences have given us a good lesson in this aspect. This kind of concept and practice is very harmful and should be corrected as soon as possible. That is, on the one hand, part of the foreign capital should be channelled to some SOEs, helping the SOEs to rearrange their industrial and regional distribution according to their comparative advantage. On the other hand, foreign capital should also be channelled to local industries in accordance with local comparative advantage, paving the way for a sustainable economic growth of the local economy.

To conclude, the problem of SOEs, especially the large-sized SOEs, is rooted in their choices of technology and industry, which deviate from China's comparative advantage and make them not viable in an open, competitive market. Therefore, to compensate for the "strategic burdens" arising from this inappropriate selection of industry and technology, the government created a whole set of price distortions and relied on administrative measures to subsidize and protect the SOEs. The ultimate solution for the SOEs, however, is to adjust their technologies and industries according to China's comparative advantage so that they can be viable in a competitive market. The WTO accession will deprive the Chinese government of the means to further subsidize and protect its SOEs. Therefore, the WTO accession will prompt the Chinese government to adopt reform measures along the lines suggested in this book so as to make the SOEs viable. In effect, the 10th Five-year Plan adopted by the Chinese government in March 2001 has embraced all the reform measures suggested in this chapter.[20] It can be expected that, with the suggested reforms, many SOEs will become viable, making it possible for China to complete other necessary reforms and realize its transition from a planned economy to a market economy.

---

20. Justin Yifu Lin and Liu Peilin, "The 10th Five-year Plan and the SOE Reform", *CCER Newsletter*, No. 38 (August 2001).

CHAPTER 11

The Characteristics and General Implications of China's Reform

It has been more than 20 years since China first introduced its economic reform, beginning with the household responsibility system in rural areas. In view of the economic growth and social stability during the reform process, China's economic reform has been a success. It is true that, as discussed in Chapter 7, the reform has suffered repeated vigour/chaos cycles and many other problems, which are the result of inadequate reform in development strategy and macro-policy environment. The reform process has thus been impeded and the public confidence in reform impaired. However, since the reform of the traditional economic system has been an incremental reform, conflicts of interest between different segments of society did not intensify while the traditional patterns of interests were adjusted. The reform could thus follow a gradual approach. Therefore, an economic analysis on the unique path of China's reform can help the country to carry on with the gradual reform and consciously adjust the development strategy and accelerate the reform accordingly.

China's reform can be used as a point of reference for other economies. Economists were once keen on a "quick, direct and radical economic reform plan" as a way to move most effectively from a centralized planning system to a market economy.[1] Such an approach is often termed "radical reform", "big bang", "one package plan", or "shock therapy". Each of these reform types is different.

1. David Lipton and Jeffrey Sachs, "Creating a Market Economy in Eastern Europe: The Case of Poland", *Brookings Papers on Economic Activities*, No. 2 (1990), pp. 293–341.

The most typical and popular type is that recommended in recent years by Western economists to Eastern European countries and the Commonwealth of Independent States (CIS). Marketization, privatization, and liberalization are the essential aspects of such a plan. These economists suggest that since God created the world in seven days, the economic reform should be conducted just as swiftly.[2] Such policy recommendations were once very popular and considered as perfect in theory and feasible in practice. But all of these suggestions are merely theoretical products and their feasibility should be subject to practical tests. In reality, they have all generated poor outcomes. China's experience in the last two decades will not only serve as a reference for other economies in transition, but also contribute to the theory of institutional change.

11.1 The Starter and Propellers of Reform

Before 1978, China had tried to get out of the economic inefficiency caused by distortions in industrial structure and the ineffective incentive mechanism. Usually it was done through adjustments to the existing policies. For instance, after Mao Zedong's *On Ten Major Relationships* was published in 1956, the government established an industrial structure that prioritized agriculture, light industries and heavy industries, in that order. The decentralization of economic administration to lower levels also led to attempts to improve incentives for enterprises and local government, although only within the framework of the traditional economic system. China's economic reform initiated from the Third Plenary Session of the 11th Conference of the Chinese Communist Party in 1978 did not have a clear goal initially. It was only intended to adjust traditional economic structures and improve the incentive mechanism. However, because of the distorted price system resulting from the macro-policy

2. Some other Western scholars recommend alternative strategies, which can be called the "step-by-step" plan and "evolutionary". See A. Walters, "Misapprehensions on Privatisation", *International Economic Insights,* Vol. 2, No. 1 (1991); J. Komai, *The Road to a Free Economy*. New York: Norton, 1990.

environment, the industrial structure in line with traditional strategic objectives still had a high degree of inertia. The reform at that time could not even touch upon the macro-policy environment. What did come through was the reform in micro-management system.

For this reason, the reform of the micro-management system is considered as the starter of China's economic reform. Once the government control on the micro-management institution was relaxed, industries previously suppressed under the traditional development strategy began to develop and to incrementally adjust the distorted industrial structure. The growth of the economy outside the traditional economic system in return imposed further challenges on the traditional economic system. As a result, a new resource allocation system and a new price system took shape outside the traditional economic system. Some of these previously suppressed sectors enjoyed high economic growth and provided the economy with a positive feed back that strengthened the momentum for reform. We call these sectors as the propeller for economic reform. Once reform took place in these sectors, it will naturally spill over to other sectors and gradually lead to further economic reforms.

The reform of the traditional economic system began in SOEs and in rural areas. In 1979, pilot reforms were carried out in some SOEs. The reform was intended to increase enterprise' decision-making power. Because of the adoption of a profit-retention scheme and other measures, enterprises had a higher incentive to increase their production and sales . Since SOEs at the time could to a certain degree decide their internal welfare and rewarding arrangements, they have the means to reward and penalize workers according to their work performance. This improved SOEs' incentive mechanism to some extent. Accordingly, incremental resources were created.[3]

At the same time, the reform of the micro-management system made a break-through in rural areas. The household responsibility system, chosen spontaneously by farmers themselves, was at first

3. Incremental resource is a term used in contrast to the original stock of resources. It refers to the newly created economic resources through reform.

"The 4 Modernizations"

adopted only in poor and remote areas. This system effectively solved the supervision problem in agricultural production, and linked farmers' incomes directly to their performance. As a result, it dramatically improved their working incentive and increased production significantly. This reform generated high returns at low costs for both the government and farmers. More flexible policies were subsequently introduced to promote its adoption. In just a few years, the household responsibility system became prevalent in rural areas, and finally led to the collapse of the People's Commune system.

The direct outcome of this agricultural reform was a dramatic increase in farm production.[4] From 1978 to 1984, the national output of grain increased by 33.65%, that of cotton increased by 188.80%, and oil crops 128.24%. The total agricultural output value increased by 127.66%, as calculated by current prices. A more important effect is that this economic growth has stimulated further reform in various ways.

Firstly, agricultural growth ameliorated the distortion of industrial structure.[5] If the output is weighted by current prices, in the gross value of industrial and agricultural output in 1978, agriculture, light industry and heavy industry made up 27.8%, 31.1%, and 41.1%, respectively. This structure illustrates that the proportion of heavy industry at the time was too high, while that of the light industry (which was consistent with China's comparative advantages) was too low. Compared with industrial sectors, the development of

4. According to estimates by Justin Yifu Lin, of the increase in total output value of the planting industry in the period 1978–84, 46.89% came from productivity increases that resulted from the household contract responsibility system, and 32.2% resulted from the increased use of chemical fertilizer. See Justin Yifu Lin, "Rural Reforms and Agricultural Growth in China", *American Economic Review,* Vol. 82, No. 1 (March 1992), pp. 34–51.
5. There are four conditions, Peter Harrold believes, that help agriculture become the first sector to carry out reform: (1) infrastructure and technological conditions, (2) the management system, (3) the social service system, and (4) diversification of agricultural economy. See Peter Harrold, "China's Reform Experience to Date", The World Bank Discussion Paper, 1992, p. 180. We believe, however, that the fundamental condition is the suppressed and controlled status of agriculture in the traditional industrial pattern.

agricultural sector was suppressed. By 1984, these three sectors made up 35.0%, 30.8%, and 34.2% of the gross value, respectively. The growth in agricultural output increased its proportion in the gross output value. Such a growth also provided the light industry with more raw materials and a larger market and thus promoted the development of non-state sectors, which correspondingly led to a relative decrease in the proportion of heavy industry.

Secondly, the inappropriate internal structure in agriculture was rectified. In agriculture, non-grain crops, forestry, animal husbandry, sideline occupations and fishery, which had been strictly controlled in the past, began to enjoy faster growth. From 1978 to 1984, in the gross agricultural output value, the proportion of cropping decreased from 67.8% to 58.1%, and in the gross output value of cropping, the output value of grains decreased from 76.7% to 66.2%. As comparative advantages in agriculture was better exploited to some extent, the rural market began to develop, and a market for production factors gradually emerged.

Finally, the increase in agricultural surplus and in the rural people's disposable income led to the rapid development of TVEs. From 1980 to 1984, on average, rural people's per capita net income in real terms increased by 14.5% annually. When price factors are deducted, productive net income per capita increased from RMB 166.39 to RMB 291.10, while per capita cash-in-hand plus the outstanding amount of savings deposit in rural areas (year-end) increased from RMB 26.55 to RMB 85.3. At the same time, this increase in agricultural productivity led to a surplus in rural labour. These two factors together laid the foundation for the development of TVEs. And thereafter, the rural industrial sector became another propeller for further economic reform.

In the early 1970s, in order to raise fund for agricultural mechanization, the development of TVEs was encouraged. They did develop to some extent, but only to a limited scale. By 1978, their gross output value accounted for just 7.2% of China's total output value. Since the 1980s, as the agricultural sector developed rapidly, it created not only a surplus of labour but a surplus of fund as well which greatly expanded the source of funds for TVEs. Meanwhile, in the 1980s, as the expansion of dual track system proceeded into China's resource allocation and price system, which was originally intended to improve the efficiency of resource allocation in SOEs, it also provided TVEs with opportunities to participate in the resource allocation process.[6]

The role of TVEs as a propeller of reform manifests itself in the following three ways. Firstly, TVEs was an outcome of marketization process, and in return it greatly pushed forward the economic reform toward a market economy. The energy and raw materials used by TVEs came from the competitive market, which was not included in the government plan. The marketing and sales of their products depended on their competitiveness and their sales promotion. They had hard budget constraints. TVE workers did not enjoy the guarantee of lifelong employment, known in China as the "iron rice bowl". Mismanaged TVEs were eliminated through competition. This style of operation put a great deal of pressure on the state sector, forcing the latter to adopt additional market-oriented reforms. Secondly, the development of TVEs had, to a great extent, corrected the distorted industrial structure. As they obtained most of their resources at market prices, to be competitive they had to choose a product mix closer to China's comparative advantages. In this way, it allocated much of the incremental resources into previously suppressed industries, and thus partially corrected the traditional development strategy. Thirdly, TVEs' rapid development promoted the expansion of market track in the dual-track system in areas of both resource allocation and price formation. This development also

6. A survey conducted in China by the World Bank in early 1984 found that "Trading prices of many less important materials as well as some important materials have begun to be decided on market." See The World Bank, *China: Issues for Long Term Development and Plans*. Beijing: China Finance and Economics Press, 1985, p. 233. Another survey conducted during the same period shows that 72.1% of the supply of raw materials to TVEs were purchased on market at high prices. See China Academy of Social Sciences, Institute of Economy, *The Economic Development and Economic System for China's Town and Village Enterprises*. Beijing: China Economy Press, 1987, pp. 141–45.

imposed more and more pressure on the traditional resource-allocation system and the macro policy environment. This made it possible to successfully implement these two reforms at low risk and cost.

The emergence of non-state sectors (represented by TVEs) inevitably imposed competition pressures on the state sector. The dual-track price system, in particular, subjected SOEs' production and input procurement decisions to the influence of marginal prices. SOEs began to face competition from TVEs for energy, raw materials and market. Following the unleashing of all-round urban reforms in 1984, a number of reform measures were tried in SOEs. These included converting profit delivery into tax payment and appropriation into loans, the introduction of the contract responsibility system, and the introduction of the joint stock system. All these reform measures were, in fact, the result of competitive pressure mentioned above. Although the competition mechanism of SOEs at the time was far from being completely on the market track, those reform measures already in place helped improve the operational efficiency of SOEs. Studies by Jefferson, Rawski, and Zheng in 1980–88 and 1992, showed that the annual growth rate of the total factor productivity of the state-owned industry sector averaged 2.4% from 1980 to 1988, with an accelerating trend, particularly after 1984.[7]

The initial motive for the reform in foreign trade system was to stimulate exports and assist the introduction of advanced technology and equipment. Thereafter, the reform was carried out to narrow the range of the mandatory foreign trade plan, expand local decision-making powers for foreign trade, and increase the share of foreign exchange retained by enterprises. These measures granted foreign trade opportunities to local government and companies, and improved enterprises' incentives to participate in foreign trade. As

7. G. Jefferson, T. Rawski, and Yuying *Zheng*, "Growth, Efficiency and Convergence in China's State and Collective Industry", *Economic Development and Cultural Change*, Vol. 40, No. 2 (January 1992), pp. 239–66.

the reform in this area proceeded and the foreign trade grew larger and larger, their role as a driving force for further economic reform became more and more evident: (1) Because a large proportion of export products were labour-intensive products produced by TVEs, the growth of foreign trade helped the growth of depressed sectors and partially ameliorated the distorted industrial structure. (2) After the adoption of the opening-up policy, price information on the international market became available, which imposed more imminent competition pressures on domestic producers. (3) The expansion of foreign trade and the introduction of foreign investment made it necessary to adjust the exchange rate and to establish a foreign exchange adjustment market. Hence, breakthroughs in the macro-policy environment were first made in the area of exchange rate.

An analysis of the reform and growth in SOEs, agriculture, and foreign trade illustrates that China began its reform from the micro-management institution, with the aim of improving the incentive mechanism. Then as several important sectors grew rapidly under the newly-formed market mechanism and in light of their demand for further reform in other areas, the economic reforms were extended to the resource-allocation system and the macroeconomic policy environment. Therefore, we regard the reform of micro-economic management mechanism as the starter of China's reform, and regard such rapidly growing sectors like agriculture, rural industry, and foreign trade as the propellers.

11.2 The Approach and Characteristics of Economic Reform

Recent literature has raised some counter-arguments to the big bang reform approach. Firstly, one of the main causes of inefficiency in a planned economy is the planners' inability to obtain the necessary information. In a market economy, however, all the information necessary for making production decisions is reflected in prices. In the transition from a planned to a market economy, the designers and executors conducting the reform according to a pre-determined timetable will face the same problem of insufficient information as planners do in a planned economy.[8]

Secondly, market is not just a pair of abstract supply and demand curves; it is an institution.[9] It is governed by a set of rules and common practices. In an economy undergoing reform, it is necessary not only to design these rules and norms but also to cultivate and develop them. The big bang type of reform may abolish old rules and practices, but it cannot immediately establish new ones.

Thirdly, reform must be paid for in terms of the costs of execution and friction. Such a cost increases as reform becomes more radical. The more radical the reform, the more violent will be the destructive social conflicts and opposition to reform.[10] If these problems are not properly addressed, it may put an end to the whole reform process. An incremental reform approach is therefore more effective. China's reform experience since the end of the 1970s is a convincing empirical counter-evidence to big bang arguments. So far, China's reform has followed a gradual approach or an evolutionary one. It has the following four characteristics.

1. A Bigger Pie

From the outset, China's economic reform has been accompanied by economic growth. Each step in the reform process was aimed at improving the incentive mechanism so as to enlarge the national economy, whether it involved the decentralization and profit

---

8. J. McMillan, and B. Naughton, "How to Reform a Planned Economy: Lessons from China", *Oxford Review of Economic Policy*, Vol. 8, No. 1 (1992), pp. 130–43.
9. Fan Gang, "Two Kinds of Reform Cost and Two Approaches of Reform", *Economic Research*, No. 1 (1993).
10. A "Pareto improvement" refers to a change that will benefit at least one person without hurting anyone else. A "Kaldor improvement" refers to a change in which the total gains outweigh the total losses so that it is possible for beneficiaries to compensate non-beneficiaries for the losses they suffer. As a result, no one suffers in the end. See N. Kaldor, "Welfare Propositions of Economics and Interpersonal Comparisons of Utility", *Economic Journal,* Vol. 49 (September 1939), pp. 549–51.

retention of state sectors, or the introduction of the household responsibility system, whether it be the opening up to the outside world, or the foreign exchange retention arrangement for relevant enterprises. Indeed, reform measures that have been implemented to date have already created a "bigger pie".

The traditional economic system created two basic dilemmas that stood in the way of China's economic growth. Firstly, the distorted economic structure led to disproportionate industrial structure, an increasing segregation in the urban-rural dual economy, a low level of urbanization, and slow improvement in people's living standards. The other was low economic efficiency caused by inadequate incentives, which kept the production within the PPF (production probability frontier) and inhibited the growth speed. Through delegation of autonomy and profit retention, the economic reform since the end of the 1970s tightened the connection between remuneration and efficiency. It motivated the initiatives of peasants, workers and enterprises, improved their working performance and increased production efficiency. In this way, it raised the production level closer to the PPF. After they have obtained autonomy in management decisions, micro units simultaneously acquired the right to allocate their newly-created resources, which made for more efficient use of the resources and resulted in an even bigger pie.

Firstly, when sectors traditionally under government protection achieved some economic growth and thus acquired some newly-created disposable resources, in order to get more profit, they usually tended to invest the newly-created resources into those traditionally suppressed sectors. For instance, some state-owned heavy-industry enterprises allocated new disposable resources to light industrial sectors or to the tertiary sector to provide jobs for the children of its working staff or in forms of cooperation with TVEs. Secondly, when traditionally suppressed sectors developed, they usually allocated newly-created disposable resources to their own or other related suppressed sectors. For instance, rural workers used newly acquired resources to develop forestry, animal husbandry, sidelines, fishery, and TVEs.

Since the pie had been made larger than before, it became

possible to implement the incremental reform (which is another characteristic of China's reform and will be discussed later). It was also instrumental in reducing resistance to reforms. In theory, there are two ways of pushing the reform forward. One is to change the transaction environment to improve efficiency without altering the pattern of vested interests in the process of institutional reforms. This can be called a Pareto improvement or a Kaldor improvement.[11] The other is to institute a new system by adjusting the vested interest pattern. This process hurts some interest groups and is known as a non-Pareto improvement. The first one causes only small frictions among interest groups and enjoys a low implementation cost. But as we know the pattern of vested interest groups is a product of the traditional macro-policy environment. If the reform could not change this pattern, it would be difficult for the new resource-allocation system to take shape. Because of this, the non-Pareto improvement type of reform is inevitable in the end. The interest groups who have anticipated a loss will of course take measures to resist the reform, which induces greater frictions and reform cost. However, a reform that continuously increases the size of the pie can also continuously increase the amount of available resources in the national economy, thus making it possible to increase the amount of resources to be allocated to all interest groups. Consequently, the reform would come as close as possible to a Pareto improvement or a Kaldor improvement, while minimizing costs and risks.

2. Incremental Reform

China's economic reform has not proceeded according to an ideal model or a fixed timetable. It is also impossible for a new and effective resource-allocation system and an incentive mechanism to function all at once in every economic field. Instead, they can only take effect first in the sectors that took the initial steps of reform and

---

11. In the reform of micro management system, it was the incremental element that brought timely gains to reform. In places where the stock of assets was radically reallocated, a certain degree of disorder resulted.

in the new ones that formed in the reform process. They can only affect the newly created resources. For instance, in the contract responsibility system, after SOEs had paid profits to the state in line with the fixed amount specified in their contracts, they can retain a certain proportion of the profit. In the dual-track system, these resources were allocated according to market signals. The TVE is one typical example of the sectors that formed in the reform process. They grew up outside the traditional economic system. Their operations were guided by market forces, and their growth helped to reduce the distortion of industrial structure. Such a reform approach, which began not with the reallocation of the existing stock of resources but by allowing the market to play its role in the allocation of the incremental resources, is known as "incremental reform". This is an important feature of China's economic reform.

First of all, incremental reform can avoid the adjustment cost of reform, while it corrects the inappropriate industrial structure. Because it can reduce reform cost and have immediate gains, it can secure maximum support and maintain consistency in its policies. In this sense, the most advantageous path for economic reform to follow is one that can ensure sustained growth rather than a "J-curve" pattern in which growth slows down before it speeds up.

As is shown in Figure 11.1, production is initially conducted at point B in the interior of the production probability set. In a reform that follows the "shock therapy" (as in Figure 11.1), it tries to adjust the industrial structure directly through reallocating the existing stock of assets.While production capacity shifts from priority sectors to suppressed sectors, part of the equipment and resources will remain idle for a period of time, and the working staff also need time to learn the necessary skills for their new jobs. Therefore, in this transition period, economic growth is impeded and cannot generate in-time profits. GNP will inevitably decrease at first.In Figure 11.1 (a), this means instead of moving directly from point B to point E, the economy moves from point B to point F before reaching point E. The resulting GNP growth path follows a J-curve pattern, as shown in Figure 11.1(b). However, if the reform follows the incremental approach (Figure 11.2), the reform of the micro-management system

Figure 11.1 The effect of shock therapy

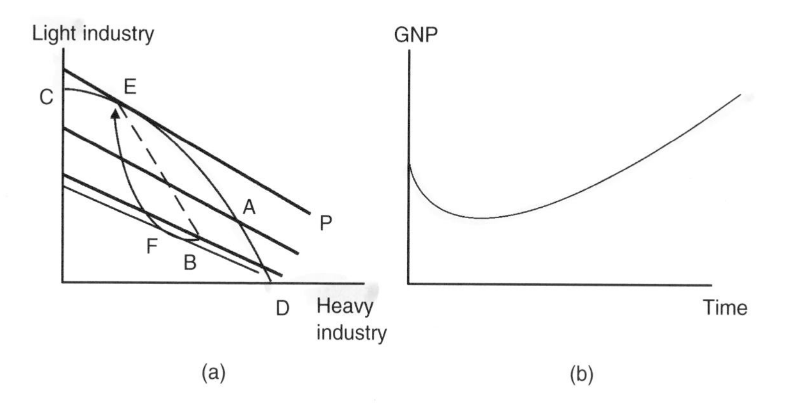

improves the incentive mechanism and the economy becomes more efficient. This means in Figure 11.2(a) the economy moves from point B to A, a point which is closer to the production probability frontier. Newly-created resources are then allocated to suppressed sectors. This not only corrects the distorted production structure in the margins but also accelerates output growth and generates immediate returns. The economy may then move gradually from point A to G. The resulting GNP growth will follow the path in Figure 11.2(b). The more the newly-created resources are invested in the suppressed sectors, the faster the growth will be. Therefore, throughout the reform process, it is possible for the economy to experience continuous growth, as in the figure. In reality, under the traditional development strategy, heavy industry was given priority. At the same time, agriculture, light industry, and tertiary industry were suppressed. When reform began, they became the leading sectors and developed rapidly. Their development provided the society with immediate proceeds and helped to sustain further reform.[12]

12. J. McMillan and B. Naughton, "How to Reform a Planned Economy: Lessons from China", *Oxford Review of Economic Policy*, Vol. 8, No. 1 (1992), pp. 130–43.

Figure 11.2 The effect of incremental reform

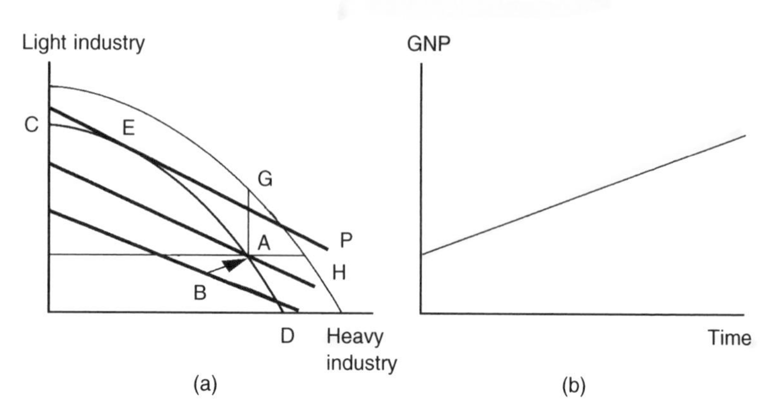

Secondly, incremental reform is conducive to maintaining the balance between stability and speed during the reform process. During the process, the economy formed a dual structure. In other words, the national economy could be divided into two sectors: one was formed by the newly-created resources, in which the market mechanism played an important role, the other was formed under the traditional development strategy, which was governed, to a large extent, by plans and administrative orders. The second sector played a stabilizing role in the actual process of reform. For example, SOEs had absorbed large numbers of workers from cities and towns and were responsible for the distribution of social welfare funds. Although there were losses in efficiency, the existence of SOEs helped prevent massive unemployment and social conflicts. When vicious inflation occurs, stabilization policy measures could have immediate effects in this part of the national economy, which helped to maintain social stability. As for the first sector, because their industrial and technical structures were more consistent with China's comparative advantages and because their managerial system was more flexible, they could maintain growth when the government imposes non-reform retrenchment programmes, thus helping to meet society's demand for an acceptable growth rate.

However, incremental reform also has its costs. Because of the conflicts between the two sectors of the economy and the alternation in the sector that the government endorses, for every two steps forward, the reform takes one step back. In terms of economic efficiency in general, it is not the best reform approach. It is a second-best option suited to China's particular situation,[13] but it has greatly reduced serious conflicts and retrogression. In addition, incremental reform is pre-conditioned by the existence of the dual-track system of resource allocation and prices, which induces economic agents to gain by rent-seeking instead of by relying entirely on market competition. The greater the opportunities for rent-seeking, the less likely it is that a competitive market will form and that market behaviour will be established.

3. Experiments and Popularization

Most of China's economic reform measures have not been applied simultaneously throughout the country. Each measure was first tried as an experiment in selected areas. In general, a reform is not introduced to the rest of the nation until the experiment has proven successful. Thus, China's reform has been local in nature. This is true of both spontaneous reforms, such as the introduction of the household responsibility system, and of reform measures imposed by the government, such as experiments in the enterprise contract system and the creation of SEZs.

The main advantages of this method of reform are as follows: (1) It can minimize risks. Before any reform measure is taken there is always the problem of inadequate information and uncertainty regarding possible obstacles and results. Since the success of the overall economic reform hinges on whether or not the reforms can benefit society, it is necessary to make every effort to avoid errors and excessively high costs. Localizing reform measures through experiments may minimize the cost of failure. (2) The combination

13. K. Chen, G. Jefferson, and I. J. Singh, "Lessons from China's Economic Reform", *Journal of Comparative Economics*, Vol. 16, No. 2 (June 1992), pp. 201–25.

of experimental spontaneous reform and incremental reform can provide timely signals about how and where further reform can maximize gains.[14] Most of the reforms that have already been introduced were initially aimed at solving specific problems. It is just this approach that has led the reform toward the right direction and created a kind of self-reinforcing mechanism. (3) It allows the market to be established and fostered gradually. The development of the market depends on the establishment of a set of rules and norms and on the existence of hardware infrastructure. All these will take time. Beginning with local reforms has thus made it possible to create gradually the market environment that the economy requires.

But this reform approach has its drawbacks as well. Firstly, the functions of the market mechanism are open. They cannot be fully employed by reforms that are confined to certain sectors or areas. Reformed and unreformed sectors or regions must be artificially separated through administrative means. When such an artificial separation fails, friction arises. For example, when Guangdong Province liberalized its control over the prices of agricultural products, it triggered price rises in the neighbouring provinces. Since its neighbours could not follow suit, this led to frictions in the inter-provincial trade between Guangdong and its neighbouring provinces. Secondly, the non-uniform progress of reform among different sectors and regions resulted in a series of problems, including disparity in development and inequality in income distribution, thus threatens social stability. Thirdly, inconsistency among piecemeal elements of the reform has often delayed the introduction of necessary measures, resulting in an incomplete coordination mechanism. For instance, since the traditional taxation system was built on the profits of the state-owned sectors and the price distortion in the macro-policy environment, the state suffered from the loss of tax sources when the mono-state ownership was broken by reforms and price distortion was alleviated. The relatively slow progress of

14. K. Chen, G. Jefferson, and I. J. Singh, "Lessons from China's Economic Reform", *Journal of Comparative Economics*, Vol. 16, No. 2 (June 1992), pp. 201–25.

taxation reform then led to fiscal problems. Fourthly, based on the logic of the formation of the traditional economic system, the price-distorting macro-policy environment was vital to the existence of the planned resource-allocation mechanism. Reform of the macro-policy environment, however, would have required a certain degree of unity. Because of this localized approach, the reform of the macro-policy environment lagged behind, and China's economy fell victim to the vigour/chaos cycle. The sectors propelling reforms were not able to produce and trade entirely based on the rules of the market economy.

4. Non-radical Reform

China's economic reform was carried out under the leadership of the Chinese Communist Party and under the premise of preserving the basic socialist system. This means that the objectives and measures of reforms had to be non-radical. As is pointed out in the preceding chapters, the inappropriate structure and the low efficiency of China's traditional economic system were caused by the leap-forward strategy and its corresponding arrangements like: macro-policy environment, the planned resource-allocation system, and the absence of autonomy in the micro-management institution. In other words, specific political system may not necessary constitutes an obstacle for reform.[15] World development shows that countries that have adopted the leap-forward strategy, irrespective of the nature of their social systems, have all established similar economic systems that have caused similar structural and efficiency problems. It also shows that countries, whether capitalist or socialist, will experience successful economic development if they make full use of their comparative advantages. The key to implementing the comparative-advantage strategy is the establishment of a price system that reflects

15. Susan L. Shirk, *The Political Logic of Economic Reform in China*. Berkeley: University of California Press, 1933, p. 6; Peter Nolan, *China's Rise, Russia's Fall: Politics, Economics and Planning in the Transition From Stalinism*. New York: St. Martin's Press, 1995, pp. 69–70.

the relative scarcities of production factors. This can be achieved only through competition in the factor markets. The central problem of China's economic reform is thus to establish a market economy and to change the country's economic development strategy.[16]

Non-radical reform has the following advantages. First of all, in the process of institutional innovation, it can make a full use of existing organizational resources, maintain the relative stability and ensure a smooth transition in the institutions. "Institution" in this context refers to both the institutional arrangements and the institutional structure, which consist of all institutional arrangements in the economy. The effectiveness of any institutional arrangement is determined not only by the arrangement itself but also by many other arrangements within the institutional structure. Any isolated radical reform will render the new institutional arrangements incompatible with the old institutional structure and will lack the support of other required arrangements. Because of this, new institutional arrangements often fail to perform their intended roles. Therefore, the basic requirement of incremental reform is that the process be controllable. As for the implementation of a certain reform, the selection of appropriate timing, the determination of its procedures, the trade-off between its gains and losses, the coordination and control of the process, and the maintenance of the achievement all depend on the government's role. Only when institutional reforms are pushed forward in a stable and smooth manner is it possible for the government to coordinate and control the reform process while at the same time making changes in itself.

Secondly, the incremental reform approach can avoid social turbulence and prevent the waste of resources. On the contrary, a radical reform will surely hurt some vested interest groups, and will thus incur severe resistance and induce waste of social resources. Moreover, those vested interest groups usually have significant

16. Justin Yifu Lin and Li Zhou, "Choice of Development Strategy is the Key to Economic Development — Perspective View of the Successes and Failures of Economic Development in Capitalist Countries after World War II", *Comparison of Economic and Social Systems*, No. 1 (1992).

political and social influence, and their resistance to reform will substantially increase the cost and risk of reform.

Finally, because it does not centre on privatization, this reform approach can prevent the inequality that arises from the reallocation of the stock of state assets and avoid the conflicts arising from this inequality. This makes it possible for each social group to share in the economic property. As almost every social group can benefit in the short or the long run from the reforms, the economic reform becomes a consensus among most people and becomes an irreversible process.

11.3 General Implications of China's Reform Approach

In contrast to the radical, comprehensive reform chosen by Eastern European countries, the CIS, and some developing countries[17] (Poland and Russia were two typical examples), China, as already mentioned, has taken an incremental reform approach, which has been proved successful in the last two decades. While successfully maintaining social stability, China has achieved a high economic growth rate, improved significantly the economic efficiency and has made great success in the market-oriented reform. It is thus worthwhile, for both theoretical and practical purposes, to sum up China's experience with this approach, to look at the general implications of China's reform experience, and to discuss whether China will be able to continue with this approach and whether the approach is the best choice for the country.

Chinese and foreign scholars have praised China's approach to reform, but some have over-emphasized China's particular situation at the time when reforms first began, thereby placing too much

17. India's economic system shares a lot of similarities with that of China and former Soviet Union. It has also carried out reforms in past decades. For detailed descriptions on these similarities, and further discussions on the Indian economic development and reform, see William H. Overholt, *The Rise of China: How Economic Reform is Creating a New Superpower*. New York and London: W.W. Norton Company, 1993, pp. 356–59.

importance on the particularity of China's experience.[18] They tend to prefer shock therapy or the big bang approach when recommending reform measures for Eastern European countries and the former Soviet Union. But as we have shown in previous chapters, most countries under reform had once adopted a leap-forward strategy and had accordingly put into place a price-distorting macro-policy environment, a highly centralized planned resource-allocation mechanism, and a micro-management institution devoid of autonomy, just as China did. All these countries have felt pressure to improve micro-incentive and managerial efficiency. They have all experienced an urgent need to correct the distorted industrial structure (or to develop suppressed industrial sectors), and to identify and develop the price signals needed for such adjustments. In fact, China's reform is just the kind of reform in need. It begins with the reform of micro-management system to improve the incentive mechanism, and then extends to the resource-allocation system and pushes forward further reform in the price system. During this process, it gradually adjusts the industrial structure through more efficient allocation of incremental resources.

In other countries that are carrying out economic reforms, traditional economic systems are also the result of their leap-forward strategy. This is similar to the situation in China. Moreover, the problems in front of them are also problems in front of China. Therefore, China's gradual reform should have some general implications for them. It is necessary for us to sum up the experience of Chinese

18. J. Sachs and W. Woo, "Structural Factors in the Economic Reforms of China, Eastern Europe and the Former Soviet Union". Paper presented at the Economic Policy Panel Meeting in Brussels, Belgium, 22–23 October 1993; Y. Y. Qian and C. G. Xu, "Why China's Economic Reforms Differ: The M-Form Hierarchy and Entry/Expansion of the Non-state Sector", *The Economics of Transition*, Vol. 1, No. 2 (June 1993), pp. 135–70. These authors look only at the differences in initial conditions that reduced the costs of incremental reform in China and neglect the fact that incremental reforms might result in greater benefits in Eastern Europe and the former Soviet Union because price distortions have been more serious in those countries. It cannot be denied that China's reforms have general implications for other economies in transition.

reform and the reasons behind its success, and recapitulate the characteristics and advantages of this gradual approach.

1. A Pareto Improvement

A gradual reform is close to a Pareto improvement or Kaldor improvement. Economic reforms necessarily involve a large-scale adjustment to the structure of vested interests. Under China's price-distorting macro-policy environment, according to the government plan, cheap resources flowed toward heavy-industry enterprises and sectors that were consistent with strategic goals. The vested interests of these enterprises and sectors will inevitably suffer as a result of reforms in the resource-allocation mechanism and macro-policy environment, although such reforms will bring about gains through structural adjustments and efficiency improvements. Reform that starts with the macro-policy environment is bound to be a non-Pareto improvement. If such a reform approach cannot adequately compensate the harmed vested interest groups, that is, if it is not a Kaldor improvement, it will meet with resistance. Reform that starts with the micro-management institution (i.e., it improves the incentive mechanism and efficiency in micro units by the delegation of managerial autonomy and the sharing of profits) can accelerate the growth of new resources and can enable the state, enterprises and workers to increase their income without harming anyone. Such a reform is a Pareto improvement. The first stage of reform in China has resulted in a rapid increase in social wealth, which has helped boost the economy's capacity for compensation during the reform process, thus creating the conditions necessary for the reform of the macro-policy environment and making it possible for the next stage of reform to assume the nature of a Kaldor improvement.

The shock therapy approach begins with price reform and reallocation of the existing stock of assets, not the reform of micro-management institution aimed at creating a new stream of resources. Therefore, such an approach is certainly a non-Pareto and non-Kaldor improvement. China took a different approach to reform. Its reform was targeted to provide incentives to people at the micro-management level enabling them to gain economic benefits and powers in the process (through delegating autonomy and profit-sharing). Even the units under reform may gain from this delegation of autonomy and sharing of profit. They may even become new vested interest groups for further reform. Such a reform therefore can gain the maximum support and avoid social commotions that a reform of the non-Pareto-improvement or non-Kaldor-improvement type might bring about.

Under gradual reform, when the micro-management institution is allowed to dispose part of the newly created resources, it will distribute the new resources to sectors that were traditionally suppressed. Lack of autonomy and incentives in the micro-management institutions are problems common to all countries that adopted the leap-forward strategy. Although suppressed sectors differ from country to country depending on each country's developmental stage and resource endowment, these sectors still have many common features.

Firstly, products of these sectors have relatively high price levels. Because they were suppressed under the traditional development strategy, their products were in short supply. This protracted shortage was gradually reflected in the adjustment of planned prices, making the prices of these products very high. In China, for instance, agriculture and light industry were suppressed under the traditional development strategy. Taking 1952 as the base period, the output value index of heavy industry in 1979 had increased by 28.9 times, while that of agriculture and light industry increased only by 16.3 times and 9.6 times, respectively, amounting to only about 57.9% and 35.5%, of the heavy industry growth. When it was reflected in prices, this uneven development increased the prices of agricultural and light industrial goods at a rate faster than that of heavy industry goods. Taking 1950 as the base period, the general index of state procurement prices of agricultural and sideline products was 265.5 in 1979. The consumer retail price index (including agricultural and sideline products) at state stores was 135.1, and the price index of daily use articles (light industrial products) was 127.1, while the price index of agricultural capital goods (heavy industrial goods) was only 100.5. Such relatively favourable prices have provided strong motivation for the development of these suppressed sectors and for the entry of new producers.

Secondly, the demand far exceeds the supply. Planned prices were unable to balance the demand and supply of the goods and services provided by the suppressed sectors. This resulted in a shortage of supply. Such a shortage was resolved by rationing. In fact, there was a widespread shortage of foodstuffs and daily necessities in China prior to the 1980s. These goods could only be obtained with coupons or by a small number of people with special privileges. The supply shortage constituted a driving force behind the development of suppressed sectors, and served as an irresistible enticement for new entrants.

Thirdly, the cost of entry was low. The sectors suppressed under the traditional development strategy were those in which the Chinese economy has comparative advantages, namely, labour-intensive industries. Based on relevant data,[19] we have calculated the content of fixed capital in the value-added of several sectors in the typical low-income economy, they are 53.4%, 67.2%, and 80% in agriculture, light industry and heavy industry, respectively. Under China's endowment structure, the reform-propelling sectors are labour-intensive and have a low threshold for capital formation. It is precisely by exploiting the comparative advantages of abundant and cheap labour resources that TVEs entered the industry and pushed the reform forward.

The improvement in incentives that came about as a result of the reform in the micro-management institution, and the allocation of newly acquired resources to the suppressed sectors, have brought about rapid economic growth and tremendous benefits. In terms of this process alone, there have been almost no victims of reforms. However, both the state sector, which has obtained autonomy in the production and allocation of resources, and the non-state sectors,

19. Wang Huijiong and Yang Guanghui, *Possibility and Options for China's Economic Structural Changes and Growth*. Beijing: Meteorological Press, 1984, pp. 65, 68.

which have edged themselves into the industry, have demanded a reform of the planned resource-allocation mechanism and the traditional macro-policy environment, thus bringing the reforms into a sensitive non-Pareto improvement stage. But the improved incentives and reduced structural distortion have contributed considerably to economic growth, resulting in tremendous benefits to society that are reflected in the increasing abundance of products, an improvement in the per capita income, and an increase in the fiscal revenue of the government at all levels. Thus enterprises and individuals have increased their capacity to withstand the losses caused by price reform, and the government has acquired the ability to subsidize enterprises and industries that have fallen victim to the price reform. Although such subsidies to SOEs are protective in nature and are in line with the traditional strategic thinking, they are worthwhile because they make it possible to correct price signals at minimal social cost. Subsidies to residents during the reform of consumer prices were in effect correcting distortion in consumer prices and wages, a practice known in China as converting implicit subsidies into explicit subsidies.

2. Intrinsic Logic and Irreversibility

As we showed in Chapters 2 and 3, the traditional economic systems of China and all other countries that adopted the leap-forward strategy had an intrinsic logic. With the objectives of developing heavy industry or import-substitution industries, and in order to obtain the large amount of capital needed in a capital-scarce environment, these countries artificially suppressed interest rates, exchange rates, and wages, and they under-priced energy, raw materials, and consumer goods, giving rise to a distorted macro-policy environment. To realize the objectives of the development strategy, which were to address the shortage of resources, it was necessary to establish a highly centralized planned resource-allocation mechanism. The state then proceeded to control the use of surplus and to prevent micro-management units from pocketing excessive profits by depriving managers of autonomy. This shows that such an economic system is endogenously formed with a high degree of intrinsic unity. Every component of this system is interconnected with one another, and adaptive to the whole system.

As illustrated by the process of China's economic reform, the reform started with the micro-management units with the purpose of improving the incentive mechanism, including the delegation of autonomy, and the sharing of profits in SOEs, and the introduction of the household responsibility system in rural areas. As a result, SOEs obtained the right to allocate a portion of the newly acquired resources, and TVEs rapidly entered the industrial sectors.

As newly created resources are more and more often being allocated to the traditionally suppressed sectors, China has seen enormous growth. SOEs' use of newly-created resources and the entry of non-state enterprises represented by TVEs have, in turn, pushed forward the reform of the resource-allocation mechanism, giving rise to the dual-track system in resource-allocation and prices. The emergence of market prices of products and factors and the adjustments of the economy at the margin have resulted in the demand for the reform of the macroeconomic policy environment and have created the conditions necessary for such a reform. Although China's reforms have had no clear objective or blueprint at the beginning, because of the intrinsic nature of the trinity of the economic system, reforms that began with the micro-management unit have proceeded from the outset in a *de facto* distinct logic or order.

Moreover, incremental reform is also irreversible. As we have seen when the macro-policy environment remained basically intact, reform in the micro-management institution and the resource-allocation system resulted in institutional incompatibility and in a disruption of the internal integrity of the traditional system, thus giving rise to the bottlenecks, inflation, rent-seeking, and other elements of the vigour/chaos cycle discussed in Chapter 7. At this time, the government had to choose between two options to maintain the integrity of the economic system. One was to take away the autonomy delegated to micro-management units so that they would be consistent with the traditional macro-policy environment. The other was to extend reforms to the macro-policy environment, and try to achieve a new internal consistency on the basis of market economy. The government, on many occasions, chose the first option, but for two reasons this did not achieve the hoped-for result and could not be sustained.

Firstly, the reform of the micro-management institution has provided SOEs, rural residents, and non-state sectors with operational autonomy and economic benefits, who all became the beneficiaries of the reform. Depriving them of this autonomy hurt their interests and aroused their resistance.

Secondly, the reform of the micro-management institution brought about impressive gains in the allocation of newly acquired resources. In this sense, the state was also a beneficiary of the reform. When SOEs were once again stripped of autonomy, and when the development of TVEs was contained, economic growth slowed dramatically, and the state's revenues dwindled. This forced the state to decentralize once again and to move forward in the reform of the macro-policy environment to make the economic system internally consistent. It is in this way that China's reform has proceeded. Although setbacks have halted progress for brief periods, the general direction of the reform is irreversible.

3. Crossing a Chasm in Two Steps

Price distortion is a major defect in the traditional economic systems of all countries undergoing reform. No matter which reform approach they adopt and how the reform schedule is drafted, price reform or the reform of the macro-policy environment is inevitable. Under the shock therapy reform method adopted by Eastern European countries and the former Soviet Union, prices were usually completely liberalized in a single step. The reasoning behind this approach is that one cannot cross a chasm in two steps. In other words, the price signal either has to be distorted or it has to truly reflect supply and demand and the relative scarcity of resources. There is no in-between. Multiple prices will inevitably lead to multiple rules and multiple behaviours. It is therefore necessary to cross the chasm in just one step. However, price-distorting macro-policy environments produce corresponding vested interest groups. To liberalize prices in one step is very risky. In other words, if the gap between the distorted price and the market price is so great that crossing the chasm in one step is impossible, one will fall into the chasm when trying to cross it in a single step.

The risk arises from two sources. Firstly, vested interest groups can oppose reform. In China, large and medium-sized SOEs were the beneficiaries of low factor prices and low-priced energy and raw materials. Therefore, they were potential opponents of the price reform. Since the leaders of large and medium-sized SOEs had close relationships with government officials, and because they hired large quantities of workers, they had strong resistance power. Urban residents were the beneficiaries of low-priced consumption goods. They also had close relationships with government officials. It was cheaper for them to organize and easier for them to form groups to oppose the reform. If the losses felt by these two interest groups were great enough, and if compensation was impossible, the price reform could not be implemented successfully.

Secondly, the price reform can lead to a slowdown in economic growth or even to economic recession. The correction of price signals will undoubtedly induce enterprises to become more competitive, and the resulting production structure will conform more closely to the economy's comparative advantage. However, under the traditional economic system, the distortion in the production structure is directly related to price distortion. After price controls are relaxed, the structural adjustment necessarily involves the reallocation of the existing stock of assets and resources, which will result in the J-shaped economic growth curve, which drops first and rises later, or even the L-shaped long-term recession curve.

China's price reform adopted the dual-track transition approach, i.e., adjusting planned prices and allowing market prices to emerge alongside. First, reform of the micro-management institution gave enterprises opportunities to retain a portion of the newly-created resources. Correspondingly, the enterprises demanded that they could allocate these resources according to market price signals instead of administrative plans. Thus the dual-track resource-allocation mechanism and price system were formed. Owing to the practice of "selling products at high prices if production used high-priced inputs" and "selling products at low prices if production used low-priced inputs", enterprises did not oppose the resource-allocation system outside the plan, or the introduction of market prices. Legitimization of market prices provided reference and demand for the adjustment of planned prices. Therefore, adjustments in planned prices could be carried out to the appropriate extent and using the method (e.g., by subsidizing) acceptable to enterprises. Since the rapid economic growth was mainly attributable to non-SOEs outside the planning system, the scope and quantity of production governed by market prices were expanding. In fact, even if the scope and quantity of production governed by planned prices had remained unchanged, or even if they had increased a bit, the influence of the plan mechanism on economic operations would have shrunk as its share became smaller and smaller. In addition, through incremental adjustment, the difference between planned prices and market prices was greatly reduced, and the resultant rent created by planned prices was smaller. At this point, the chasm had nearly been filled and narrowed, and it was almost completely safe to cross it. Thus, although the reform of the macro-policy environment in China lagged behind the reform of the micro-management institution and the resource-allocation mechanism, it was less risky and less costly. The method used shows that, at least in this particular case, crossing a chasm in two steps is possible.

The reform of the foreign exchange system provides a good illustration of the above analysis. A proportional foreign exchange retention system was put into practice to improve the micro-operational organization's incentive to earn foreign exchange and to expand its decision-making power. The foreign exchange allocation system and dual-track exchange rate emerged as a result. In 1988, a swap market was officially opened. The market track of exchange rate and foreign exchange allocation system continued to expand so much that, before the unification of the exchange rate in 1994, 80% of the total foreign exchange was allocated based on the market exchange rate on the swap market. Meanwhile, the official rate had been adjusted for several times to narrow the gap between the two tracks. As a result, the unification of the exchange rate, an important measure, proceeded smoothly.

4. Maintaining Speed and Stability

To gain support for reform from most social groups and most people, the political party or the government leading the reform must adopt a non-radical reform approach that could maintain the balance between growth speed and social stability during the reform process.

To illustrate the point, let us turn to a "voting model"[20] (see Figure 11.3). Suppose there are two attitudes to reform, one emphasizing stability (left of the median line at M) and the other emphasizing speed (right of the median line). Accordingly, there are two different views on reform among leaders (W and S). Members of society with extreme views toward reform have a clear objective to support: those on the left side of W support W, while those on the

Figure 11.3 Voting model for reform opinions

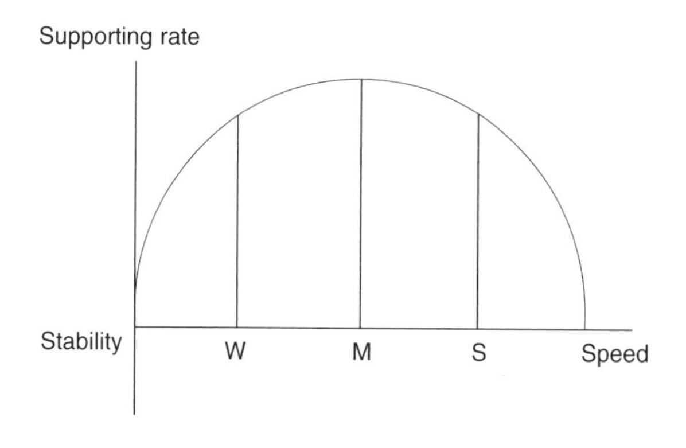

20. W. L. David, *Political Economy of Economic Policy — The Quest for Human Betterment*. Praeger, 1998, pp. 189–91.

right side of S support S. Under the condition that both policies remain unchanged, the social members tend to support either W or S, with the median line as the dividing line. The figure shows that if W or S shifts its view toward the other side, it will win more supporters. If both sides do this, the degree of extremity of the two reform views will decrease. Thus, advocates of stability show concern about speed, while advocates for speed also want stability.

Based on the mechanism illustrated by the model, it can be seen that when two views are equally influential, their coexistence and the checks and balances of one against the other are necessary and conducive for the non-radical reform. However, to function, this mechanism requires that the reform process be incremental in nature. Once the shock therapy approach has been adopted, there is no longer any opportunity for social groups or the general public to make choices. The reform process and the degree of how radical the reform should be can no longer be put in control.

China's reform has been carried out under the leadership of the Chinese Communist Party. Although no faction within the leadership is strong enough to challenge the mainstream views (i.e., to continue the reform), there are different views within the leadership as to the scope, orientation, and timing of reforms. The two predominant views within the leadership stress either stability or speed. The former emphasizes that we should maintain the stability of the social system in the reform process, and therefore should slow the pace of reform and growth, while the latter emphasizes that reform is an urgent task and should not be delayed, and therefore we should make swift changes and accelerate growth rate so as to build up public confidence in the reform.

As China has opted for incremental reform, members of society and those within the ruling party have frequent opportunities to make choices and to correct overly radical measures. Moreover, the mechanism illustrated in the model can push reform forward when it stagnates as a result of political obstructions. In fact, it is exactly such a correcting mechanism that has enabled China's reform process to move forward steadily over the past 20 years despite many ups and downs. So long as this balance between speed and stability is maintained, people will have confidence in the eventual success of the reform.

[Four Fundamentals Failures]

* Failure to create a new fiscal system
* to clarify or restructure property rts (听话 "necessary component of mkt sys.")
* to put real accountability into the investment system
* repeated & excessive delays in reforming some of the more distorted aspects of the price system

[Third Plenum Achievements]

Deng Xiaoping came up '78, '79

Chen Yun economist leader

CHAPTER 12

Concluding Remarks

The economic reforms that have taken place in China since 1979 have been extremely successful. China's national economy has grown rapidly as a result of the reforms, and its people's living standards have improved steadily. As the world's most populous country, China's resurgence has aroused worldwide interest. This book has systematically described the traditional economic system that impeded China's economic development. It analyzes the logic of the traditional economic system, the intrinsic unity of the system, the process of the reform, the conflicts arising from the reform, the causes and solutions of the current deflation, and the implication of WTO access to reform. It has also pointed out the direction in which further reform should proceed and its general implications for other transitional countries with similar circumstances to China.

The logical starting point for the formation of China's traditional economic system was the adoption of the heavy-industry-oriented development strategy. To give priority to the development of capital-intensive heavy industries in a capital-scarce under-developed economy, the Chinese government had to artificially suppress the prices of capital, foreign exchange, energy, raw materials, labour, and daily necessities to lower the capital-formation threshold in heavy industries. Distorted prices of production factors and products resulted in a shortage economy. In order to allocate scarce resources to heavy industries, the government had to establish a non-market resource-allocation mechanism. To guarantee that the surplus of grassroot economic entities were used to promote the development of heavy industries, corresponding micro-management mechanism were created through the nationalization of industry and the establishment of rural communes. In the price-distorting macro-policy environment, profits ceased to be an indicator of enterprise management performance and no objective substitute could be found. To prevent managers and workers from embezzling profits and state property, the government had to deprive micro-management units of autonomy.

Under the traditional economic system, the government's choice of the heavy-industry-oriented development strategy was exogenously determined. The choice led endogenously to the formation of a price-distorting macro-policy environment, a planned-resource-allocation mechanism, and a microeconomic management system lacking in autonomy. These institutional arrangements constitute an organic whole.

The traditional economic system was formed to facilitate the implementation of the heavy-industry-oriented development strategy and to achieve the goal of catching up with and overtaking developed countries. However, the fact that the micro-management system was without autonomy led to low work incentives. The non-market resource-allocation mechanism resulted in inefficient resource allocation. The price-distorting macroeconomic environment resulted in a distorted economic structure. Therefore, the traditional economic system, instead of enabling China to catch up with and overtake developed countries, impeded economic growth and resulted in low living standards for the Chinese people.

China's economic reform started in the late 1970s. It began with the delegation of autonomy and profit-sharing with micro-management units. In the state-owned sector, these reform measures helped improve the incentive mechanism and increased productivity. They also granted enterprises the right to allocate a proportion of newly created resources. Driven by profit motives, enterprises channelled the newly created resources into sectors that had been suppressed under the traditional economic system. In rural areas, the introduction of household responsibility system improved rural residents' incentives. Along with the development of TVEs, it created new resources that were also channelled into traditionally suppressed sectors.

The objective of the heavy-industry-oriented development strategy was to give priority to the development of capital-intensive heavy industries. One of the side effects of the strategy was the suppression of labour-intensive industries, in which China enjoys a comparative advantage. The development of previously suppressed sectors reduced the distortion in industrial structure and resulted in better use of the country's comparative advantages. The improvement in both incentives and industrial structure brought about tremendous growth. China's GDP has risen by an annual average of 9.6% since 1978. After the micro-management units had acquired the right to dispose of some newly created resources at their own discretion, they needed a corresponding channel other than the planned-resource-allocation system with which to allocate resources under their control. At first, the government allowed only barter trade and prohibited cash trade. However, the shadow prices formed through barter trade exerted great challenge on the macro-policy environment and created further demand for reforms in the resource-allocation mechanism and the macro-policy environment. Hence, the dual-track price system and resource-allocation system were adopted.

The price-distorting macro-policy environment was the basic institutional arrangement for the maintenance of the heavy-industry-oriented development strategy. The gradual loosening of control over the macro-policy environment reduced the influence of the traditional economic strategy. As we know, large and medium-sized SOEs were the basic vehicles for the implementation of the traditional development strategy, but because of the rapid development of non-state sectors represented by TVEs, the relative and then absolute importance of SOEs in the national economy diminished, stimulating an increasingly strong attack on the traditional development strategy.

We are now in a position to answer the first question raised in the introduction of this book. That is: why the Chinese economy developed so slowly before the reform, and why it developed so rapidly thereafter? The root of China's slow development before the introduction of reform was the government's adoption of the heavy-industry-oriented development strategy, which was inconsistent with China's comparative advantages. The key to the rapid economic growth after reform lies in the better exploitation of China's comparative advantages, which was made possible through the reform of the trinity in the traditional economic system. All developing economies that adopted the leap-forward strategy (e.g., South American countries and Asian countries such as India and the Philippines) suffered because of their inefficient economic system and unsatisfactory economic performances, while all those that relied on the market mechanism to exploit their comparative advantages (e.g., the four Little Dragons) created efficient economic systems and achieved rapid economic growth. The core of the successful Chinese economic reform, in the final analysis, is to shift to the new development strategy through the reform of the trinity in the traditional economic system.

China's economic reform is far from complete. It still faces a series of dilemmas. Under the traditional economic system, every individual arrangement within the institutional structure was preconditioned by and adapted to another. Although the reform started with the micro-management institution and inevitably spilled over into the resource-allocation system and the macro-policy environment, the government still has not formally renounced the leap-forward strategy and still protects large and medium-sized SOEs embodying the strategic goal. Therefore, price reforms, particularly the reform of factor prices, were bound to lag behind.

As the newly created resources increased, the amount that the micro entities could freely dispose of increased, and the traditional government control on resource-allocation loosened. These changes in micro-management system and resource-allocation system sharpened their conflict with the traditional macro-policy environment, in particular the distortion in interest rates, exchange rates and prices of energy and raw materials. Because of the slow reform in the traditional macro-policy environment, enterprise expansion was often constrained by the shortage of goods and services such as energy and transportation. These shortages became bottlenecks for economic growth and contributed to the great fluctuations in economic growth. In the low-interest-rate policy environment, non-state sectors were more competitive than state sectors in the race for funds, resulting in a shortage of funds for state sectors. To ensure SOEs' survival, the government had no choice but to issue more money and thus caused endogenous inflation. Under the dual-track system in resource allocation and prices, enterprises' profit motives gave rise to a strong desire for rent-seeking, leading to corruption. As long as the government has not shifted away from the leap-forward strategy, SOEs have to bear all the policy burdens and the reform of SOEs will not succeed, which will also impede the financial reforms.

When the vigour/chaos cycle became so extreme that it threatened the economy's normal operation, the government more often than not resorted to traditional planning, forcing the economy into retrenchment, and suppressing the expansion of non-state sectors, thereby causing a recurring cycle within the reform process. We can thus answer the second question raised in the introduction of this book. That is: what is the underlying reason for the vigour/chaos cycle in China's economic development and how can we get rid of it? The underlying reason is that the uncoordinated reform has led to the institutional incompatibility. During the economic reform process, the reform in some areas made significant achievement while the reform in other areas lagged far behind. This made the institutional components of the economic system uncompatible with one another, and the vigour/chaos cycle took place. The key to eliminating the cycle is to extend the reform to the macro-policy environment and to replace the trinity in the traditional economic system with a new structure by adopting a strategy of comparative advantages.

In spite of various snags and setbacks, China's reform has proceeded steadily, and its ultimate goal is becoming more evident. Through the delegation of autonomy and the sharing of profits, the government has stimulated the creation of new resources, which have been allocated to previously suppressed sectors, resulting in industrial structure adjustment and rapid economic growth. The reform has benefited not only the micro-management units but also the whole society.

When conflicts within the trinity arose, the government often chose traditional retrenchment measures to resolve institutional incompatibility. However, re-centralization not only fails to win the support of micro-management units but also causes a decline in fiscal revenue. Finally, the government had to reform the macro-policy environment to make it compatible with the reformed micro-management institution and the resource-allocation mechanism. Thus, incremental reform is logically irreversible. If the government could recognize this and accept the urgency of adopting the comparative-advantage strategy, reform would proceed more smoothly and quickly. The answer to the third question posed in the introduction is that as long as the orientation of the reform remains correct, difficulties on the path to reform can be overcome. Successful reforms will effectively support sustainable, healthy, and rapid economic growth. And China will probably catch up with and overtake the United States and Japan early in the 21st century and to become the largest economy in the world.

In contrast to the Eastern European countries and the former Soviet Union, both of which adopted the shock therapy type of reform, China chose the incremental reform. Instead of starting with the macro-policy environment, which required a major adjustment of vested interest structure, China began with the reform of micro-management units by improving their incentive mechanisms, granting greater autonomy in operations, allowing them to share more profits so as to create more new resources and to allocate resources to sectors suppressed under the traditional system. The approach made the whole society the beneficiary of the reform. When the reform of the micro-management institution and the resource-allocation mechanism called for corresponding price reforms, the increased social wealth put the government in a better position to compensate the vested interest groups that suffered losses. Thus, China's reform has the nature of a Pareto improvement or a Kaldor improvement.

China's reform has a logical order. Once micro-management units could allocate a portion of the newly created resources, it was impossible to cling to the unitary system of planned resource allocation and state-controlled prices. Reform thus naturally extended from the micro-management system to the resource-allocation system and the macro-policy environment. The dual-track system of resource allocation and prices was the logical outcome of the process. The formation of the dual-track system and the expansion of the market, in turn, pressed for a compatible macro-policy environment. The upshot was the deepening of reform. In the process, when the dual-track system was in operation, the market expanded gradually and the prices in the planned track are constantly adjusted toward the market level. As this process goes on, the price distortion in the macro-policy environment diminished and so did its impact on the economic activities. In the end, it will be possible to abandon the traditional macro-policy environment with little risk and at a low cost.

In addition, incremental reform has provided the Chinese people and political leaders with many opportunities to choose concrete reform measures and the appropriate timing, and has thus helped to guarantee a proper balance between growth speed and social stability and to avoid excessive friction. Our answer to the fourth question posed in the introduction is that China has chosen a low-cost, low-risk incremental reform with timely returns. The Eastern European countries and the former Soviet Union chose the opposite, and their choice has resulted in tremendous friction and social shocks. Since the reasons for the establishment of traditional economic systems and the problems experienced by these economies in transition are very similar, their approaches to effective reform should have something in common. As proven in this book, China's experiences are not at all peculiar to China's specific conditions. Instead, they have general implications and can be applied to other countries.

Bibliography

(The original bibliographical data of those works in Chinese are given after their translation.)

Amsden, Alice H. *Asia's Next Giant: South Korea and Late Industrialization*. Oxford: Oxford University Press, 1989.

Anderson, Kym. *Changes of Comparative Advantages in Chinese Economy*, Chinese edition. Beijing: Economic Science Press, 1992. (基姆•安德森：《中國經濟比較優勢的變化》。北京：經濟科學出版社，1992。)

Anderson, Kym. *Changing Comparative Advantages in China: Effects on Food, Feed and Fiber Markets*. Paris: Development Studies Center, OCED, 1990.

Annual Analysis of the Rural Economy Project Group. *Annual Report on China's Rural Economic Development in 1993*. Beijing: China Social Sciences Press, 1994 (in Chinese). (農村經濟年度分析課題組：《1993年中國農村經濟發展年度報告》。北京：中國社會科學出版社，1994。)

Aoton, Basil; Hill, Kenneth; Piazza, Alan and Zeitz, Robin. "Famine in China, 1958–1961", *Population and Development Review*, Vol. 10 (December 1984), pp. 613–45.

Asia Development Bank. *Asia Development Outlook 1990*. Manila: Asian Development Bank, 1991.

Balass, B., et al. *Development Strategies in Semi-industrial Economics*. Baltimore: Johns Hopkins University Press, 1982.

Bank of China, Institute of International Finance. *Analysis of the Current International and Domestic Economic and Financial Situation*. Beijing: Bank of China, 1999 (in Chinese). (中國銀行國際金融研究所：《當前國際國內經濟金融形勢分析》(內部資料)，1999年7月。

Brada, J. C. "The Economic Transition of Czechoslovakia: From Plan to Market", *Journal of Economic Perspectives*, Vol. 3 (1989), pp. 171–77.

Brada, J. C. and King, A. E. *Sequencing Measures for the Transformation of Socialist Economies to Capitalism: Is There a J-Curve for Economic Reform?* Research Paper Series, No. 13. Washington, DC: Socialist Economic Reform Unit, The World Bank, 1991.

Cai, Fang. "Positive Analysis and Strategic Thought about the Unevenness of Rural Economic Development", *Rural Economy and Society*, No. 3 (1994), pp. 7–15 (in Chinese).（蔡昉：〈農村經濟發展不平衡的實證分析與戰略思考〉，《農村經濟與社會》，第3期（1994），頁7–15。）

Cai, Fang. "The New Stage in China's Urbanization", *Future and Development*, No. 5 (1990), pp. 5–9 (in Chinese).（蔡昉：〈我國城市化的新階段〉，《未來與發展》，第5期（1990），頁5–9。）

Chen, K.; Jefferson, G. and Singh, I. J. "Lessons from China's Economic Reform". *Journal of Comparative Economics*, Vol. 16, No. 2 (June 1992), pp. 201–25.

Chen, K.; Wang, H.; Zheng, Y.; Jefferson, G. and Rawski, T. "Productivity Change in Chinese Industry: 1953–1985", *Journal of Comparative Economics*, Vol. 12 (1988), pp. 570–91.

Chen, Licheng, et al. *Economic Development in Developing Countries and the New International Economic Order*. Beijing: Economic Science Press, 1987 (in Chinese).（陳立成等：《發展中國家的經濟發展戰略與國際經濟新秩序》。北京：經濟科學出版社，1987。）

Chen, Wenhong, et al. *Where Should the East Asian Economies Head For — A Review and Outlook of '97 East Asian Financial Storms*. Beijing: Economic Management Press, 1998 (in Chinese).（陳文鴻等：《東亞經濟何處去 —— '97東亞金融風暴的回顧與展望》。北京：經濟科學出版社，1998。）

Chenery, Hollis B. "Comparative Advantage and Development Policy", *American Economic Review*, Vol. 51 (March 1961), p. 21.

Chenery, Hollis B., et al. *Patterns of Development, 1950–1970*. London: Oxford University Press, 1975; Chinese edition, Beijing: Economic Science Press, 1988.（錢納里等：《發展的型式（1950–1970）》。北京：經濟科學出版社，1988。）

China Academy of Social Sciences, Institute of Economy. *The*

Economic Development and Economic System for China's Town and Village Enterprises. Beijing: China Economy Press, 1987 (in Chinese).（中國社會科學院經濟研究所：《中國鄉鎮企業的經濟發展與經濟體制》。北京：中國經濟出版社，1987。）

China Center for Economic Research, Macroeconomic Research Group, Peking University. "Take the Deflation Pressure Seriously and Expedite the Micro-mechanism Reform", *Economic Research*, No. 7 (1999), pp. 10–17 (in Chinese).（《經濟研究》，第7期（1999），頁10–17。）

China Economic Yearbook 1981, abridged edition. Beijing: Economic Management Press, 1982 (in Chinese).（中國經濟年鑑編輯委員會編：《1981年中國經濟年鑑（簡編）》。北京：經濟管理出版社，1982。）

China Encyclopaedia, Economics Editorial Board, ed. *China Encyclopaedia: Economics*, Vol. 2. Beijing & Shanghai: China Encyclopaedia Press, 1988 (in Chinese).（中國大百科全書編輯委員會、《經濟學》編輯委員會編：《中國大百科全書·經濟卷》（第二卷）。北京、上海：中國大百科全書出版社，1988。）

China Yearbook, 1988. Hong Kong: New China Media Co. and Beijing: Xinhua Press, 1988 (in Chinese).（《中國年鑑（1988）》。香港：新中國新聞有限公司、北京：新華出版社，1988。）

Cipolla, Carlo M. *Before the Industrial Revolution: European Society and Economy, 1000–1700*, 2nd ed. New York: Norton, 1980.

Coase, R. H. "The Nature of the Firm", *Economica*, Vol. 3, No. 19, pp. 386–405.

Cody, John, *et al.*, eds. *Industrial Development Policies in the Developing Countries*, Chinese edition. Beijing: Economic Science Press, 1986.（約翰·科迪等主編：《發展中國家的工業發展政策》。北京：經濟科學出版社，1986。）

CPC Central Committee, Documentation and Research Office. *Documents of the Second Session of the First National People's Congress of the PRC*. Beijing: People's Press, 1955 (in Chinese).（中華人民共和國全國人民代表大會編：《中華人民共和國第一次全國人民代表大會第二次會議文件》。北京：人民出版社，1955。）

CPC Central Committee, Documentation and Research Office. *Selected Important Documents since the 12th National Congress of the Communist Party of China*, Vol. 2. Beijing: People's Press, 1986 (in Chinese). (中共中央文獻研究室編：《十二大以來重要文獻選編(中)》。北京：人民出版社，1986。)

CPC Central Committee Secretariat, Research Office and CPC Central Committee, Documentation and Research Office. *Persisting in Reform, Opening Up and Revitalizing the Economy — Selected Important Documents Issued since the Third Plenary Session of the CPC 11th Central Committee*. Beijing: People's Press, 1987 (in Chinese). (中共中央書記處研究室、中共中央文獻研究室編：《堅持改革、開放、搞活 —— 十一屆三中全會以來有關重要文獻摘編》。北京：人民出版社，1987。)

David, W. L. *Political Economy of Economic Policy — The Quest for Human Betterment*. London: Praeger, 1988.

Davies, R. W. *The Industrialization of Soviet Russia*, Vol. 3: *The Soviet Economy in Turmoil, 1929–1930*. Cambridge, MA: Harvard University Press, 1989.

Debate on Important Questions Concerning Plutonomy since the Foundation of the PRC (1949–1980). Beijing: China Finance and Economics Press, 1981 (in Chinese). (《建國以來政治經濟學重要問題爭論(1949–1980)》。北京：中國財政經濟出版社，1981。)

Deng, Yingtao. *New Development Models and the Future of China*. Beijing: China Trust and Investment Press, 1992 (in Chinese). (鄧英陶：《新發展方式與中國未來》。北京：中信出版社，1992。)

Desai, P. and Martin, R. "Efficiency Loss from Resource Misallocation in Soviet Industry", *Quarterly Journal of Economics*, Vol. 98, No. 3 (1983), pp. 117–29.

Development Research Institute. *Reform Facing Institutional Challenges*. Shanghai: Shanghai Sanlian Bookstore, 1988 (in Chinese). (發展研究所綜合課題組：《改革面臨制度創新》。上海：上海三聯書店，1988。)

Dewatripont, M. and Roland, G. "The Virtues of Gradualism and Legitimacy in the Transition to a Market Economy", *Economic Journal*, Vol. 102 (1992), pp. 291–300.

Dollar, D. "Economic Reform and Allocative Efficiency in China's State-owned Industry", *Economic Development and Cultural Change*, Vol. 39 (1990), pp. 89–105.

Domar, E. D. *Essays on the Theory of Economic Growth*. New York: Oxford University Press, 1957; Chinese edition, Beijing: Commercial Press, 1983. (多馬：《經濟增長理論》。北京：商務印書館，1983。)

Domar, Evsey. "Capital Expansion, Rate of Growth, and Employment", *Econometrica*, Vol. 14, No. 2 (April 1946), pp. 137–47.

Dong, Fureng. "On the Nature and Status of State Enterprises", in *Selected Works of Dong Fureng*. Shanxi: Shanxi People's Press, 1985 (in Chinese). (董輔礽：〈全民所有制企業的性質和地位問題〉，載《董輔礽選集》。山西：山西人民出版社，1985。)

Du, Haiyan, et al. "Decision-making Power of the State-owned Enterprise, Market Structure and the Bonus System", *Economic Research*, No. 1 (1990), pp. 3–14 (in Chinese). (杜海燕等：〈國有企業自主權、市場結構和激勵制度〉，《經濟研究》，第1期(1990)，頁 3–14。)

Eatwell, John; Milgate, Murray and Newman, Peter, eds. *The New Palgrave: A Dictionary of Economics*, Chinese edition. Beijing: Economic Science Press, 1992. (伊特韋爾、米爾蓋特和紐曼編：《新帕爾格雷夫經濟學大詞典》。北京：經濟科學出版社，1992)。

Economic Institute of the Chinese Academy of Social Sciences. *The Economic Development of China's Township Enterprises and the Economic System*. Beijing: China Economics Press, 1987 (in Chinese). (中國社會科學院經濟研究所：《中國鄉鎮企業的經濟發展與經濟體制》。北京：中國經濟出版社，1987。)

Fan, Gang. "Two Kinds of Reform Cost and Two Approaches of Reform", *Economic Research*, No. 1 (1993), pp. 3–15 (in Chinese). (樊綱：〈兩種改革成本與兩種改革方式〉，《經濟研究》，第1期(1993)，頁 3–15。)

Fan, Q. and Schaffer, M. E. *Enterprise Reform in Chinese and Polish State-owned Industries*. Research Paper Series No. 11. Washington, DC: Socialist Economic Reform Unit, The World Bank, 1991.

Fei, John and Ranis, Gustav. *Development of the Labor Surplus*

Economy: Theory and Policy. Homewood, III: Richard D. Irwin. Inc, 1964.

Feng, Ruilan and Zhao, Lukuan. *China Urban Employment and Salary*. Beijing: People's Press, 1982 (in Chinese). (馮瑞蘭、趙履寬：《中國城鎮的就業和工資》。北京：人民出版社，1982。)

Food and Agriculture Organization (FAO). "FAOSTAT", at http://www.fao.org.

Freeman, C. *Technology Policy and Economic Performance: Lessons from Japan*. London and New York: Pinter Publishers, 1987.

Fu, Zhengluo, et al. *The Four Little Asian Dragons and the Export-oriented Economy*. Beijing: China Foreign Trade Press, 1990 (in Chinese). (傅政羅等：《亞州"四小龍"與外向型經濟》。北京：中國對外貿易出版社，1990。)

Garnaut, Ross and Ma, Guonan. *Grain in China*. Canberra: East Asia Analytical Unit, Department of Foreign Affairs and Trade, 1993.

Gordon, R. and Li, W. "Chinese Enterprise Behavior Under the Reforms", *American Economic Review, Papers and Proceedings*, Vol. 81 (1991), pp. 202–206.

Griffin, Keith. *The Alternative Strategies for Economic Development*. London: Macmillan, 1989; Chinese edition, Beijing: Economic Science Press, 1992. (格里芬：《可供選擇的發展戰略》。北京：經濟科學出版社，1992。)

Groves, Theodore; Hong, Yongmiao; McMillan, John and Naughton, Barry. *Autonomy and Incentives in Chinese State Enterprises*. Mimeo. UCSD, 1992.

Groves, Theodore., Hong, Yongmian, McMillan, John and Naughton, Barry. "China's Evolving Managerial Labour Market", *Journal of Political Economy*, Vol. 103 (1995), pp. 873–92.

Haggard, S. "The Politics of Industrialization in the Republic of Korea and Taiwan", in Hughes, H. ed. *Achieving Industrialization in Asia*. Cambridge: Cambridge University Press, 1988.

Hall, Thomas E. and Ferguson, J. David. *The Great Depression: An International Disaster of Perverse Economic Policies*. Ann Arbor: The University of Michigan Press, 1998.

Harrold, Peter. "China's Reform Experience to Date" (The World Bank Discussion Paper). Washington, DC: The World Bank, 1992.

Harrold, Roy F. Harrold. "An Essay in Dynamic Theory", *Economic Journal,* Vol. 49, No. 193 (March 1939), pp. 14–33.

Hayami, Yujiro. "A Commentary on the 'East Asian Miracle': Are There Lessons to Be Learned — Review Essay", *Journal of the Japanese and International Economies*, Vol. 10, No. 3 (September 1996), pp. 318–25.

Hayami, Yujiro and Ruttan, Vernon W. *Agricultural Development: An International Perspective.* Baltimore: Johns Hopkins University Press, 1985.

Hoffmann, Walter. *Growth of Industrial Economics.* Manchester: Manchester University Press, 1958.

Hsu, R. C. *Economic Theories in China, 1979–1988.* Cambridge: Cambridge University Press, 1991.

Hu, Heli. "An Estimation of Part of the Rents in China in 1988", in *Corruption: Trading of Power for Money.* Beijing: China Outlook Press, 1989 (in Chinese).（胡和立：〈1988年我國部分租金的估算〉，載《腐敗：貨幣與權力的交換》。北京：中國展望出版社，1989。）

Hu, Heli. "Three Measures for a Clean Government", in *Corruption: Trading of Power for Money.* Beijing: China Outlook Press, 1989 (in Chinese).（胡和立：〈廉政三策〉，載《腐敗：貨幣與權力的交換》。北京：中國展望出版社，1989。）

Hu, Shengyi. *Economic Development and Social Welfare.* Taipei: Zhongyang Wenwu Gongyingshe, 1980 (in Chinese).（胡勝益：《經濟發展與社會福利》。台北：中央文物供應社，1980。）

Hu, Zhuliu. "The Road to Prosperity — How China's Economic Position is Evaluated in the World", *Economic Research Materials*, No. 21 (November 1993), pp. 57–63 (in Chinese).（胡祖六：〈走向富強 —— 國際上怎樣評估中國的經濟地位〉，《經濟研究資料》，第21期（1993年11月），頁57–63。）

Ikeda, Tetsuo and Hu, Xin. *Economic Restructuring in Taiwan and Its Prospects of Development.* Beijing: China Economics Press, 1993 (in Chinese).（池田哲夫、胡欣：《台灣經濟結構重組及其發展前景》。北京：中國經濟出版社，1993。）

Ito, Takatoshi. "Japanese Economic Development: Are Its Features Idiosyncratic or Universal?" Paper presented at the XIth Congress of the International Economic Association at Tunis, 17–22 December 1995.

Ito, Takatoshi. *The Japanese Economy*. Cambridge, MA: The MIT Press, 1982.

James, William E.; Naya, Seiji and Meier, Gerald M. *Asian Development: Economic Success and Policy Lessons*. San Francisco: ICS Press, 1987.

Jefferson, G.; Rawski, T. and Zheng, Yuying. "Growth, Efficiency and Convergence in China's State and Collective Industry", *Economic Development and Cultural Change*, Vol. 40, No. 2 (January 1992), pp. 239–66.

Jiang, Yiwei. "On Enterprise as Base Unit", *China Social Sciences*, No. 1 (1980), pp. 21–36 (in Chinese). (蔣一葦：〈企業本位論〉，《中國社會科學》，第1期（1980），頁21–36。)

Jin, Yaoji. "An Explanation of the East Asian Economic Development from a Cultural Perspective", *Information Newspaper Finance and Economy Monthly*, No. 11 (1987) (in Chinese). (金耀基：〈東亞經濟發展的一個文化詮釋〉，《信報財經月刊》，1987年11月。)

Johnson, C. *MITI and the Japanese Miracle*. Stanford: Stanford University Press, 1982.

Johnson, D. Gale. "WTO and Chinese Agriculture". Paper presented in a seminar at the China Center for Economic Research, Peking University, 23 March 2000.

Jones, Hywel G. *An Introduction to Modern Theories of Economic Growth*. New York: McGraw-Hill, 1976.

Kaldor, N. "Welfare Propositions of Economics and Interpersonal Comparisons of Utility", *Economic Journal*, Vol. 49 (September 1939), pp. 549–51.

"Keeping the Hot Money Out", *The Economist*, 24 January 1998, p. 71.

Kemp, Tom. *Industrialization in the Non-West World*. London: Longman, 1983.

Kemp, Tom. *Modern Industrialization Model —The Soviet Union, Japan and Developing Countries*. Beijing: China Outlook Press, 1985 (in Chinese). (湯姆•肯普：《現代工業化模式 —— 蘇日及發展中國家》。北京：中國展望出版社，1985。)

Kornai, J. *Shortage Economics*. Amsterdam: North-Holland Publishing Company, and New York: Oxford University Press, 1980; Chinese edition, Beijing: Economic Science Press, 1986.（科爾內：《短缺經濟學》。北京：經濟科學出版社，1986。）

Kornai, J. *The Road to a Free Economy*. New York: Norton, 1990.

Krueger, Anne O. *Economic Policy Reform in Developing Countries*. Oxford: Basil Blackwell, 1992.

Krueger, Anne O. *Foreign Trade Regimes and Economic Development: Liberalization Attempts and Consequences*. Cambridge: Cambridge University Press, 1978.

Krueger, Anne O. "The Political Economy of the Rent-seeking Society", *American Economic Review*, Vol. 64, No. 3 (June 1974), pp. 291–303.

Krugman, Paul. "The Myth of Asia's Miracle", *Foreign Affairs*, Vol. 73, No. 6 (November/December 1994), pp. 62–78.

Krugman, Paul. "What Happened to Asia?", at http://web.mit.edlu/krugman/www/DISINTER.html, January 1998.

Kuznetz, Simon. *Economic Growth of Nations: Total Output and Production Structure*. Cambridge, MA: Harvard University Press, 1971.

Lal, Deepak. *Political Economy and Public Policy* (Occasional Paper No. 9). San Francisco: International Center for Economic Growth, 1990.

Lal, Deepak. *The Poverty of Development Economics*. Cambridge, MA: Harvard University Press, 1985.

Lapres, Arthur. "The E.U.-China WTO Deal Compared", at http://www.gyoza.com/lapres.

Lardy, Nicholas R. *China in the World Economy*. Washington, DC: Institute for International Economics, 1994.

Lardy, Nicholas R. *China's Unfinished Economic Revolution*. Washington, DC: Brookings Institution Press, 1998.

Lawrence, Robert Z. and Weinstein, David E. "Trade and Growth: Import-led or Export-led? Evidence from Japan and Korea", in Stiglitz, Joseph E. and Yusuf, Shahid, eds. *Rethinking the East Asia Miracle*. Oxford: Oxford Universtiy Press, 2001.

Lecaillon, Jacques, et al. *Income Distribution and Economic Development*. Geneva: International Labour Office, 1984.

Lees, Francis A. *China Superpower: Requisites for High Growth*. New York: St. Martin's Press, 1997.

Leong, Liew. *The Chinese Economy in Transition: From Plan to Market*. Cheltenham, UK and Brookfield, USA: Edward Elgar, 1997.

Lewis, Arthur. *The Theories of Economic Growth*, Chinese edition. Shanghai: Shanghai Sanlian Bookstore and Shanghai People's Press, 1994.（上海：上海三聯書店、上海人民出版社，1989。）

Lewis, W. A. "Economic Development with Unlimited Supplies of Labour", *Manchester School of Economics and Social Studies*, Vol. 28 (1954), pp. 139–91.

Lewis, W. A. *Economic Dualism*, Chinese edition. Beijing: Beijing Economics Academy Press, 1989.（劉易斯：《二元經濟論》。北京：北京經濟學院出版社，1989。）

Li, Debin. *A Concise Economic History of the PRC (1949–1985)*. Changsha: Hunan People's Press, 1987 (in Chinese).（李德彬：《中華人民共和國經濟史簡編（1949–1985年）》。長沙：湖南人民出版社，1987。）

Li, Jingwen and Zheng, Youjing, eds. *Technological Progress and the Choice of Industrial Structure*. Beijing: Science Press, 1989 (in Chinese).（李京文、鄭友敬編：《技術進步和產業結構選擇》。北京：科學出版社，1989。）

Li, Ming and Yuan, Guoliang. "Debt Financing and Sustainable Development for Firms", *Jingrong Yanjiu*, July 1999, pp. 34–39 (in Chinese).（劉明、袁國良：〈債務融資與上市公司可持續發展〉，《金融研究》，第7期（1999），頁34–39。）

Li, Shantong; Wang, Zhi; Qu, Fan and Wang, Lin. *WTO: China and the World*. Beijing: China Development Press, 2000 (in Chinese).（李善同、王直、翟凡：《WTO：中國與世界》。北京：中國發展出版社，2000。）

Li, Wei. *Rural Surplus and Industrial Capital Accumulation*. Kunming City: Yuannan People's Press, 1993 (in Chinese).（李溦：《農業剩餘與工業化資本積累》。昆明：雲南人民出版社，1993。）

Li, Xiaoxi. "Deflation, Insufficient Demand and Policy Option", *Caimao Jingji*, No. 8 (August 1999), pp. 9–13 (in Chinese).（李曉

西：〈通貨緊縮、需求不足與政策思路〉，《財貿經濟》，第8期（1999年8月），頁9–13。）

Li, Yining. *An Exploratory Study of Economic Structural Reforms*. Beijing: People's Daily Press, 1987 (in Chinese).（厲以寧：《經濟體制改革的探索》。北京：人民日報出版社，1987。）

Liao, Jili. "On China's Reforms of Economic System", in *China Economic Yearbook 1981*, abridged edition. Beijing: Economic Management Press, 1982 (in Chinese).（廖季立：〈關於中國經濟體制改革的問題〉，載《1981年中國經濟年鑑（簡編）》。北京：經濟管理出版社，1982。）

Lin, Justin Yifu. "An Economic Theory of Institutional Change: Induced and Imposed Change", *The Cato Journal*, Vol. 9, No. 1 (1989), pp. 1–33.

Lin, Justin Yifu. "Can China's Mini-bang Succeed?" *Comtemporary Economic Policy*, Vol. 13, No. 1 (Janaury 1995), pp. 10–14.

Lin, Justin Yifu. "Collectivization and China's Agricultural Crisis in 1959–1961", *Journal of Political Economy*, Vol. 98, No. 6 (December 1990), pp. 1228–52.

Lin, Justin Yifu. "Deepening Market-oriented Reform is the Only Way to Solve the Current Peasant Problem", *Economic Research*, No. 11 (1998), pp. 19–23 (in Chinese).（林毅夫：〈深化市場改革是解決當前農民問題的關鍵〉，《經濟研究》，第11期（1998），頁19–23。）

Lin, Justin Yifu. "Development Strategy, Viability and Economic Convergence". Inaugural D. Gale Johnson Lecture, Department of Economics, the University of Chicago, 14 May 2001.

Lin, Justin Yifu. *Institution, Technology and China's Agricultural Development*. Shanghai: Shanghai Sanlian Bookstore, 1992 (in Chinese).（林毅夫：《制度、技術與中國農業發展》。上海：上海三聯書店，1992。）

Lin, Justin Yifu. "Prohibition of Factor Market Exchanges and Technological Choice in Chinese Agriculture", *Journal of Development Studies*, Vol. 27, No. 4 (July 1991), pp. 1–15.

Lin, Justin Yifu. "Rural Reforms and Agricultural Growth in China", *American Economic Review*, Vol. 82, No. 1 (March 1992), pp. 34–51.

Lin, Justin Yifu. "Supervision, Peer Pressure, and Incentive in a Labor-managed Firm", *China Economic Review*, No. 2 (October 1991), pp. 213–29.

Lin, Jusitn Yifu. "The Current Deflation in China: Causes and Policy Options", *Asian Pacific Journal of Economics and Business*, Vol. 4, No. 2 (December 2000), pp. 4–21.

Lin, Justin Yifu. "The Household Responsibility System in China's Agricultural Reform: A Theoretical and Empirical Study", *Economic Development and Cultural Change*, Vol. 36, No. 3 (April 1988) (Supplement), pp. S199–S224.

Lin, Justin Yifu. "The Needham Puzzle: Why the Industrial Revolution Did Not Originate in China", *Economic Development and Cultural Change*, Vol. 43, No. 2 (January 1995), pp. 269–92.

Lin, Justin Yifu. "The Outlook of China's Economy at the New Millennium", in Lin, Justin Yifu, Hai, Wen; and Ping, Xinqiao, eds. *Economic Research on China*. Beijing: Peking University Press, 1999 (in Chinese). (林毅夫：〈展望新千年的中國經濟〉，載林毅夫、海聞、平新喬主編：《中國經濟研究：北京大學中國經濟研究中心內部討論稿選編1995–1999》。北京：北京大學出版社，2000。)

Lin, Justin Yifu. "What is the Direction of China's Financial Reform?", in Hai, Wen and Lu, Feng, eds. *China: Economic Transition and Economic Policy*. Beijing: Peking University Press, 2000 (in Chinese). (林毅夫：〈我國金融體制改革的方向是什麼？〉，載海聞、盧鋒主編：《中國：經濟轉型與經濟政策》。北京：北京大學出版社，2000。)

Lin, Justin Yifu. "WTO Accession and China's Agriculture", *China Economic Review*, Vol. 11, No. 4 (2000), pp. 405–408.

Lin, Justin Yifu. "WTO Accession and China's SOE Reform", in Lee, Kyung Tae; Lin, Justin Yifu and Kim, Si Joong, eds. *China's Integration with the World Economy: Repercussions of China's Accession to the WTO*. Seoul: Korea Institute for International Economic Policy, 2001.

Lin, Justin Yifu. "WTO Accession and Financial Market Reform in China", *The Cato Journal*, Vol. 21, No. 1 (Spring/Summer 2001), pp. 13–19.

Lin, Justin Yifu and Cai, Fang. "On China's Inflation, Its Prevention and Control", *Newsletter on Development Research*, No. 2 (1989) (in Chinese).（林毅夫、蔡昉：〈論我國通貨膨脹及其治理〉，《發展研究通訊》，第2期（1989）。）

Lin, Justin Yifu and Hu, Shudong. "To be a Member of WTO: Challenges and Opportunities for China". Working paper of China Center for Economic Research, Peking University, No. C2000004, March 2000.

Lin, Justin Yifu and Li, Zhou. "Choice of Development Strategy is the Key to Economic Development — Perspective View of the Successes and Failures of Economic Development in Capitalist Countries after World War II", *Comparison of Economic and Social Systems*, No. 1 (1992), pp. 1–5 (in Chinese).（林毅夫、李周：〈戰略抉擇是經濟發展的關鍵 — 二戰以後資本主義國家經濟發展成敗的透視〉，《經濟社會體制比較》，第1期（1992），頁1–5。）

Lin, Justin Yifu and Liu, Peilin. "The 10th Five-year Plan and the SOE Reform", *CCER Newsletter*, No. 38 (August 2001).（林毅夫、劉培林：〈十五計劃和國企改革〉，《中國經濟研究中心簡報》，第38期（2001年8月）。）

Lin, Justin Yifu and Tan, Guofu. "Policy Burdens, Accountability and Soft-budget Constraint", *American Economic Review*, Vol. 89, No. 2 (May 1999), pp. 426–31.

Lin, Justin Yifu; Cai, Fang and Li, Zhou. "Competition, Policy Burdens and State-owned Enterprises Reform", *American Economic Review,* Vol. 88, No. 2 (May 1998), pp. 422–27.

Lin, Justin Yifu; Cai, Fang and Li, Zhou. "Consequences des Reformes Economicques sur les Disparites Regionales en Chine", *Revue d'Economie du Development*, Vol. 1, No. 2 (1999), pp. 7–32.

Lin, Justin Yifu; Cai, Fang and Li, Zhou. *State-owned Enterprise Reform in China*. Hong Kong: Chinese University Press, 2001.

Lin, Justin Yifu; Cai, Fang; Li, Zhou and Shen, Gaoming. "The Major Problems in the Current Economic Reform and Development and Their Solutions", *Study Materials for Economists*, No. 23 (1993) (in Chinese).（林毅夫、蔡昉、李周、沈高明：〈當前經濟改革

與發展中的主要問題及其對策〉，《經濟工作者學習資料》，第23期（1993）。）

Lin, Justin Yifu; Shen, Minggao and Zhou, Hao. *Agricultural Research Priorities: An Demand and Supply Analysis of Grain Technology in China*. Beijing: Agriculture Press, 1996 (in Chinese).（林毅夫、沈明高、周浩：《農業科研優先序研究》。北京：農業出版社，1996。）

Lipton, David and Sachs, Jeffrey. "Creating a Market Economy in Eastern Europe: The Case of Poland", *Brookings Papers on Economic Activities*, Vol. 2 (1990), pp. 293–341.

List, Georg Friedrich. *The National System of Political Economics,* Chinese edition. Beijing: Commercial Press, 1961.（李斯特：《政治經濟學的國民體系》。北京：商務印書館，1961。）

Liu, Guoguang. "On China's Economic Development Strategy", in *Selected Works of Liu Guoguang*. Shanxi: Shanxi People's Press, 1986 (in Chinese).（劉國光：〈中國經濟發展戰略問題〉，載《劉國光選集》。山西：山西人民出版社，1986。）

Liu, Guoguang. "On the Change-over of Two Models", *World Economic Herald*, 26 August 1985.

Liu, Guoguan, ed. *On China's Economic Reform Models*. Beijing: China Social Science Press, 1988 (in Chinese).（劉國光主編：《中國經濟體制改革的模式研究》。北京：中國社會科學出版社，1988。）

Liu, Guoguang and Zhao, Renwei. "Some Problems Concerning the Relationship between Planning and Market", *Red Flag*, No. 9 (1979), pp. 20–26 (in Chinese).（劉國光、趙人偉：〈計劃和市場關係的幾個問題〉，《紅旗》，第9期（1979），頁20–26。）

Liu, Hongru and Li, Zhiling. "The Reform of China's Financial System and the Role of the Stock Market", *Jingrong Yanjiu*, August 1999, pp. 19–26 (in Chinese).（劉鴻儒、李志玲：〈中國融資體制的變革及股票市場的地位〉，《金融研究》，第8期（1999年8月），頁19–26。）

Lu, Feng. "The Comparative Advantage and the China's Structure of Grain Trade: The Third Choice for Restructuring China's Agriculture Policy", in Lin, Justin Yifu, Hai, Wen; and Ping, Xinqiao, eds. *Economic Research on China*. Beijing: Peking University Press,

1999 (in Chinese). (盧鋒：〈比較優勢與中國糧食貿易結構：中國糧食政策調整的第三種選擇〉，載林毅夫、海聞、平心喬主編：《中國經濟研究：北京大學中國經濟研究中心內部討論稿選編1995–1999》。北京：北京大學出版社，1999。)

Lu, Wen. "The Development of the Property Right System Reform in the TVEs", *Rural Economy in China*, No. 11 (1997), pp. 4–9 (in Chinese). (盧文：〈鄉鎮企業產權制度改革的發展〉，《中國農村經濟》，第11期 (1997)，頁4–9。)

Lu, Zhongyuan. "Actively Push Forward the Reform of the Small State-owned Enterprises", *China Industrial Economy*, No. 4 (1996), pp. 30–32 (in Chinese). (盧中原：〈積極推進國有小型企業改革〉，《中國工業經濟》，第4期 (1996)，頁30–32。)

Luo, Hanxian. *Economic Change in Rural China*. Beijing: New World Press, 1985.

Ma, Hong, ed. *Dictionary of Economic Affairs in Contemporary China*. Beijing: China Social Sciences Press, 1982 (in Chinese). (馬洪主編：《現代中國經濟事典》。北京：中國社會科學出版社，1982。)

Ma, Hong and Sun, Shangqing, eds. *China's Economic Situation and Prospects (1991–1992)*. Beijing: China Development Press, 1992 (in Chinese). (馬洪、孫尚清主編：《中國經濟形勢與展望 (1991–1992)》。北京：中國發展出版社，1992。)

Ma, Hong and Sun, Shangqing, eds. *China's Economic Structural Problems*. Beijing: People's Press, 1981 (in Chinese). (馬洪、孫尚清主編：《中國經濟結構問題研究》。北京：人民出版社，1981。)

Ma, Hong and Sun, Shangqing, eds. *Contemporary Dictionary of Chinese Economic Events*. Beijing: China Finance and Economics Press, 1993 (in Chinese). (馬洪、孫尚清主編：《現代中國經濟大事典》。北京：中國財政經濟出版社，1993。)

Maddison, Augus. *Chinese Economy: Performance in the Long Run*. Paris: OECD, 1998.

Maddison, Angus. *Monitoring the World Economy, 1820–1992*. Paris: OECD, 1995.

Mao, Zedong. *Collected Works of Mao Zedong*, Vol. 5. Beijing: People's Press, 1977 (in Chinese). (毛澤東：《毛澤東選集》，第5卷。北京：人民出版社，1977。)

"Mao Zedong's Visit to the Villages in Shangdong", *People's Daily*, 13 August 1958, p. 1 (in Chinese).（〈毛澤東視察山東農村〉，《人民日報》，1958年8月13日，頁1。）

Mao, Zong. "What were Covered by 'Over-capacity'?", *China's National Situation and Power*, No. 4 (1999), pp. 21–22 (in Chinese).（毛宗：〈"過剩"掩蓋了什麼？〉，《中國國情國力》，第4期（1999），頁21–22。）

Mckinnon, R. I. "Gradual versus Rapid Liberalization in Socialist Economics: Financial Policies and Macroeconomic Stability in China and Russia Compared", in *Proceedings of the World Bank Annual Conference on Development Economics, 1993*. Washington, DC: The World Bank, 1993.

McMillan, J. and Naughton, B. "How to Reform a Planned Economy: Lessons from China", *Oxford Review of Economic Policy*, Vol. 8, No. 1 (1992), pp. 130–43.

Meier, G. M. *Leading Issues in Economic Development*. New York: Oxford University Press, 1998.

Meier, G. M. and Seers, D. *Pioneers of the Development Economics*. Beijing: Economic Science Press, 1988 (in Chinese).（邁耶、西爾斯編，譚崇台等譯：《發展經濟學的先驅》。北京：經濟科學出版社，1988。）

Murphy, K.; Schleifer, A. and Vishny, R. "The Transition to a Market Economy: Pitfall of Partial Reform", *Quarterly Journal of Economics*, Vol. 107, No. 3 (1992), pp. 889–906.

Murrel, P. and Wang, Y. "When Privatization Should Be Delayed: The Effect of Communist Legacies on Organizational and Institutional Reforms", *Journal of Comparative Economics*, Vol. 17 (1993), p. 385.

National Bureau of Statistics of China. *20 Years of Magnificent Achievement*. Beijing: China Statistics Press, 1998 (in Chinese).（國家統計局編：《成就輝煌的20年》。北京：中國統計出版社，1998。）

National Bureau of Statistics of China. *A Statistical Survey of China, 1995*. Beijing: China Statistics Press, 1995 (in Chinese).（國家統計局編：《中國統計摘要（1995）》。北京：中國統計出版社，1995。）

National Bureau of Statistics of China. *China Development Report, 1998*. Beijing: China Statistics Press, 1998 (in Chinese). (國家統計局編：《98中國發展報告》。北京：中國統計出版社，1998。)

National Bureau of Statistics of China. *China Statistical Abstract, 1993*. Beijing: China Statistics Press, 1993 (in Chinese). (國家統計局編：《中國統計摘要 (1993)》。北京：中國統計出版社，1993。)

National Bureau of Statistics of China. *China Statistical Abstract, 1999*. Beijing: China Statistics Press, 1999 (in Chinese). (國家統計局編：《中國統計摘要 (1999)》。北京：中國統計出版社，1999。)

National Bureau of Statistics of China. *China Statistical Abstract, 2000*. Beijing: Statistics Press, 2000 (in Chinese). (國家統計局編：《中國統計摘要 (2000)》。北京：中國統計出版社，2000。)

National Bureau of Statistics of China. *China Statistical Abstract, 2001*. Beijing: Statistics Press, 2001 (in Chinese). (國家統計局編：《中國統計摘要 (2001)》。北京：中國統計出版社，2001。)

National Bureau of Statistics of China. *China Statistical Yearbook, 1987*. Beijing: China Statistics Press, 1987 (in Chinese). (國家統計局編：《中國統計年鑑 (1987)》。北京：中國統計出版社，1987。)

National Bureau of Statistics of China. *China Statistical Yearbook, 1989*. Beijing: China Statistics Press, 1989 (in Chinese). (國家統計局編：《中國統計年鑑 (1989)》。北京：中國統計出版社，1989。)

National Bureau of Statistics of China. *China Statistical Yearbook, 1992*. Beijing: China Statistics Press, 1992 (in Chinese). (國家統計局編：《中國統計年鑑 (1992)》。北京：中國統計出版社，1992。)

National Bureau of Statistics of China. *China Statistical Yearbook, 1993*. Beijing: China Statistics Press, 1993 (in Chinese). (國家統計局編：《中國統計年鑑 (1993)》。北京：中國統計出版社，1993。)

National Bureau of Statistics of China. *China Statistical Yearbook,*

1994. Beijing: China Statistics Press, 1994 (in Chinese).（國家統計局編：《中國統計年鑑（1994）》。北京：中國統計出版社，1994。）

National Bureau of Statistics of China. *China Statistical Yearbook, 1995*. Beijing: China Statistics Press, 1995 (in Chinese).（國家統計局編：《中國統計年鑑（1995）》。北京：中國統計出版社，1995。）

National Bureau of Statistics of China. *China Statistical Yearbook, 1997*. Beijing: China Statistics Press, 1997 (in Chinese).（國家統計局編：《中國統計年鑑（1997）》。北京：中國統計出版社，1997。）

National Bureau of Statistics of China. *China Statistical Yearbook, 1998*. Beijing: China Statistics Press, 1998 (in Chinese).（國家統計局編：《中國統計年鑑（1998）》。北京：中國統計出版社，1998。）

National Bureau of Statistics of China. *China Statistical Yearbook, 1999*. Beijing: China Statistics Press, 1999 (in Chinese).（國家統計局編：《中國統計年鑑（1999）》。北京：中國統計出版社，1999。）

National Bureau of Statistics of China. *China Statistical Yearbook, 2001*. Beijing: China Statistics Press, 2001 (in Chinese).（國家統計局編：《中國統計年鑑（2001）》。北京：中國統計出版社，2001。）

National Bureau of Statistics of China. *China's Industrial Economic Statistical Data*. Beijing: China Statistics Press, 1987 (in Chinese).（國家統計局編：《中國工業經濟統計資料》。北京：中國統計出版社，1987。）

National Bureau of Statistics of China. *The Statistical Data of Fixed Asset Investment in China, 1950–1985*. Beijing: China Statistics Press, 1987 (in Chinese).（國家統計局編：《中國固定資產投資統計資料（1950–1985）》。北京：中國統計出版社，1987。）

National Bureau of Statistics of China, Comprehensive Division. "Assessment of Current Money Supply Growth and Policy Recommendations", *Statistical Data*, No. 30 (October 1999), pp. 3–8 (in Chinese).（國家統計局綜合司：〈對當前貨幣供應量增速的判斷和建議〉，《統計資料（內參版）》，第30期（1999年10月），頁3–8。）

National Bureau of Statistics of China, National Economic Accounting Division. *The Gross Domestic Product of China, 1952–1995*. Beijing: Northeast Finance University Press, 1997 (in Chinese). (中國國家統計局國民經濟核算司：《中國國內生產總值核算歷史資料1952–1995》。北京：東北財經大學出版社，1997。)

National Bureau of Statistics of China, National Economic Balance Statistics Division. *A Compilation of National Income Statistics Data (1949–1985)*. Beijing: China Statistics Press, 1987 (in Chinese). (國家統計局國民經濟平衡統計司編：《國民收入統計資料匯編 (1949–1985)》。北京：中國統計出版社，1987。)

Newbery, D. M. "Transformation in Mature Versus Emerging Economies: Why Hungary Has Been Less Successful Than China?" Paper presented to the "International Symposium on the Theoretical and Practical Issues of the Transition towards the Market Economy in China", Hainan, China, 1–3 July 1993.

Nolan, Peter. *China's Rise, Russia's Fall: Politics, Economics and Planning in the Transition From Stalinism*. New York: St. Martin's Press, 1995.

North, D. C. *Institutions, Institutional Change and Economic Performance*. Cambridge: Cambridge University Press, 1990.

Ohlin, Bertil. *Interregional and International Trade*. Cambridge, MA: Harvard University Press, 1968.

Overholt, William H. *The Rise of China: How Economic Reform is Creating a New Superpower*. New York and London: W.W. Norton Company, 1993.

Palgrave, R. H., ed. *Dictionary of Political Economy*. New York: Macmillan, 1896.

People's Bank of China. *Statistical Quarterly*, Vol. 4 (1998) (in Chinese). (中國人民銀行：《中國人民銀行統計季報》，第4期 (1998) 。)

Perkins, Dwight H. "China's Gradual Approach to Market Reform". Paper presented at the "Conference on Comparative Experiences of Economic Reform and Post-Socialist Transformation", El Escorial, Spain, 6–8 July 1992.

Preobrazhensky, E. A. *New Economics,* Chinese edition. Beijing: Sanlian Bookstore, 1984 (in Chinese). (普列奧•布拉任斯基：《新經濟學》。北京：三聯書店，1984。)

Qian, Y. Y. and Xu, C. G. "Why China's Economic Reforms Differ: The M-Form Hierarchy and Entry/Expansion of the Non-state Sector", *The Economics of Transition*, Vol. 1, No. 2 (June 1993), pp. 135–70.

Ranis, Gustav and Syed, Mahmood. *The Political Economy of Development Policy Change*. Cambridge: Blackwell, 1992.

Rawski, Thomas G. *Economic Growth and Employment in China*. Oxford: Oxford University Press, published for the World Bank, 1979.

Ricardo, David. "Political Economy and the Principle of Taxation", in Sraffa, Piero, ed. *The Works and Correspondence of David Ricardo*, Vol. 1. Cambridge: Cambridge University Press, 1951.

Riedel, James. "The Transition to Market Economy in Vietnam", *HKCER Letters*, No. 35 (November 1995).

Riedel, James and Comer, Bruce. "Transition to Market Economy in Viet Nam", in Woo, Wing Thye; Parker, Stephen and Sachs, Jeffrey D., eds. *Economies in Transition: Comparing Asia and Europe*. Cambridge, MA: MIT Press, 1997.

Rodrik, D. *The New Global Economy and Developing Countries: Making Openness Work*. Washington, DC: Overseas Development Council, 1999.

Rodriquez, Francisco and Rodrik, D. "Trade Policy and Economic Growth: A Skeptic's Guide to the Cross-national Evidence", in Bernanke, B. and Rogoff, K. *NBER Macroeconomics Annual 2000*. Cambridge, MA: MIT Press, 2000.

Romer, Paul. "Increasing Returns and Long-Run Growth", *Journal of Political Economy*, Vol. 94, No. 5 (1986), pp. 1002–1037.

Rural Development Research Center. *Rural Reform*, No. 125 (1987) (in Chinese). (農村發展研究中心：《農村改革》，第125期（1985）。)

Sachs, J. and Woo, W. "Structural Factors in the Economic Reforms of China, Eastern Europe and the Former Soviet Union". Paper presented at the Economic Policy Panel Meeting, Brussels, Belgium, 22–23 October 1993.

Sah, Raj K. and Stiglitz, Joseph E. *Peasants Versus City-dwellers*. Oxford: Clarendon Press, 1992.

Sah, Raj K. and Stiglitz, Joseph E. "Price Scissors and the Structure of the Economy", *The Quarterly Journal of Economics*, No. 102 (1987), pp. 109–34.

Selected Documents of the 14th CPC National Congress. Beijing: People's Press, 1992 (in Chinese).（《中國共產黨第十四次全國代表大會文件匯編》。北京：人民出版社，1992。）

Sheng, Bin and Feng, Lun. *Census Report on China*. Shenyang: Liaonin People's Press, 1991 (in Chinese).（盛斌、馮侖主編：《中國國情報告》。瀋陽：遼寧人民出版社，1991。）

Shinohara, M. *Industrial Growth, Trade, and Dynamic Patterns in the Japanese Economy*. Tokyo: University of Tokyo Press, 1982.

Shirk, Susan L. *The Political Logic of Economic Reform in China*. Berkeley: University of California Press, 1933.

Singh, I. J. *China and Central and Eastern Europe: Is There a Professional Schizophrenia on Socialist Reform?* Research Paper Series No. 17. Washington, DC: Socialist Economics Reform Unit, The World Bank, 1991.

Solow, Robert M. *Growth Theory: An Exposition*. Oxford: Oxford University Press, 1988.

State Administration for Exchange Control. *Exchange Rate Manual*. Beijing: China Finance Press, 1986 (in Chinese).（國家外匯管理局編：《匯價手冊》。北京：中國金融出版社，1986。）

State Commission for the Restructuring of the Economic System, ed. *China's Economic Restructuring Yearbook, 1992*. Beijing: Reform Press, 1992 (in Chinese).（國家經濟體制改革委員會編：《中國經濟體制改革年鑒，1992》。北京：改革出版社，1992。）

State Planning Commission, Price Administration Bureau. "The Weights and Changes of Three Patterns of Prices", *Price in China*, No. 12 (1997), pp. 31–34 (in Chinese).（國家計委價格管理司：〈三種價格形式所占比重及其變化〉，《中國物價》，第12期（1997），頁31–34。）

State Planning Council, Research Group on Macroeconomic Situation. "Managing Deflation with All Efforts", *People's Daily*, 28 June 1999, p. 9 (in Chinese).（國家計委宏觀研究院形勢課題組：〈集中力量治理通貨緊縮〉，《人民日報》，1999年6月28日，頁9。）

State Planning Council, Research Group on Macroeconomic Situation. "Proposal for Stopping Deflation", *People's Daily*, 5 July 1999 (in Chinese). (國家計委宏觀研究院形勢課題組：〈遏制通貨緊縮的對策建議〉，《人民日報》，1999年7月5日，頁9。)

Su, Xing. *The Socialist Transformation of Agriculture in China*. Beijing: People's Press, 1980 (in Chinese). (蘇星：《我國農業的社會主義改造》。北京：人民出版社，1980。)

Sun, Peijun, ed. *A Comparative Study on China's and India's Economic Development*. Beijing: Peking University Press, 1991 (in Chinese). (孫培均主編：《中印經濟發展比較研究》。北京：北京大學出版社，1991。)

Sun, Tanzhen and Zhu, Gang. "Analysis on China's Finance Outside the System in the Towns and Villages", *Economic Research*, No. 9 (1993), pp. 38–44 (in Chinese). (孫潭鎮、朱鋼：〈我國鄉鎮制度外財政分析〉，《經濟研究》，第9期（1993），頁38–44。)

Sung, Y. "An Appraisal of China's Foreign Trade Policy, 1950–1992", in Srinivasan, T. N., ed. *The Comparative Experience of Agricultural and Trade Reforms in China and India*. San Francisco: International Center for Economic Growth, 1993.

Sung, Yeung Kwack. "The Economic Development of the Republic of Korea, 1965–81", in Lau, Lawrence J., ed. *Models of Development*, revised and expanded edition. San Francisco: ICS Press, 1990.

"The Central Bank Lowered the Interest Rates Seven Times", *China Security News*, 12 June 1999, p. 1 (in Chinese). (〈央行七次降息對照〉，《中國證券報》，1999年6月12日，頁1。)

Todaro, Michael P. *Economic Development of the Third World*. New York & London: Longman Inc., 1985; Chinese edition, Beijing: China People's University Press, 1988. (托達羅：《第三世界的經濟發展》。北京：中國人民大學出版社，1988。)

Tsiang, S. C. "The Economic Take-off of the Four Little Dragons in Asia", *China Times* (Taiwan), 29 March 1984 (in Chinese). (蔣碩傑：〈亞洲四條龍的經濟起飛〉，台灣《中國時報》，1984年3月29日。)

Tsiang, S. C. "The Implications of Taiwan's Economic Development". *China Times* (Taiwan), 13 June 1983 (in Chinese). (蔣碩

傑：〈臺灣經濟發展的啟示〉，台灣《中國時報》，1983年6月13日。）

United Nations, The, Industrial Development Organization. *Basics and Trends of Industrialization in World Countries and Regions.* Beijing: China Foreign Translation Publishing Co., 1980 (in Chinese).（聯合國工業發展組織：《世界各國工業化概況和趨向》。北京：中國對外翻譯出版公司，1980。）

Wade, Robert. *Governing the Market: Economic Theory and the Role of Government in East Asian Industrialization.* Princeton: Princeton University Press, 1990.

Walters, A. "Misapprehensions on Privatisation", *International Economic Insights,* Vol. 2, No. 1 (1991).

Wang, Dafu, ed. *Commerce in the Transitional Period.* Shanghai: New Knowledge Press, 1955 (in Chinese).（王達夫編著：《過渡時期的商業》。上海：新知出版社，1955。）

Wang, Huijiong and Yang, Guanghui. *Possibility and Options for China's Economic Structural Changes and Growth.* Beijing: Meteorological Press, 1984 (in Chinese).（王慧炯、楊光輝主編：《中國經濟結構變化與增長的可能性和選擇方案》。北京：氣象出版社，1984。）

Wang, Y. *Communist Legacy, Pattern of Post Communism Organization and the Problem of Transition.* Mimeo. Minnesota: Industrial Relations Center, University of Minnesota, 1992.

Weber, Max. *The Protestant Ethic and the Spirit of Capitalism.* London: Harper, 1991.

Website at www.worldbank.org/data/countrydata/countrydata.html.

"When China Wakes, A Survey of China", *The Economist,* 28 November 1992.

White House Office of Public Liaison. *Summary of U.S.-China Bilateral WTO Agreement,* available at the website of U.S.-China Business Council at www.uschina.org.

Whitesell, R. and Barreto, H. *Estimation of Output Loss from Allocative Inefficiency: Comparisons of the Soviet Union and the U.S.* Research Memorandum RM-109. Center for Development Economics, Williams College, 1988.

Wilber, Charles, ed. *The Political Economy of Development and*

Underdevelopment. New York: Random House, 1979; Chinese edition, Beijing: China Social Sciences Press, 1984.（查爾斯•威爾伯主編：《發達與不發達問題的政治經濟學》。北京：中國社會科學出版社，1984。）

Woo, J. E. *Race to the Swift: State and Finance in Korean Industrialization*. New York: Columbia University Press, 1991.

Woo, W. T. "The Art of Reforming Centrally-planned Economies: Comparing China, Poland and Russia". Paper presented at the "Conference on the Transition of Centrally-planned Economies in Pacific Asia", Asia Foundation in San Francisco, 7–8 May 1993.

World Bank, The. *Annual Conference on Development Economics, 1993*. Washington, DC: The World Bank, 1993.

World Bank, The. *China: Issues for Long Term Development and Plans*. Beijing: China Finance and Economics Press, 1985 (in Chinese).（世界銀行1984年經濟考察團：《中國：長期發展的問題和方案》。北京：中國財政經濟出版社，1985。）

World Bank, The. *East Asian Miracle*. Beijing, China Finance and Economics Press, 1995 (in Chinese).（世界銀行：《東亞的奇蹟》。北京：中國財經經濟出版社，1995。）

World Bank, The. *How to Manage Technological Development, Some Questions for China to Consider*. Beijing, Meteorological Press, 1984 (in Chinese).（世界銀行：《如何管理技術發展：可供中國考慮的一些問題》。北京：氣象出版社，1984。）

World Bank, The. *PR China: Development of Socialist Economy*. Washington, DC: The World Bank, 1983.

World Bank, The. *Reform and the Role of Planning in the 1990s*. Washington, DC: The World Bank, 1992.

World Bank, The. *The Chinese Economy: Fighting Inflation, Deepening Reforms*, Vol. I. Report No. 15288-CNA. Washington, DC: The World Bank, 1996.

World Bank, The. *The East Asian Miracle: Economic Growth and Public Policy*. New York: Oxford University Press, 1993.

World Bank, The. *The World Bank Report, 1985*. Oxford: Oxford University Press, 1985.

World Bank, The. *World Development Report, 1983*. Beijing: China Finance and Economics Press, 1983 (in Chinese).（世界銀行：

《世界發展報告(1983)》。北京：中國財政經濟出版社，1983。)

World Bank, The. *World Development Report, 1986*. Beijing: China Finance and Economics Press, 1986 (in Chinese). (世界銀行：《世界發展報告(1986)》。北京：中國財政經濟出版社，1986。)

World Bank, The. *World Development Report, 1988*. Oxford: Oxford University Press, 1988; Chinese edition, Beijing: China Finance and Economics Press, 1988. (世界銀行：《世界發展報告(1988)》。北京：中國財政經濟出版社，1988。)

World Bank, The. *World Development Report, 1989*. Oxford: Oxford University Press, 1989.

World Bank, The. *World Development Report, 1990*. Beijing: China Finance and Economics Press, 1990 (in Chinese). (世界銀行：《世界發展報告(1990)》。北京：中國財政經濟出版社，1990。)

World Bank, The. *World Development Report, 1991*. Beijing: China Finance and Economics Press, 1991 (in Chinese). (世界銀行：《世界發展報告(1991)》。北京：中國財政經濟出版社，1991。)

World Bank, The. *World Development Report, 1992*. Beijing: China Finance and Economics Press, 1992 (in Chinese). (世界銀行：《世界發展報告(1992)》。北京：中國財政經濟出版社，1992。)

World Bank, The. *World Development Report, 1993*. Oxford: Oxford University Press, 1993; Chinese edition, Beijing: China Finance and Economics Press, 1993. (世界銀行：《世界發展報告(1993)》。北京：中國財政經濟出版社，1993。)

World Bank, The. *World Development Report, 1994*. Beijing: China Finance and Economics Press, 1994 (in Chinese). (世界銀行：《世界發展報告(1994)》。北京：中國財政經濟出版社，1994。)

World Bank, The. *World Development Report, 1995*. Beijing: China Finance and Economics Press, 1995 (in Chinese). (世界銀行：《世界發展報告(1995)》。北京：中國財政經濟出版社，1995。)

World Bank, The. *World Development Report, 1996*. Beijing: China Finance and Economics Press, 1996 (in Chinese). (世界銀行：

《世界發展報告(1996)》。北京：中國財政經濟出版社，1996。)

World Bank, The. *World Development Report, 1997.* Beijing: China Finance and Economics Press, 1997 (in Chinese).(世界銀行：《世界發展報告(1997)》。北京：中國財政經濟出版社，1997。)

World Bank, The. *World Development Report, 2000/2001.* Oxford: Oxford University Press, 2001.

World Bank, The. *World Table, 1992.* Baltimore: Johns Hopkins University Press, 1992.

World Bank, The, 1984 Economic Study Tour. *China: Long-term Issues and Options.* Washington, DC: The World Bank, 1985; Chinese edition, Beijing: China Finance and Economics Press, 1987. (世界銀行1984年經濟考察團：《中國：長期發展的問題和方案》。北京：中國財政經濟出版社，1987。)

Wu, Harry Xiaoying. *Measuring China's GDP* (EAAU Briefing Paper No. 8). Sydney: Department of Foreign Affairs and Trade of Australia, 1997.

Wu, Jinglian, Li, Jiansge and Ding, Ningning. "Current Economic Development Stage and Basic Contradictions of China's Economy", *Management World*, No. 1 (1987), pp. 1–18 (in Chinese). (吳敬璉、李劍閣、丁寧寧：〈中國當前的經濟發展階段和基本矛盾〉，《管理世界》，第1期(1987)，頁1–18。)

Wu, Jinglian, Zhou, Xiaochuan, et al. *Overall Design of China's Economic Reform.* Beijing: China Prospects Press, 1990 (in Chinese). (吳敬璉、周小川等：《中國經濟改革的整體設計》。北京：中國展望出版社，1990。)

Xie, Baisan. *Economic Policies and Their Theories in Contemporary China*, revised edition. Beijing: Chinese People's University Press, 1992 (in Chinese). (謝百三：《當代中國的若干經濟政策及其理論》(增訂本)。北京：中國人民大學出版社，1992。)

Xie, Ping. "Analysis of China's Financial Capital Structure", *Economics Research*, No. 11 (1992), p. 34 (in Chinese). (謝平：〈中國金融資產結構分析〉，《經濟研究》，第11期(1992)，頁34。)

Xie, Ping and Shen, Bingxi. "Deflation and Monetary Policy",

Economic Research, No. 8 (1999), pp. 14–22 (in Chinese). (《經濟研究》，第8期（1999），頁14–22。)

Xinhau Daily Telegraph, 6 January 1994 (in Chinese). (《新華每日電訊》，1994年1月6日。)

Xinhua Monthly, various issues. Beijing: People's Press, 1996–99 (in Chinese). (《新華月報》。北京：人民出版社，1996–99各期。)

Xu, Tianqing. *World Pattern and the Economic Development Strategy of China — The Theoretical Meditation at the Turn of the Century*. Beijing: Economic and Science Press, 1998 (in Chinese). (徐滇慶：《世界格局與中國經濟發展策略 —— 世紀之交的理論思考》。北京：經濟科學出版社，1998。)

Xue, Muqiao. *A Study of Problems Concerning China's Socialist Economy*. Beijing: People's Press, 1979 (in Chinese). (薛暮橋：《中國社會主義經濟問題研究》。北京：人民出版社，1979。)

Yang, Jianbai. "Speed, Structure and Efficiency", *Economic Research*, No. 9 (1991), pp. 37–44 (in Chinese). (楊堅白：〈速度・結構・效率〉，《經濟研究》，第9期（1991），頁37–44。)

Yang, Peixin. *Contract System — An Inevitable Road to Prosperity of Enterprises*. Beijing: China Economics Press, 1990 (in Chinese). (楊培新：《承包制 —— 企業發達必由之路》。北京：中國經濟出版社，1990。)

Yi, Gang. "China's Financial Assets: Structural Analysis and Policy Implications", in Hai, Wen; Lu, Feng and Ping, Xinqiao, eds. *Economic Research on China*. Beijing: Peking University Press, 1999 (in Chinese). 易綱：〈中國金融資產結構分析及政策含義〉，載海聞、盧峰和平新喬編：《中國經濟研究》。北京：北京大學出版社，1999。)

Yu Guangyuan, ed. *ABC of Socialist Economic Construction*, Vol. 3. Jiangxi: Jiangxi People's Press, 1984 (in Chinese). (于光遠主編：《社會主義經濟建設常識》(第3冊)。江西：江西人民出版社，1984。)

Yu, Guangyuan, ed. *China's Socialist Modernization*. Beijing: Foreign Languages Press, 1984.

Yu, Yongding. "Breaking the Vicious Cycle of Deflation: A New Challenge to China's Economic Development", *Economic Research*,

No. 7 (1999), pp. 3–9 (in Chinese). (《經濟研究》，第7期 (1999)，頁3–9。)

Yusuf, S. *The Rise of China's Non-state Sector*. Mimeo. Washington, DC: The World Bank, 1993.

Zhao, Dexin, ed. *The Economic History of the PRC*. Zhengzhou: Henan People's Press, 1989 (in Chinese). (趙德馨主編：《中華人民共和國經濟史》。鄭州：河南人民出版社，1989。)

Zhao, Ziyang. *Advance Along the Socialist Road with Chinese Characteristics*. Beijing: People's Press, 1987. (趙紫陽：《沿著有中國特色的社會主義道路前進》。北京：人民出版社，1987。)

Zheng, Jingping. "How Many US Dollars Is China's Per Capita GNP?" *Economics Information*, 13 September 1996 (in Chinese). (鄭京平：〈中國人均GDP到底為多少美元〉，《經濟學消息報》，1996年9月13日。)

Zheng, Xianbing. *An Introduction to Interest Rate*. Beijing: China Finance Press, 1991 (in Chinese). (鄭先炳：《利率導論》。北京：中國金融出版社，1991。)

Zheng, Youjing and Fang, Hanzhong. "A Study on the Trend of Economic Growth", *Economic Research*, No. 2 (1992), pp. 23–28 (in Chinese). (鄭友敬、方漢中：〈經濟增長趨勢研究〉，《經濟研究》，第2期 (1992)，頁23–28。)

Zhou, Qiren. "China's Rural Reform: The Changes in the Country and the Relationship of Ownership — A Retrospect into the Vicissitudes of Economic *Institutions*", in Unirule Institute, ed. *China Economics, 1994*. Shanghai: Shanghai People's Press, 1995 (in Chinese). (周其仁：〈中國農村改革：國家和所有權關係的變化 —— 一個經濟制度變遷史的回顧〉，載《中國經濟學，1994》。上海：上海人民出版社，1995。)

Zou, G. *Enterprise Behavior Under the Two-tier Plan Market System*. Mimeo. Los Angelis: IBEAR/SBA/USC, 1992.

Index

156 key projects, 36

agricultural collectivization, 50, 55–59, 238
Amsden, A. H., 107
arbitrage by officials (*guandao* 官倒), 212
arbitrage by private individuals (*sidao* 私倒), 212
Argentina,
  adoption of leap forward strategy, 92–93, 95, 114, 363
  economic growth, 92–93, 114
  and inflation, 95
Asian Development Bank, 72n
Australia and comparative advantage strategy 114
autonomy,
  and SOE reform, 149–55
  in production and management, 55, 137, 149–55, 177, 179, 316, 323, 327–32, 340, 344
  in foreign trade, 162

barter trade, 341
Brazil,
  adoption of leap forward strategy, 64, 92–95
  foreign debt in, 95
  economic growth in, 92–94
  inflation in, 95
  rent seeking in, 94
Bukharin, 33, 34

capital-intensive industries, 25, 37–39, 93, 95, 113, 119, 122, 135, 249, 294
  and their conflicts with China's comparative advantage, 29, 37–39, 69
Chenery, H. B., 62, 77
Chenery Large Country Model, the, 77–78
Chile, 92, 126, 363
China,
  devaluation of official exchange rate, 11, 41–42, 46
  economic size, 11
  economic growth of, 2, 8–12, 72, 73, 94, 198, 304, 316
  exchange rate policy reform, 172–75
  urbanization in, 69, 80–82, 199, 281, 316
  see also China-India comparison
China-India comparison, 96–97
CIS (Commonwealth of Independent States), 308, 325
Civil Service examination, 1
commodities,
  first-category, 52
  second-category, 52
  third-category, 52
Commonwealth of Independent States, see CIS
Commune, People's,
  and agricultural crisis, 57

and grass-root organization 146–49
and working incentives, 17, 140, 141–42, 191
disintegration of, 143–45, 310
size of, 55–59, 97
comparative advantage,
and competitiveness, 86, 119, 252, 299
and change of industrial structure, 190–96, 299
and development of science and technology, 1, 18, 297–99
and development theory, 62–63, 100
and economic efficiency, 69, 79–80
and economic growth, 119, 299, 342
and economic structure, 69, 77–78, 122, 311
and employment, 119, 254–56
and factor endowments, 115–20, 122
and financial crisis, 127–36, 252–54
and government functions, 120–27
and grain production, 287–89
and income disparity, 244, 247–51
and industrial structure, 122, 132, 190–96
and international trade, 119–20
and success of four Little Dragons, 103, 108–14, 117, 126–27
and technological choice, 297–99
and the upgrading of endowment structure, 115–20, 234, 299
and township and village enterprise, 200–201, 247, 311–12, 329, *see also* TVE
and viability, 64, 187, 218, 294–305
China's, 145, 183, 189–90, 197, 200, 238, 239, 254, 293, 296
dynamic, 119, 298
static, 119
comparative-advantage-defying development strategy, *see* leap forward development strategy
comparative-advantage development strategy,
and Argentina and Uruguay, 114
and Australia and New Zealand, 114
and avoidance of Kuznetz's inverted U curve in Taiwan and Korea, 248
and competitive labour market, 117
and competitive product market, 118
and employment, 117, 119, 192, 280
and equity, 119
and flexible and effective financial market, 117
and income distribution, 58, 244, 247–51
and role of government, 120–27
and Taiwan's development, 104–107, 132, 134–36, 248–49, 300–301
in South Korea, Taiwan and Singapore, 103

macro-policy environment of, 120–27
and the development of four Little Dragons, 108–14, 117, 126–27
competition and enterprise performance, 151, 179–80, 186
contract responsibility system, 153, 155, 313, 318, 310n,
convertible currency, 130, 133, 174
cooperatives,
advanced, 57
elementary, 56
coordinated development and Bukharin, 33–34
CPC Central Committee, 51, 63, 143, 144, 163, 166, 303
"crossing the river by groping the stones", 177
Cultural Revolution, 139, 140, 176
Czechoslovakia, 5, 7

Deng, Xiaoping, 24, 283
decentralization, 22, 141, 150, 178, 185, 205, 207–208, 216–17, 238–43, 308, 315
deflation,
and bubbles in stock market, 262–64
and consumption 265
and counter fiscal and monetary measures, 271–75
and credit supply, 259–62
and New Village Movement, 275-81
and production capacity, 266–71, 271–75
and the bust in real estate market, 264–65
development economics, xxviii, xxix, xxxiii, xxxiv, 62, 99–100
development strategy, *see* comparative-advantage development strategy *and* leap forward development strategy
development theory, radical, 62
dual track
price system, xxxvi, xl, 151, 171–72, 313, 341
resource allocation system, 178–79, 212–13, 312, 318, 321, 331, 334, 341, 343, 345
system and development of labour-intensive sectors, 312–13, 318, 341
foreign exchange rate, 174, 334

employment structure, 81, 97, 191–93, 199
exchange rate,
internal settlement, 173, 173n , 175
managed flexible, 174
official, 19, 43, 49, 175
exit right, 58n, 148–49

FDI (foreign direct investment), 3, 253, 284, 304
Fei, John, 104n
Feldman, G. A., 35
financial suppression, 65, 140, 253
financial crisis and capital inflow, 304–305
five-year plan,
first, 36–37, 47–49, 54, 60, 73, 75, 179

second, 60, 75
foreign direct investment, *see* FDI
foreign exchange,
adjustment market, 314, 334–35
control, 48, 49, 172–77
flexible single system, 175
multiple system, 65, 175
swap market, 161, 174
foreign trade, as propeller of reform, 313–14
foreign trade companies, 161
Fujian, 193, 225n

Gang of Four, 140
Garnaut, R., xliii, 12
Great Leap Forward, xxiii, 57, 63, 75, 191
and the greatest famine, xxiii, 58
Guangdong, 180, 193, 225n, 229, 278, 332

Hainan, 193, 225, 289
Harrold, Peter, 310n
heavy industry-oriented development strategy,
and capital scarcity, 30, 37–39, 218, 222
and conflicts with China's endowment structure, 37–39, 112–13, 114, 197
and former Soviet Union, 4, 27, 32–33, 35–37, 59, 92, 112–13
and the import of equipments, xxiii, 37–38, 40–41,
and international competition, 31, 87, 101
and market mechanism, xxxv, 29, 34, 37, 40, 44, 46–47, 139, 164
and military, 32, 98, 112
and mobilization of funds, 25, 38–40, 93n, 111–12, 129
and planning, xxxv, 29, 34, 49, 51, 53, 55, 73–74, 78–79, 84, 100, 127, 210, 238, 242, 294
and traditional economic system, xxxiii–xxxv, 17, 27, 29–67, 69–102, 138, 140, 178, 197, 238, 340, 342
see also leap forward development strategy
Hoffmann, Walter, 31
Hoffmann Coefficient, 31
Hong Kong,
economic growth in, 103–105
emphasis on comparative advantage, 109, 198, 218
household responsibility system,
and working incentives, 17, 141–43, 145, 340
and method of income distribution, 142–43, 145
and output growth, 17, 145, 147, 184–85, 310
and dual-level operation system, 146–48
and TVEs, 179, 185–86, 311
household output-quota contract phase, 142–44
work-quota contract phase, 142–44
hyper-industrialization and Preobrazhensky, 33, 34, 35
hyper-inflation, 41

IMF, *see* International Monetary Fund

import substitution, xxiv, 31, 47, 86
  primary, 86
  secondary, 86
import substitution strategy, 86
  Central and South America's adoption of, 63, 92
  see also leap forward development strategy
incentive,
  and micro-management system, 52–59, 84–91, 140–56, 184–85
  lack of, 52–59, 84–91
  mechanism, 88, 91, 148, 181, 184–86, 216–17, 238, 308–309, 314–15, 317, 319, 326–27, 331, 340, 344
income disparities,
  and economic development, 248–49
  and migration, 231
  proposals in China for reducing, 249–50
  widening regional, 223–31, 244
  widening rural-urban, xxiv, 224
India,
  and the heavy-industry-oriented develop- ment strategy, 60, 96–97, 342
  and the leap forward strategy, 60, 96–97, 342
  economic growth, 92, 93
  growth rate of total factor productivity in, 94
  see also China-India comparison
indicative plan, 139, 158, 159, 241
Indonesia, 21, 132, 136, 222, 290n
industrial revolution, 1, 2, 18
inflation,
  and credit control, 206
  and low interest rates, 206, 240–44
  and money supply, 240, 243, 261
  endogenous, 242–43, 343
information asymmetry, 55, 180, 181, 216, 216, 239
institutional economics, new, xxxiii, xxxiv
institutional incompatibility, 203, 331, 343–44
International Monetary Fund (IMF), 11, 12
iron rice bowls, 312

Japan, 2, 3, 11, 16, 18, 19, 92, 103–109, 113–14, 117, 120, 124–28, 132, 134–36, 162, 231, 254, 262, 275–76, 298, 344
J-curve, 318
Jefferson, G., 313
Jiang, Shuojie, 104n
Jiangsu, 225n
Johnson, D. G., xxv, 37n, 288n
Joint state-private venture, 54
joint stock system, 313

Kaldor improvement, xxxvi, xl, 315n, 317, 327, 344
Kaldor, N., 315n
Keynesian economics, 100
Korea, South,
  and comparative advantage strategy, 108–14, 249
  and financial crisis, 21, 127–28, 132–36, 254, 300
  China's conditions for economic

development compared with, 71
economic growth in, 70, 103–105, 126
income disparity in, 249
Korean war, 31
Kornai, J., 46n
Krugman, Paul, 19n
Kuomintang (Nationalist Party), 32
Kuznetz, Simon, 248
Kuznetz's inverted U Curve, 248
Taiwan's avoidance of, 249

Large-country Model a la Chenery, 77
law of socialist primitive accumulation, 34
law of value, 34
leading coefficient of
heavy industry, 74
TVEs, 200
fixed asset investment over the household consumption, 266
leap forward development strategy, 29–102
and aspirations of "leaping forward", 98
and deterioration in the terms of trade 61, 100–101
and deterioration of fiscal condition, 95
and distorted industrial structure, 69–70, 84, 113, 190, 218, 312
and dynamic change of comparative advantage, 119, 298
and economic performance, 59, 69–74, 84–91, 91–102
and exchange rate policy, xxiii, 41–42, 41n, 46, 48–49, 64, 108, 140, 172–77, 207, 211, 330, 342
and import substitution strategy, 86
and improvement of living standard, 25, 73–74, 78, 82–83, 92, 95, 113, 140, 316, 340
and inefficiency, 70, 94, 137, 141, 148, 156, 240, 250, 308, 314
and inflation, 95, 103, 109, 177, 205–209, 214, 220, 241–43, 331, 343
and inward looking, 83
and level of urbanization, 69, 80–82, 199, 316
and low interest rate policy, 40–41, 46–48, 206, 240–44
and low nominal wages, 43–44
and low price policy for agricultural products, 44–45, 46, 50–51, 56, 244
and macro-policy environment, 29–30, 37–39, 40, 44–46, 48, 53, 59, 64–67, 140–41, 238, 241–42, 247–49, 341–45
and micro-management institution, 26, 52–59, 84–90, 137, 140–45, 156, 171, 178, 215–20, 326
and nationalization, 49, 52–55, 60, 64–65, 339
and planned resource allocation mechanism, 46–52, 156–71, 208, 344, 367
and polarization of wealth distribution, 61

and rate of economic growth in pre-reform China, 70–74
and rent seeking, xxx, 20–21, 94, 101, 115, 119, 151, 203, 208, 210–14
and slow growth in capitalist and socialist countries, 27, 92
and state-owned enterprise, 52–55, 84–88, 149–56
and trinity of traditional economic system, xxix, xxxv, xxxvii, xl, 59–68, 91, 137, 138, 140, 178, 238, 331, 342
and worker's and farmer's incentives, 84–91, 140–56, 184–86
Central and Eastern Europe's adoption of, xxiv
market failures and choice of, 100
political independence and choice of, 31, 72, 99
Lenin, 33, 35
Lewis, W. A., 69n, 120
Li, Fuchun, 36
Li, Wei, 148
Little Dragons, Asia's four, xxx, xxxi,xxxviii, 2, 16, 91–92, 102, 104–109, 113–17, 120, 124–27, 134, 140, 182–84, 298, 342
Liu, G. G., xliii
L-shaped long-term recession curve, 333

macro-policy environment, distorted, xxxv, 39–46, 55, 56, 59, 64, 97, 137–38, 140, 141, 150, 189, 217, 330
Mahalanobis, 60
Malaysia, 21, 132, 222
management autonomy, *see* autonomy
management system,
credit, 164–65
foreign exchange rate, 48
international trade, 48–49, 165
material, 49–50, 157
Mao, Zedong, 53n, 55n, 56, 140, 308
market competition, 24, 116–7, 121, 151, 179–80, 186, 189, 299, 321
market mechanism xxxv, xxxviii, 26, 29, 34, 37, 40, 44, 46, 47, 118, 121–22, 139, 164, 171, 197, 246, 251, 314, 320, 322, 342
Marx, 35
Mexico, 95
micro-management institution,
and low incentives and efficiency, 84–91
as starter of reform, 308
as starting point of reform, 33, 117, 238, 250, 339
difficulties in the reform of, 215–21
reform of, 140–56,
under leap-forward strategy, 52–59,
Ministry of International Trade, 49
monitoring costs, 55
mutual aid team, 58n

Nehru, 60
New Democracy Policy, 53
New Economic Policy, 33

New Zealand and comparative advantage strategy, 114

Ohlin, B., 116
open-door policy, 3, 24, 193
Overall Guidelines and Tasks in the Transition Period, 55–56

Pareto improvement, xxxvi, xxxix, 315n, 317, 327, 330, 344
People's Bank of China, 47, 163–64, 163n, 168, 260, 289
Perkins, Dwight H., 118
permit system, import and export, 49
Philippines,
  adoption of leap forward strategy, xxiv, 92, 93, 342
  and economic growth, 92, 106, 254, 342
  and the Green Revolution, 233
  rising star in Asia, 92
plan,
  indicative, 139, 158, 159, 241
  mandatory (or compulsory), 53, 112, 152, 158–59, 162, 241
  number of materials distributed by, 158
planning system
  and endogenous inflation, 242
  and the leap forward strategy, 29, 46–53, 238
  and SOEs, 52–55, 215–20, 294
  reform of, 156–71
Poland, 325, 307n
Preobrazhensky, E. A., 33, 34, 111n
price control, 220, 333,
price policy reform, 171–72, 207–208, 246–47, 330, 332–33
privatization, 182, 308, 325
procurement
  and marketing system, xxxv, 50–52
  and collectivization movement, 50
  contracted, 143
  state monopoly of, 52
production possibility frontier (PPF), 17, 70, 78–79, 316
production team system, 141, 231
profit retention, 150, 216, 316
profit sharing, 141, 178, 185, 214, 216
Purchasing Power Parity (PPP), 11

Qian, Y. Y., 326n

radical development theory, 62
rationality assumption, xlii
Rawski, T. G., 313
reform,
  and awakening of China — the sleeping lion, 10–11
  and capital inflow, 193, 296, 304–305
  and change in employment structure, 199
  and China's economic growth, 8–12
  and commercialization of state-owned banks, 177, 222, 240, 253
  and correction of industrial structure, 190–16, 312, 318, 319, 326

and development of financial market, 166–70
and diversification of sources of investment, 194–96
and dual-track system, 171–75, 179, 212, 312, 318, 321, 331
and economic opening, 193–95
and establishment of policy banks, 170, 222
and exploitation of comparative advantage, 197–202
and foreign exchange adjustment market, 314, 334–35
and foreign exchange retention system, 160, 162, 173, 334
and improvement of incentives and efficiency, 184–90
and improvement of living standard, 9–13, 140, 204, 339
and increase of per capita consumption, 9–10
and increase of per capita income, 113
and market mechanism, 164, 171, 197, 251, 314, 320, 322, 342
and regional disparities, 22, 200, 223–31
and exchange rate system, 172–75
and utilization of comparative advantage, 197–202
general implications of China's approach to, 325–37
in China and economic growth, 8–12, 198, 316
of the credit management system, 164–65
of the credit system, 165–66
of the exchange rate policy, 172–75
of the financial management system, 162–70
of the interest rate management system, 165
of the interest rate policy, 175–77
of the macro-policy environment, 171–77
of the material management system, 157–59
of the planned resource allocation mechanism, 156–71
of the price policy, 171–72, 207–208, 330, 332–33
of the single banking system, 163–64
the starter and propellers of, 308–14
reform approach,
advantage of incremental, 317–21
big bang, 315–17
characteristics of China's, 315
comparison of big bang and incremental, 314–15, 318–21, 324–25, 336
dual track system and reform approach, incremental, 312, 318, 321, 331
experiments and popularization, 321–23
general implications of China's, 325–37
gradual and evolutionary, *see* reform approach, incremental
incremental, xxxi, 178, 215, 307,

315, 317–21, 322, 324, 325, 326n, 331, 336, 344, 345
incremental reform as a second-best, 321
intrinsic logic and orderliness of incremental, 330–32
irreversibility of incremental, 330–32
non-radical reform, 323–25
radical and one-package, 325–37
rent seeking and incremental, 210–14, 321, 331, 343
shock therapy, xxiv, xxx, 307, 318, 326–27, 332, 336, 344, *see also* reform approach, big bang
social stability and incremental, 320, 325, 345
reform of foreign-trade management system, 159–62
and the shift from the single-commodity based operation system, 159
and foreign trade responsibility system, 159–61, 174
phase one, 159–60
phase two, 160–61
phase three, 161–62
reform of state-owned enterprise, 149–56
and asset contract responsibility system, 155
and competitive markets, 155–56
and dual-track price system, 151, 312
and enterprise contract responsibility system, 153, 155, 313, 318
and manager responsibility system, 151
and increase of enterprise autonomy, 149–56
and poor delineation of property rights, 155
and profit-retention system, 150, 216, 316
and replacement of profit remittance with corporate income tax, 153
and shareholding system, 152, 154–55, 168
first phase, 149–51
second phase, 151–54
third phase, 154–56
the major purpose of, 154
reform performance, compared China with former Soviet Union and Eastern Europe in, 4–8
regional disparity, 22, 200, 223–31
relative price regression, 246
rent seeking, 119, 210, 368
and dual track system, 210–11
retrenchment, xxxiii, 205, 208, 257, 264, 271, 320, 343, 344
Russia, xxvii, xxxi, 323n, 325

Sachs, J., 326n
savings deposit, value-guaranteed, 176
scientific discoveries,
and casual observation, 1
and science-based experiment, 1, 16
scientific revolution, 1

SEZ (special economic zone), 193, 321
Shandong, 55n, 151, 180, 225n
Shandong Peninsula, 193
Shantou, 193
Shenzhen, 193, 289
Shijiazhuang City, 158
shortage economy, 339
Singapore, xxx, 12, 103, 104, 105, 126, 132
socialist market economy, 21
soft budget constraints, 37n, 40n, 84, 84n, 134, 221, 295
SOE, *see* state-owned enterprise
Soviet State Planning Commission, 35
Soviet Union, former, 4, 27, 32–33, 35–37, 59, 92, 112–13, 326, 332, 344–45
  adoption of heavy-industry oriented strategy, 32–35
  adoption of leap forward development strategy, 32–35
special economic zone, *see* SEZ
state capitalism, 36
state enterprise, *see* state-owned enterprise
State Planning Commission, 35, 36, 49, 50, 152, 159
state-owned enterprise,
  and employment, 80–82
  and need of government protection, 64, 187, 206, 294–95, 301
  and urban economic reform, 149–59, 313
  and WTO, 289–305
  difficulties of reform in, 215–21
  joint stock system and reform of, 313
  policy suggestions for further SOE reform, 297–305
Summers, Lawrence, 19n
suppressed sectors, 309, 316, 318–19, 328–30, 331, 340, 343
  common features of, 328–30

Taiwan,
  China's conditions for economic development compared with, 70–71
  and the comparative advantage strategy, 103, 134–36, 198, 300–301
  economic growth in, 71, 104–105, 107
  income distribution, 248–49
technological innovation, induced, 15–16
technological invention,
  advantage of backwardness in, 15
  and economic growth, 13
  and experience, 1
  and science-based experiment, 18
Thailand, 21, 132, 136, 222, 254
Third Plenum of the 11th CPC Central Committee, 53n, 163, 166
township and village enterprise, *see* TVE
trade dependent ratio, 194n, 195
traditional economic system, 17, 25, 27, 39–67
  and vigour/chaos cycle, 208–10, 244, 343,

basic dilemmas of, 316
endogeny of, 29–67, 140, 189, 197, 331, 340
intrinsic logic of, xxviii, 138, 330–32
leap forward development strategy and trinity of, xxix, xxxv, xxxvii, xl, 59–68, 91, 137, 138, 140, 178, 238, 331, 342
trinity of, xxix, xxxv, xxxvii, xl, 30, 59–68, 91, 137, 138, 140, 178, 238, 331, 342
TVE (township and village enterprise), 147, 151, 179–82, 185, 189, 192, 198–201, 223, 240, 247, 311–14, 316, 329, 331, 332, 340, 341
and economic growth, 199–200, 316
and household responsibility system, 179, 185–86, 311
and labour-intensive industries, 200-201, 247
and regional disparity, 200, 247
and rural employment, 192, 199
and rural industrialization, 199
and rural surplus labour, 199, 311
and state revenue, 199
as the propeller of reform, 312–14
China's comparative advantage and growth of, 198, 312–14

unified state distribution system 158
United Nations Industrial Development Organization, 72n
Uruguay
and adoption of leap forward strategy, xxiv, 92–93, 114
and economic growth, 92, 93, 114
USSR, xxiv, 63

vested interests 138, 324
adjustment to the structure of, 327
groups, 138, 324
groups as opponents of price reform, 324
pattern of, 317
Vietnam, xxvii
vigour/chaos cycle, xxxiii, xxxiv, xxxv, xxxvi, xxxiv, xxxix, xl, 26, 30, 244, 251, 256, 257, 307, 323, 331, 343
and cycle of institutional reform, 26, 204–10
and corruption, 331, 343
and inflation, 26, 205, 207, 244, 331, 343
and internal inconsistency of economic system, xl, 178
approaches for solving, 251, 256
and experimental and localized reform, 323
readjustment measures in, 207–208
rent seeking, 244, 331, 343
voting model, 335

Wade, R., 107
Woo, W., 326n

work point, 141
World Bank, 4, 11, 13, 19, 33n, 62, 72n, 91, 106, 116, 185, 312n
World Trade Organization, *see* WTO
World War II, 31, 61, 72, 99, 101, 104, 111, 126, 275, 276, 298
WTO (World Trade Organization)
and China's agriculture, 285-89
and China's financial sector, 289–93
and SOE reform, 293–305,
and the viability problem, 294
policy suggestions for further SOE reform, 297–305

Xiamen, 193
Xu, C. G., 326n
Xue, Muquio, 33n

Yalu River, 32
Yang, Jianbai, 185
Yangtze River Delta, 193

Zhejiang, 225n
Zhou, Qiren, 148
Zhuhai, 193